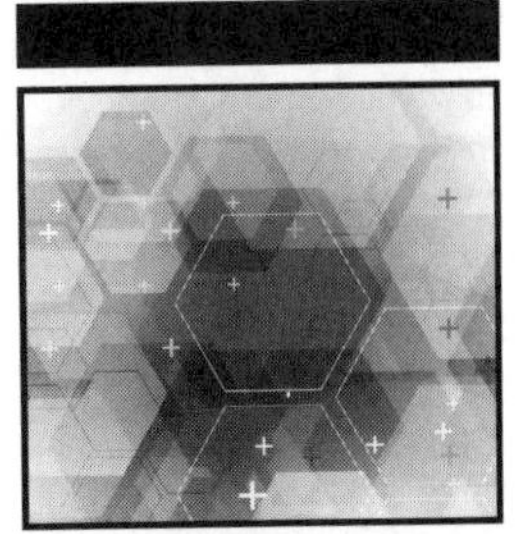

Microsoft® Big Data Solutions

Adam Jorgensen
James Rowland-Jones
John Welch
Dan Clark
Christopher Price
Brian Mitchell

WILEY

Microsoft® Big Data Solutions

Published by
John Wiley & Sons, Inc.
10475 Crosspoint Boulevard
Indianapolis, IN 46256
www.wiley.com

ISBN: 978-1-118-72908-3
ISBN: 978-1-118-74209-9 (ebk)
ISBN: 978-1-118-72955-7 (ebk)

Manufactured in the United States of America

10 9 8 7 6 5 4 3 2 1

Library of Congress Control Number: 2013958290

Executive Editor
Robert Elliot

Project Editor
Jennifer Lynn

Technical Editors
Rohit Bakhshi
John Hoang
Josh Luedeman

Production Editor
Christine Mugnolo

Copy Editor
Keith Cline

Editorial Manager
Mary Beth Wakefield

Freelancer Editorial Manager
Rosemarie Graham

Associate Director of Marketing
David Mayhew

Marketing Manager
Ashley Zurcher

Business Manager
Amy Knies

Vice President and Executive Group Publisher
Richard Swadley

Associate Publisher
Jim Minatel

Project Coordinator, Cover
Todd Klemme

Proofreader
Sarah Kaikini, Word One New York

Indexer
Robert Swanson

Cover Image
©traffic_analyzer/iStockphoto.com

Cover Designer
Ryan Sneed/Wiley

I am honored to dedicate this book to my author team who pulled together and created a wonderful project for the community they love as I do.

— Adam Jorgensen

For my beautiful and eternally patient wife, Jane, and our three children Lucy, Kate, and Oliver. I will love you all forever.

— James Rowland-Jones

To my lovely wife, Marlana, and my children, Kayla and Michael, thanks for the support and understanding during the late nights while I was writing.

— John Welch

To my family, thank you for your unconditional support throughout this process. I'd especially like to thank my wife Shannon for believing in me.

— Brian Mitchell

Acknowledgments

I would like to thank my Lord and Savior Jesus Christ for all He has blessed me with. Thank you to my wife and family for their support and love. This author team has been incredible and has responded to constantly changing platforms and market factors to deliver a great title on this fast changing subject area. Special thanks to the tech editors and vendor editors from Hortonworks and Microsoft. Last, but certainly not least, thank you to the readers and those data professionals whose passion makes a book like this worthwhile. It's for you we do what we do!

— Adam Jorgensen

I have come to know many people through the SQL community. Some I know professionally while others I know a bit better than that and consider friends. Adam definitely falls into the latter category. I'd like to start by thanking him not only for the opportunity to collaborate on this book, but also for his friendship, especially as we've journeyed on the PASS rollercoaster together.

I'd like to thank my copy editor Keith Cline and my official technical reviewers, Josh Luedemen (InfoTech), Michael Reed (PragmaticWorks), and John Hoang (Microsoft Azure CAT). John's help and support in particular has been invaluable to me for several years: I'd like to take this moment to give him a special mention and express my sincere thanks.

I'd also like to thank our oft-suffering editor Jennifer Lynn (www.pageoneediting.com). I know I didn't make your life very easy on this one, Jennifer, and would like to take this moment to both thank you and apologize for my seemingly never-ending list of excuses.

Last but by no means least, I'd like to thank my unofficial reviewer who gave up her time to offer me her feedback, insights, and sagely advice. Lara Rubbelke, you are nothing if not thought provoking and inspirational. Thank you so much for taking the time to help me shape my thoughts, bounce ideas, and for being my naïve friend.

—James Rowland-Jones

About the Authors

Adam Jorgensen is the president of Pragmatic Works and the executive vice president of the Professional Association for SQL Server (PASS). He has gained extensive experience with SQL Server, SharePoint, and analytics over the past 13 years. His primary focus is helping organizations and executives drive value through new technology solutions, management techniques, and financial optimization. He specializes in the areas of cloud and big data analytics and works on solutions to make those technologies real for enterprises. He lives in Jacksonville, Florida, with his wife, Cristina.

James Rowland-Jones is a principal consultant for The Big Bang Data Company. His focus and passion is to architect and deliver highly scalable, analytical platforms that are creative, simple, and elegant in their design. James specializes in big data warehouse solutions that leverage both SQL Server PDW and Hadoop ecosystems. James is a keen advocate for the SQL Server community, both internationally and in the United Kingdom. He currently serves on the board of directors for PASS and sits on the organizing committee for SQLBits (Europe's largest event for the Microsoft Data Platform). James has been awarded Microsoft's MVP accreditation since 2008 for his services to the community.

John Welch works at Pragmatic Works, where he manages the development of a suite of BI products that make developing, managing, and documenting BI solutions easier. John has been working with BI and data warehousing technologies since 2001, with a focus on Microsoft products in heterogeneous environments. He is a Microsoft Most Valued Professional (MVP), an award given due to his commitment to sharing his knowledge with the IT community, and an SSAS Maestro. John is an experienced speaker, having given presentations at PASS conferences, the Microsoft Business Intelligence conference, Software Development West (SD West), Software Management Conference (ASM/SM), and others. He has also contributed to multiple books on SQL Server, including *Smart Business Intelligence Solutions with Microsoft SQL Server 2008* (Microsoft Press, 2009) and the *SQL Server MVP Deep Dives* (Manning Publications) series.

John writes a blog on BI and SQL Server Information Services (SSIS) topics at `http://agilebi.com/jwelch`. He is active in open source projects that help ease the development process for Microsoft BI developers, including ssisUnit (`http://ssisunit.codeplex.com`), a unit testing framework for SSIS.

Dan Clark is a senior BI consultant for Pragmatic Works. He enjoys learning new BI technologies and training others how to best implement the technology. Dan is particularly interested in how to use data to drive better decision making. Dan has published several books and numerous articles on .NET programming and BI development. He is a regular speaker at various developer/BI conferences and user group meetings, and enjoys interacting with the Microsoft developer and database communities.

Chris Price is a senior consultant with Microsoft based out of Tampa, Florida. He has a Bachelor of Science degree in management information systems and a Master of Business Administration degree, both from the University of South Florida. He began his career as a developer, programming with everything from Visual Basic and Java to both VB.Net and C# as he worked his way into a software architect role before being bitten by the BI bug. Although he is still passionate about software development, his current focus is on ETL (extract, transform, and load), Data integration, data quality, MDM (master data management), SSAS (SQL Server Analysis Server), SharePoint, and all things big data.

He regularly speaks at SQL Saturdays, PASS Summit, conferences, code camps, and other community events. He blogs frequently and has also authored multiple books and whitepapers and has served as technical editor for a range of BI and big data topics. You can follow Chris on his blog at `http://bluewatersql.wordpress.com/` or on Twitter at `@BluewaterSQL`.

Brian Mitchell is the lead architect of the Microsoft Big Data Center of Expertise. Brian focuses exclusively on data warehouse/business intelligence (DW/BI) solutions, with the majority of his time focusing on SQL Server Parallel Data Warehouse (PDW) and HDInsight. He has spent more than 15 years working with Microsoft SQL Server and Microsoft Business Intelligence. Brian is a Microsoft Certified Master–SQL Server 2008. You can find his blog on topics such as Big Data, SQL Server Parallel Data Warehouse, and Microsoft Business Intelligence at `http://brianwmitchell.com`. Brian earned his Master of Business Administration degree from the University of Florida. When he is not tinkering with SQL Server or Hadoop, Brian enjoys spending time exploring his adopted home state of Florida with his wife, Shannon, and their kids.

About the Technical Editors

Rohit Bakhshi is a product manager at Hortonworks, a leading provider of support and services for Apache Hadoop. Hortonworks builds and distributes the Hortonworks Data Platform (HDP), which is a 100% open source data management software powered by Hadoop available on Windows and Linux OS platforms.

Rohit is responsible for the HDP for the Windows product line, core Apache Hadoop components, and Platform Services for HDP. He has worked with Microsoft to bring the entire stack of Apache Hadoop components to Windows to enable Windows developers and system administrators to harness the full power of Apache Hadoop. Before Hortonworks, Rohit was a consultant in the Accenture Technology Labs R & D consulting group, where he focused on architecting and delivering big data solutions to Fortune 500 clients.

John Hoang is a senior program manager based out of Aliso Viejo, California, on the Azure Customer Advisory Team (AzureCAT). He has more than 20 years of experience working in various roles, including developer, business analyst, and project manager implementing software solutions to manufacturing, retail, and healthcare. He currently specializes in the SQL Server PDW. In his free time, John enjoys bike riding, tennis, and spending time with his two children.

Josh Luedeman has been working with SQL Server for more than eight years. He is currently a solutions architect with Data Structures, Inc., where he is working with customers to help them utilize business intelligence (BI) tools and big data. He has worked in IT for more than 10 years, holding positions in application support, database administration, and BI. In these industries, Josh has held integral roles in Fortune 500 companies, major institutions of higher education, small-medium businesses, and startups. Josh is a speaker at software development and data conferences including Code On The Beach and multiple SQL Saturdays. He is originally from Corning, New York, and currently resides in Orlando, Florida, with his wife and children. Josh can be found online at `www.joshluedeman.com`, `josh@joshluedeman.com`, `www.linkedin.com/in/joshluedeman`, and `@joshluedeman` on Twitter.

Michael Reed has a long history of designing innovative solutions to difficult business problems. During the last 14 years, he focused on database development and architecture, and more recently business intelligence and analytics. He is currently employed by Pragmatic Works as a Senor BI Consultant. Previously he was director of Insight and Analytics at a healthcare claim processor. Prior to that he held operations, data, and information delivery centric roles in Microsoft's Online Services Division; specifically the AdCenter Behavioral Targeting group, which is the primary research unit for mining social behaviors at Microsoft supporting the Bing decision search engine and BingAds advertising services.

In a prior life, he was co-owner of a multimillion dollar manufacturing business, grown from a startup, where he gained much of the business knowledge and insight he employs in his work today.

Contents

Introduction

This book was built for those of you who are searching. Those of you who are wondering. Searching and wondering what on earth big data will mean for your data world. IT takes a different approach, however, than the litany of titles designed to spend hundreds of pages beating you over the head telling you that you need big data, that everyone is doing it, and that you have to be "cool," too!

This author team wanted to create something that would be your go-to resource for moving from your existing relational world and provide you not only the roadmap forward but also practical experience for those of you who don't need the click here, move the mouse to the left, and click again level of instruction. We do explain some things in greater detail, but these are things that require this due to their newness or relative complexity.

We are focused on making sure you can ease your transition to using these tools and technologies because we have been where you are. Your boss came back from a conference and said, "We need a big data solution." When you inquire what he would like it to solve, he doesn't really know, but he knows how critical it is that the organization have one. You will become the responsible party for making these big data dreams come true.

Normally, this would entail training classes and long hours combing the Internet like you did when they told you they needed a data warehouse or a cube, those other words once foreign to you. You will learn through this text that big data is really big—no pun intended. It can do big things, solve big problems, and is a big ecosystem of tools and platforms. However, like most other ecosystems (RDBMSs, programming languages, mobile, and cloud), there are really only a few foundational things, and if you can come up to speed on those, you will be rocking and rolling when you need to apply more advanced tools, or automation, and so on.

Our Team

We have assembled a strong international team of authors to make sure that we can provide a sound perspective and knowledge transfer on the right topics (we'll discuss those shortly). Those topics include:

1. Accelerated overview of Big Data, Hadoop, NoSQL, and key industry knowledge
2. Key problems people are trying to solve and how to identify them
3. Delivering big data in a Microsoft world
4. Tool and platform choice
5. Installation, configuration, and exploration
6. Storing and managing big data
7. Working with, adding structure, and cleansing your data
8. Big data and SQL Server together
9. Analytics in the big data world
10. How this works in the cloud
11. Case studies and real world applications
12. Moving your organization forward in this new world

This team includes members of Pragmatic Works, a global leader in information services, software, and training; Microsoft Research; Microsoft Consulting Services; Azure Customer Advisory Team; and some other industry firms making a big impact in this expanding space.

All Kidding Aside

Big data is coming on strong. You will have these solutions in your environment within 24 months, and you should be prepared. This book is designed to help you make the transition with practical skills from a relational to a more "evolved" view of the data worlds. This includes solutions that will handle data that does not fit nicely into a tabular structure, but is nonetheless just as or more important in some cases as the data that you have curated so carefully for so many years.

You will learn some new terms as well. This will be almost as much a vocabulary lesson as a technical lesson.

Who Is This Book For?

This book is for those data developers, power users, and executives looking to understand how these big data technologies will impact their world and how to properly approach solutions in this new ecosystem. Readers will need a basic understanding of data systems and a passion for learning new technologies and techniques. Some experience with developing database or application solutions will be helpful in some advanced topic areas.

What You Need to Use This Book

We have designed this book to make extensive use of cloud resources so, as the reader, you will need to have a newer model computer PC or Mac that can access the Internet reliably. In addition, you will want to be able to install additional programs and tools as advised by the authors, so please ensure you have that access on the machine you're using. Different chapters will have different tools or data sets, so please follow the authors' instructions in those chapters to get the most out of your experience. Having access to a SQL Server database will be required in certain chapters, and if you wish to set up your environment on premise, then a virtualization technology such as Hyper-V, VMWare, or Virtual box is recommended.

Chapter Overview

Now we'll go through the chapters in this text and discuss what you'll be learning from each one.

- **Chapter 1: Industry Needs and Solutions**
  No book on big data would be complete without some coverage of the history, origins, and use cases in this ecosystem. We also need to discuss the industry players and platforms that are in scope for the book. Other books spend 5 to 6 chapters rehashing this information; we have done it efficiently for you so you can get to work on more fun topics!
- **Chapter 2: Microsoft's Approach to Big Data**
  Doing this in a Microsoft world is a little different that the traditional UNIX or Linux deployment. We chose this approach since we feel it makes this technology more accessible to millions of windows administrators, developers and power users. Many of the folks were surveyed before this writing, we heard overwhelmingly that we needed a Windows-focused solution to help the largest population of enterprise users access this new technology.

- **Chapter 3: Installing HDInsight**
  In this chapter, you'll get started configuring your big data environment.
- **Chapter 4: HDFS, Hive, HBase and HCatalog**
  These are some key data and metadata technologies. We'll make sure you understand when to use each one and how to get the most out of them.
- **Chapter 5: Storing and Managing data in HDFS**
  A distributed file system might be a new concept for most readers, so we are going to make sure we go through this core component of Hadoop and ensure you're prepared for designing with this incredible feature.
- **Chapter 6: Adding Structure with Hive**
  We need to go deeper into Hive because you'll use it a lot. Let's dive in with this chapter to make sure you understand commands and the logic behind using Hive efficiently.
- **Chapter 7: Expanding your Capability with HBase and HCatalog**
  Dealing with large tables and metadata requires some new tools and techniques. HBase and HCatalog will help you manage these types of challenges, and we're going to take you through using them. Get ready to put the BIG in big data.
- **Chapter 8: Effective Big Data ETL with SSIS, Pig, and Sqoop**
  We have to load this data, and there is no better way to do it than with our ETL expert authors. Come along while they take you through using favorite and familiar tools, along with some new ones, to load data quickly and effectively.
- **Chapter 9: Data Research and Advanced Data Cleansing with Pig and Hive**
  Now we've installed, configured, explored, and loaded some data. Let's get buys researching and cleansing this data with our new tools and platform.
- **Chapter 10: Data Warehouses and Hadoop Integration**
  How do SQL Server and business intelligence fit in with big data? Very closely. Most of the time they will work in tandem. We will show you when to use each solution and how they work together in scale-up and scale-out solutions.
- **Chapter 11: Visualizing Big Data with Microsoft BI**
  Now that we have the analysis, how do we visualize this for our users? Do we have new tools? Do we use our familiar tools? Yes! Let's do this together so we can understand how to combine these solutions for the best results for our users and customers.

- **Chapter 12: Big Data Analytics**
  You've heard about analytics. This chapter includes advanced statistical analysis, social sentiment analysis, forecasting, modeling, and much more! No PhD required.
- **Chapter 13: Big Data In the Cloud**
  Do you need a lot of servers in your data center to do the things in this book? No way! We can do it in the cloud in an elastic and scalable fashion.
- **Chapter 14: SQL Server Big Data Case Examples**
  How are other firms succeeding and failing in this ecosystem. We will take you through some of the best wins and losses and why these outcomes happened so you can model after them or avoid them.
- **Chapter 15: Building and Executing your Big Data Plan**
  How do we take what we've done and make it real? This chapter will help you write your big data plan.
- **Chapter 16: Operational Big Data Management**
  Administering these technologies and integrating them into your existing infrastructure will take planning and careful execution, just like your other critical systems. Let's plan this out together!

Features Used in This Book

The following features and icons are used in this book to help draw your attention to some of the most important or useful information in the book:

WARNING Be sure to take heed when you see one of these asides. When particular steps could cause damage to your electronics if performed incorrectly, you'll see one of these asides.

TIP These asides contain quick hints about how to perform simple tasks that might prove useful for the task at hand.

NOTE These asides contain additional information that may be of importance to you, including links to videos and online material that will make it easier to following along with the development of a particular project.

SAMPLE HEADING

These asides go into additional depth about the current topic or a related topic.

Part I

What Is Big Data?

In This Part

CHAPTER 1

Industry Needs and Solutions

WHAT YOU WILL LEARN IN THIS CHAPTER:

- Finding Out What Constitutes "Big Data"
- Appreciating the History and Origins of Hadoop
- Defining Hadoop
- Understanding the Core Components of Hadoop
- Looking to the Future with Hadoop 2.0

This first chapter introduces you to the open source world of Apache and to Hadoop, one of the most exciting and innovative platforms ever created for the data professional. In this chapter we're going to go on a bit of a journey. You're going to find out what inspired Hadoop, where it came from, and its future direction. You'll see how from humble beginnings two gentlemen have inspired a generation of data professionals to think completely differently about data processing and data architecture.

Before we look into the world of Hadoop, though, we must first ask ourselves an important question. Why does big data exist? Is this name just a fad, or is there substance to all the hype? Is big data here to stay? If you want to know the answers to these questions and a little more, read on. You have quite a journey in front of you...

What's So *Big* About Big Data?

The world has witnessed explosive, exponential growth in recent times. So, did we suddenly have a need for big data? Not exactly. Businesses have been tackling the capacity challenge for many years (much to the delight of storage hardware vendors). Therefore the *big* in big data isn't purely a statement on size.

Likewise, on the processing front, scale-out solutions such as high-performance computing and distributed database technology have been in place since the last millennium. There is nothing intrinsically new there either.

People also often talk about unstructured data, but, really, this just refers to the format of the data. Could this be a reason we "suddenly" need big data? We know that web data, especially web log data, is born in an unstructured format and can be generated in significant quantities and volume. However, is this really enough to be considered big data?

In my mind, the answer is no. No one property on its own is sufficient for a project or a solution to be considered a big data solution. It's only when you have a cunning blend of these ingredients that you get to bake a big data cake.

This is in line with the Gartner definition of big data, which they updated in Doug Laney's publication, *The Importance of Big Data: A Definition* (Gartner, 2012): "High volume, high velocity, and/or high variety information assets that require new forms of processing to enable enhanced decision making, insight discovery and process optimization."

What we do know is that every CIO on the planet seems to want to start a big data project right now. In a world of shrinking budgets, there is this sudden desire to jump in with both feet into this world of big data and start prospecting for golden nuggets. It's the gold rush all over again, and clearly companies feel like they might miss out if they hesitate.

However, this is a picture that has been sharpening its focus for several years. In the buildup to this ubiquitous acceptance of big data, we've been blessed with plenty of industry terms and trends, web scale, new programming paradigms of "code first," and of course, to the total disgust of data modelers everywhere, NoSQL. Technologies such as Cassandra and MongoDB are certainly part of the broader ecosystem, but none have resonated as strongly with the market as Hadoop and big data. Why? In essence, unless you were Facebook, Google, Yahoo!, or Bing, issues like web scale really didn't apply.

It seems as though everyone is now building analytics platforms, and that, to be the king of geek chic, requires a degree in advanced statistics. The reason? Big data projects aren't defined by having big data sets. They are shaped by big ideas, by big questions, and by big opportunities. Big data is not about one technology or even one platform. It's so much more than that: It's a mindset and a movement.

Big data, therefore, is a term that underpins a raft of technologies (including the various Hadoop projects, NoSQL offerings, and even MPP Database Systems, for example) that have been created in the drive to better analyze and derive meaning from data at a dramatically lower cost and while delivering new insights and products for organizations all over the world. In times of recession, businesses look to derive greater value from the assets they have rather than invest in new assets. Big data, and in particular Hadoop, is the perfect vehicle for doing exactly that.

A Brief History of Hadoop

Necessity is the mother of invention, and Hadoop is no exception. Hadoop was created to meet the need of web companies to index and process the data tsunami courtesy of the newfangled Internetz. Hadoop's origins owe everything to both Google and the Apache Nutch project. Without one influencing the other, Hadoop might have ended up a very different animal (joke intended). In this next section, we are going to see how their work contributed to making Hadoop what it is today.

Google

As with many pioneering efforts, Google provided significant inspiration for the development that became known as Hadoop. Google published two landmark papers. The first paper, published in October 2003, was titled "The Google File System," and the second paper, "MapReduce: Simplified Data Processing on Large Clusters," published just over a year later in December 2004, provided the inspiration to Doug Cutting and his team of part-time developers for their project, Nutch.

MapReduce was first designed to enable Google developers to focus on the large-scale computations that they were trying to perform while abstracting away all the scaffolding code required to make the computation possible. Given the size of the data set they were working on and the duration of tasks, the developers knew that they had to have a model that was highly parallelized, was fault tolerant, and was able to balance the workload across a distributed set of machines. Of course, the Google implementation of MapReduce worked over Google File System (GFS); Hadoop Distributed File System (HDFS) was still waiting to be invented.

Google has since continued to release thought-provoking, illuminating, and inspirational publications. One publication worthy of note is "BigTable: A Distributed Storage System for Structured Data." Of course, they aren't the only ones. LinkedIn, Facebook, and of course Yahoo! have all contributed to the big data mind share.

There are similarities here to the SIGMOD papers published by various parties in the relational database world, but ultimately it isn't the same. Let's look at an example. Twitter has open-sourced Storm—their complex event processing engine—which has recently been accepted into the Apache incubator program. For relational database vendors, this level of open sharing is really quite unheard of. For more details about storm head over to Apache: `http://incubator.apache.org/projects/storm.html`.

Nutch

Nutch was an open source crawler-based search engine built by a handful of part-time developers, including Doug Cutting. As previously mentioned Cutting was inspired by the Google publications and changed Nutch to take advantage of the enhanced scalability of the architecture promoted by Google. However, it wasn't too long after this that Cutting joined Yahoo! and Hadoop was born.

Nutch joined the Apache foundation in January 2005, and its first release (0.7) was in August 2005. However, it was not until 0.8 was released in July 2006 that Nutch began the transition to Hadoop-based architecture.

Nutch is still very much alive and is an actively contributed-to project. However, Nutch has now been split into two codebases. Version 1 is the legacy and provides the origins of Hadoop. Version 2 represents something of a re-architecture of the original implementation while still holding true to the original goals of the project.

What Is Hadoop?

Apache Hadoop is a top-level open source project and is governed by the Apache Software Foundation (ASF). Hadoop is not any one entity or thing. It is best thought of as a platform or an ecosystem that describes a method of distributed data processing at scale using commodity hardware configured to run as a cluster of computing power. This architecture enables Hadoop to address and analyze vast quantities of data at significantly lower cost than traditional methods commonly found in data warehousing, for example, with relational database systems.

At its core, Hadoop has two primary functions:

- Processing data (MapReduce)
- Storing data (HDFS)

With the advent of Hadoop 2.0, the next major release of Hadoop, we will see the decoupling of resource management from data processing. This adds a third primary function to this list. However, at the time of this writing, Yarn, the Apache project responsible for the resource management, is in alpha technology preview modes.

That said, a number of additional subprojects have been developed and added to the ecosystem that have been built on top of these two primary functions. When bundled together, these subprojects plus the core projects of MapReduce and HDFS become known as a *distribution*.

Derivative Works and Distributions

To fully understand a distribution, you must first understand the role, naming, and branding of Apache Hadoop. The basic rule here is that only official releases by the Apache Hadoop project may be called *Apache Hadoop* or *Hadoop*. So, what about companies that build products/solutions on top of Hadoop? This is where the term *derivative works* comes in.

What Are Derivative Works?

Any product that uses Apache Hadoop code, known as *artifacts*, as part of its construction is said to be a *derivative work*. A derivative work is *not* an Apache Hadoop release. It may be true that a derivative work can be described as "powered by Apache Hadoop." However, there is strict guidance on product naming to avoid confusion in the marketplace. Consequently, companies that provide distributions of Hadoop should also be considered to be derivative works.

NOTE I liken the relationship between Hadoop and derivative works to the world of Xbox games development. Many Xbox games use graphics engines provided by a third party. The Unreal Engine is just such an example.

What Is a Distribution?

Now that you know what a derivative work is, we can look at distributions. A *distribution* is the packaging of Apache Hadoop projects and subprojects plus any other additional proprietary components into a single managed package. For example, Hortonworks provides a distribution of Hadoop called "Hortonworks Data Platform," or HDP for short. This is the distribution used by Microsoft for its product, HDInsight.

You may be asking yourself what is so special about that? You could certainly do this yourself. However, this would be a significant undertaking. First, you'd need to download the projects you want, resolve any dependencies, and then compile all the source code. However, when you decide to go down this route, all the testing and integration of the various components is on you to manage and maintain. Bear in mind that the creators of distributions also employ the committers of the actual source and therefore can also offer support.

As you might expect, distributions may lag slightly behind the Apache projects in terms of releases. This is one of the deciding factors you might want to consider when picking a distribution. Frequency of updates is a key factor, given how quickly the Hadoop ecosystem evolves.

If you look at the Hortonworks distribution, known as Hortonworks Data Platform (HDP), you can see that there are a number of projects at different stages of development. The distribution brings these projects together and tests them for interoperability and stability. Once satisfied that the projects all hang together, the distributor (in this case, Hortonworks) creates the versioned release of the integrated software (the distribution as an installable package).

The 1.3 version made a number of choices as to which versions to support. Today, though, just a few months later, the top-line Hadoop project has a 1.2.0.5 release available, which is not part of HDP 1.3. This and other ecosystem changes will be consumed in the next release of the HDP distribution.

To see a nice graphic of the Hortonworks distribution history, I will refer you to `http://hortonworks.com/products/hdp-2/`. Hadoop is a rapidly changing and evolving ecosystem and doesn't rest on its laurels so including version history is largely futile.

Hadoop Distributions

Note that there are several Hadoop distributions on the market for you to choose from. Some include proprietary components; others do not. The following sections briefly cover some of the main Hadoop distributions.

Hortonworks HDP

Hortonworks provides a distribution of Apache Hadoop known as Hortonworks Data Platform (HDP). HDP is a 100% open source distribution. Therefore, it does not contain any proprietary code or licensing. The developers employed by Hortonworks contribute directly to the Apache projects. Hortonworks is also building a good track record for regular releases of their distribution, educational content, and community engagement. In addition, Hortonworks has established a number of strategic partnerships, which will stand them in good stead. HDP is available in three forms. The first is for Hadoop 1.x, and the second is for Hadoop 2.0, which is currently in development. Hortonworks also offers HDP for Windows, which is a third distribution. HDP for Windows is the only version that runs on the Windows platform.

MapR

MapR is an interesting distribution for Hadoop. They have taken some radical steps to alter the core architecture of Hadoop to mitigate some of its single points of failure, such as the removal of the single master name node for an alternative architecture that provides them with a multimaster system. As a result, MapR has also implemented its own JobTracker to improve availability.

MapR also takes a different approach to storage. Instead of using direct attached storage in the data nodes, MapR uses mounted network file storage, which they call Direct Access NFS. The storage provided uses MapR's file system, which is fully POSIX compliant.

MapR is available both within Amazon's Elastic MapReduce Service and within Google's Cloud Platform. MapR also offers a free distribution called M3. However, it is not available in Azure or on Windows and is missing some of the high-availability (HA) features. For those goodies, you have to pay to get either the M5 or M7 versions.

Cloudera CDH

Cloudera, whose chief architect is Doug Cutting, offers an open source distribution called Cloudera Distribution Including Apache Hadoop (CDH). Like MapR, Cloudera has invested heavily in some proprietary extensions to Hadoop for their Enterprise distribution. Cloudera, however, also has an additional release, Cloudera Standard, which combines CDH with their own cluster management tool: Cloudera Manager. Cloudera Manager is proprietary, but it is a free download. As far as competition goes, this puts Cloudera Standard firmly up against Hortonworks's HDP distribution, which includes Ambari for its cluster management.

Cloudera's big-ticket item is Impala. Impala is a real-time, massively parallel processing (MPP) query engine that runs natively on Hadoop. This enables users to issue SQL queries against data stored in HDFS and Apache HBase without having to first move the data into another platform.

IS HDINSIGHT A DISTRIBUTION?

In a word, no. HDInsight is a product that has been built on top of the Hortonworks HDP distribution (specifically the HDP distribution for Windows). At the time of this writing, HDP 1.3 is the currently available version.

Core Hadoop Ecosystem

Some projects in the world of Hadoop are simply more important than others. Projects like HDFS, the Hadoop Distributed File System, are fundamental to the operation of Hadoop. Similarly, MapReduce currently provides both the scheduling and the execution and programming engines to the whole of Hadoop. Without these two projects there simply is no Hadoop.

In this next section, we are going to delve a little deeper into these core Hadoop projects to build up our knowledge of the main building blocks. Once we've done that, we'll be well placed to move forward with the next section, which will touch on some of the other projects in the Hadoop ecosystem.

HDFS

HDFS, one of the core components of Apache Hadoop, stands for Hadoop Distributed File System. There's no exotic branding to be found here. HDFS is a Java-based, distributed, fault-tolerant file storage system designed for distribution across a number of commodity servers. These servers have been configured to operate together as an HDFS *cluster*. By leveraging a scale-out model, HDFS ensures that it can support truly massive data volumes at a low and linear cost point.

Before diving into the details of HDFS, it is worth taking a moment to discuss the files themselves. Files created in HDFS are made up of a number of HDFS *data blocks* or simply HDFS *blocks*. These blocks are not small. They are 64MB or more in size, which allows for larger I/O sizes and in turn greater throughput. Each block is replicated and then distributed across the machines of the HDFS cluster.

HDFS is built on three core subcomponents:

- NameNode
- DataNode
- Secondary NameNode

Simply put, the NameNode is the "brain." It is responsible for managing the file system, and therefore is responsible for allocating directories and files. The NameNode also manages the *blocks*, which are present on the DataNode. There is only one NameNode per HDFS cluster.

The DataNodes are the workers, sometimes known as *slaves*. The DataNodes perform the bidding of the NameNode. DataNodes exist on every machine in the cluster, and they are responsible for offering up the machine's storage to HDFS. In summary, the job of the DataNode is to manage all the I/O (that is, read and write requests).

HDFS is also the point of integration for a new Microsoft technology called Polybase, which you will learn more about in Chapter 10, "Data Warehouses and Hadoop Integration."

MapReduce

MapReduce is both an engine and a programming model. Users develop MapReduce programs and submit them to the MapReduce engine for processing. The programs created by the developers are known as *jobs*. Each *job* is a combination of Java ARchive (JAR) files and classes required to execute the MapReduce program. These files are themselves collated into a single JAR file known as a *job file*.

Each MapReduce job can be broken down into a few key components. The first phase of the job is the *map*. The *map* breaks the input up into many tiny pieces so that it can then process each piece independently and in parallel. Once complete, the results from this initial process can be collected, aggregated, and processed. This is the *reduce* part of the job.

The MapReduce engine is used to distribute the workload across the HDFS cluster and is responsible for the execution of MapReduce jobs. The MapReduce engine accepts jobs via the JobTracker. There is one JobTracker per Hadoop cluster (the impact of which we discuss shortly). The JobTracker provides the scheduling and orchestration of the MapReduce engine; it does not actually process data itself.

To execute a job, the JobTracker communicates with the HDFS NameNode to determine the location of the data to be analyzed. Once the location is known, the JobTracker then speaks to another component of the MapReduce engine called the *TaskTracker*. There are actually many TaskTracker nodes in the Hadoop cluster. Each node of the cluster has its own TaskTracker. Clearly then, the MapReduce engine is another master/slave architecture.

TaskTrackers provide the execution engine for the MapReduce engine by spawning a separate process for every task request. Therefore, the JobTracker must identify the appropriate TaskTrackers to use by assessing which are available to accept task requests and, ideally, which trackers are closest to the data. After the decision has been made, the JobTracker can submit the workload to the targeted TaskTrackers.

TaskTrackers are monitored by the JobTracker. This is a bottom-up monitoring process. Each TaskTracker must "report in" via a heartbeat signal. If it fails to do so for any reason, the JobTracker assumes it has failed and reassigns the tasks accordingly. Similarly, if an error occurs during the processing of an assigned task, the TaskTracker is responsible for calling that in to the JobTracker. The decision on what to do next then lies with the JobTracker.

The JobTracker keeps a record of the tasks as they complete. It maintains the status of the job, and a client application can poll it to get the latest state of the job.

NOTE **The JobTracker is a single point of failure for the MapReduce engine. If it goes down, all running jobs are halted, and new jobs cannot be scheduled.**

Important Apache Projects for Hadoop

Now that we have a conceptual grasp of the core projects for Hadoop (the brain and heart if you will), we can start to flesh out our understanding of the broader ecosystem. There are a number of projects that fall under the Hadoop umbrella.

Some will succeed, while others will wither and die. That is the very nature of open source software. The good ideas get developed, evolve, and become great—at least, that's the theory.

Some of the projects we are about to discuss are driving lots of innovation—especially for Hadoop 2.0. Hive is the most notable project in this regard. Almost all the work around the Hortonworks Stinger initiative is to empower SQL in Hadoop. Many of these changes will be driven through the Hive project. Therefore, it is important to know what Hive is and why it is getting so much attention.

Hive

Apache Hive is another key subproject of Hadoop. It provides data warehouse software that enables a SQL-like querying experience for the end user. The Hive query language is called Hive Query Language (HQL). (Clearly, the creators of Hive had no time for any kind of creative branding.) HQL is similar to ANSI SQL, making the crossover from one to the other relatively simple. HQL provides an abstraction over MapReduce; HQL queries are translated by Hive into MapReduce jobs. Hive is therefore quite a popular starting point for end users because there is no need to learn how to program a MapReduce job to access and process data held in Hadoop.

It is important to understand that Hive does not turn Hadoop into a relational database management system (RDBMS). Hive is still a batch-processing system that generates MapReduce jobs. It does not offer transactional support, a full type system, security, high concurrency, or predictable response times. Queries tend to be measured in minutes rather in than milliseconds or seconds. This is because there is a high spin-up cost for each query and, at the end of the day, no cost-based optimizer underpins the query plan like traditional SQL developers are used to. Therefore, it is important not to overstate Hive's capabilities.

Hive does offer certain features that an RDBMS might not, though. For example, Hive supports the following complex types: structs, maps (key/value pairs), and arrays. Likewise, Hive offers native operator support for regular expressions, which is an interesting addition. HQL also offers additional extensibility by allowing MapReduce developers to plug in their own custom mappers and reducers, allowing for more advanced analysis.

The most recent and exciting developments for Hive have been the new *Stinger* initiatives. Stinger has the goal of delivering 100X performance improvement to Hive plus SQL compatibility. These two features will have a profound impact on Hadoop adoption; keep them on your radar. We'll talk more about Stinger in Chapter 2, "Microsoft's Approach to Big Data."

Pig

Apache Pig is an openly extensible programmable platform for loading, manipulating, and transforming data in Hadoop using a scripting language called Pig

Latin. Pig is another abstraction on top of the Hadoop core. It converts the Pig Latin script into MapReduce jobs, which can then be executed against Hadoop.

Pig Latin scripts define the flow of data through transformations and, although simple to write, can result in complex and sophisticated manipulation of data. So, even though Pig Latin is SQL-like syntactically, it is more like a SQL Server Integration Services (SSIS) Data Flow task in spirit. Pig Latin scripts can have multiple inputs, transformations, and outputs. Pig has a large number of its own built-in functions, but you can always either create your own or just "raid the piggybank" (`https://cwiki.apache.org/confluence/display/PIG/PiggyBank`) for community-provided functions.

As previously mentioned, Pig provides its scalability by operating in a distributed mode on a Hadoop cluster. However, Pig Latin programs can also be run in a local mode. This does not use a Hadoop cluster; instead, the processing takes place in a single local Java Virtual Machine (JVM). This is certainly advantageous for iterative development and initial prototyping.

SQOOP

SQOOP is a top-level Apache project. However, I like to think of Apache SQOOP as a glue project. It provides the vehicle to transfer data from the relational, tabular world of structured data stores to Apache Hadoop (and vice versa).

SQOOP is extensible to allow developers to create new connectors using the SQOOP application programming interface (API). This is a core part of SQOOP's architecture, enabling a plug-and-play framework for new connectors.

SQOOP is currently going through something of a re-imagining process. As a result, there are now two versions of SQOOP. SQOOP 1 is a client application architecture that interacts directly with the Hadoop configurations and databases. SQOOP 1 also experienced a number of challenges in its development. SQOOP 2 aims to address the original design issues and starts from a server-based architecture. These are discussed in more detail later in this book.

Historically, SQL Server had SQOOP connectors that were separate downloads available from Microsoft. These have now been rolled into SQOOP 1.4 and are also included into the HDInsight Service. SQL Server Parallel Data Warehouse (PDW) has an alternative technology, Polybase, which we discuss in more detail in Chapter 10, "Data Warehouses and Hadoop Integration."

HCatalog

So, what is HCatalog? Simply put, HCatalog provides a tabular abstraction of the HDFS files stored in Hadoop. A number of tools then leverage this abstraction when working with the data. Pig, Hive, and MapReduce all use this abstraction to reduce the complexity and overhead of reading and writing data to Hadoop.

HDFS files can, in theory, be in any format, and the data blocks can be placed anywhere on the cluster. HCatalog provides the mechanism for mapping both the file formats and data locations to the tabular view of the data. Again, HCatalog is open and extensible to allow for the fact that some file formats may be proprietary. Additional coding would be required, but the fact that a file format in HDFS was previously unknown would not be a blocker to using HCatalog.

Apache HCatalog is technically no longer a Hadoop project. It is still an important feature, but its codebase was merged with the Hive Project early in 2013. HCatalog is built on top of the Hive and leverages its command-line interface for issuing commands against the HCatalog.

One way to think about HCatalog is as the master database for Hive. In that sense, HCatalog provides the catalog views and interfaces for your Hadoop "database."

HBase

HBase is an interesting project because it provides NoSQL database functionality on top of HDFS. It is also a column store, providing fast access to large quantities of data, which is often sparsely populated. HBase also offers transactional support to Hadoop, enabling a level of Data Modification Language (DML) (that is, inserts, updates, and deletes). However, HBase does not offer a SQL interface; remember, it is part of the NoSQL family. It also does not offer a number of other RDBMS features, such as typed columns, security, enhanced data programmability features, and querying languages.

HBase is designed to work with large tables, but you are unlikely to ever see a table like this in an RDBMS (not even in a SharePoint database). HBase tables can have billions of rows, which is not uncommon these days; but in conjunction with that, those rows can have an almost limitless number of columns. In that sense, there could be millions of columns. In contrast, SQL Server is limited to 1,024 columns.

Architecturally, HBase belongs to the master/slave collection of distributed Hadoop implementations. It is also heavily reliant on Zookeeper (an Apache project we discuss shortly).

Flume

Flume is the StreamInsight of the Hadoop ecosystem. As you would expect, it is a distributed system that collects, aggregates, and shifts large volumes of event streaming data into HDFS. Flume is also fault tolerant and can be tuned for failover and recovery. However, in general terms, faster recovery tends to mean trading some performance; so, as with most things, a balance needs to be found.

The Flume architecture consists of the following components:

- Client
- Source
- Channel
- Sink
- Destination

Events flow from the client to the source. The *source* is the first Flume component. The source inspects the event and then farms it out to one or more *channels* for processing. Each channel is consumed by a *sink*. In Hadoop parlance, the event is "drained" by the sink. The channel provides the separation between source and sink and is also responsible for managing recovery by persisting events to the file system if required.

Once an event is drained, it is the sink's responsibility to then deliver the event to the destination. There are a number of different sinks available, including an HDFS sink. For the Integration Services users out there familiar with the term backpressure, you can think of the channel as the component that handles backpressure. If the source is receiving events faster than they can be drained, it is the channel's responsibility to grow and manage that accumulation of events.

A single pass through a source, channel, and sink is known as a *hop*. The components for a hop exist in a single JVM called an *agent*. However, Flume does not restrict the developer to a single hop. Complex multihop flows are perfectly possible with Flume. This includes creating fan-out and fan-in flows; failover routes for failed hops; and conditional, contextual routing of events. Consequently, events can be passed from agent to agent before reaching their ultimate destination.

Mahout

Mahout is all about machine learning. The goal of the project is to build scalable machine-learning libraries. The core of Apache Mahout is implemented on top of Hadoop using MapReduce. However, the project does not limit itself to that paradigm. At present, Mahout is focused on four use cases:

- **Recommendation mining**: Recommendation mining is the driving force behind several recommendation engines. How many of you have seen something like this appear in your inbox: "Because you bought this New England Patriots shirt, you might also like this NFL football."
- **Clustering**: Clustering is the grouping of text documents to create topically related groupings or categories.

- **Classification**: Classification algorithms sit on top of classified documents and subsequently learn how to classify new documents. You could imagine how recruitment agents would love clustering and classification for their buzzword bingo analysis. If Apache Mahout is able to reduce the number of calls received for the wrong job, that's a win for everyone in my book.
- **Frequent item set mining**: Frequent item set mining is a way to understand which items are often bucketed together (for example, in shopping basket analysis).

Ambari

Ambari is the system center of the Hadoop ecosystem. It provides all the provisioning, operational insight, and management for Hadoop clusters. Remember that Hadoop clusters can contain many hundreds or thousands of machines. Keeping them configured correctly is a significant undertaking, and so having some tooling in this space is absolutely essential.

Ambari provides a web interface for ease of management where you can check on all the Hadoop services and core components. The same web interface can also be used to monitor the cluster, configuring notification alerts for health and performance conditions. Job diagnostic information is also surfaced in the web UI, helping users better understand job interdependencies, historic performance, and system trends.

Finally, Ambari can integrate with other third-party monitoring applications via its RESTful API. So when I say it is the system center of Hadoop, it literally is!

Oozie

Oozie is a Java web scheduling application for Hadoop. Often, a single job on its own does not define a business process. More often than not, there is a chain of events, processing, or processes that must be initiated and completed for the result to have meaning. It is Oozie's lot in life to provide this functionality. Simply put, Oozie can be used to compose a single container/unit of work from a collection of jobs, scripts, and programs. For those familiar with enterprise schedulers, this will be familiar territory. Oozie takes these units of work and can schedule them accordingly.

It is important to understand that Oozie is a trigger mechanism. It submits jobs and such, but MapReduce is the executor. Consequently, Oozie must also solicit status information for actions that it has requested. Therefore, Oozie has callback and polling mechanisms built in to provide it with job status/completion information.

Zookeeper

Distributed applications use Zookeeper to help manage and store configuration information. Zookeeper is interesting because it steps away from the master/slave model seen in other areas of Hadoop and is itself a highly distributed architecture and consequently highly available. What is interesting is that it achieves this while providing a "single view of the truth" for the configuration information data that it holds. Zookeeper is responsible for managing and mediating potentially conflicting updates to this information to ensure synchronized consistency across the cluster. For those of you who are familiar with managing complex merge replication topologies, you know that this is no trivial task!

The Future for Hadoop

You don't have to look too far into the future to discern the future direction of Hadoop. Alpha code and community previews are already available for Hadoop 2.0, which is fantastic to see. Aside from this, the projects we've talked about in the previous section continue to add new features, and so we should also expect to see new V1 distributions from the likes of Hortonworks for the foreseeable future.

Of course, one of the most exciting things to happen to Hadoop is the support for Hadoop on Windows and Azure. The opportunity this presents for the market cannot be overstated. Hadoop is now an option for all data professionals on all major platforms, and that is very exciting indeed.

So, what can we expect in Hadoop 2.0? Two projects that are worth highlighting here (at least in summary): YARN and Tez.

Summary

In this first chapter, you learned all about what big data is, about the core components of the Hadoop ecosystem, and a little bit about its history and inspiration. The stage is set now for you to immerse yourself in this new and exciting world of big data using Hadoop.

CHAPTER

2

Microsoft's Approach to Big Data

WHAT YOU WILL LEARN IN THIS CHAPTER:

- Recognizing Microsoft's Strategic Moves to Adopt Big Data
- Competing in the Hadoop Ecosystem
- Deciding How to Deploy Hadoop

In Chapter 1 we learned a bit about the various projects that comprise the Hadoop ecosystem. In this chapter we will focus on Microsoft's approach to big data and delve a bit deeper into the more competitive elements of the Hadoop. Finally, we'll look at some of the considerations when deploying Hadoop and evaluate our deployment options. We'll consider how these deployment factors might manifest themselves in our chosen topology and what, if anything, we can do to mitigate them.

A Story of "Better Together"

Back in 2011, at the PASS Summit Keynote, then Senior Vice President Ted Kummert formally announced the partnership with Hortonworks as a central tenet of Microsoft's strategy into the world of "big data." It was quite a surprise.

Those of us who had been following Microsoft's efforts in this space were all waiting for Microsoft to release a proprietary product for distributed scale-out compute (for example, the Microsoft Research project known as Dryad). However, it was not to be. Microsoft elected to invest in this partnership and work with the open source community to enable Hadoop to run on Windows and work with Microsoft's tooling. It was more than a bold move. It was unprecedented.

Later that week, Dave DeWitt commented in his keynote Q&A that the "market had already spoken" and had chosen Hadoop. This was a great insight into Microsoft's rationale; they were too late to launch their own product. However, this is just the beginning of the story. Competition is rife, and although Hadoop's core is open source, a number of proprietary products have emerged that are built on top of Hadoop. Will Microsoft ever build any proprietary components? No one knows. Importantly, though, the precedent has been set. As product companies look to monetize their investment, it seems inevitable that there will ultimately be more proprietary products built on top of Hadoop.

Microsoft's foray into the world of big data and open source solutions (OSS) has also overlapped with the even broader, even more strategic shift in focus to the cloud with Windows Azure. This has led to some very interesting consequences for the big data strategy that would have otherwise never materialized. Have you ever considered Linux to be part of the Microsoft data platform? Neither had I!

With these thoughts in your mind, I now urge you to read on and learn more about this fascinating ecosystem. Understand Microsoft's relationship with the open source world and get insight on your deployment choices for your Apache Hadoop cluster.

NOTE **If you want to know more about project Dryad, this site provides a great starting point:** `http://research.microsoft.com/en-us/projects/dryad/`. **You will notice some uncanny similarities.**

Competition in the Ecosystem

Just because Hadoop is an open source series of projects doesn't mean for one moment that it is uncompetitive. Quite the opposite. In many ways, it is a bit like playing cards but with everyone holding an open hand; everyone can see each other's cards. That is, until they can't. Many systems use open source technology as part of a mix of components that blend in proprietary extensions. These proprietary elements are what closes the hand and fuels the competition. We will see an example of this later in this chapter when we look at Cloudera's Impala technology.

Hadoop is no exception. To differentiate themselves in the market, distributors of Hadoop have opted to move in different directions rather than collaborate on a single project or initiative. To highlight how this is all playing out, let's focus on one area: SQL on Hadoop. No area is more hotly contested or more important to the future of adoption of a distribution than the next generation of SQL on Hadoop.

SQL on Hadoop Today

To recap what you learned in Chapter 1, "Industry Needs and Solutions": SQL on Hadoop came into being via the Hive project. Hive abstracts away the complexity of MapReduce by providing a SQL-like language known as Hive Query Language (HQL). Notice that it does not suddenly mean that Hadoop observes all the ACID (atomicity, consistency, isolation, durability) rules of a transaction. It is more that Hadoop offers through Hive a querying syntax that is familiar to end users. However, you want to note that Hive works only on data that resides in Hadoop.

The challenge for Hive has always been that dependency on MapReduce. Owing to the tight coupling between the execution engine of MapReduce and the scheduling, there was no choice but to build on top of MR. However, Hadoop 2.0 and project YARN changed all that. By separating scheduling into its own project and decoupling it from execution, new possibilities have surfaced for the evolution of Hive.

Hortonworks and Stinger

Hortonworks has focused all its energy on Stinger. Stinger is not a Hadoop project as such; instead, it is an initiative to dramatically improve the performance and completeness of Hive. The goal is to speed up Hive by 100x. No mean feat. What is interesting about Stinger is that all the coding effort goes directly into the Hadoop projects. That way everyone benefits from the changes made. This completely aligns with Hortonworks's commitment and charter to Hadoop.

So what is Stinger? It consists of three phases. The first two phases have already been delivered.

Stinger Phase 1

Phase 1 was primarily aimed at optimizing Hive within its current architecture. Hence it was delivered in Hive 0.11 in May 2013, forming part of Hortonworks Data Platform (HDP) 1.3 release. Phase 1 delivered three changes of notable significance:

- Optimized RC file (ORCFile): Optimizations to the ORC File format have contributed enormously to Hive's data access patterns. By adding metadata at the file and block level, queries can now be run faster. In addition, much like SQL Server's column store technology, only the bytes from the required columns are read from HDFS; reducing I/O and again adding a further performance boost.

NOTE **ORCFile stands for Optimized Record Columnar File. This file format allows for the data to be partitioned horizontally (rows) and vertically (columns). In essence, it's a column store for Hadoop.**

- SQL compatibility: Decimal as a data type was introduced. Truncate was also added. Windowing functions also made the list, so Hive picked up support for `RANK`, `LAG & LEAD`, `FIRST & LAST`, and `ROW_NUMBER` in addition to the `OVER` clause. Some improvements were also made in the core syntax, so `GROUP BY` allowed aliases and `ALTER VIEW` was also included.
- Query and join optimizations: As with most releases of database software, query optimizations are often featured, and Hive 0.11 was no exception. Hive had two major changes in this area. The first was to remove redundant operators from the plan. It had been observed that these operators could be consuming up to 10% of the CPU in simple queries. The second improvement was to `JOIN` operators with the de-emphasis of the `MAPJOIN` hint. This was in part enabled by another change, which changed the default configuration of `hive.auto.convert.join` to `true` (that is, on).

Stinger Phase 2

Phase 2 was implemented as part of Hive 0.12, which was released in October 2013. Note that this release followed only 5 months after phase 1. The community behind Stinger are moving at a fast pace.

To continue with Stinger's three-pronged focus on speed, scale, and SQL, phase 2 also needed to cut over to Hadoop 2.0. This enabled the engineers working on Hive to leverage YARN and lay the groundwork for Tez.

NOTE **Refer back to Chapter 1 for definitions of Hadoop projects YARN and Tez.**

Phase 2 included the following enhancements:

- Performance: Queries got faster with Stinger phase 2 thanks to a number of changes. A new logical optimizer was introduced called the Correlation Optimizer. Its job is to merge multiple correlated MapReduce jobs into a single job to reduce the movement of data. `ORDER BY` was made a parallel operation. Furthermore, predicate pushdown was implemented to allow ORCFile to skip over rows, much like segment skipping in SQL Server. Optimizations were also added for `COUNT (DISTINCT)`, with the `hive.map.groupby.sorted` configuration property.

- SQL compatibility: Two significant data types were introduced: `VARCHAR` and `DATE`. `GROUP BY` support was enhanced to enable support for struct and union types. Lateral views were also extended to support an "outer" join behavior, and truncate was extended to support truncation of columns. New user-defined functions (UDFs) were added to work over the Binary data type. Finally partition switching entered the product courtesy of `ALTER TABLE..EXCHANGE PARTITION`.

NOTE **SQL Server does not support lateral views. That's because SQL Server doesn't support a data type for arrays and functions to interact with this type. To learn about lateral views, head over to `https://cwiki.apache.org/confluence/display/Hive/LanguageManual+LateralView`.**

- End of HCatalog project: With Hive 0.12, HCatalog ceased to exist as its own project and was merged into Hive.

NOTE **HCatalog is defined in Chapter 1.**

Stinger Phase 3

Stinger phase 3 is underway, but will see Hadoop introduce Apache Tez, thus moving away from batch to a more interactive query/response engine. Vectorized queries (batch mode to SQL Server Query Processor aficionados) and an in-memory cache are all in the pipeline. However, it is still the early days for this phase of the Stinger initiative.

Cloudera and Impala

Cloudera chose a different direction when defining their SQL in Hadoop strategy. Clearly, they saw the limitations of MapReduce and chose to implement their own engine: Impala.

Cloudera took a different approach to Hortonworks when they built Impala. In effect, they chose to sidestep the whole issue of Hadoop's legacy with MapReduce and started over. Cloudera created three new daemons that drive Impala:

- Impala Daemon
- Impala Statestore
- Impala Catalog Service

Impala Daemon

The Impala daemon is the core component, and it runs on every node of the Hadoop cluster. The process is called impalad, and it operates in a decentralized, multimaster pattern; that is, any node can be the controlling "brain" for a given query. As the coordinating node is decided for each query, a common single point of failure and bottleneck for a number of massively parallel-processing (MPP) systems is elegantly removed from the architecture. Note, however, that the Impala daemon you connect to when submitting your query will be the one that will take on the responsibility of acting as the coordinator. This could be load balanced by the calling application. However, it is not automatically load balanced.

Once one node has been defined as the coordinator, the other nodes act as workhorses performing delegated tasks on data subsets as defined by the coordinator. Each workhorse operates over data and provides interim results back to the coordinator, who will be responsible for the final result set.

The Impala daemons are in constant contact with the Statestore daemon to see which nodes in the cluster are healthy and are accepting tasks.

Impala Statestore

The Statestore is another daemon known as statestored. Its job is to monitor all the Impala daemons, confirming their availability to perform tasks and informing them of the health of other Impala daemons in the cluster. It therefore helps to make sure that tasks are not assigned to a node that is currently unreachable. This is important because Impala sacrifices runtime resilience for speed. Unlike MapReduce, queries that experience a node failure are canceled; so, the sooner the cluster knows about an issue, the better.

Note that only one Statestore daemon is deployed on the cluster. However, this is not an availability issue per se. This process is not critical to the operation of Impala. The cluster does become susceptible to runtime stability for query operation, but does not go offline.

Impala Catalog Service

The Catalog Service is the third daemon and is named catalogd. Its job is to distribute metadata changes to all nodes in the cluster. Again, only one Catalog Service daemon is in operation on the cluster, and it is commonly deployed on the same node as the Statestore owing to the fact that it uses the Statestore as the vehicle for transmitting its messages to the Impala daemons.

The catalog service removes the need to issue `REFRESH` and `INVALIDATE METADATA` statements, which would otherwise be required when using Data Definition Language (DDL) or Data Modification Language (DML) in Impala. By distributing metadata changes it ensures that any Impala daemon can act as a coordinator without any additional actions on the part of the calling application.

As with the Statestore, the Catalog Service is not mission critical. If the Catalog Service is down for any reason, users would need to execute `REFRESH` table after performing an insert or `INVALIDATE METADATA` after DDL operations on any Impala daemon they were connecting to.

IS IMPALA OPEN SOURCE?

The simple answer is yes. Impala is an open source product. However, there is a catch. It's an extension to CDH (Cloudera Distribution Including Apache Hadoop). This last point is important. You cannot use Impala on any old Hadoop distribution; it is unique to Cloudera. So although it is open source, it is in many ways proprietary. Just because something is open source doesn't mean that there is no vendor lock-in.

Like Hortonworks, Cloudera monetizes their investment in Hadoop through support and training. Impala is no exception. Real Time Query (RTQ) is the technical support package for Impala and is an extension of Cloudera Enterprise (their base enterprise technical support offering). To get RTQ, you have to purchase both Cloudera Enterprise and RTQ.

Microsoft's Contribution to SQL in Hadoop

Microsoft's initial contribution was really focused on getting Hadoop (specifically Hortonworks HDP) running on Windows. This has become the basis upon which HDInsight, Microsoft's platform as a service Hadoop offering, has been built. More recently, Microsoft has been collaborating with Hortonworks on the Stinger initiative. Personally speaking, that is clear given the obvious commonality between SQL Server Column Store and batch mode processing and Hadoop's OCFile optimizations and the vectorized query processing seen in Tez. Tez also introduces a more general, expressive, cost-based optimizer for executing complex directed acyclic graphs (DAGs). Because SQL Server has one of the most sophisticated and complex cost-based optimizers on the market today, I am certain that the team will be able to make a significant and positive contribution to this new processing paradigm for Hadoop.

Deploying Hadoop

Now that you have a firm grip on the ecosystem that surrounds Hadoop, both from a technology and business perspective, you'll want to actually consider deploying Hadoop and trying it yourself.

As you might expect, Microsoft offers a number of choices when it comes to deploying Hadoop. However, we really need to set a benchmark to help us consider all the angles as we evaluate which is the most appropriate option for a given environment. This next section first discusses a number of the considerations. The discussion then turns to possible topologies. Ultimately, you want a scorecard to help you make some objective decisions.

Deployment Factors

Which deployment option you choose will be dictated by several factors, many of which are intertwined like the fibers of a shredded-wheat biscuit. It's therefore worth keeping them all, as follows, in mind as we work through this section:

- Elasticity
- Flexibility
- Scalability
- Security
- Proximity
- Functionality
- Usability
- Manageability

Elasticity

Think of your elasticity requirement as a rubber band:

Do you need to be able to stretch your performance requirement to enable faster processing or to cope with spikes/surges in demand?

Elastic scale is the sweet spot for cloud services such as those offered by Windows Azure. I can alter the size and compute power of my cluster at will. With an on-premise service, I am always able to grow, albeit more slowly, but shrinking the topology isn't possible. Once I've bought the kit, I am stuck with it for three years—even if I don't want it any more.

Also, ask:

- Would you like to be able to reduce your outlay/capacity when there is little or no work to do?
- Do you know your workload and could you characterize it?
- Is it predictable and constant, or is it volatile in nature?
- How quickly can you scale your target environment?
- Is this even important to you?

These are tough questions to answer, especially at the outset of a project. Each deployment option offers varying degrees of elasticity, and your understanding of your environment will be an important factor for your desired deployment option.

Flexibility

Closely tied to elasticity is the concept of flexibility:

- Are you sure of your processing requirements?
- How dynamic are your requirements?
- How complete is the vision driving your project?
- Is it possible you may need to change your mind as you enter into a voyage of discovery with big data?

Different models offer the opportunity for greater flexibility in terms of dynamic change. Buying hardware also tends to be a fixed commitment with a three-year write-down.

Scalability

You can look at the scalability factor quite simplistically and answer the following question: How many data nodes do you need?

However, this answer also drives a number of follow-up questions for you to consider:

- Where will you put these nodes?
- How will you manage and monitor them?
- Who will manage and monitor them?

Because Hadoop is a scale-out architecture, the first question of quantity is really a trigger point to think about the broader issues associated with the scale of the deployment. In actuality, the answer to the scale question provides additional context into the decision making of other factors, particularly flexibility and elasticity.

In terms of scale, there are also considerations that relate to limitations. For example, in HDInsight, Microsoft currently allows a maximum of 40 data nodes. However, this is merely an artificial cap placed on the service and can be lifted. *Architecturally* no limit applies.

One might say the same about an on-premise deployment. Certainly, the largest clusters in the world are on premise. However, practicalities will often get in the way. In truth, the same challenges exist for Azure. There has to be capacity in the data center to take your request. However, I have to say, I quite like the idea of making this Microsoft's problem.

Security

Hadoop doesn't have a very sophisticated method of securing the data that is resident in the Hadoop Distributed File System (HDFS). The security models range from weak to none. Therefore, your approach to meeting your security needs is an important factor in your decision-making process. You might want to consider the network layer in addition to the operating system and physical hardware when evaluating all these options. Other options include a "secure by default" configuration, which may well be worth replicating if you want to lock down your deployment.

Proximity

When addressing the question of proximity, you must know where the data is born. This is relevant for a number of reasons, but the prime reason is latency. We do not want the source and analytical systems to be far apart, because if they are, this distance will add latency to the analysis. That latency can often be directly correlated back to cost; a short local network can often be significantly cheaper and result in less impact that than a geographically dispersed network.

The value of the insights from the data may depreciate significantly as the data ages. In these situations, therefore, we may want to keep in close proximity to the data to reduce the mean time to value when analyzing the data.

In addition, the farther apart the systems are, the more expensive and potentially brittle the networking becomes. This is especially apparent in ultra-low latency network topologies where expensive InfiniBand cables may be used to move data at significant velocity. For example, FDR InfiniBand networks can move data at 56Gbps. However, that performance comes at a price, so the shorter the network cables are the better.

Consequently, and by way of simple example, if the data is born in the cloud, it will often make sense to provide analytics in the cloud. By doing so, your network will be local, and the performance between environments will be LAN Ethernet speed rather than Internet/VPN (virtual private network) speed. Your environment and total cost of ownership (TCO) will also benefit because you will avoid data egress charges.

Functionality

Although perhaps not immediately obvious, you need to make sure that your target platform offers the functionality you want to use. Not all Hadoop distributions are created equally. A simple example is differing support for versions of Hive or the inclusion of HBase in a Hadoop distribution. That is not to say that you cannot add/upgrade Hadoop projects to your deployment. However, when you do this, you are stepping outside of the boundaries of the hardened distribution.

Your choice of operating system also dictates the range of distributions of Hadoop available to you and therefore your deployment options.

Usability

Getting started with Hadoop can sometimes feel like a rather daunting prospect, especially if you are exclusively used to the Microsoft ecosystem. At its most extreme, you could download the source code from the Apache website, compile the code yourself, and then manually deploy the code to build the cluster. However, deployment can be as simple as configuring a wizard. Usability therefore is a sliding scale, and the spin-up cost you can accept will help to drive you toward one solution vs. another.

Whichever solution you decide on, you are probably going to want to roll your own PowerShell scripts to build your cluster so that it is a repeatable process.

Manageability

Operational considerations are often overlooked when considering deployment factors. Consider the following:

- How will the system be monitored?
- Which human resources will be needed to support the environment?
- What availability requirements exist, and what disaster recovery strategy is in place?
- How will security be addressed?

These are all common operational questions that you need to answer.

Deployment Topologies

Now that we have an understanding of the factors that might influence a deployment, we can focus on the topologies themselves before moving on to compare them with each other.

In this next section we'll compare the following options:

- On-Premise Hadoop
- Infrastructure as a Service Hadoop
- Platform as a Service Hadoop

Hadoop on Premise

You can always follow the traditional path, which is to build your Hadoop cluster on premise. Most Hadoop clusters in the world today are built using Linux as the operating system. However, as you learned in Chapter 1, Hortonworks has a distribution for Windows.

The biggest challenge when picking Hadoop on premise as your deployment option is knowing how to size it. How many data nodes will you really *need*?

Of course, after you have done that, you then need to procure all the hardware and rack and configure it. You will also have taken on the management and monitoring of the cluster and so will need to figure that out as well. You might choose to use the Ambari project for this purpose. Alternatively, you could stay within the Microsoft ecosystem and use System Center to drive your monitoring. An Ambari SCOM Management Pack has been created so that you can monitor Hadoop using the same infrastructure as the rest of your enterprise. Either way, you need to ensure that you have integrated the new infrastructure into your environment and make sure that all the feeds of data can access the new cluster.

So, why follow this model? Speaking personally, it often comes down to flexibility, proximity, security, and functionality. However, proximity is one factor to emphasize here. If the data is born on premise, and in significant volume, it may make greater sense to retain the data in an on-premise environment. Pushing large volumes of data to the cloud might be impractical and might introduce too much latency prior to the analysis. That said, this issue may be tempered once the initial data load has been accomplished. Subsequent loads will contain only delta changes which would hopefully reduce the burden of the latency.

Remember, though, the second part of proximity, which pertains to integration with other data environments. Business users don't actually care where or what store their data is; they just want to query (and that might be a query across environments).

PDW Integration

Querying across environments was one of the three key design goals for project Polybase, one of the stand-out features in SQL Server Parallel Data Warehouse (PDW) 2012. Polybase provides the glue between Hadoop and the data warehouse for the parallel import and export of data. However, it also enables a unified heterogeneous querying platform for end users. In other words, I can write the following and it just works:

```
SELECT          COUNT(*)
,               SUM(s.Value) AS Total_Sales
,               p.Category_name
,               d.CalendarMonth_name
FROM            dbo.hdfs_Sales s
JOIN            dbo.pdw_Product p       ON s.Product_key        = p.Product_key
JOIN            dbo.pdw_Date d          ON s.Date_              = p.Date_key
WHERE           d.CalendarYear_nmbr = 2012
GROUP BY        p.Category_name
,               d.CalendarMonth_name
```

In the preceding code, I am able to query data held in Hadoop and join it to data held in PDW with a single logical declarative statement. This is important because it enables consumers of data to work with data irrespective of the data source. They are just tables of data.

That said, project Polybase is not without its restrictions. In the release-to-manufacturing (RTM) version of PDW 2012, Polybase only currently supports a delimited file format and works with a limited number of distributions: HDP on Windows, HDP on Linux, and Cloudera. Furthermore, the RTM version does not leverage any of the compute resources of the Hadoop cluster. PDW is simply importing (at great speed) all the data held in Hadoop and holding it in temporary tables inside PDW. This model will evolve over time, and we should look forward in the future to the automatic generation of MapReduce jobs as query optimizations. One might imagine that a slightly rewritten query like the following one might trigger a MapReduce job to enable the where clause to be applied to the query as part of the Hadoop subtree of the query plan:

```
SELECT          COUNT(*)
,               SUM(s.Value) AS Total_Sales
,               p.Category_name
,               d.CalendarMonth_name
FROM            dbo.hdfs_Sales s
JOIN            dbo.pdw_Product p      ON s.Product_key       = p.Product_key
JOIN            dbo.pdw_Date d         ON s.Date_key          = p.Date_key
WHERE           s.Date_key >=  20120101
AND             s.Date_key <   20130101
GROUP BY        p.Category_name
,               d.CalendarMonth_name
```

Exciting times lie ahead for PDW with Polybase integration into Hadoop. We will dive into PDW and Polybase in much greater detail in Chapter 10, "Data Warehouses and Hadoop Integration."

HDInsight

When HDInsight was announced as being generally available (GA), the team also announced an HDInsight emulator. This is designed for developer scenarios in an on-premise environment. Because it is targeted for development, it can be deployed in a single node configuration only. However, you could also opt for a custom one-data-node configuration of an HDInsight cluster using the Azure benefits accompanying an MSDN subscription or Azure trial.

For some simple instructions on getting started with the emulator, head over to the following article: `http://www.windowsazure.com/en-us/manage/services/hdinsight/get-started-with-windows-azure-hdinsight-emulator/`.

If you don't like either of these options, Hortonworks offers either a sandbox virtual machine or you can build a one-node development environment on Windows. The advantage of this is that as HDInsight uses HDP under the hood you can be confident of developing portable code. Either way, you certainly aren't short of choices!

Hadoop in the Cloud

The single biggest transformation to occur to IT in recent times has been the advent of the cloud. By leveraging cloud computing, we can take advantage of a more dynamic, elastic service that can expand and contract as we need. However, what has also become apparent is that the drive to the cloud has forced providers to openly embrace heterogeneity. For example, in September 2013 Microsoft announced its new partnership with Oracle to run its software on Windows Azure. Who would have thought that Oracle would be offered on a service run by Microsoft? The same could also be said for Linux virtual machines.

This has all been great news for users of Hadoop. It means that customer choice is as broad as it has ever been. Do you want to run on premise using Windows or Linux? You can. Would you rather use a cloud offering and use either Linux or Microsoft? You can do that as well. Would you prefer to use a managed service? Go for it. All these options are not only available but are also actively supported and driving new meaning into what Microsoft calls its data platform.

This section delves into the two primary options for deployment with Windows Azure. At the one end, we have infrastructure as a service (IAAS), where you get to roll your own infrastructure. At the other end, there's platform as a service (PAAS) offering a managed service. Which one is most appropriate? Let your requirements decide!

Platform as a Service (PAAS)

Hadoop is offered in a PAAS configuration courtesy of HDInsight on Windows Azure. HDInsight is Microsoft's branding and value-added components based on the Hortonworks distribution HDP. It is a secured, managed service that you can spin up and tear down very easily. Spin-up is measured in minutes and teardown seconds. In that sense, it is very easy to get started with HDInsight and so it scores highly in terms of usability.

To create an HDInsight Hadoop cluster, you can either use one of the two wizards available to you via the management portal or use a PowerShell script. It is also simple to tear down an HDInsight Hadoop cluster. You simply log in to the Azure Management Portal, locate the cluster, and then click the Delete button (and it's gone). This is important because Azure will be charging you for all the time your HDInsight cluster is up and running.

> **WHAT HAPPENS TO THE DELETED DATA?**
>
> You might be wondering what happens to the data in an HDInsight cluster that has just been deleted. That is a good question. On the face of it, one could be forgiven for thinking that the data is lost. However, that is not the case. One of the most interesting parts of HDInsight is the fact that it separates data storage from the compute nodes. HDInsight uses Windows Azure Storage Blob (WASB) accounts to actually hold the data. HDFS is literally treated like a caching tier for the data. No data is actually persisted there by default. You can, of course, override this and treat HDInsight like a "normal" cluster, but then you would have to keep the cluster up and running for as long as you want the data or accept that you will lose the data if/when you decided to delete it.

HDInsight is a secure-by-default configuration. It disables access to the cluster via Remote Desktop by default and also provides (for free) a secure gateway virtual machine that performs the authorization/authentication and exposes endpoints on port 443. Similarly, you can also retrieve Ambari metrics using the REST API via the secure gateway on port 443.

HDInsight is using HDP as its base distribution, but limitations apply. For example, at the moment, HBase is not included in HDInsight. However, on the plus side, it means complete ubiquity. You can take your data set and export it from HDInsight if you want and install it in an on-premise or IAAS installation running HDP, and it will just work.

In late 2013, Microsoft released HDInsight to general availability. It currently is not installed in all Azure data centers, but I expect that to change as the space is provisioned in each data center.

Infrastructure as a Service (IAAS)

Much of what can be achieved currently with HDInsight and PAAS can also be achieved using a combination of IAAS and scripting. You can automate the process of creating your environment and also elastically adjust the resources each time you spin up a Hadoop cluster. Granted, you will have to roll your own scripts to build this environment, but you will have ultimate flexibility in your deployment during the installation process. You may find that it takes you more time to configure and build your IAAS environment as opposed to using the PAAS option with HDInsight.

Note, however, that some additional tasks do become your responsibility. For example, the secure node in HDInsight isn't automatically provisioned, and neither is the metastore. Also, if you want to save money and keep hold of your data, you will need to have your own automated process of detaching disks, deleting virtual machines and performing any additional cleanup. The same clearly is also true (in the inverse) for creating the cluster.

Interestingly enough, the IAAS option opens up the opportunity to run Linux or Windows virtual machines inside of Windows Azure. Therefore, you can actually run any flavor of Hadoop you like on Windows Azure including the latest and greatest versions of Hortonworks or even Cloudera's Impala. You simply aren't constrained to Windows as an operating system on the Microsoft data platform. If you said that to me a few years ago, I'd have looked at you somewhat quizzically. However, the world has simply moved on. Cloud platforms are more interested in managing the compute resources at massive scale than in eliminating workloads based on technology choices.

Deployment Scorecard

So what have we learned? See Figure 2.1.

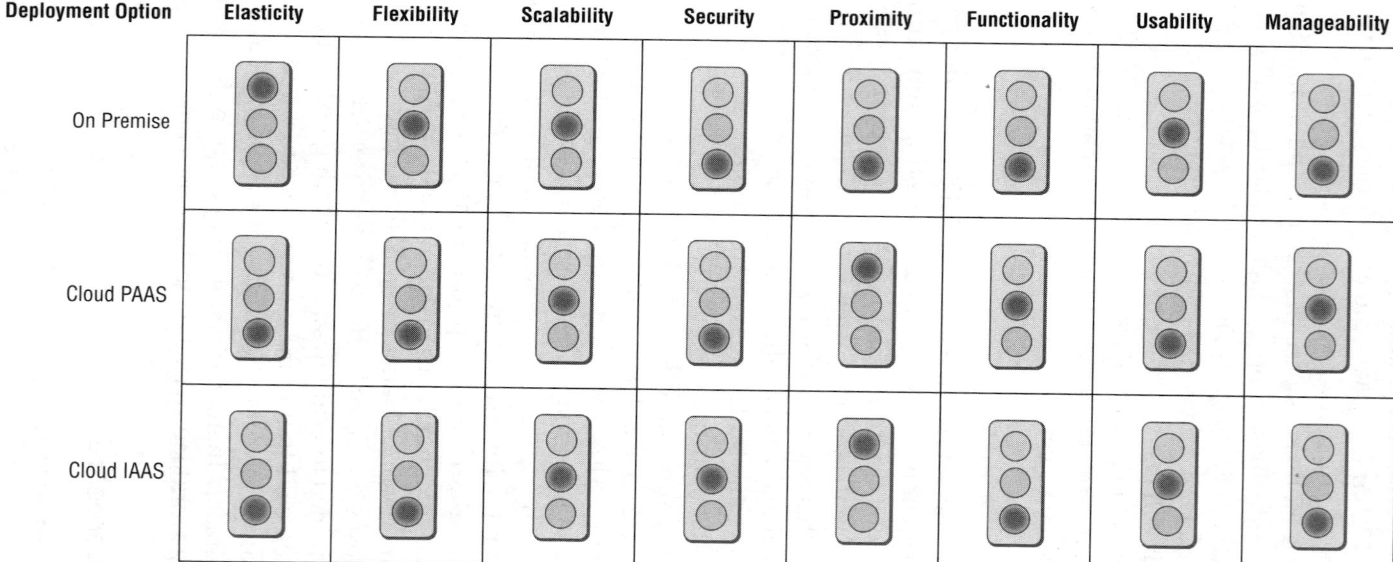

Figure 2.1: The deployment scorecard

We've learned that some of this is relative. Security, for example, is not a great situation for any option, because it is not a strength of Hadoop. Likewise, proximity depends on where the data is actually born. When data is born in the cloud, proximity of cloud offerings would be better (assuming the same service provider was used). However, for proximity I've scored this based on a more general ability to integrate with other disparate data sources throughout out an enterprise. At the time of this writing, the majority of this kind of enterprise data sits on premise, which explains the scoring.

Cloud deployments work well for the following:

- Elastic scale
- Kicking the tires
- Prototyping

On our scorecard, shown in Figure 2.1, what shines through is that the cloud offers that elusive flexibility and elastic scale that encourages experimentation and works brilliantly for "bursty" workloads. However, unless the data is consistently being born in the cloud (a mighty big *if*), the proximity question will probably be an issue. Remember proximity is a two-part measure:

- The distance to the system managing the data (i.e., the bandwidth question)
- The distance to other enterprise data sources (i.e., the integrated analysis dilemma)

The magnitude of this first element may be mitigated if the burden is only endured for an initial or historic load. If the subsequent deltas are of a manageable size, then the concerns may be significantly reduced. The second element is a ratio. If there is little or no integrated analysis with on-premise data sources, then the proximity issue is again less of a concern. If there is a significant amount of integrated analysis, this may prove to be a cloud deployment deal breaker.

On-premise deployments work well for the following:

- Custom deployments
- Data born on premise
- Secure data

An on-premise deployment is best suited for data that is born on premise and that perhaps also needs to be integrated with other data sources that may also reside locally. Having your own environment, although flexible, is also a commitment of both compute and human resources. It therefore suits predictable workloads, which can be more readily sized.

Summary

What have you learned? The world isn't quite what it once seemed. In the time it has taken to move from SQL Server 2008 to SQL Server 2012 the world has been turned upside down. Microsoft's data platform now includes and embraces Linux deployments of open source technology running Apache Hadoop. What's more, we have a variety of options available in terms of our deployment choices. What we choose is largely down to business need and data value (as it should be).

You should now understand the factors that could influence your deployment choice and how to evaluate the options before you. You should also have a better understanding of the Hadoop ecosystem and some of the drivers influencing its future direction.

Part

II

Setting Up for Big Data with Microsoft

In This Part

CHAPTER

3

Configuring Your First Big Data Environment

WHAT YOU WILL LEARN IN THIS CHAPTER:

- Getting Started
- Finding the Installation Tools
- Running the Installation
- Validating Your New Cluster
- Learning Post Install Tasks

In this chapter, you learn the steps necessary to get Hortonworks Data Platform (HDP) and HDInsight Service installed and configured for your use. You'll first walk through the install of HDP on a local Windows Server. Next you'll walk through installing HDInsight on Windows Azure. You'll then follow up on some basic steps on verifying your installs by analyzing log files. Finally, you'll load some data into the Hadoop Distributed File System (HDFS) and run some queries against it using Hive and Pig. This chapter will introduce you to and prepare you for many of the big data features you will be using throughout the rest of the book.

Getting Started

This chapter covers two common scenarios: a single-node Hadoop cluster for simple testing and kicking-the-tires Hadoop; and then we configure an HDInsight cluster in Windows Azure with four nodes to understand the vagaries of the cloud environment. This chapter assumes that the on-premise cluster is being built in a Hyper-V environment or other similar virtualization technology for your initial development environment. (Later in this book, Chapter 16, "Operational Big Data Management," shows what an enterprise class cluster may look like when built so that you have a guideline for a production-class Hadoop cluster.)

Hadoop is an enterprise solution that requires server-class software to run. Therefore, the first thing you need for the installation of the HDP is a copy of one of the following:

1. Windows Server 2008 R2 (64-bit)
2. Windows Server 2012 (64-bit)

NOTE **Windows 7 and Windows 8 are not supported. But one of the best reasons to upgrade from Windows 7 to Windows 8 is that it includes Windows Hyper-V, which means that you can have all the benefits of your client desktop but drive enterprise software from the Hyper-V environment.**

For the development environment, this chapter uses Windows Server 2012 Standard Edition (64-bit) with a graphical user interface (GUI). You should allocate at least 2GB of memory for the virtual machine (VM) of your HDP server.

Getting the Install

Because HDInsight and the HDP are a collaboration between Microsoft and Hortonworks, you can get information about the product in multiple places. The Microsoft website has a number of resources about Microsoft's overall plan for big data and HDInsight in particular. You can find the information at `http://www.microsoft.com/bigdata`. Here you will find information about HDInsight Service that runs on Windows Azure (Microsoft's cloud service) and more about the Microsoft and Hortonworks partnership. In addition, Hortonworks provides a plethora of material for their HDP on Windows on their website at `http://hortonworks.com/products/hdp-windows/`. Here you will find the download link to install HDP and plenty of documentation and support forums for HDP on Windows.

Running the Installation

Now it is time for you to install Hadoop for the first time. In this section you are going to install all the prerequisites for the HDP, configure your server and configuration file, download HDP, and finally run the installation.

BEFORE YOU INSTALL HADOOP

Hadoop is a large distributed product, and understanding how it all ties together is fundamental to successfully installing, configuring, and implementing a cluster. Each distribution from the various vendors has a slightly different look and feel to it, so it is essential to spend a few minutes getting to know what makes a particular flavor of Hadoop tick before diving head first into it.

For HDP, Hortonworks has a short introductory "Getting Started Guide" available online and in a PDF for download. You can find the guide at `http://docs.hortonworks.com/HDPDocuments/HDP1/HDP-Win-1.3.0/bk_getting-startedguide/content/ch_about-hortonworks-data-platform.html`.

You can find the installation documentation for HDP from Hortonworks at `http://docs.hortonworks.com/HDPDocuments/HDP1/HDP-Win-1.3.0/bk_installing_hdp_for_windows/content/win-getting-ready.html`.

On-premise Installation: Single-node Installation

After you have built your base Windows server for installation of HDP, there are several prerequisites for HDP to install, as follows:

1. Install Microsoft Visual C++ 2010 Redistributable Package (64-bit).
2. Install Microsoft .NET framework 4.0.
3. Install Java Development Kit (JDK) 6u31.
4. Install Python 2.7.

WARNING **To be clear, these prerequisites are mandatory. Skipping any of these steps will likely result in a failed installation.**

One of the advantages to using virtualization for installation of a complex product like Hadoop is the ability to take snapshots of your server along the installation process. It is highly recommended that you take a snapshot of your Windows server environment after you have successfully installed all of your prerequisites and before attempting to install the HDP.

Microsoft Visual C++ 2010 Redistributable Package (64-Bit)

To begin, you need to install Microsoft Visual C++ 2010 Redistributable Package (64-bit) from `http://www.microsoft.com/en-us/download/details.aspx?id=14632`. Download and install this package with all the defaults.

Microsoft .NET Framework 4.0

Now you need to install Microsoft.NET Framework 4.0. If you are installing HDP on a Windows 2012 server, you can skip this step because it is already installed with the base operating system. If you are installing on Windows Server 2008 R2, this is a required step. Use the instructions provided here to download and install Microsoft.NET Framework 4.0: `http://www.microsoft.com/en-us/download/confirmation.aspx?id=17851`.

Java JDK 6u31

To begin, you need to download Java JDK located here: `http://www.oracle.com/technetwork/java/javase/downloads/java-archive-downloads-javase6-419409.html#jdk-6u31-oth-JPR`. You want to choose the Windows x64 (64-bit) version, which is at the bottom of the table. Ensure that you accept the license at the top of the table before clicking the link. You need to sign in with your Oracle account. If you do not have one, sign up for one to proceed.

Then, complete the following steps:

1. Install the Java JDK to a directory path that has no whitespace characters in its path; the default path will not work! For example, `C:\program files\Java\` is not a valid path. It is recommended to use `C:\Software\JAVA\`, which is a valid path (see Figure 3.1).

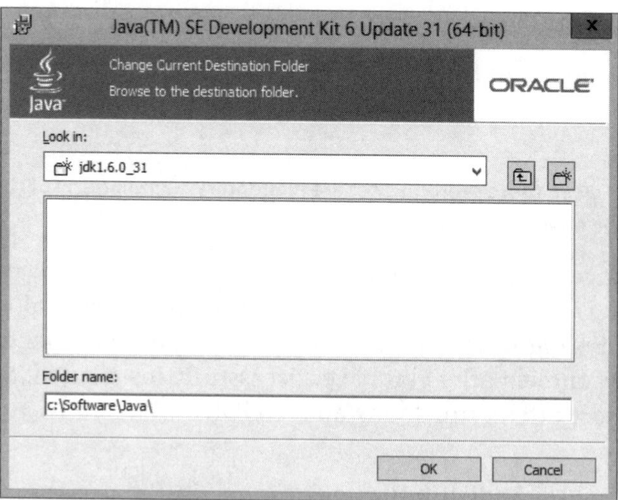

Figure 3.1: Java directory path.

2. If prompted, register your Java JDK.

3. Create a system variable named `JAVA_HOME`. The value of this variable is the full path to the installation directory defined earlier for JDK.
4. Open the Control Panel's System pane and click Advanced system settings. Click the Advanced tab.
5. Click the Environment Variables button. Under System variables, click New. Enter the variable name as **`JAVA_HOME`**.
6. Enter the variable value, as the installation path for the JDK. If you followed the earlier direction, this variable value will be `C:\Software\JAVA` (see Figure 3.2).

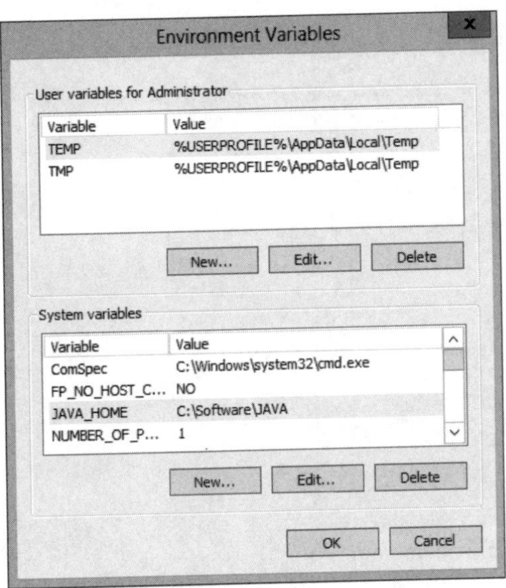

Figure 3.2: Setting the JAVA_HOME path.

7. Click OK.
8. Click Apply Changes.

Python 2.7

You must install Python 2.7. Download Python from `http://www.python.org/download/`. Choose Python 2.7.6 Windows Installer (Windows binary, does not include source). Install Python using all the default configurations.

Then, complete the following steps:

1. Update the `PATH` environment variable. Using Administrator privileges, open the Control Panel's System pane and click Advanced system settings. Click the Advanced tab.

2. Click the Environment Variables button. Under System Variables, find PATH and click Edit.
3. In the Edit windows, modify PATH by appending the installation path for your Python directory to the value of PATH. For example, if the Python executable is installed at C:\Python27\, you must append this value to PATH (see Figure 3.3).

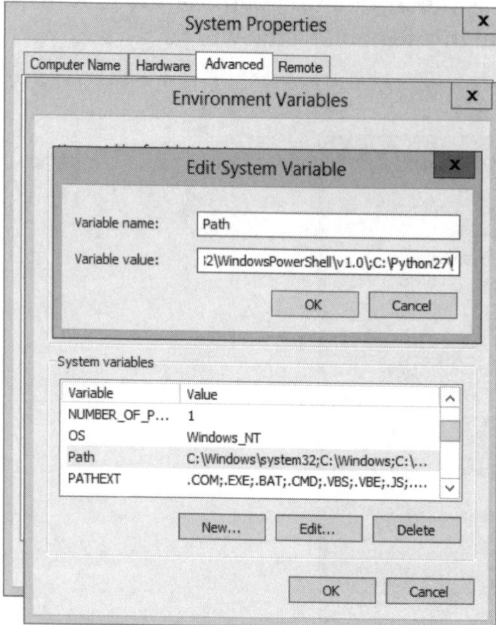

Figure 3.3: Adding Python to your default path.

4. To validate your settings, from a command shell or PowerShell window, type **Python**. If you set your path properly, you will get a response shown in Figure 3.4.

At this point, take a snapshot of the VM image and name it something like **HDP_1-3_PreReqs_Installed.**

Server Configuration

Now it's time to begin configuring your server. You need the hostname of the server you are installing to for later configuration tasks. On the desktop of your server, right-click and select New and the select Text Document. Name it **HDP**

`Configuration`. You will use this document for a few pieces of information you will need later.

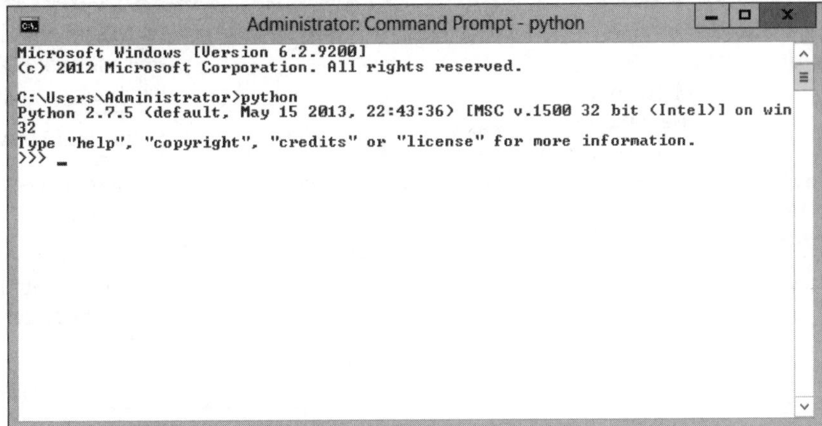

Figure 3.4: Verifying Python.

Next, complete the following steps:

1. Get your hostname. At a command prompt on the cluster host, execute the following command: `Hostname`. You will receive back the hostname of your server. Copy and paste this text into the HDP configuration file you created and save the file.
2. Now you configure a firewall. For the purposes of a development environment, the easiest thing to do is to disable the firewall completely and open all ports.
3. Open the Control Panel. Type **`firewall`** into the search box. Click Check Firewall Status. Click Turn Windows Firewall on or off. Click Turn off Windows Firewall for all available networks.

   If your corporate firewall policies require you to have firewalls turned on, you must open up all of the necessary ports. One way to do it is to open an administrative command prompt (Shift+right-click, Run as Administrator) and type the following command for each port:

   ```
   netsh advfirewall firewall add rule name=AllowRPCCommunication dir=in
   action=allow protocol=TCP localport=135
   ```

   Table 3.1 through Table 3.4 list the default ports used by the various services. Make sure the appropriate ports are opened before you install HDP.

Table 3.1: Default Ports Used by the Hadoop Distributed File System (HDFS)

SERVICE	SERVERS	DEFAULT PORTS USED	PROTOCOL	DESCRIPTION
NameNode web UI	Master nodes (NameNode and any backup NameNodes)	50070	HTTP	Web UI to look at current status of HDFS, explore file system
		50470	HTTPS	Secure HTTP service
NameNode metadata service		8020/9000	IPC	File system metadata operations
DataNode	All slave nodes	50075	HTTP	DataNode web UI to access the status, logs, and so on
		50475	HTTPS	Secure HTTP service
		50010		Data transfer
		50020	IPC	Metadata operations
Secondary NameNode	Secondary NameNode and any backup secondary NameNode	50090	HTTP	Checkpoint for NameNode metadata

Table 3.2: Default Ports Used by MapReduce

SERVICE	SERVERS	DEFAULT PORTS USED	PROTOCOL	DESCRIPTION
JobTracker web UI	Master nodes (JobTracker node and any backup JobTracker node)	50030	HTTP	Web UI for JobTracker
JobTracker	Master nodes (JobTracker node)	8021	IPC	For job submissions
TaskTracker web UI and shuffle	All slave nodes	50060	HTTP	DataNode web UI to access status, logs, and so on
History server web UI		51111	HTTP	Web UI for job history

Table 3.3: Default Ports Used by Hive

SERVICE	SERVERS	DEFAULT PORTS USED	PROTOCOL	DESCRIPTION
HiveServer2	HiveServer2 machine (usually a utility machine)	10001	Thrift	Service for programmatically (Thrift/JDBC) connecting to Hive
HiveServer	Hive Server machine (usually a utility machine)	10000	Thrift	Service for programmatically (Thrift/JDBC) connecting to Hive
Hive Metastore		9083	Thrift	Service for programmatically (Thrift/JDBC) connecting to Hive metadata

Table 3.4: Default Port Used by WebHCat

SERVICE	SERVERS	DEFAULT PORTS USED	PROTOCOL	DESCRIPTION
WebHCat server	Any utility machine	50111	HTTP	Web API on top of HCatalog and other Hadoop services

Table 3.5: Default Ports Used by HBase

SERVICE	SERVERS	DEFAULT PORTS USED	PROTOCOL	DESCRIPTION
HMaster	Master nodes (HBase master node and any backup HBase master node)	60000		
HMaster Info web UI	Master nodes (HBase master node and backup HBase master node if any)	60010	HTTP	The port for the HBaseMaster web UI. Set to –1 if you do not want the info server to run.
Region server	All slave nodes	60020		

Continues

Table 3.5 (*continued*)

SERVICE	SERVERS	DEFAULT PORTS USED	PROTOCOL	DESCRIPTION
Region server	All slave nodes	60030	HTTP	
ZooKeeper	All ZooKeeper nodes	2888		Port used by ZooKeeper peers to talk to each other. See here for more information.
ZooKeeper	All ZooKeeper nodes	3888		Port used by ZooKeeper peers to talk to each other. Refer to `http://zookeeper.apache.org/doc/r3.4.3/zookeeperStarted.html#sc_RunningReplicatedZooKeeper`
		2181		Property from ZooKeeper's config zoo.cfg. The port at which the clients will connect.

4. Download HDP from `http://public-repo-1.hortonworks.com/HDP-Win/1.3/hdp-1.3.0.0-GA.zip`.
5. Go to your downloads folder and extract the zipped file. Within the extracted folder, you should find four files (see Figure 3.5).

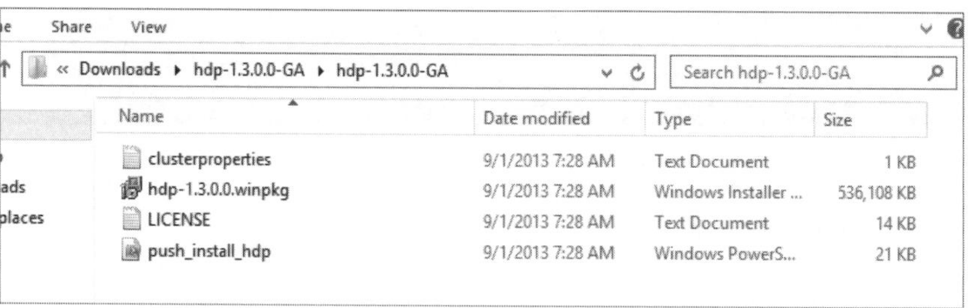

Figure 3.5: Installation files for Hortonworks Data Platform.

6. Open up cluster properties to make configuration changes to it. Here, you want to copy your server name from your HDP Configuration file on your desktop and replace the server names for all the nodes under #Hosts and for the `DB_HOSTNAME` under #Database Host. Additionally, be sure to change the Log and Data directories to the appropriate drive for your server, most likely the C drive. The final `clusterproperties.txt` file

should look similar to the file shown in Figure 3.6 (with your hostname for your single node cluster). Save your file.

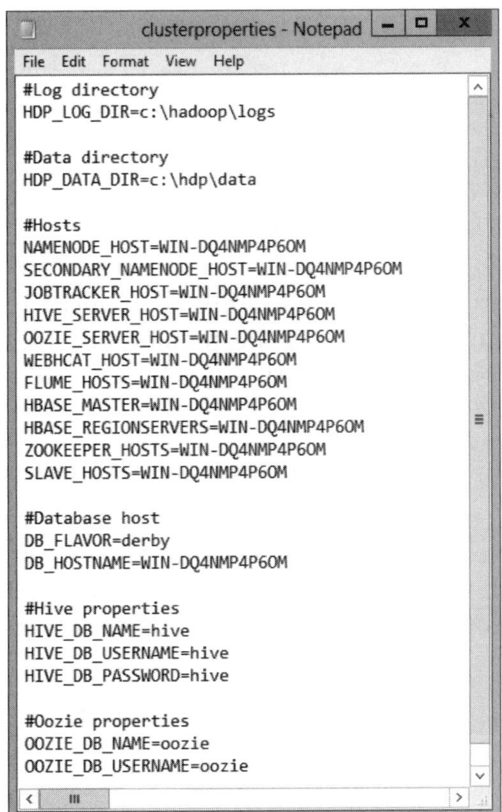

clusterproperties - Notepad
File Edit Format View Help
#Log directory
HDP_LOG_DIR=c:\hadoop\logs
#Data directory
HDP_DATA_DIR=c:\hdp\data
#Hosts
NAMENODE_HOST=WIN-DQ4NMP4P6OM
SECONDARY_NAMENODE_HOST=WIN-DQ4NMP4P6OM
JOBTRACKER_HOST=WIN-DQ4NMP4P6OM
HIVE_SERVER_HOST=WIN-DQ4NMP4P6OM
OOZIE_SERVER_HOST=WIN-DQ4NMP4P6OM
WEBHCAT_HOST=WIN-DQ4NMP4P6OM
FLUME_HOSTS=WIN-DQ4NMP4P6OM
HBASE_MASTER=WIN-DQ4NMP4P6OM
HBASE_REGIONSERVERS=WIN-DQ4NMP4P6OM
ZOOKEEPER_HOSTS=WIN-DQ4NMP4P6OM
SLAVE_HOSTS=WIN-DQ4NMP4P6OM
#Database host
DB_FLAVOR=derby
DB_HOSTNAME=WIN-DQ4NMP4P6OM
#Hive properties
HIVE_DB_NAME=hive
HIVE_DB_USERNAME=hive
HIVE_DB_PASSWORD=hive
#Oozie properties
OOZIE_DB_NAME=oozie
OOZIE_DB_USERNAME=oozie

Figure 3.6: Setting clusterproperties.txt values.

7. Within your HDP Configuration file on your desktop, type the following command for installation of HDP. It is recommended to keep a copy of this command here in case you need multiple installation attempts. Replace any location values (`HDP.msi`, `clusterproperties.txt`) if they differ from the example:

```
Msiexec /i "C:\Users\Administrator\Downloads\hdp-1.3.0.0-GA\
hdp-1.3.0.0-GA\hdp-1.3.0.0.winpkg.msi" /lv "hdp.log"
HDP_LAYOUT="C:\Users\Administrator\Downloads\hdp-1.3.0.0-GA\
hdp-1.3.0.0-GA\clusterproperties.txt" HDP_DIR="C:\hdp\hadoop"
DESTROY_DATA="yes"
```

8. From an elevated command prompt with administrative privileges, run the preceding command. A successful installation will give you back the

dialog box shown in Figure 3.7. Otherwise, you will have some investigating to do, as explained later in the chapter.

Figure 3.7: Successful installation.

9. On the desktop of your server, you will have three new icons. Click the Hadoop command prompt. This opens up a command prompt to the Hadoop install directory. Now, navigate back a directory:

   ```
   cd ..
   ```

10. Next we want to start all the services associated with your HDP installation:

    ```
    start_local_hdp_services
    ```

    This job will take a couple minutes to complete. In the next step, we evaluate the success of our installation with a smoke test that validates the installation. Ideally, you will get a message like the one shown in Figure 3.8 that validates the starting of all services.

```
starting metastore
starting derbyserver
starting templeton
starting oozieservice
Sent all start commands.
total services
16
running services
16
not yet running services
0
Failed_Start

C:\hdp\hadoop>_
```

Figure 3.8: Successful starting of all services.

11. From the same command prompt, enter the following:

    ```
    Run-SmokeTests
    ```

This command runs a variety of tests against your installation to verify that MapReduce, Hive, Pig, Hcat, ZooKeeper and other services are running as expected. It does this by actually creating tables, describing them, querying them, and dropping them from your installation. This command takes several minutes to run and the output will provide you with the confidence that you have installed HDP correctly and can begin using your installation.

Once complete, read through the output in your command shell and look for any errors. If you find none, congratulations, you have successfully installed HDP onto a single node "cluster."

HDInsight Service: Installing in the Cloud

HDInsight Service is Microsoft's cloud-based Hadoop solution built from the HDP. HDInsight Service is a great solution for both test and production data. For test, there is no easier way to spin up a Hadoop cluster and start loading data and running jobs. For production, HDInsight is a wonderful elastic solution for organizations that want their clusters to grow both with their size and complexity of their data.

You will now set up the storage containers needed for your data to reside in Azure Storage Vault (ASV) and then create an HDInsight cluster:

1. After signing in to your Windows Azure portal, click the Storage icon and click the New icon in the bottom-left corner. Create a new storage container using a unique name. Choose a location that is appropriate for you (see Figure 3.9). Later when you create your HDInsight Service cluster, you will choose the same location as you want to collocate your data with your computer nodes.

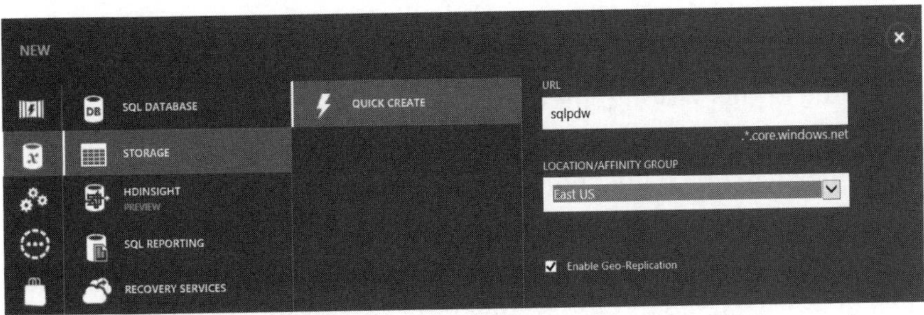

Figure 3.9: Configuring your Windows Azure storage.

2. Click the HDInsight icon and click Create an HDInsight Cluster or click New in the bottom-left corner of the web page. You have two choices at this point: to either use the Quick Create or Custom Create paths to create a new cluster. The Quick Create path is great for getting a development cluster up and running swiftly.
3. Choose a unique cluster name. You get a green check box when you choose a unique name; otherwise, you get a red explanation point telling you that you have chosen a name already in use.

4. Choose a cluster size. Quick Create allows you to choose clusters of sizes 4, 8, 16, and 32. If you are creating a development environment for you to learn on, start with a small size, such as 4 nodes.

CHOOSING THE RIGHT CLUSTER SIZE

Choosing cluster size is an important decision in the cluster creation process. The larger your cluster size, the more compute cycles that you will use. You pay for these compute cycles while your cluster is running, which is the entire time from cluster creation until you delete the cluster. The main reason Microsoft decouples the storage container for HDInsight from the HDInsight cluster is so that you don't have to keep the compute clusters running at all times. You simply pay for what you use.

However, if you spin up a cluster and forget to delete after you have finished, you may be in for a shock at the end of the month when your bill arrives. If you are using your MSDN benefits and spin up a 32-node cluster, you will use your free monthly benefits very quickly. Be cognizant of spinning up the appropriate size of the cluster you need and then spinning it down when you have finished with your processing of data. It is recommended to use four- or eight-node clusters for your testing environments and save the larger cluster sizes for your production workloads.

5. Provide an appropriate password. The password must be at least 10 characters and contain all of the following: an uppercase letter, a lowercase letter, a number, and a special character.
6. Choose the storage account you created in the previous section. At the time of this writing, the supported locations are West US, East US, and North Europe.
7. Click Create HDInsight Cluster at the lower right of the web page (see Figure 3.10).

You created your HDInsight Cluster and ASV storage environment. Now you need to move data to the environment for processing. We'll speak more about data movement from an enterprise perspective in Chapter 16.

Windows Azure Storage Explorer Options

You can choose from several options for data movement to Azure Storage. Azure Storage Explorer (`http://azurestorageexplorer.codeplex.com/`) is a free tool available from CodePlex that enables you to manage your ASV data. To set up any Storage Explorer with your ASV account, navigate to your Storage page in Windows Azure and click the storage container that you want to associate with the Storage Explorer. Then click Manage Access Keys at the bottom of the web page. The pop-up web page provides you with your storage account name and primary and secondary access keys. Ideally, you will keep the primary access key to yourself and share the secondary access key with someone else who might need to access your data. You can always regenerate access keys, which will force users to reset them in their client tool.

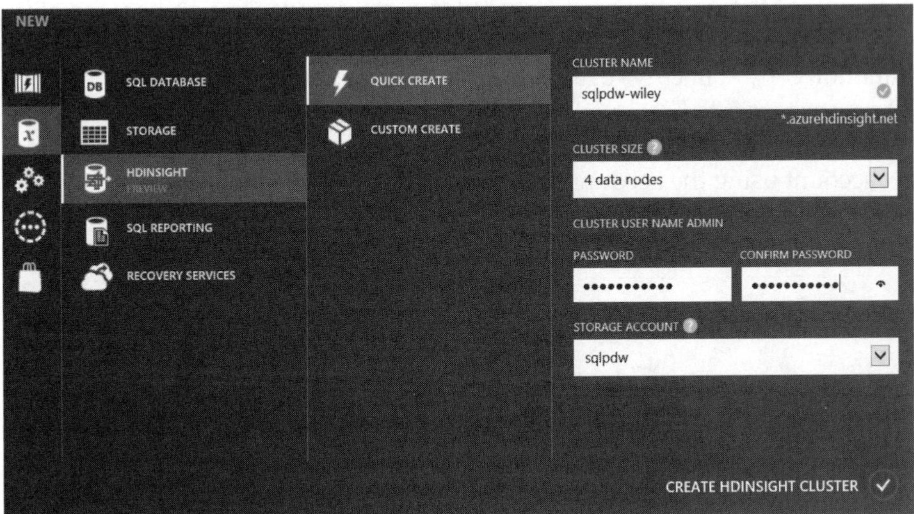

Figure 3.10: Configuring your HDInsight Service Cluster.

Configuring Azure Storage Explorer

To configure Azure Storage Explore, click Add Account and enter the storage account name and storage account key from your Manage Access Keys page in Windows Azure. Click Add Storage Account when complete (see Figure 3.11).

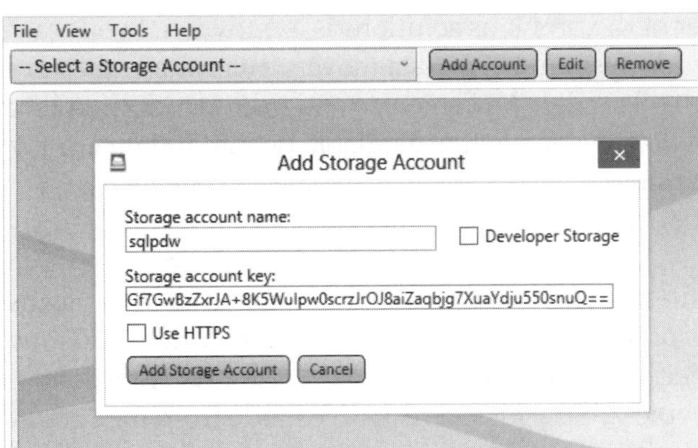

Figure 3.11: Connecting Azure Storage Explorer to your storage account.

With Storage Explorer, you can both explore previously created containers while also providing capabilities to add and delete containers or upload and download files. In other words, it works and feels much like Windows Explorer.

ClumsyLeaf's CloudXplorer

Another popular option is ClumsyLeaf Software's CloudXplorer. Although not free like Storage Explorer, CloudXplorer is a popular option because of its modern interface and simple functionality (see Figure 3.12). You can find an evaluation copy at `http://clumsyleaf.com/products/cloudxplorer`. You can add new accounts to CloudXplorer very similarly to Storage Explorer. Click the Accounts icon on the Windows ribbon and walk through the steps of creating a new account using the account name and secret key from your Manage Access Keys page in Windows Azure.

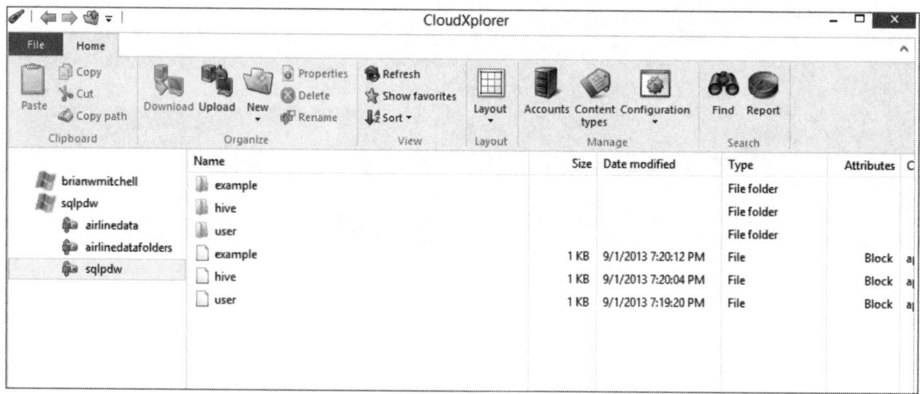

Figure 3.12: CloudXplorer's clean user interface.

AZCopy

As you can imagine, neither of the previous solutions is exactly what you want when developing a production system where data movement is one of the keys to success. A command-line tool for data movement to and from Windows Azure storage is needed. AZCopy to the rescue. It is available on GitHub (`https://github.com/downloads/WindowsAzure/azure-sdk-downloads/AzCopy.zip`).

AZCopy is similar to Robocopy in functionality except that it can natively connect to your ASV storage. Among its many features, AZCopy enables you to copy nested directories of files, use wildcards, and is restartable, which means that you can resume a copy process from where it left off. In addition, AZCopy has a verbose logging mode that is essential to an enterprise-class process.

The following example copies all the files in recursive mode from the `localdata` folder to the container called `newcontainer` in ASV. You would replace `key` with a copy of your secret key from your Azure storage account:

```
AzCopy C:\localdata https://sqlpdw.blob.core.windows.net/newcontainer/
/destkey:key /S
```

AZCopy can easily be wrapped in a robust program written by you or called from a SQL Server Integration Services (SSIS) package as needed. It could also be called from a SQLAgent job for scheduling of data movement both to or from your Azure storage account.

Validating Your New Cluster

Now that you have created your new cluster, it is time to validate it. Validating that everything is installed and working as expected is vital to your understanding of the system and gives you confidence that what you hand over is ready for use.

Logging into HDInsight Service

After you have successfully created your HDInsight cluster, you may want to verify its functionality. HDInsight includes some sample data that enables you to do this very quickly.

From the HDInsight tab, choose your cluster (see Figure 3.13).

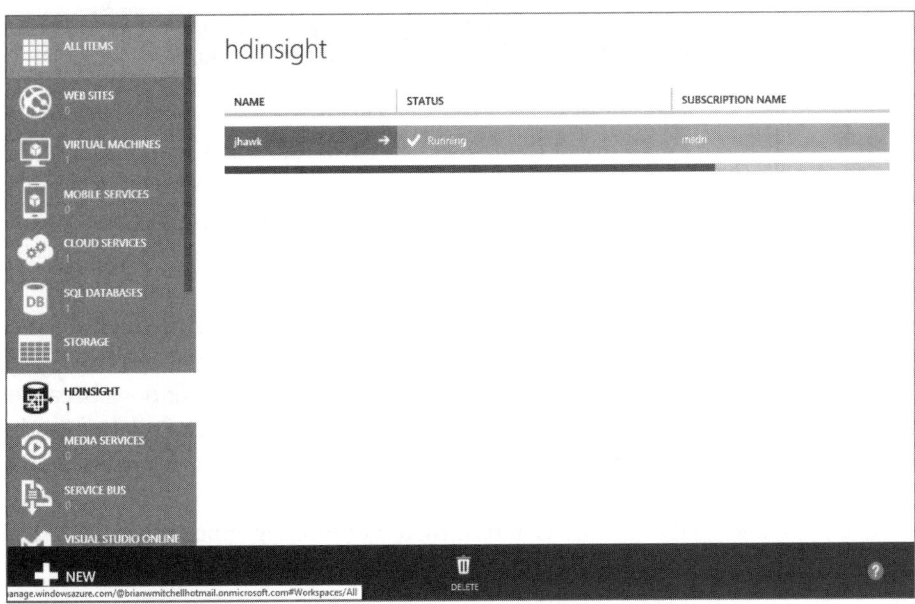

Figure 3.13: HDInsight Service interface.

Click Configuration on the top menu. Next, click Enable Remote. A pop-up box will ask you for a username and password for connecting to the HDInsight NameNode. Finally, you will need to provide an expiration, after which the remote access expires. You should now have a Connect button as shown in Figure 3.14.

It is at the bottom of your configuration page, and clicking the Connect button will allow you to receive the Remote Desktop (RDP) file that will allow you to access the NameNode. Go ahead and click Connect.

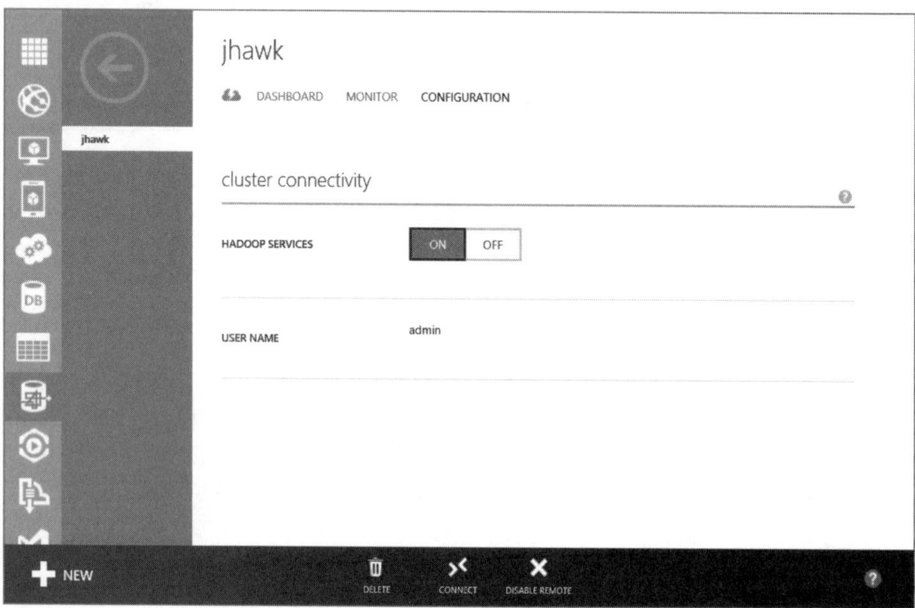

Figure 3.14: Clicking the Connect button.

In Internet Explorer, a request to open or save the file will appear on screen. Choose Open, and an RDP session will begin. Log in to the NameNode with your admin password you chose during the cluster creation process. You'll see here that the desktop of the NameNode in HDInsight Service looks very similar to the single-node cluster we built with our HDP on-premise solution. You can use all the same commands in this environment that you can in the on-premise version.

Generally you shouldn't have to verify HDInsight Service installations because these are highly engineered solutions that have been tested and executed thousands of times. If you happen to run into a problem, you will most likely either just delete that and create a new one or contact Microsoft Support through the Azure website. However, installing HDP locally will require a bit more vigilance on your part.

Verify HDP Functionality in the Logs

Chances are decent that the first few times you attempt to install HDP, you will get an error. This is due to the many pre-installation steps that are vital to the successful installation of Hadoop. Now's not the time to get frustrated, but to follow what the logs tell you and make the adjustments necessary to try the installation again. Here we will walk you through where to find the information you'll need to be successful.

Installation Logs

If you have any failures during the installation of HDP, check the installation log files located at `C:\HadoopInstallFiles`. Specifically, you'll want the file located at `C:\HadoopInstallFiles\HadoopSetupTools\hdp-1.3.0.0.winpkg.install.txt`. If the package did not install correctly, details in this file can help guide you in fixing the solution. Generally, the issues revolve around not paying attention to the details of the installation instructions, such as creating the appropriate environmental variables, making all the changes in the configuration file, or disabling the firewall. If the error seems to involve one of these steps in the pre-installation phase, go back and double-check that you did everything correctly. Make sure that all paths and names are exactly as they are supposed to be, because this is where most people make mistakes.

Individual Service Logs

If you had a successful installation of HDP but are having trouble starting the services, look into the product log directory that was specified in the `cluster-properties.txt` file during installation. Recall that the example in this book had them located at `C:\hadoop\logs`.

Each one of the services has a separate folder. Each folder has multiple files in it, and you might have to open a few to determine the correct one for a particular problem. For example, if you are having a problem starting the Hive service, you navigate to the `C:\hadoop\logs\hive\hive.txt` file. See Figure 3.15.

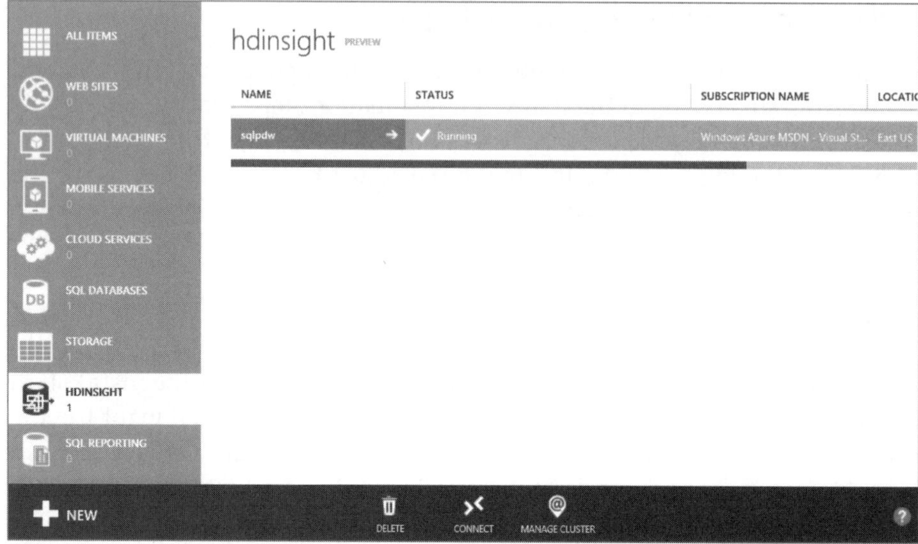

Figure 3.15: Connecting to the RDP session.

Common Post-setup Tasks

Once you have successfully created your cluster and verified its success, you should be itching to get some data on it and start kicking the tires. In the next few steps, we'll load some real data into Hadoop and then check out a couple of the most useful tools, Hive and Pig. (You'll learn more about Hive and Pig in Chapter 6, "Adding Structure with Hive," and Chapter 8, "Effective Big Data ETL with SSIS, Pig, and Sqoop.")

Loading Your First Files

Now that you have successfully installed HDP, it is time to get some data loaded into HDFS so that you can verify the functionality of the system. A favorite data set for playing around in HDP (and Hive in particular) is an airline data set that shows all the flight and on-time information for airline flights within the United States from 1987 to 2008. You can find the original files at `http://stat-computing.org/dataexpo/2009/the-data.html`.

Basic File system Operations

The HDFS is available and ready to be loaded with data. Using the file system command `fs`, you can list and create directories, read and move files, and delete data. Use the `hadoop fs -help` command to get all the functionality available.

Start by loading the airline data into HDFS. In the following example, a folder `C:\SourceData` was created on the HDP server, but it can be a share anywhere in your network. Four of the files from the airline data set have been downloaded into the `SourceData` folder for loading into HDFS. First, create a folder in HDFS to store the data. Then complete the following steps to import the data into HDFS:

1. Open the Hadoop command console from the desktop and enter the following command:

   ```
   hadoop fs -mkdir flightinfo
   ```

2. Import the all files from the `SourceData` folder into the `flightinfo` folder:

   ```
   hadoop fs -put c:\SourceData\*.* flightinfo
   ```

3. To verify the files were copied as expected, you can run the `-ls` command:

   ```
   hadoop fs -ls flightinfo
   ```

The output of the preceding steps should look like Figure 3.16.

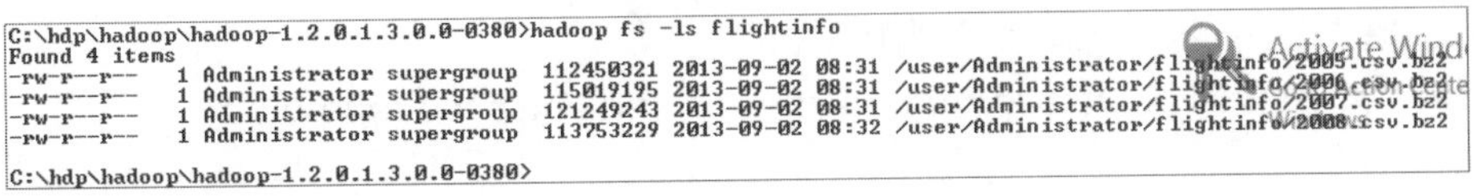

```
C:\hdp\hadoop\hadoop-1.2.0.1.3.0.0-0380>hadoop fs -ls flightinfo
Found 4 items
-rw-r--r--   1 Administrator supergroup  112450321 2013-09-02 08:31 /user/Administrator/flightinfo/2005.csv.bz2
-rw-r--r--   1 Administrator supergroup  115019195 2013-09-02 08:31 /user/Administrator/flightinfo/2006.csv.bz2
-rw-r--r--   1 Administrator supergroup  121249243 2013-09-02 08:31 /user/Administrator/flightinfo/2007.csv.bz2
-rw-r--r--   1 Administrator supergroup  113753229 2013-09-02 08:32 /user/Administrator/flightinfo/2008.csv.bz2

C:\hdp\hadoop\hadoop-1.2.0.1.3.0.0-0380>
```

Figure 3.16: Verifying files in HDFS.

A few of the file system commands that you will use often are listed in Table 3.6. For a full list of available commands, enter **`hadoop fs -help`** at the prompt in the Hadoop command console.

Table 3.6: Common File system Commands

FILE SYSTEM COMMANDS	DESCRIPTION
`cat`	Copies source paths to `stdout`
`copyFromLocal`	Similar to `put` command, except that the source is restricted to a local file reference
`count`	Counts the number of files within a directory
`cp`	Copies files from source to destination
`get`	Copies files to the local file system (opposite of `put`)
`mv`	Moves files from source to definition within HDFS
`rm`	Deletes specified files
`tail`	Displays last KB of the file to `stdout`

Verifying Hive and Pig

Two tools that you will find yourself using often are Hive and Pig. Both of these tools are higher-level languages that allow developers to work with data stored in HDFS without having to write Java programs. Hive is a SQL-like language that allows developers to apply a table-like structure to the data so that they can invoke Hive queries in much the same manner that they invoke SQL Queries. These HiveQL queries are translated into MapReduce jobs that are submitted to Hadoop for execution.

Pig is another abstracted language, which is scripting in nature. Because of the scripting nature of Pig, it is very useful as an extract, translate, and load (ETL) tool for data movement and manipulation. The next couple of sections introduce these two tools.

Verifying Hive

To verify Hive, follow these steps:

1. Open the Hadoop command console and enter the following:

   ```
   cd..
   ```

   This brings us up one level in the folder structure.

2. Next, enter the following:

   ```
   cd hive-0.11.0.1.3.0.0-0380\bin
   ```

   Alternatively, type `hive` and then press Tab; it will fill in the rest of the folder name for you and then add `\bin`).

3. Then enter the following:

   ```
   hive
   ```

This brings up the Hive prompt, and the fact that it comes up is the first thing that lets us know that the service is running as expected.

To find out what objects already exist in your Hive database, enter the following command:

```
show tables;
```

There may be a few tables listed from the previous smoke tests that were run.

NOTE Make sure to include the semicolon after each command; otherwise, the Hive prompt will simply go to the next line and await further commands.

To create your own table based on the airline data that you loaded earlier, run the following command. Note that you may need to replace "administrator" in the location path with your username that you used to log into Windows:

```
CREATE EXTERNAL TABLE flightinfo (
Year int,
     Month int,
     DayofMonth int,
     DayOfWeek int,
     DepTime int,
     CRSDepTime int,
     ArrTime int,
     CRSArrTime int,
     UniqueCarrier string,
     FlightNum int,
     TailNum string,
     ActualElapsedTime int,
     CRSElapsedTime int,
     AirTime int,
     ArrDelay int,
     DepDelay int,
     Origin string,
     Dest string,
     Distance int,
     TaxiIn int,
     TaxiOut int,
     Cancelled int,
     CancellationCode string,
     Diverted string,
     CarrierDelay int,
     WeatherDelay int,
     NASDelay int,
     SecurityDelay int,
     LateAircraftDelay int
     )ROW FORMAT DELIMITED FIELDS TERMINATED BY ',' LOCATION
/user/administrator/flightinfo';
```

This should take very little time to finish. Once completed, you can run a query against the table, such as the following:

```
SELECT COUNT (*) FROM flightinfo;
```

A successful query will look like Figure 3.17.

```
MapReduce Total cumulative CPU time: 4 minutes 6 seconds 694 msec
Ended Job = job_201309010803_0003
MapReduce Jobs Launched:
Job 0: Map: 8  Reduce: 1   Cumulative CPU: 246.694 sec   HDFS Read: 463514236 HDFS Write: 9 SUCCESS
Total MapReduce CPU Time Spent: 4 minutes 6 seconds 694 msec
OK
28745465
Time taken: 300.049 seconds, Fetched: 1 row(s)
hive> _
```

Figure 3.17: Results of Hive query.

As you can see, it provides a great deal of information beyond just the answer to the query (28, 745, 465). Your answer may differ depending on which and how many of the flight info files you loaded into HDFS. Hive also tells us the time it took for the query to complete, how many reads and writes occurred, and the name of the job used in the process. The name of the job is vitally important if you need to troubleshoot for errors.

Finally, you can drop the table:

```
DROP TABLE IF EXISTS flightinfo;
```

And exit Hive:

```
exit;
```

Open up a new Hadoop command prompt and enter the following:

```
hadoop fs -ls flightinfo
```

Notice that the data is still there. Hive external tables such as what we created earlier are simply metadata explanations of the data residing in HDFS. You can create and drop tables without affecting the underlying data; this is one of the great powers of Hive that you will learn more about in Chapter 10, "Adding Structure with Hive."

Verifying Pig

Pig is a procedural scripting language that you will learn more about in Chapter 8, "Effective Big Data ETL with SSIS, Pig, and Sqoop." To quickly test Pig, you are going to run a word-count program that you often see in MapReduce examples. Any `*.txt` file will do, but one good example is the `Davinci.txt` file available from the examples in the HDInsight Service Samples directory. You can get to this directory by logging in to the Windows Azure portal and clicking Manage Cluster. Samples is one of the choices on the screen, and WordCount is a choice on the next screen. On this screen, is the `Davinci.txt` download link.

Now, complete the following steps to verify Pig:

1. Download `Davinci.txt` or any text file into a new folder `C:\PigSource`. Put the data into HDFS:

   ```
   hadoop fs -mkdir wordcount
   ```

2. Import the all files from the `SourceData` folder into the `flightinfo` folder:

   ```
   hadoop fs -put c:\PigSource\davinci.txt wordcount/
   ```

3. To verify the file was copied as expected, run the `-ls` command:

   ```
   hadoop fs -ls wordcount
   ```

   Now let's log in to the Pig console.

4. Navigate to the `hadoop\pig-0.11.0.1.3.0.0-0380\bin` directory and enter the following:

   ```
   pig
   ```

You will find yourself at the grunt prompt:

```
Grunt>
```

5. To get used to the interactive console, type each one of the following lines at the `Grunt` prompt. Press Enter after each line and the Grunt command should reappear for the next line:

```
myinput = LOAD 'wordcount/davinci.txt' USING TextLoader();
words = FOREACH myinput GENERATE FLATTEN(TOKENIZE($0));
grouped = GROUP words BY \$0;
counts = foreach grouped generate GROUP, count(words);
ordered = ORDER counts BY \$0;
STORE ordered INTO 'output/pigout' USING PigStorage;
```

   The final line will kick off a MapReduce job and store the output in the `pigout` folder.

6. Run the following command to read the output of the Pig job:

```
hadoop fs -cat output/pigout/part-r-00000
```

The output is a list of every word in the document and the count of the times it was used. You will get more exposure to Pig in later chapters, but this should give you a good idea of the procedural methods used by Pig to move data through a pipeline and transform it to a useful final state. Of course, you could have written the preceding code as a Pig script and saved the text file and simply called it from Pig. You will learn how to do this in Chapter 8.

Summary

In this chapter, you learned how to install Hortonworks Data Platform into a single-node cluster, how to configure HDInsight Service in Windows Azure, and how to use the tools available in each to quickly validate their installs. You were also introduced to moving data into HDFS and the tools available to move data into your Azure storage. Finally, this chapter gave you a primer in Hive and Pig so that you can quickly evaluate that they are running as expected in your environment.

Part III

Storing and Managing Big Data

In This Part

CHAPTER

4

HDFS, Hive, HBase, and HCatalog

WHAT YOU WILL LEARN IN THIS CHAPTER:

- Exploring HDFS
- Working with Hive
- Understanding HBase and HCatalog

One of the key pieces of the Hadoop big data platform is the file system. Functioning as the backbone, it is used to store and later retrieve your data, making it available to consumers for a multitude of tasks, including data processing.

Unlike the file system found on your desktop computer or laptop, where drives are typically measured in gigabytes, the Hadoop Distributed File System (HDFS) must be capable of storing files where each file can be of gigabyte or terabyte sizes. This presents a series of unique challenges that must be overcome.

This chapter discusses the HDFS, its architecture, and how it solves many of the hurdles, such as reliably storing your big data, efficient access, and other tasks like replicating data throughout your cluster. We will also look at Hive, HBase, and HCatalog, all platforms or tools available within the Hadoop ecosystem that help simplify the management and subsequent retrieval of data out of HDFS.

Exploring the Hadoop Distributed File System

Originally created as part of a web search engine project called Apache Nutch, HDFS is a distributed file system designed to run on a cluster of cost-effective commodity hardware. Although there are a number of distributed file systems in the marketplace, several notable characteristics make HDFS really stand out. These characteristics align with the overalls goals as defined by the HDFS team and are enumerated here:

- **Fault tolerance:** Instead of assuming that hardware failure is rare, HDFS assumes that failures are instead the norm. To this end, an HDFS instance consists of multiple machines or servers that each stores part of the data. Because the data is distributed, HDFS can quickly detect faults and failures and subsequently automatically and transparently recover.
- **High throughput:** Where most file systems strive for low-latency operations, HDFS is more focused on high throughput, even at the expense of latency. This characteristic means that HDFS can stream data to its clients to support analytical processing over large sets of data and favors batch over interactive operations. With forward-looking features like caching and tiered storage, it will no longer be the case that HDFS is not good for interactive operations.
- **Support for large data sets:** It's not uncommon for HDFS to contain files that range in size from several gigabytes all the way up to several terabytes and can include data sets in excess of tens of millions of files per instance (all accomplished by scaling on cost-effective commodity hardware).
- **Write-once read-many (WORM) principle:** This is one of the guiding principles of HDFS and is sometimes referred to as coherency. More simply put, data files in HDFS are written and when closed are never updated. This simplification enables the high level of throughput obtained by HDFS.
- **Data locality:** In a normal application scenario, a process requests data for a source; the data is then transferred from the source over a network to the requestor who can then process it. This time tested and proven process often works fine on smaller data sets. As the size of the data set grows, however, bottlenecks and hotspots begin to appear. Server resources and networks can quickly become overwhelmed as the whole process breaks down. HDFS overcomes this limitation by providing facilities or interfaces

for applications to move the computation to the data, rather than moving the data to the computation.

As one of the more critical pieces of the Hadoop ecosystem, it's worth spending a little extra time to understand the HDFS architecture and how it enables the aforementioned capabilities.

Explaining the HDFS Architecture

Before discussing machine roles or nodes, let's look at the most fundamental concept within HDFS: the block. You may already be familiar with the block concept as it is carried over from the file system found on your own computer. *Blocks*, in this context, are how files are split up so that they can be written to your hard drive in whatever free space is available.

A lot of functional similarities exist between your file system blocks and the HDFS block. HDFS blocks split files, some which may be larger than any single drive, so that they can be distributed throughout the cluster and subsequently written to each node's disk. HDFS blocks are also much larger than those in use on your local file system, defaulting to an initial size of 64MB (but often being allocated much larger).

Within an HDFS cluster, two types or roles of machines or servers make up what is often referred to as the master/slave architecture. The first, called the NameNode, functions as the master or controller for the entire cluster. It's responsible for maintaining all the HDFS metadata and drives the entire file system namespace operation. There can be only one single NameNode per cluster, and if it is lost or fails, all the data in the HDFS cluster is gone.

The second type of role within an HDFS cluster is the DataNode. And although there is only one NameNode, there are usually many DataNodes. These nodes primarily interact with HDFS clients by taking on the responsibility to read and write or store data or data blocks. This makes scaling in your cluster easy, as you simply add additional DataNodes to your cluster to increase capacity. The DataNode is also responsible for replicating data out when instructed to do so by the NameNode (more on HDFS replication shortly).

HDFS Read and Write Operations

To get a better understanding of how these parts or pieces fit together, Figure 4.1 and Figure 4.2 illustrate how a client reads from and writes to an HDFS cluster.

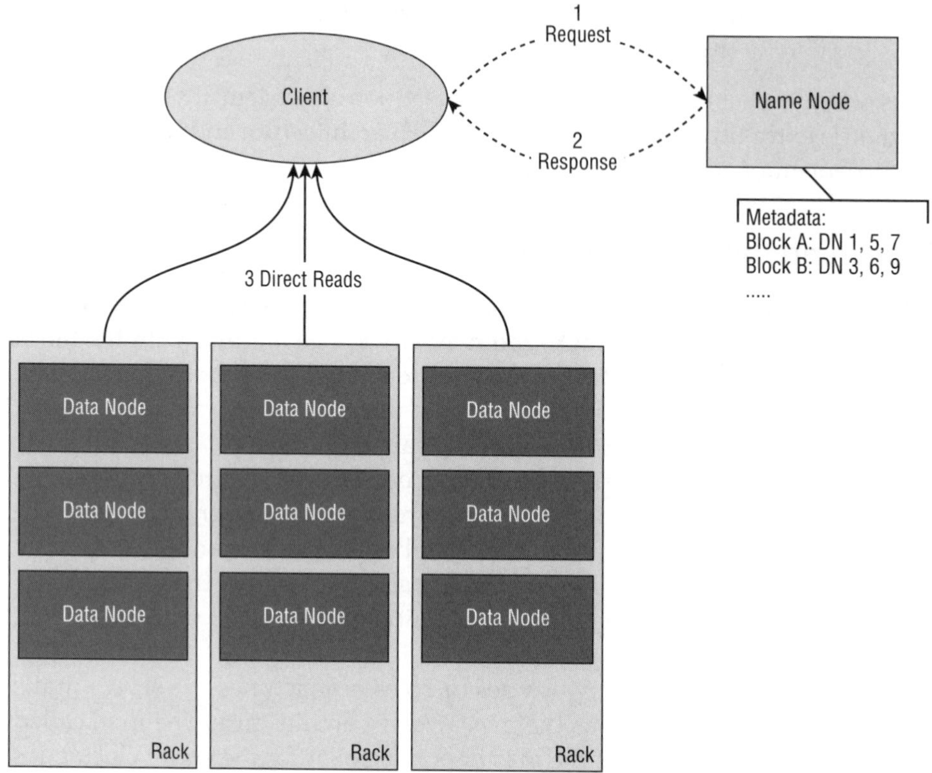

Figure 4.1: HDFS read operation

When a client needs to read a data set from HDFS (see Figure 4.1), it must first contact the NameNode. The NameNode contains all the metadata associated with the data set or file, including its blocks and all the block storage locations. The NameNode passes this metadata or information back to the client. The client then subsequently requests the data directly for each DataNode.

The pattern of this interaction is important. Although the NameNode acts as a gatekeeper, after the metadata is provided to the client, it gets out of the way and allows the client to interact directly with the DataNode. This provides the foundation for the extremely high level of throughput in HDFS.

Much like the read operation, an HDFS write-operation begins with the NameNode (see Figure 4.2). First, the client requests that the NameNode create a new empty file with no blocks associated with it. Next, the client streams data directly to the DataNode using an internal queue to reliably manage the process of sending and acknowledging the data.

Throughout the streaming process, as new blocks are allocated, the NameNode is updated. After the client has completed the write operation, it closes out the process with the NameNode. The NameNode only verifies that the minimum set of replicas have been created before returning successfully.

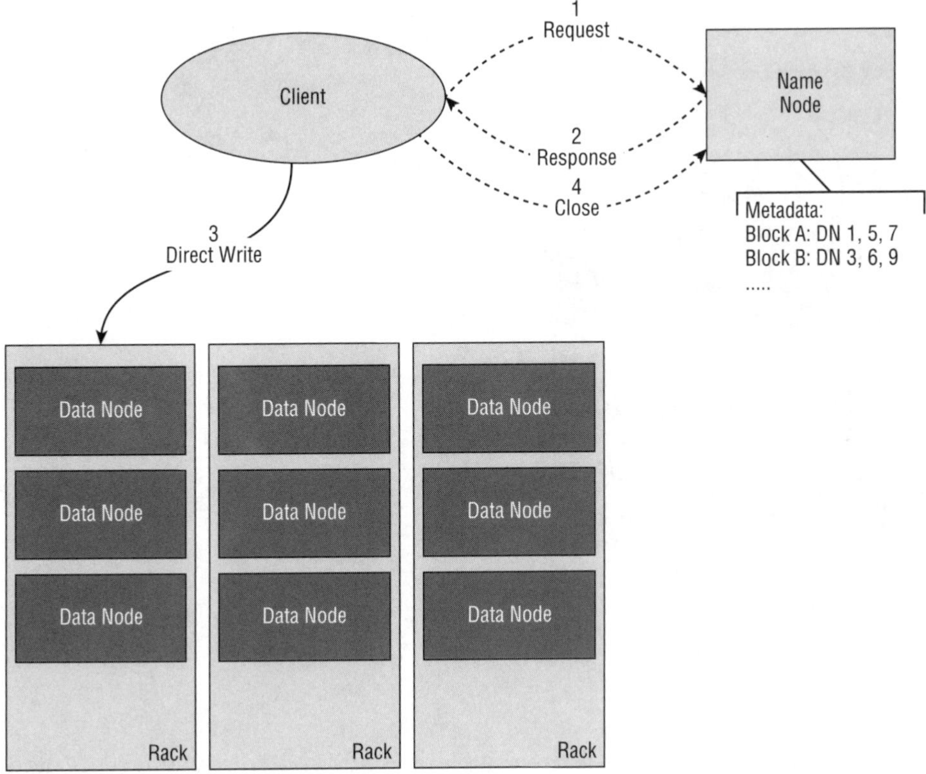

Figure 4.2: HDFS write operation

NOTE **Throughout this process, any write failures are handled silently and transparently to the client. If a node fails during the write or during the replicate process, it will be reattempted on an alternative node automatically.**

Replication

Replication provides for fault tolerance within HDFS and occurs as part of each write or whenever the NameNode detects a DataNode failure. Out of the box, the default HDFS replication factor is three (controlled by the `dfs.replication` property), meaning that each block is written to three different nodes. Figure 4.3 elaborates on the previous write operation example to illustrate how replication occurs.

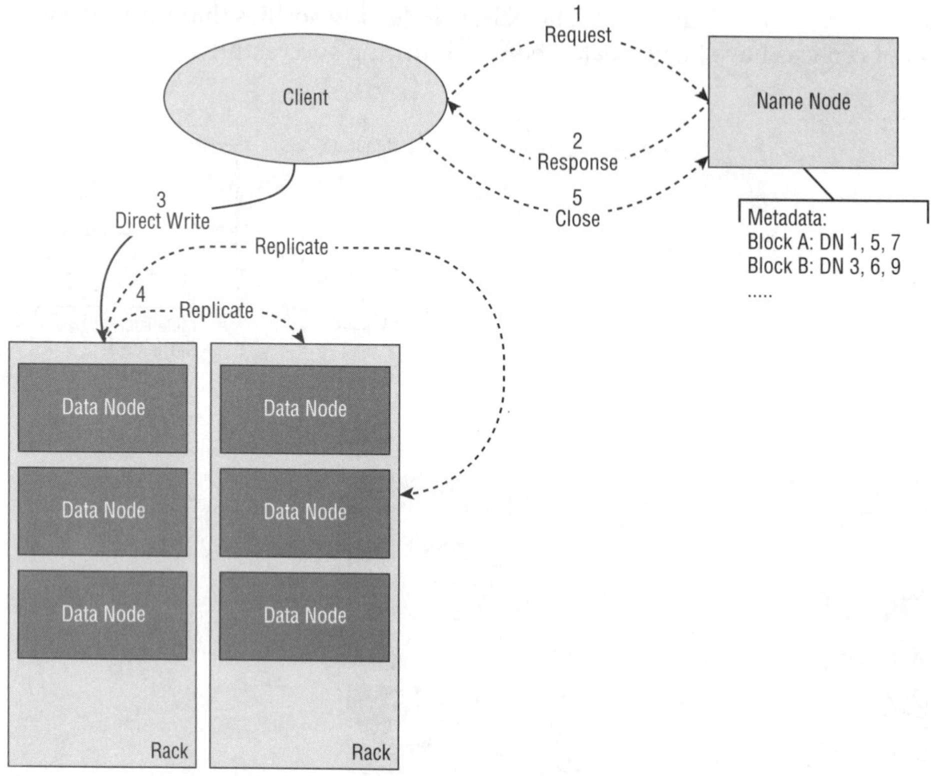

Figure 4.3: HDFS replication

During the course of the write the NameNode controls where replicated blocks are created and HDFS will create a minimum number of replicated blocks before the write is considered successful. Selecting the location for replicas is important for both fault tolerance and availability. HDFS is server, rack, and data center aware and is sophisticated in placement of replicated data so that maximum fault tolerance is achieved.

NOTE **The `dfs.replication.min` property controls the minimum number of replicas that must be created. If there is a difference between the `dfs.replication` and `dfs.replication.min` properties, the additional replicas are created asynchronously.**

Interacting with HDFS

Because HDFS is built on top of the Java platform, the majority of integration and interaction options all require some level of Java development. Although these options, which range from the HDFS application programming interface (API) to Apache Thrift, are important (particularly if you are writing native client interactions), this chapter introduces only two of those most commonly used on the Microsoft platform: the HDFS command shell and WebHDFS. This is not intended to discount the other available options; instead, it is intended to help you get your feet wet as you get started with HDFS.

Hadoop File System (FS) Shell

Whether you realized it or not, you've already seen the HDFS command shell in action. As you worked through the Hortonworks Data Platform On-Premise introduction, the commands used to both upload and retrieve data from HDFS were all handled by the File System (FS) shell.

```
Administrator: Hadoop Command Line
Usage: hadoop [--config confdir] COMMAND
where COMMAND is one of:
  namenode -format       format the DFS filesystem
  secondarynamenode      run the DFS secondary namenode
  namenode               run the DFS namenode
  datanode               run a DFS datanode
  dfsadmin               run a DFS admin client
  mradmin                run a Map-Reduce admin client
  fsck                   run a DFS filesystem checking utility
  fs                     run a generic filesystem user client
  balancer               run a cluster balancing utility
  snapshotDiff           diff two snapshots of a directory or diff the
                         current directory contents with a snapshot
  lsSnapshottableDir     list all snapshottable dirs owned by the current user
  oiv                    apply the offline fsimage viewer to an fsimage
  fetchdt                fetch a delegation token from the NameNode
  jobtracker             run the MapReduce job Tracker node
  pipes                  run a Pipes job
  tasktracker            run a MapReduce task Tracker node
  historyserver          run job history servers as a standalone daemon
  job                    manipulate MapReduce jobs
  queue                  get information regarding JobQueues
  version                print the version
  jar <jar>              run a jar file

  distcp <srcurl> <desturl> copy file or directories recursively
  distcp2 <srcurl> <desturl> DistCp version 2
  archive -archiveName NAME <src>* <dest> create a hadoop archive
  daemonlog              get/set the log level for each daemon
 or
  CLASSNAME              run the class named CLASSNAME
Most commands print help when invoked w/o parameters.

c:\hdp\hadoop\hadoop-1.2.0.1.3.0.0-0380>_
```

Figure 4.4: HDFS shell

The FS shell is actually part of Hadoop and uses commands that primarily align with UNIX commands. The FS shell commands all take the following format:

```
hadoop fs -<CMD> <ARGS>
```

The `CMD` is a specific file system command, and `ARGS` are the arguments needed to execute the command. The FS shell commands all use uniform resource indicators (URIs) in the format of `[schema]://[authority]/[path]`. For HDFS, these paths look like this: `hdfs://node/mydata`. The `hdfs://` prefix is optional and is often left off for simplicity.

Table 4.1 lists some of the most common commands and shows usage examples.

Table 4.1: Hadoop File System Shell Commands

FS COMMAND	DESCRIPTION	USAGE
`cp`	Copies a files from a source to a destination	`hadoop fs -cp /user/hadoop /file1 /user/hadoop/file2`
`get`	Copies a file to the local file system	`hadoop fs -get /user/hadoop /file localfile`
`ls` and `lsr`	Lists the files containing the specified directory; can be used recursively	`hadoop fs -ls /user/hadoop/` `hadoop fs -lsr /user/hadoop/`
`mkdir`	Creates an HDFS directory	`hadoop fs -mkdir /user/hadoop /dir1`
`put`	Copies a file from the local file system to HDFS	`hadoop fs -put localfile /user /hadoop/hadoopfile`
`rm` and `rmr`	Removes a file or directory; can be used recursively	`hadoop fs -rm /user/hadoop/dir` `hadoop fs -rmr /user/hadoop/dir`

WebHDFS

The Hadoop FS shell is simple to get started with and straightforward to use for data management operations, but it has one potential weakness: The shell commands are just that, shell commands. Therefore, they require access to a machine with Hadoop installed to execute the commands.

NOTE **WebHDFS is just one of the many approaches for working with HDFS. There are advantages and disadvantages associated with each option.**

An alternative to this approach, and one that overcomes this limitation, is WebHDFS. WebHDFS is an HTTP-based REST (Representational State Transfer) API that fully implements the same file system commands found in the FS shell.

Accessing this API is accomplished by embedding commands into HTTP URL requests and taking advantage of the standard HTTP operations (`GET`, `POST`, `PUT`, `DELETE`). To better illustrate, consider the following example to open a file via WebHDFS:

```
http://<HOST>:<PORT>/webhdfs/v1/<PATH>?op=OPEN
```

To deconstruct this URL for better understanding, note the following:

- The `<HOST>` and `<PORT>` arguments point to the location of the NameNode.
- The `<PATH>` argument is the file being requested.
- The `op` querystring parameter passes in the file system operation.

An HTTP `GET` request is issued using the example URL. After the path and location metadata is queried from the NameNode, an HTTP 307 temporary redirect is returned to the requestor, as shown here:

```
HTTP/1.1 307 TEMPORARY_REDIRECT
Location: http://<DATANODE>:<PORT>/webhdfs/v1/<PATH>?op=OPEN...
Content-Length: 0
```

The redirect contains the actual path to the DataNode that hosts the data file or block. The client can then follow the redirect to stream the data directly from the source.

As previously mentioned, the WebHDFS offers a complete implementation of the FS shell commands, Table 4.2 list some of the file system commands and their WebHDFS equivalents.

Table 4.2: WebHDFS Access Commands

FILE SYSTEM COMMAND	WEBHDFS EQUIVALENT
`mkdir`	`PUT "http://<HOST>:<PORT>/<PATH>?op=MKDIRS"`
`rm`	`DELETE "http://<host>:<port>/webhdfs/v1/<path>?op=DELETE"`
`ls`	`"http://<HOST>:<PORT>/webhdfs/v1/<PATH>?op=LISTSTATUS"`

Now that you are familiar with the basic concepts behind HDFS, let's look at some of the other functionality that is built on top of HDFS.

Exploring Hive: The Hadoop Data Warehouse Platform

Within the Hadoop ecosystem, HDFS can load and store massive quantities of data in an efficient and reliable manner. It can also serve that same data back up to client applications, such as MapReduce jobs, for processing and data analysis.

Although this is a productive and workable paradigm with a developer's background, it doesn't do much for an analyst or data scientist trying to sort through potentially large sets of data, as was the case with Facebook.

Hive, often considered the Hadoop data warehouse platform, got its start at Facebook as their analyst struggled to deal with the massive quantities of data produced by the social network. Requiring analysts to learn and write MapReduce jobs was neither productive nor practical.

Instead, Facebook developed a data warehouse-like layer of abstraction that would be based on tables. The tables function merely as metadata, and the table schema is projected onto the data, instead of actually moving potentially massive sets of data. This new capability allowed their analyst to use a SQL-like language called Hive Query Language (HQL) to query massive data sets stored with HDFS and to perform both simple and sophisticated summarizations and data analysis.

Designing, Building, and Loading Tables

If you are familiar with basic T-SQL data definition language (DDL) commands, you already have a good head start in working with Hive tables. To declare a Hive table, a `CREATE` statement is issued similar to those used to create tables in a SQL Server database. The following example creates a simple table using primitive types that are commonly found elsewhere:

```
CREATE EXTERNAL TABLE iislog (
       date STRING,
       time STRING,
       username STRING,
       ip STRING,
       port INT,
       method STRING,
       uristem STRING,
       uriquery STRING,
       timetaken INT,
       useragent STRING,
       referrer STRING
)
ROW FORMAT DELIMITED FIELDS TERMINATED BY ',';
```

Two important distinctions need to be pointed out with regard to the preceding example. First, note the `EXTERNAL` keyword. This keyword tells Hive that for this table it only owns the table metadata and not the underlying data. The opposite of this keyword (and the default value) is `INTERNAL`, which gives Hive control of both the metadata and the underlying data.

The difference between these two options is most evident when the table is dropped using the `DROP TABLE` command. Because Hive does not own the data for an `EXTERNAL` table, only the metadata is removed, and the data continues to live on. For an `INTERNAL` table, both the table metadata and data are deleted.

The second distinction in the `CREATE` statement is found on the final line of the command: `ROW FORMAT DELIMITED FIELDS TERMINATED BY ','`. This command instructs Hive to read the underlying data file and split the columns or fields using a comma delimiter. This is indicative that instead of storing data in an actual table structure, the data continues to live in its original file format.

At this point, in this example, although we have defined a table schema, no data has been explicitly loaded. To load data after the table is created, you could use the following command to log all of your IIS web server log files that exist in the logs directory:

```
load data inpath '/logs'
overwrite into table iislog;
```

This demonstration only scratches the surface of the capabilities in Hive. Hive supports a robust set of features, including complex data types (maps, structs, and arrays), partitioning, views, and indexes. These features are beyond the scope of this book, but they certainly warrant further exploration if you intend to use this technology.

Querying Data

Like the process used previously to create a Hive table, HQL can be subsequently used to query data out for the purposes of summarization or analysis. The syntax, as you might expect, is almost identical to that use to query a SQL Server database. Don't be fooled, though. Although the interface looks a lot like SQL, behind the scenes Hive does quite a bit of heavy lifting to optimize and convert the SQL-like syntax to one or more MapReduce jobs that is used to satisfy the query:

```
SELECT *
FROM iislog;
```

This simple query, much like its counterparts in the SQL world, simply returns all rows found in the iislog table. Although this is not a sophisticated query, the HQL supports both basic operations such as sorts and joins to more sophisticated operations, including group by, unions, and even user-defined functions. The following example is a common example of a group by query to count the number of times each URI occurs in the web server logs:

```
SELECT uristem, COUNT(*)
FROM iislog
GROUP BY (uristem);
```

Configuring the Hive ODBC Driver

A wealth of third-party tools, such as Microsoft Excel, provide advanced analytic features, visualizations, and toolsets. These tools are often a critical part of a data analyst's day-to-day job, which make the Hive Open Database Connectivity

(ODBC) driver one of the most important pieces of Hive. You can download the Hive ODBC driver from `http://www.microsoft.com/en-us/download/details.aspx?id=40886`. It allows any ODBC-compliant application to easily tap into and integrate with your big data store.

Configuring the Hive ODBC driver (see Figure 4.5) is handled using the ODBC Data Sources configuration tool built in to the Microsoft Windows operating system. After configuration is complete, Hive tables can be accessed directly from not only analytics tools such as Microsoft Excel but also from other ODBC-compliant tools such as SQL Server Integration Services (SSIS).

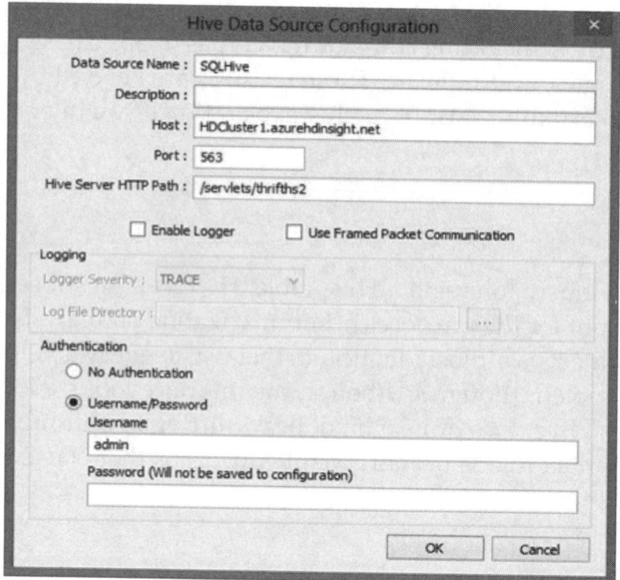

Figure 4.5: Hive ODBC configuration

Exploring HCatalog: HDFS Table and Metadata Management

In the previous examples, the source use for our Hive table is an HDFS path. This is common within the Hadoop ecosystem. While referencing these paths directly works fine and is perfectly acceptable in many scenarios, what it does is bind your Hive table or Pig job to a specific data layout within HDFS.

If this data layout were to change during an activity like data maintenance or simply because the size of the data outgrew the initial HDFS organizational structure, your script or job would be broken. This would require you to revisit every script or job that referenced this data, which in large systems could be potentially unpleasant.

This scenario is just one of the reasons the Apache HCatalog project was created. HCatalog started as an abstraction of the Hive metadata management functionality (currently is part of the larger Apache Hive project) and is intended to allow for shared metadata across the Hadoop ecosystem.

Table definitions and even data type mappings can be created and shared, so users can work with data stored in HDFS without worrying about the underlying details such as where or how the data is stored. HCatalog currently works with MapReduce, Hive, and of course, Pig; and as an abstraction of the Hive platform, the syntax for creating tables is identical, except that we have to specify the data location during creation of the table:

```
CREATE EXTERNAL TABLE iislog (
       date STRING,
       time STRING,
       username STRING,
       ip STRING,
       port INT,
       method STRING,
       uristem STRING,
       uriquery STRING,
       timetaken INT,
       useragent STRING,
       referrer STRING
)
ROW FORMAT DELIMITED FIELDS TERMINATED BY ','
STORED AS TEXTFILE
LOCATION '/data/logs';
```

Our iislog table can now be referenced directly one or more times in Hive by simply using the table name, as seen previously. Because HCatalog is integrated across platforms, the same table can also be referenced in a Pig job.

Let's look first at an example of a simple Pig Latin script that references the data location directly and includes the column schema definition:

```
A = load '/data/logs' using PigStorage() as (date:chararray,
time:chararray, username:chararray, ip:chararray,
port:int, method:chararray, uristem:chararray,
uriquery:chararray, timetaken:int,
useragent:chararry, referrer:chararray);
```

You can compare and contrast the code samples to see how HCatalog simplifies the process by removing both the data storage location and schema from the script:

```
A = load 'iislog' using HCatLoader();
```

In this example, if the underlying data structure were to change and the location of the logs were moved from the `/data/logs` path to `/archive/2013/weblogs`, the HCatalog metadata could be updated using the `ALTER` statement.

This allows all the Hive script, MapReduce, and Pig jobs that are using the HCatalog to continue to run without modification:

```
ALTER EXTERNAL TABLE iislog
LOCATION '/archive/2013/weblogs ';
```

Together, these features allow Hive to look and act like a database or data warehouse over your big data. In the next section, we will explore a different implementation that provides a No-SQL database on top of HDFS.

Exploring HBase: An HDFS Column-oriented Database

So far, all the techniques presented in this chapter have a similar use case. They are all efficient at simplifying access to your big data, but they have all largely been focused on batch-centric operations and are mostly inappropriate for interactive or real-time data access purposes. Apache HBase fills the gap in this space and is a NoSQL database built on top of Hadoop and HDFS that provides real-time, random read/write access to your big data.

The Apache HBase project is actually a clone modeled after the Google BigTable project defined by Chang et al. (2006) in the paper "BigTable: A Distributed Storage System for Structured Data." You can review the whole paper at `http://research.google.com/archive/bigtable.html`, but a summary or overview of columnar databases in general will suffice to get you going.

NOSQL DATABASE TYPES

The term NoSQL often refers to nonrelational databases. There are four common types of NoSQL databases:

- **Key/value: The simplest of the NoSQL databases, key/value databases are essentially hash sets that consist of a unique key and a value that is often represented as a schema-less blob.**
- **Document: Similar to key/value databases, document databases contain structured documents (such as XML, JSON, or even HTML) in place of the schema-less blob. These systems usually provide functionality to search within the stored documents.**
- **Columnar: Instead of storing data in a row/column approach, data in a columnar database is organized by column families which are groups of related columns, as discussed in more detail in the following section.**
- **Graph: The graph database consists of entities and edges, which represent relationships between nodes. The relationships between nodes can contain properties, which include items like direction of the relationship. This type of NoSQL database is commonly used to traverse organization or social network data.**

Columnar Databases

If you are familiar with relational database systems, you are without a doubt familiar with the traditional column and row layout used. To demonstrate the differences, let's look at a concrete example.

Consider the entity-relationship diagram (ERD) shown in Figure 4.6. It uses a pretty common approach to model a one-to-many relationship between customers and addresses. Like you've probably been taught throughout the years, it is highly normalized and follows good relational database design principles. Figure 4.7 illustrates a populated customer and address model based on the ERD found in Figure 4.6.

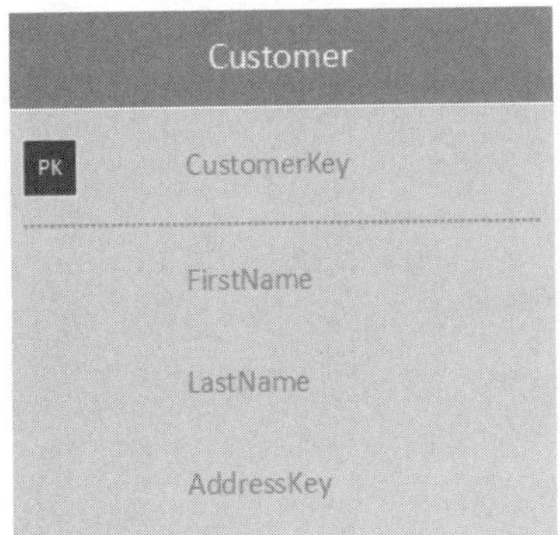

Figure 4.6: Entity-relationship diagram

Customer

CustomerKey	FirstName	LastName	AddressKey
10	Chris	Price	901
20	Adam	Jorgensen	902
30	Donald	Duck	903

Address

AddressKey	Address1	City	State	Country	ZipCode
901	123 Main St	Tampa	FL	US	33555
902	123 Beach Ave	Jacksonville	FL	US	33666
903	123 Mickey Lane	Orlando	FL	US	33777

Figure 4.7: Traditional database structure

Relational designs and databases do not easily scale and cannot typically handle the volumes, variety, and velocity associated with big data environments. This is where NoSQL databases such as HBase were designed to excel, yet they represent a very different way of thinking about and ultimately storing your data.

HBase is a columnar database, which means that instead of being organized by rows and columns, it is organized by column families, which are sets of related columns. Restructuring the data presented in Figure 4.7 using the columnar approach results in a layout that although similar is actually very different (see Figure 4.8).

Row Key	Column Families	
Customer ID	Customer	Address
10	FirstName: Chris LastName: Price	Street1: 123 Main St. City: Tampa State: FL Country: US Zip: 33555
20	FirstName: Adam LastName: Jorgensen	Street1: 123 Beach Ave. City: Jacksonville State: FL Country: US Zip: 33666
30	FirstName: Donald LastName: Duck	Street1: 123 Mickey Circle City: Orlando State: FL Country: US Zip: 33777

Figure 4.8: Columnar database structure

The columnar layout has many advantages over a relational model in the context of handling big data, including the following:

- Can handle very large (even massive) quantities of data through a process known as sharding
- Allows flexible data formats that can vary from row to row
- Typically scales linearly

For a more thorough discussion on columnar database capabilities and HBase in general, check out the HBase website at `http://hbase.apache.org/`.

Defining and Populating an HBase Table

HBase is installed and configured for you as part of the Hortonworks Data Platform. You can work with HBase directly from the HBase command shell.

To define a table, you specify a table name and the column family or families. In the following example, a basic customer table with a single column family for addresses is created:

```
create 'customer', 'address'
```

Take note that no schema or columns were defined for the actual table or the column family. This is intentional because the actual columns contained within an address could vary.

At this point, you may be questioning why this is a desirable behavior. There are actually a number of use cases; the easiest involves international addresses. Consider a U.S. address that has parts like address1, address2, city, state, and ZIP code. Other regions and countries do not necessarily follow this same format, so the flexibility is desirable in this scenario.

Now, let's take a quick look at how we put data into our customer table using the `put` statement:

```
put 'customer', 'row01', 'address:street', '123 Main St.'
put 'customer', 'row01', 'address:city', 'Tampa'
put 'customer', 'row01', 'address:state', 'Florida'
put 'customer', 'row01', 'address:country', 'United States of America'
put 'customer', 'row01', 'address:zip', '34637'
```

The format of this command specifies the table name (`customer`), the row identifier (`row01`), the column family and column name (`address: [xxx]`), and finally the value. When the commands complete, the data is available for query operations.

NOTE **To drop an HBase table, you must first disable it, and then drop it. The syntax to perform this operation is as follows:**

```
disable 'customer'
drop 'customer'
```

Using Query Operations

To retrieve the data from the HBase table you just created, there are two fundamental methods available through the HBase shell. The `scan` command indiscriminately reads the entire contents of your table and dumps it to the console window:

```
scan 'customer'
```

For small tables, this command is useful for verifying that the table is configured and set up correct. When working with a larger table, it is preferable to use a more targeted query. The `get` command accomplishes this:

```
get 'customer' 'row01'
```

To use the `get` command, you specify the table name (`customer`) followed by the row key (`row01`). This returns all the column families and associated columns for the given key.

A more thorough discussion of HBase is beyond the scope of this book, but it's worth noting that HBase supports updating and deleting rows. There are also robust and fully functional Java and REST APIs available for integrating HBase outside the Hadoop ecosystem.

Summary

Hadoop offers a number of different methods or options for both storing and retrieving your data for processing and analytical purposes. HDFS is the Hadoop file system that provides a reliable and scalable platform for hosting your data. HDFS is also well suited to serve your data to other tools within the Hadoop ecosystem, like MapReduce and even Pig jobs.

Hive, the Hadoop Data Warehousing platform, is also built on top of HDFS. Using the HQL, you can easily project a schema onto your data and then use SQL-like syntax to summarize and analyze your data.

To build more robust solutions, you can implement HCatalog to abstract the details of how your big data is stored. HCatalog provides table and metadata management that is built on top of Hive and integrates well into the Hadoop stack of tools.

Finally, when it becomes necessary to provide real-time, random read/write capabilities to your data, the Apache HBase project provides a columnar NoSQL database implementation also built on top of HDFS. Together, these tools and platforms give you many different options to tackle a number of different use cases in the diverse big data space.

CHAPTER

5

Storing and Managing Data in HDFS

WHAT YOU WILL LEARN IN THIS CHAPTER

- Getting to Know the History and Fundamentals of HDFS
- Interacting with HDFS to Manage Files
- Administering HDFS Environments
- Managing Your HDFS Data

This chapter discusses the basics of storing and managing data for use in your big data system. The options for storing data can vary, depending on whether you are using the HDInsight Service or the Hortonworks distribution. Both options offer the Hadoop Distributed File System (HDFS), which is the standard file storage mechanism. HDInsight also offers the option of using Azure Storage Vault (ASV), which presents a full HDFS file system that uses Azure Blob storage "under the hood."

Quite a bit of complexity underlies the full HDFS implementation, and a complete description of it would take a book of its own. This chapter instead focuses on the core knowledge you need to leverage HDFS. It also provides some details of what happens under the hood, where appropriate, to help you understand how to best use the system. Fortunately, HDFS is a stable, mature product and used by a large number of companies on an ongoing basis. In the same way that you can use SQL Server to accomplish a great deal of work without understanding its internal workings, you can use HDFS without worrying about the low-level details.

Understanding the Fundamentals of HDFS

HDFS's origin can be traced back to the Google File System (GFS) (`http://research.google.com/archive/gfs.html`), which was designed to handle Google's needs for storing and processing large amounts of data. Google released a paper on its file system in 2003, and when Doug Cutting began working on Hadoop, he adopted the GFS approach for HDFS.

The design goals for HDFS were threefold:

- To enable large-scale data sets to be stored and processed
- To provide reliable data storage and be fault tolerant
- To provide support for moving the computation to the data

HDFS addresses these goals well and offers a number of architectural features that enable these goals to be met. These goals also logically lead to some constraints, which HDFS had to address. (The next section breaks down these features and how they address the goals and constraints of a distributed file system designed for large data sets.)

HDFS is implemented using the Java language. This makes it highly portable because modern operating systems offer Java support. Communication in HDFS is handled using Transmission Control Protocol/Internet Protocol (TCP/IP), which also enables it to be very portable.

In HDFS terminology, an installation is usually referred to as a cluster. A cluster is made up of individual nodes. A node is a single computer that participates in the cluster. So when someone refers to a cluster, it encompasses all the individual computers that participate in the cluster.

HDFS runs beside the local file system. Each computer still has a standard file system available on it. For Linux, that may be ext4, and for a Windows server, it's usually going to be New Technology File System (NTFS). HDFS stores its files as files in the local file system, but not in a way that enables you to directly interact with them. This is similar to the way SQL Server or other relational database management systems (RDBMSs) use physical files on disk to store their data: While the files store the data, you don't manipulate the files directly. Instead, you go through the interface that the database provides. HDFS uses the native file system in the same way; it stores data there, but not in a directly useable form.

HDFS uses a write-once, read-many access model. This means that data, once written to a file, cannot be updated. Files can be deleted and then rewritten, but not updated. Although this might seem like a major limitation, in practice, with large data sets, it is often much faster to delete and replace than to perform in-place updates of data.

Now that you have a better understanding of HDFS, in the next sections you look at the architecture behind HDFS, learn about NameNodes and DataNodes, and find out about HDFS support for replication.

HDFS Architecture

Traditionally, data has been centralized rather than spread out. That worked well over the past few decades, as the capability to store ever-increasing amounts of data on a single disk continued to grow. For example, in 1981, you could purchase hard drives that stored around 20MB at a cost of approximately $ 180 per MB. By 2007, you could get a drive that stored 1TB at cost of about $ 0.0004 per MB.

Today, storage needs in big-data scenarios continue to outpace the capacity of even the largest drives (4TB). One early solution to this problem was simply to add more hard drives. If you wanted to store 1 petabyte (1,024TB) of information, you would need 256 4TB hard drives. However, if all the hard drives were placed in the same server, it introduced a single point of failure. Any problem that affected the server could mean the drives weren't accessible, and so the data on the drives could be neither read nor written. The single computer could also introduce a performance bottleneck for access to the hard drives.

HDFS was designed to solve this problem by supporting distribution of the data storage across many nodes. Because the data is spread across multiple nodes, no single computer becomes a bottleneck. By storing redundant copies of the information (discussed in more detail in the section "Data Replication"), a single point of failure is also removed.

This redundancy also enables the use of commodity hardware. (Commodity means nonspecialized, off-the-shelf components.) Special hardware or a unique configuration is not needed for a computer to participate in an HDFS cluster. Commodity hardware tends to be less expensive than more specialized components and can be acquired at a wider variety of vendors.

Many of today's server-class computers include a number of features designed to minimize downtime. This includes things like redundant power supplies, multiple network interfaces, and hard drive controllers capable of managing pools of hard drives in redundant arrays of independent/inexpensive disk (RAID) setups. Thanks to the data redundancy inherent in HDFS, it can minimize the need for this level of hardware, allowing the use of less-expensive computers.

NOTE **Just because HDFS can be run on commodity hardware and manages redundancy doesn't mean that you should ignore the reliability and performance of the computers used in an HDFS cluster. Using more reliable hardware means less time spent replacing broken components. And, just like any other application, HDFS will**

benefit from more computing resources to work with. In particular, NameNodes (discussed next in the "NameNodes and DataNodes" section) benefit from reliable hardware and high-performing components.

As already stated, the data being stored in HDFS is spread out and replicated across multiple machines. This makes the system resilient to the failure of any individual machine. Depending on the level of redundancy configured, the system may be able to withstand the loss of multiple machines.

Another area where HDFS enables support for large data sets is in computation. Although HDFS does not perform computation directly, it does support moving the computations closer to the data. In many computer systems, the data is moved from a server to another computer, which performs any needed computations. Then the data may be moved back to the original server or moved to yet another server.

This is a common pattern in applications that leverage a relational database. Data is retrieved from a database server to a client computer, where the application logic to update or process the data is applied. Finally, the data is saved to the database server. This pattern makes sense when you consider that the data is being stored on a single computer. If all the application logic were performed on the database server, a single computationally intensive process could block any other user from performing his or her work. By offloading application logic to client computers, it increases the database server's capability to serve data and spreads the computation work across more machines.

This approach works well for smaller data sets, but it rapidly breaks down when you begin dealing with data sets in the 1TB and up range. Moving that much data across the network can introduce a tremendous amount of latency. In HDFS, though, the data is spread out over many computers. By moving the computations closer to the data, HDFS avoids the overhead of moving the data around, while still getting the benefit of spreading computation over a larger number of computers.

Although HDFS is not directly responsible for performing the computation work, it does provide an interface that allows applications to place their computing tasks closer to the data. MapReduce is a prime example of this. It works hand in hand with HDFS to distribute computational tasks to DataNodes so that the work can be performed as close to the data as possible. Only the results of the data actually need to be transmitted across the network.

NOTE **You can think of moving the computation closer to the data as being similar to the way that many relational database engines optimize queries by moving filter criteria as close to the original data as possible. For example, if you are joining two**

tables, and then filtering results by a column from one table, the engine will often move that filter to the initial retrieval of data from the table, thus reducing the amount of data it has to join with the second table.

NameNodes and DataNodes

HDFS uses two primary types of nodes. A NameNode acts as a master node, managing the file system and access to files from clients. DataNodes manage the physical storage of data.

Each HDFS cluster has a single NameNode. The NameNode acts as the coordinator for the cluster and is responsible for managing and communicating to all the DataNodes in a cluster. It manages all the metadata associated with the cluster. One of its primary responsibilities is to manage the file system namespace, which is the layer that presents the distributed data stored in HDFS as though it is in a traditional file system organized as folders and files. The NameNode manages any file system namespace operations, such as creating or deleting files and folders.

The file system namespace presents the appearance that the data is stored in a folder/file structure, but the data is actually split into multiple blocks that are stored on DataNodes. The NameNode controls which blocks of data map to which DataNodes. These blocks of data are usually 64MB, but the setting is configurable.

The DataNode is responsible for the creation of blocks of data in its physical storage and for the deletion of those blocks. It is also responsible for creation of replica blocks from other nodes. The NameNode coordinates this activity, telling the DataNode what blocks to create, delete, or replicate. DataNodes communicate with the NameNode by sending a regular "heartbeat" communication over the network. This heartbeat indicates that the DataNode is operating correctly. A block report is also delivered with the heartbeat and provides a list of all the blocks stored on the DataNode.

The NameNode maintains a transaction history of all changes to the file system, known as the EditLog. It also maintains a file, referred to as the FsImage, that contains the file system metadata. The FsImage and EditLog files are read by the NameNode when it starts up, and the EditLog's transaction history is applied to the FsImage. This brings the FsImage up-to-date with the latest changes recorded by the NameNode. Once the FsImage is updated, it is written back to the file system, and the EditLog is cleared. At this point, the NameNode can begin accepting requests. This process (shown in Figure 5.1) is referred to as checkpointing, and it is run only on startup. It can have some performance impact if the NameNode has accumulated a large EditLog.

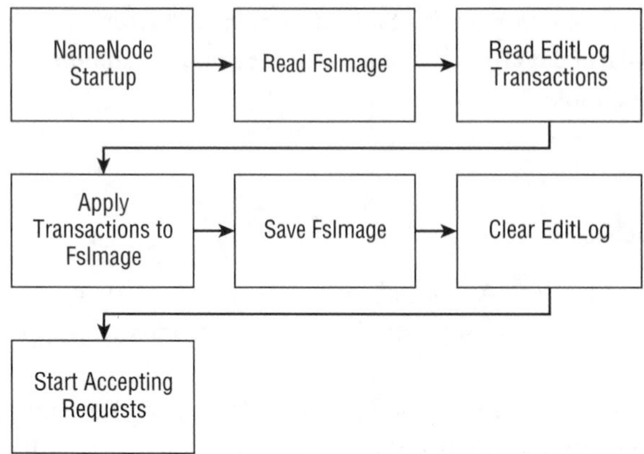

Figure 5.1: The checkpointing process

The NameNode is a crucial component of any HDFS cluster. Without a functioning NameNode, the data cannot be accessed. That means that the NameNode is a single point of failure for the cluster. Because of that, the NameNode is one place that using a more fault-tolerant hardware setup is advisable. In addition, setting up a Backup node may help you recover more quickly in the event of a NameNode failure. The Backup node maintains its own copy of the FsImage and EditLog. It receives all the file system transactions from the NameNode and uses that to keep its copy of the FsImage up to date. If the NameNode fails catastrophically, you can use the Backup node's copy of the FsImage to start up a new NameNode more quickly.

NOTE **Despite their name, Backup nodes aren't a direct backup to a NameNode. Rather, they manage the checkpointing process and retain a backup copy of the FsImage and EditLog. A NameNode cannot fail over to a Backup node automatically.**

NOTE **Hadoop 2.0 includes several improvements for improving the availability of NameNodes, with support for Active and Standby NameNodes. These new options will make it much easier to have a highly available HDFS cluster.**

Data Replication

One of the critical features of HDFS is its support for data replication. This is critical for creating redundancy in the data, which allows HDFS to be resilient to the failure of one or more nodes. Without this capability, HDFS would not be reliable to run on commodity hardware, and as a result, would require significantly more investment in highly available servers.

Data replication also enables better performance for large data sets. By spreading copies of the data across multiple nodes, the data can be read in parallel. This enables faster access and processing of large files.

By default, HDFS replicates every file three times. However, the replication level can also be specified per file. This can prove useful if you are storing transient data or data that can be re-created easily. This type of data might not be replicated at all, or only replicated once. The file is replicated at the block level. Therefore, a single file may be (and likely is) made up of blocks stored on multiple nodes. The replicas of these blocks may be stored on still more nodes.

Replicas are created as the client writes the data to HDFS. The first DataNode to receive the data gets it in small chunks. Each chunk is written to the DataNode's local storage and then transferred to the next DataNode. The receiving DataNode carries out the same process, forwarding the processed chunks to the next DataNode. That process is repeated for each chunk, for each DataNode, until the required number of replicas has been created. Because a node can be receiving a chunk to process at the same time that it is sending another chunk to the next node, the process is said to be pipelined.

A key aspect of the data replication capabilities in HDFS is that the replica placement is optimized and is continuing to be improved. The replication process is rack aware; that is, it understands how the computers are physically organized. For data centers with large numbers of computers, it is common to use network racks to hold the computers. Often, each rack has its own network switch to handle network communication between computers in the rack. This switch would then be connected to another switch, which is connected to other network racks. This means that communications between computers in the same rack is generally going to be faster than communications between computers in different racks.

HDFS uses its rack awareness to optimize the placement of replicas within a cluster. In doing so, it balances the need for performance with the need for availability in the case of a hardware failure. In the common scenario, with three replicas, one replica is stored on a node in the local rack. The other two replicas will be stored in a remote rack, on two different nodes in the rack. This approach still delivers good read performance, because a client reading the file can access two unique racks (with their own network connection) for the contents of the file. It also delivers good write performance, because writing a replica to a node in the same rack is significantly faster than writing it to a node in a different rack. This also balances availability; the replicas are located in two separate racks and three nodes. Rack failures are less common than node failures, so replicating across fewer racks doesn't have an appreciable impact on availability.

NOTE The replica placement approach is subject to change, as the HDFS developers consider it a work in progress. As they learn more about usage patterns, they plan to update the policies to deliver the optimal balance of performance and availability.

HDFS monitors the replication levels of files to ensure the replication factor is being met. If a computer hosting a DataNode were to crash, or a network rack were taken offline, the NameNode would flag the absence of heartbeat messages. If the nodes are offline for too long, the NameNode stores forwarding requests to them, and it also checks the replication factors of any data blocks associated with those nodes. In the event that the replication factor has fallen below the threshold set when the file was created, the NameNode begins replication of those blocks again.

Using Common Commands to Interact with HDFS

This section discusses interacting with HDFS. Even though HDFS is a distributed file system, you can interact with it in a similar way as you do with a traditional file system. However, this section covers some key differences. The command examples in the following sections work with the Hortonworks Data Platform environment setup in Chapter 3, "Installing HDInsight."

Interfaces for Working with HDFS

By default, HDFS includes two mechanisms for working with it. The primary way to interact with it is by the use of a command-line interface. For status checks, reporting, and browsing the file system, there is also a web-based interface.

Hadoop is a Java script that can run several modules of the Hadoop system. The two modules that are used for HDFS are `dfs` (also known as FsShell) and `dfsadmin`. The `dfs module` is used for most common file operations, such as adding or moving files. The `dfsadmin` module is used for administrative functions.

You can open the command prompt on your Windows Hortonworks Data Platform (HDP) server by double-clicking the Hadoop Command Line shortcut on the desktop or by running `cmd.exe` from the Start menu. If you start from the Hadoop Command Line shortcut, it will set your current directory to the Hadoop location automatically, as shown in Figure 5.2.

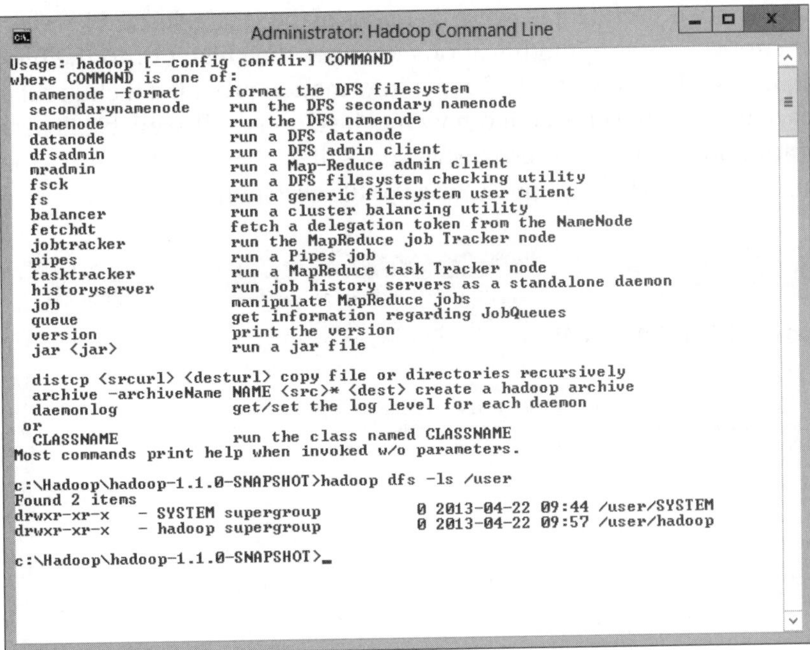

Figure 5.2: The HDFS command prompt

When running commands from the command-line interface, you must use the following format:

```
hadoop MODULE -command arguments
```

The command line starts with `hadoop`, the executable that will interpret the remaining items on the command line. *`MODULE`* designates which Hadoop module should be run. Recall that when interacting with the HDFS file system this will be `dfs` or `dfsadmin`. *`-command`* indicates the specific command in the module that should be run, and the *`arguments`* are any specific values necessary to execute the command successfully.

NOTE **You can usually find the full list of commands supported by any module by running the module with no command, as follows:**

```
hadoop dfs
```

The same holds true for commands. Running a command without arguments lists the help for that command:

```
hadoop dfs -put
```

The web interface is useful for viewing the status of the HDFS cluster. However, it does not support making modifications to either the cluster or to the files contained in it. As shown in Figure 5.3, the information provided includes the current space used by the cluster and how much space is still available. It also includes information on any unresponsive nodes. It enables you to browse the file system, as well, by clicking the Browse the file system link.

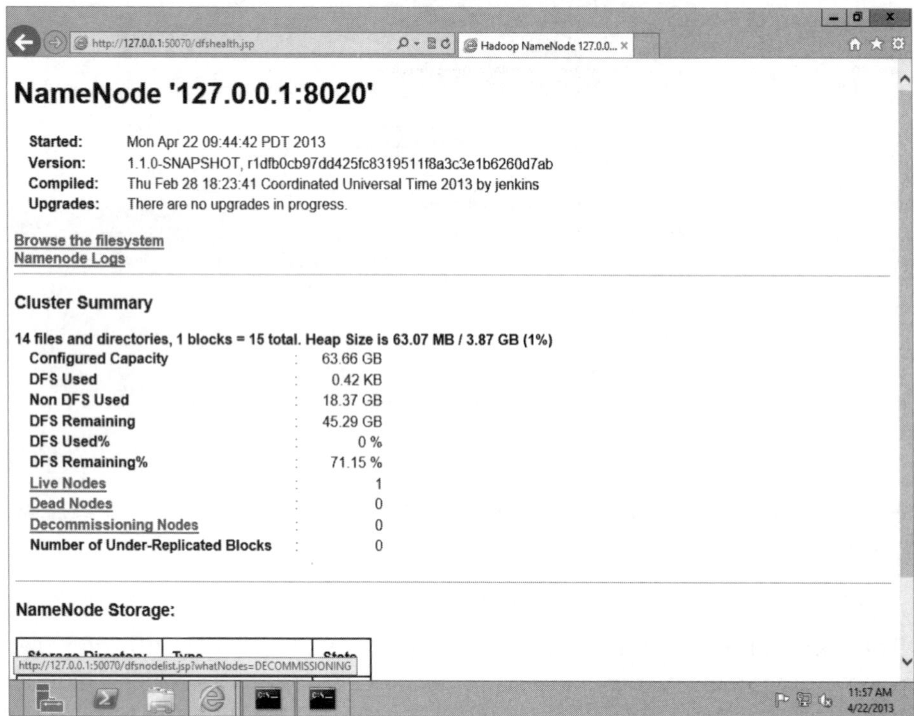

Figure 5.3: Web interface for HDFS

File Manipulation Commands

Most direct interaction with HDFS involves file manipulation—creating, deleting, or moving files. Remember that HDFS files are write-once, read-many, so there are no commands for updating files. However, you can manipulate the metadata associated with a file, such as the owner or group that has access to it.

NOTE **Unlike some file systems, HDFS does not have the concept of a working directory or a `cd` command. Most commands require that you provide a complete path to the files or directory you want to work with.**

NOTE The following commands will work on an HDInsight cluster using the standard HDFS implementation as well as ASV (discussed in Chapter 13, "Big Data and the Cloud"). However, you need to adjust the paths for each case. To reference a path in the locally attached distributed file system, use `hdfs://<namenodehost>/<path>` as the path. To reference a path in ASV, use `asv://[<container>@]<accountname>.blob.core.windows.net/<path>` as the path. You can change the `asv` prefix to `asvs` to use an encrypted connection.

By default, HDInsight creates the directories listed in Table 5.1 during the initial setup.

Table 5-1: Initial HDFS Root Directories

DIRECTORY NAME	PURPOSE
`/hive`	Directory used by Hive for data storage (see Chapter 6, "Adding Structure with Hive")
`/mapred`	Directory used for MapReduce
`/user`	Directory for user data

You can list the root directories by using the `ls` or `lsr` command:

```
hadoop dfs -ls /
hadoop dfs -lsr /
```

`ls` lists the directory contents of the specified folder. In the example, / indicates the root folder. `lsr` lists directory contents, as well, but it does it recursively for each subfolder it encounters.

Normally, user files are created in a subfolder of the `/user` folder, with the username being used for the title of the folder. However, this is not a requirement, and you can tailor the folder structure to fit specific scenarios. The following examples use a fictional user named `MSBigDataSolutions`.

Before adding data to HDFS, there must be a directory to hold it. To create a user directory for the `MSBigDataSolutions` user, you run the `mkdir` command:

```
hadoop dfs -mkdir /user/MSBigDataSolutions
```

If a directory is created by accident, or it is no longer needed, you can remove it by using the `rmr` command. `rmr` is short for remove recursive, and it removes the directory specified and any subdirectories:

```
hadoop dfs -rmr /user/DirectoryToRemove
```

After a directory has been selected or created, files can be copied to it. The most common scenario for this is to copy files from the local file system into

HDFS using the put command. This example uses the sample data files created in this chapter:

```
hadoop dfs -put C:\MSBigDataSolutions\SampleData1.txt
    /user/MSBigDataSolutions
```

This command loads a single file from the local file system (C:\MSBigDataSolutions\SampleData1.txt) to a directory in HDFS (/user/MSBigDataSolutions). You can use the following command to verify the file was loaded correctly:

```
hadoop dfs -ls /user/MSBigDataSolutions
```

put can load multiple files to HDFS simultaneously. You do that by using a folder as the source path, in which case all files in the folder are uploaded. You can also do so by using wildcards in the source system path:

```
hadoop dfs -put C:\MSBigDataSolutions\SampleData_*
    /user/MSBigDataSolutions
```

Two other commands are related to put. copyFromLocal works exactly like the put command, and is simply an alias for it. moveFromLocal also functions like put, with the difference that the local file is deleted after the specified file(s) are loaded into HDFS.

Once the files are in HDFS, you have a couple of ways to retrieve them. One option is the cat command. cat displays the contents of the file to the screen, or it can be redirected to another output device:

```
hadoop dfs -cat /user/MSBigDataSolutions/SampleData1.txt
```

You can also use the text command to display information. The only difference is that text attempts to convert the file to a text format before displaying it. However, because most data in HDFS is text already, cat will usually work.

To get the contents of a file back to the local file system from HDFS, use the get command:

```
hadoop dfs -get /user/MSBigDataSolutions/SampleData1.txt
    C:\MSBigDataSolutions\Output
```

Just like the put command, get can work with multiple files simultaneously, either by specifying a folder or a wildcard:

```
hadoop dfs -get /user/MSBigDataSolutions/SampleData_*
    C:\MSBigDataSolutions\Output
```

get also has two related commands. copyToLocal works exactly like the get command and is simply an alias for it. moveToLocal also functions like get, with the difference that the HDFS file will be deleted after the specified file(s) are copied to the local file system.

Copying and moving files and directories within HDFS can be done with the `cp` and `mv` commands, respectively:

```
hadoop dfs -cp /user/MSBigDataSolutions /user/Backup
hadoop dfs -mv /user/MSBigDataSolutions /user/Backup2
```

You can delete a file in HDFS with the `rm` command. `rm` does not remove directories, though. For that, you must use the `rmr` command:

```
hadoop dfs -rm /user/MSBigDataSolutions/SampleData1.txt
hadoop dfs -rmr /user/MSBigDataSolutions
```

NOTE **HDFS is case sensitive. `mydirectory` and `MYDIRECTORY` are treated by HDFS as two separate directories. Because HDFS automatically creates directories for you when using some commands (the `put`, `cp`, and `mv` commands, for example), paying attention to case is important, as it can be easy to accidentally create directories. `rmr` is useful to clean up these directories.**

Administrative Functions in HDFS

Security in HDFS follows a straightforward model, where files have an owner and a group. A given file or directory maintains permissions for three scenarios, which it checks in the following order:

1. **The owner identity.** This is a single-user account, and it tracks the assigned owner of the file or directory. If the user account accessing the file matches the owner identity, the user gets the owner's assigned permissions.
2. **The group identity**. This is a group account, and any user account with membership in the group gets the group permissions.
3. **All other users**. If the user account does not match the owner identity, and the user account is not a member of the group, the user will use these permissions.

NOTE **Permissions in Azure Data Storage work a bit differently. Permissions are managed in the storage account. The HDInsight cluster has full permissions to all containers in the storage account that is set as its default storage. It can also access containers in other storage accounts. If the target container is the public container, or it has the public-access level, the HDInsight cluster will have read-access without additional configuration. If the target container uses the private-access level, however, you have to update the `core-site.xml` within the HDInsight cluster to provide the key to access the container.**

In the current release of HDFS, the host operating system manages user identity. HDFS uses whatever identity the host reports to determine the user's identity. On a Windows server, the user identity reported to HDFS will be the equivalent of the `whoami` command from a command prompt. The group membership will be the same groups as reported by running `net user [username]` command.

NOTE HDFS also has a super-user account. The super user has access to view and modify everything, because permission checks are effectively bypassed for the super user. The account used to start the NameNode process is always set as the super user. Note that if the NameNode process is started under a different user identity, that account will then be the super user. This can be convenient for development purposes, because a developer starting a local NameNode to work against will automatically be the super user. However, for a production environment, a consistent, secured account should be used to start the NameNode.

Files and folders support a simple set of permissions:

- **Read (r) permission**: An account has permission to read the contents of the file or directory.
- **Write (w) permission**: An account has permission to change or modify the file or folder.
- **Execute (x) permission**: An account can enumerate the contents of a directory. This permission applies to directories only.

To modify the permissions applied to a file, you can use the `chmod` command. To add permissions, use the plus (+) sign followed by the appropriate permission letters. For example, to give all users read/write permissions to the `SampleData_4.txt` file, you use the following command:

```
hadoop dfs -chmod +rw /user/MSBigDataSolutions/SampleData_4.txt
```

To remove the permissions, use the minus (-) sign:

```
hadoop dfs -chmod -rw /user/MSBigDataSolutions/SampleData_4.txt
```

To control which user the permissions apply to, you can prefix the permission with `u`, `g`, or `o`, which respectively stand for the user who owns the file, the group assigned to the file, or all other users. The following command adds read/write permissions back, but only to the owner of the file:

```
hadoop dfs -chmod u+rw /user/MSBigDataSolutions/SampleData_4.txt
```

You can modify the owner and group associated with a file or directory by using `chown` and `chgrp`, respectively. To change the owner, you must be running the command as the super-user account:

```
hadoop dfs -chown NewOwner /user/MSBigDataSolutions/SampleData_4.txt
```

To change the group associated with a file or a directory, you must be either the current owner or the super user:

```
hadoop dfs -chgrp NewGroup /user/MSBigDataSolutions/SampleData_4.txt
```

You can apply all the preceding commands recursively to a directory structure by using `-R` as an argument to the command. This applies permissions to be changed easily for a large group of files. The following command applies the read/write permission to all files in the `MSBigDataSolutions` folder:

```
hadoop dfs -chmod -R +rw /user/MSBigDataSolutions
```

NOTE **The `chmod`, `chown`, and `chgrp` commands are common commands in UNIX-based systems, but are not found on the Windows platform. HDFS implements versions of these commands internally, and for the most part, they function like their UNIX counterparts. `chmod`, in particular, supports a number of options, such as specifying the permission set in octal notation, that aren't immediately obvious. You can find more documentation on advanced uses of `chmod` at `http://en.wikipedia.org/wiki/Chmod`.**

Managing deleted files in HDFS is normally transparent to the user. However, in some cases, it can require intervention by an administrator. By default, deleting files from HDFS does not result in immediate removal of the file. Instead, the file is moved to the `/trash` folder. (If a file is deleted accidentally, it can be recovered by simply moving it back out of the `/trash` folder using the `-mv` command.) By default, the `/trash` folder is emptied every six hours. To explicitly manage the process, you can run the `expunge` command to force the trash to be emptied:

```
hadoop dfs -expunge
```

You can access other administrative functions in HDFS through the `dfsadmin` module. `dfsadmin` can be used for a number of different activities, most of which are fairly uncommon. One useful command it offers is `report`. This command returns a summary of the space available to the HDFS cluster, how much is actually used, and some basic indicators of replication status and potential corruption. Here is an example:

```
hadoop dfsadmin -report
```

When you need to manipulate the available nodes for maintenance, a useful command is `refreshNodes`, which forces the name node to reread the list of available DataNodes and any exclusions:

```
hadoop dfsadmin -refreshNodes
```

Generally, HDFS will correct any file system problems that it encounters, assuming that the problem is correctable. In some cases, though, you might want to explicitly check for errors. In that case, you can run the `fsck` command.

This checks the HDFS file system and reports any errors back to the user. You can also use the `fsck` command to move corrupted files to a specific folder or to delete them. This command runs the file system check on the `/user` directory:

```
hadoop fsck /user
```

Overall, HDFS is designed to minimize the amount of administrative overhead involved. This section has focused on the core pieces of administrative information to provide you with enough information to get up and running without overwhelming you. For more details on administering it, you may want to review the document at `http://hadoop.apache.org/docs/stable/hadoop-project-dist/hadoop-hdfs/HdfsDesign.html`.

Moving and Organizing Data in HDFS

HDFS manages the data stored in the Hadoop cluster without any necessary user intervention. In fact, a good portion of the design strategies used for HDFS were adopted to support that goal: a system that minimizes the amount of administration that you need to be concerned with. If you will be working with small clusters, or data on the smaller end of big data, you can safely skip this section. However, there are still scenarios in Hadoop where you can get better performance and scalability by taking a more direct approach, as this section covers.

Moving Data in HDFS

As your big data needs grow, it is not uncommon to create additional Hadoop clusters. Additional clusters are also used to keep workloads separate and to manage single-point-of-failure concerns that arise from having a single NameNode. But what happens if you need access to the same data from multiple clusters? You can export the data, using the `dfs -get` command to move it back to a local file system and the `dfs -put` command to put into the new cluster. However, this is likely to be slow and take a large amount of additional disk space during the copying process.

Fortunately, a tool in HDFS makes this easier: `distcp` (Distributed Copy). `distcp` enables a distributed approach to copying large amounts of data. It does this by leveraging MapReduce to distribute the copy process to multiple DataNodes in the cluster. The list of files to be copied is placed in a list, along with any related directories. Then the list is partitioned by the available nodes, and each node becomes responsible for copying its assigned files.

`distcp` can be executed by running the `distcp` module with two arguments: the source directory and the target directory. To reference a different cluster, you use a fully qualified name for the NameNode:

```
hadoop distcp hdfs://mynamenode:50010/user/MSBigDataSolutions \
              hdfs://mybackupcluster:50010/user/MSBigDataSolutions
```

`distcp` can also be used for copying data inside the same cluster. This is useful if you need to copy a large amount of data for backup purposes.

NOTE **If you are using HDInsight with ASV, you will not have as much need to move data between clusters. That is because containers in Azure Storage can be shared between clusters; there's no need to copy it. However, you may still need to copy data from one container to another. You can do this from the Azure Storage Explorer (`http://azurestorageexplorer.codeplex.com`) if you would like a graphical user interface (GUI). You can also use the same HDFS commands (including `distcp`) to work with ASV; just use the appropriate qualifier and reference to the container (for example, `asv:///MyAsvContainer/MyData/Test.txt`).**

Implementing Data Structures for Easier Management

HDFS, being a file system, is organized into directories. Many commands work with directories as well as with files, and a number of them also support the `-R` parameter for applying the command recursively across all child directories. Security can also be managed more easily for folders than for individual files.

Given this, it is very effective to map your data files into a folder structure that reflects the use and segmentation of the data. Using a hierarchical folder structure that reflects the source, usage, and application for the data supports this.

Consider, for example, a company that manages several websites. The website traffic logs are being captured into HDFS, along with user activity logs. Each activity log has its own distinct format. When creating a folder structure for storing this information, you would consider whether it is more important to segment the data by the site that originated it or by the type of data. Which aspect is more important likely depends on the business needs. For this example, suppose that the originating site is the most critical element, because this company keeps their website information heavily separated and secured. You might use a folder structure like this one:

```
/user/CompanyWebsiteA/sitelogs
/user/CompanyWebsiteA/useractivity
/user/CompanyWebsiteB/sitelogs
/user/CompanyWebsiteB/useractivity
...
```

By structuring the folders in this manner, you can easily implement security for each folder at the website level, to prevent unauthorized access. Conversely, if security were not a critical element, you might choose to reverse the order and store the format of the data first. This would make it easier to know what each folder contains and to do processing that spans all websites.

NOTE ASV doesn't support a directory hierarchy. Instead, you have a container, and it stores key/value pairs for the data. However, ASV does allow the forward slash (/) to be used inside a key name (for example, `CompanyWebsiteA/sitelogs/sitelog1.txt`). By using the forward slash, the key keeps the appearance of a folder-based structure.

You can easily modify the folder structures by using the `dfs -cp` and `-mv` commands. This means that if a particular folder structure isn't working out, you can try new ones.

Rebalancing Data

Generally, HDFS manages the placement of data across nodes very well. As discussed previously, it attempts to balance the placement of data to ensure a combination of reliability and performance. However, as more data is added to a Hadoop cluster, it is normal to add more nodes to it. This can lead to the cluster being out of balance; that is, some nodes have more data and, therefore, more activity than other nodes. It can also lead to certain nodes having most of the more recently added data, which can create some issues, because newly added data is often more heavily accessed.

You can rebalance the cluster by using the balancer tool, which is simple to use. It takes one optional parameter, which defines a threshold of disk usage variance to use for the rebalancing process. The default threshold level is 10%, as shown here:

```
hadoop balancer -threshold .1
```

The balancer determines an average space utilization across the cluster. Nodes are considered over- or underutilized if their space usage varies by more than the threshold from the average space utilization. The balance runs until one of the following occurs:

- All the nodes in the cluster have been balanced.
- It has exceeded three iterations without making progress on balancing.
- The user who started the balancer aborts it by pressing Ctrl+C.

Balancing the data across nodes is an important step to maintaining the performance of the cluster, and it should be carried out whenever there are significant changes to the nodes in a cluster.

Summary

In this chapter, the background of the HDFS file system has been covered, along with some of the underlying details, including how NameNodes and DataNodes interact to store information in HDFS. The basic commands for working with and administering an HDFS file system—such as `ls` for listing files, `get` and `put` for moving files in and out of HDFS, and `rm` for removing unnecessary files—have been covered. In addition, some advanced administrative topics, like balancing and data movement, which are important for maintaining your HDFS cluster, have been covered. In the next chapter, these topics will be built on with a discussion of how the Hive application runs on top of the HDFS file system while presenting the appearance of a traditional RDBMS to applications.

CHAPTER

6

Adding Structure with Hive

WHAT YOU WILL LEARN IN THIS CHAPTER:

- Learning How Hive Provides Value in a Hadoop Environment
- Comparing Hive to a Relational Database
- Working With Data in Hive
- Understanding Advanced Options in Hive

This chapter discusses how you can use Hive with Hadoop to get more value out of your big data initiatives. Hive is a component of all major Hadoop distributions, and it is used extensively to provide SQL-like functionality from a Hadoop installation. For example, Hive is often used to enable common data warehouse scenarios on top of data stored in Hadoop. An example of this would be retrieving a summary of sales by store, and by department. Using MapReduce to prepare and produce these results would take multiple lines of Java code. By using Hive, you can write a familiar SQL query to get the same results:

```
SELECT Store, Department, SUM(SalesAmount)
FROM StoreSales
GROUP BY Store, Department
```

If you are familiar with SQL Server, or other relational databases, portions of Hive will seem very familiar. Other aspects of Hive, however, may feel very different or restrictive compared to a relational database. It's important to remember that Hive attempts to bridge some of the gap between Hadoop Distributed File System (HDFS) data store and the relational world, while providing some of the benefits of both technologies. By keeping that perspective, you'll find it easier to understand how and why Hive functions as it does.

Hive is not a full relational database, and limitations apply to the relational database management system (RDBMS) functionality it supports. The differences that are most likely to impact someone coming from a relational perspective are covered in this chapter. Although complete coverage of the administration and configuration of Hive is beyond the scope for this chapter, the discussion here does include basic commands for creating tables and working with data in Hive.

Understanding Hive's Purpose and Role

Hadoop was developed to handle big data. It does an admirable job of this; but in creating a new platform to solve this problem, it introduced a new challenge: people had to learn a new and different way to work with their data. Instead of using Structured Query Language (SQL) to retrieve and transform data, they had to use Java and MapReduce. Not only did this mean that data professionals had to learn a new skillset, but also that the SQL query tools that IT workers and business users traditionally used to access data didn't work against Hadoop.

Hive was created to address these needs and make it easier for people and tools to work with Hadoop data. It does that by acting as an interpreter for Hadoop; you give Hive instructions in Hive Query Language (HQL), which is a language that looks very much like SQL, and Hive translates that HQL into MapReduce jobs. This opens up Hadoop data to tools and users that understand SQL.

In addition to acting as a translator, Hive also answers another common challenge with data in Hadoop. Files stored in Hadoop do not have to share a common data format. They can be text files delimited by commas, control characters, or any of a wide variety of characters. It's not even necessary that they be delimited text files. They can be files that use binary format, XML, or any of a combination of different formats. Hive enables you to deliver the data to users in a way that adheres to a defined schema or format.

Hive addresses these issues by providing a layer on top of Hadoop data that resembles a traditional relational database. In particular, Hive is designed to support the common operations for data warehousing scenarios.

NOTE **Although Hive looks like a relational database, with tables, columns, indexes, and so on, and much of the terminology is the same, it is *not* a relational database.**

Hive does not enable referential integrity, it does not enable transactions, and it does not grant ACID (atomicity, consistency, isolation, and durability) properties to Hadoop data stores.

Providing Structure for Unstructured Data

Users and the tools they use for querying data warehouses generally expect tabular, well-structured data. They expect the data to be delivered in a row/column format, and they expect consistency in the data values returned. Take the example of a user requesting a data set containing all the sales transactions for yesterday. Imagine the user's reaction if some rows in the data set contained 10 columns, some contained 8 columns, and some contained 15. The user would also be very surprised to find that the unit cost column in the data set contained valid numeric values on some rows, and on others it might contain alpha characters.

Because Hadoop data stores don't enforce a particular schema, this is a very real scenario when querying Hadoop. Hive helps with this scenario by enabling you to specify a schema of columns and their types for the information. Then, when the data is queried through Hive, it ensures that the results conform to the expected schema.

These schemas are declared by creating a table. The actual table data is stored as files in the Hadoop file system. When you request data from the table, Hive translates that request to read the appropriate files from the Hadoop file system and returns the data in a format that matches the table definition provided.

The table definitions are stored in the Hive metadata store, or *metastore*. By default, the metastore is an embedded Derby database. This metastore is a relational database that captures the table metadata (the name of the table, the columns and data types it contains, and the format that the underlying files are expected to be in).

NOTE **In a default Hive setup, the Derby database used for the metastore may be configured for single-user access. If you are just testing Hive or running a local instance for development, this may be fine. However, for Hive implementation in a production environment, you will want to upgrade the metastore to a multiple-user setup using a more robust database. One of the more common databases used for this is MySQL. However, the metastore can be any Java Database Connectivity (JDBC)-compliant database. If you are using the Hortonworks' HDP 1.3 Windows distribution, SQL Server can be used as a supported metastore.**

Hive v0.11 also includes HiveServer2. This version of Hive improves support for multi-user concurrency and supports additional authentication methods, while providing the same experience as the standard Hive server. Again, for a production environment, HiveServer2 may be a better fit. The examples used in this chapter run against Hive Server and HiveServer2.

Another area of difference between Hive and many relational databases is its support for different data types. Due to the unstructured data that it must support, it defines a number of data types that you won't find in a traditional relational database.

Hive Data Types

Table 6.1 lists the data types supported by Hive. Many of these data types have equivalent values in SQL Server, but a few are unique to Hive. Even for the data types that appear familiar, it is important to remember that Hive is coded as a Java application, and so these data types are implemented in Java. Their behavior will match the behavior from a Java application that uses the same data type. One immediate difference you will notice is that `STRING` types do not have a defined length. This is normal for Java and other programming languages, but is not typical for relational databases.

Table 6-1: Hive Data Types

TYPE	DESCRIPTION	EXAMPLES	SQL SERVER EQUIVALENT
`STRING`	String enclosed by single or double quotation marks.	`'John Smith'` or `"John Smith"`	`varchar(n)`, `nvarchar(n)`
`TINYINT`	1-byte signed integer in the range of -128 to 127.	`10`	`tinyint`
`SMALLINT`	2-byte signed integer in the range of -32,768 to 32,767.	`32000`	`smallint`
`INT`	4-byte signed integer in the range of -2,147,483,648 to 2,147,483,647.	`2000000`	`int`
`BIGINT`	8-byte signed integer in the range of -9,223,372,036,854,775,808 to 9,223,372,036,854,775,807.	`20000000`	`bigint`
`BOOLEAN`	Boolean true or false.	`TRUE` `FALSE`	`bit`
`FLOAT`	4-byte single-precision floating point.	`25.189764`	`real`
`DOUBLE`	8-byte double-precision floating point.	`25.1897645126`	`float(53)`
`DECIMAL`	A 38-digit precision number.	`25.1897654`	`decimal`, `numeric`

TYPE	DESCRIPTION	EXAMPLES	SQL SERVER EQUIVALENT
TIMESTAMP	UNIX timestamp that can be in one of three forms: Integer: Represents the number of seconds from the UNIX epoch date and time (January 1, 1970 12:00 AM). Floating point: Represents second offset from UNIX epoch with nanosecond precision. String: JDBC-compliant timestamp format YYYY-MM-DD HH:MM:SS.fffffffff.	123412123 123412123.1234567 '2013-01-01 12:00:00'	datetime2 datetime2(7)
DATE	A date in YYYY-MM-DD format.	{{2012-01-01}}	date
BINARY	A series of bytes.		binary(n)
STRUCT	Defines a column that contains a defined set of additional values and their types.	struct('John', 'Smith')	
MAP	Defines a collection of key/value pairs.	map('first', 'John', 'last', 'Smith')	
ARRAY	Defines a sequenced collection of values.	array('John', 'Smith')	
UNION	Similar to sql_variant types. They hold one value at a time, but it can be any one of the defined types for the column.	Varies depending on column	sql_variant

NOTE **DATE types are new for Hive 0.12. The Hortonworks Data Platform (HDP) 1.3 release is built using Hive 0.11, so this data type cannot be used with it yet.**

The types that are unique to Hive are MAP, ARRAY, and STRUCT. These types are supported in Hive so that it can better work with the denormalized data that is often found in Hadoop data stores. Relational database tables are typically normalized; that is, a row holds only one value for a given column. In Hadoop, though, it is not uncommon to find data where many values are stored in a row for a "column." This denormalization of the data makes it easier and faster to write the data, but makes it more challenging to retrieve it in a tabular format.

Hive addresses this with the MAP, ARRAY, and STRUCT types, which let a developer flatten out the denormalized data into a multicolumn structure. The details of querying this denormalized data are discussed later in this chapter. For now, we will review the data types that support these structures.

A STRUCT is a column that contains multiple defined fields. Each field can have its own data type. This is comparable to structs in most programming languages. In Hive, you can declare a STRUCT for a full name using the following syntax:

```
STRUCT <FirstName:string, MiddleName:string, LastName:string>
```

To access the individual fields of the STRUCT type, use the column name followed by a period and the name of the field:

```
FullName.FirstName
```

An ARRAY is a column that contains an ordered sequence of values. All the values must be of the same type:

```
ARRAY<STRING>
```

Because it is ordered, the individual values can be accessed by their index. As with Java and .NET languages, ARRAY types use a zero-based index, so you use an index of 0 to access the first element, and an index of 2 to access the third element. If the preceding Full Name column were declared as an ARRAY, with first name in the first position, middle name in the second position, and last name in the third position, you would access the first name with index 0 and last name with index 2:

```
FullName[0], FullName[2]
```

A MAP column is a collection of key/value pairs, where both the key and values have data types. The key and value do not have to use the same data type. A MAP for Full Name might be declared using the following syntax:

```
MAP<string, string>
```

In the Full Name case, you would populate the MAP column with the following key/value pairs:

```
'FirstName', 'John'
'MiddleName', 'Doe'
'LastName', 'Smith'
```

You can access MAP column elements using the same syntax as you use with an ARRAY, except that you use the key value instead of the position as the index. Accessing the first and last names would be done with this syntax:

```
FullName['FirstName'], FullName['LastName']
```

After looking at the possible data types, you may be wondering how these are stored in Hive. The next section covers the file formats that can be used to store the data.

File Formats

Hive uses Hadoop as the underlying data store. Because the actual data is stored in Hadoop, it can be in a wide variety of formats. As discussed in Chapter 5, "Storing and Managing Data in HDFS," Hadoop stores files and doesn't impose any restrictions in the content or format of those files. Hive offers enough flexibility that you can work with almost any file format, but some formats require significantly more effort.

The simplest files to work with in Hive are text files, and this is the default format Hive expects for files. These text files are normally delimited by specific characters. Common formats in business settings are comma-separated value files or tab-separated value files. However, the drawback of these formats is that commas and tabs often appear in real data; that is, they are embedded inside other text, and not intended as delimiters in all instances. For that reason, Hive by default uses control characters as delimiters, which are less likely to appear in real data. Table 6.2 describes these default delimiters.

Table 6-2: Hive Default Delimiters for Text Files

DELIMITER	OCTAL CODE	DESCRIPTION
\n	\012	New line character; this delimits rows in a text file.
^A	\001	Separates columns in each row.
^B	\002	Separates elements in an `ARRAY`, `STRUCT`, and key/value pairs in a `MAP`.
^C	\003	Separates the key from the value in a `MAP` column.

NOTE **The default delimiters can be overridden when the table is created. This is useful when you are dealing with text files that use different delimiters, but are still formatted in a very similar way. The options for that are shown in the section "Creating Tables" in this chapter.**

What if one of the many text files that is accessed through a Hive table uses a different value as a column delimiter? In that case, Hive won't be able to parse the file accurately. The exact results will vary depending on exactly how the text file is formatted, and how the Hive table was configured. However, it's likely that Hive will find less than the expected number of columns in the text file. In this case, it will fill in the columns it finds values for, and then output null values for any "missing" columns.

The same thing will happen if the data values in the files don't match the data type defined on the Hive table. If a file contains alphanumeric characters where Hive is expecting only numeric values, it will return null values. This enables Hive to be resilient to data quality issues with the files stored in Hadoop.

Some data, however, isn't stored as text. Binary file formats can be faster and more efficient than text formats, as the data takes less space in the files. If the data is stored in a smaller number of bytes, more of it can be read from the disk in a single-read operation, and more of it can fit in memory. This can improve performance, particularly in a big data system.

Unlike a text file, though, you can't open a binary file in your favorite text editor and understand the data. Other applications can't understand the data either, unless they have been built specifically to understand the format. In some cases, though, the improved performance can offset the lack of portability of the binary file formats.

Hive supports several binary formats natively for files. One option is the Sequence File format. Sequence files consist of binary encoded key/value pairs. This is a standard file format for Hadoop, so it will be usable by many other tools in the Hadoop ecosystem.

Another option is the RCFile format. RCFile uses a columnar storage approach, rather than the row-based approach familiar to users of relational systems. In the columnar approach, the values in a column are compressed so that only the distinct values for the column need to be stored, rather than the repeated values for each row. This can help compress the data a great deal, particularly if the column values are repeated for many rows. RCFiles are readable through Hive, but not from most other Hadoop tools.

A variation on the RCFile is the Optimized Record Columnar File format (ORCFile). This format includes additional metadata in the file system, which can vastly speed up the querying of Hive data. This was released as part of Hive 0.11.

NOTE **Compression is an option for your Hadoop data, and Hive can decompress the data as needed for processing. Hive and Hadoop have native support for compressing and decompressing files on demand using a variety of compression types, including common formats like Zip compression. This can be an alternative that allows to you get the benefits of smaller data formats while still keeping the data in a text format.**

If the data is in a binary or text format that Hive doesn't understand, custom logic can be developed to support it. The next section discusses how these can be implemented.

Custom File and Record Formats

Hive leverages Hadoop's ability to use custom logic for processing files. A full discussion of the implementation of custom logic for this is beyond the scope of this chapter, but this section does cover the basics.

First, you want to understand that Hive (and Hadoop in general) makes a distinction between the file format and the record format. The file format determines how records are stored in the file, and the record format determines how individual fields are extracted from each record.

By default, Hive uses the `TEXTFILE` format for the file format. You can override this for each Hive table by specifying a custom input format and a custom output format. The input format controls how records are written to the file, and the output format controls how the record is read from the file. If the record format of the file doesn't match one of the natively supported formats, you must provide an implementation of both the input format and output format, or Hive will not be able to use the file. Implementing the custom input and output formats is usually done in Java, although Microsoft is providing support for .NET-based implementations as well.

The record format is the next aspect to consider. As discussed already, the default record format is a text with delimiters between fields. If the record format requires custom processing, you must provide a reference to a serializer/deserializer (or SerDe). SerDes implements the logic for serializing the fields in a record to a specific record format and for deserializing that record format back to the individual fields.

Hive includes a couple of standard SerDes. The delimited record format is the default SerDe, and it can be customized to use different delimiters, in the event that a file uses a record format with nonstandard delimiters.

One of the other included SerDes handles regular expressions. The `RegexSerde` is useful when processing web logs and other text files where the format can vary but values can be extracted using pattern matching.

THIRD-PARTY SERDES

Third-party SerDes are available for Hive as well. Examples include `CSVSerde` (`https://github.com/ogrodnek/csv-serde`), which handles CSV files with embedded quotes and delimiters, and a JSON `SerDe` (`https://github.com/cloudera/cdh-twitter-example/blob/master/hive-serdes/src/main/java/com/cloudera/hive/serde/JSONSerDe.java`), which will parse records stored as JSON objects.

Hive has robust support for both standard and complex data types, stored in a wide variety of formats. And as highlighted in the preceding section, if support for a particular file format is not included, it can be added via third-party add-ons or custom implementations. This works very well with the type of data that is often found in Hadoop data stores. By using Hive's ability to apply a tabular structure to the data, it makes it easier for users and tools to consume. But there is another component to making access much easier for existing tools, which is discussed next.

Enabling Data Access and Transformation

Traditional users of data warehouses expect to be able to query and transform the data. They use SQL for this. They run this SQL through applications that use common middleware software to provide a standard interface to the data. Most RDBMS systems implement support for one or more of these middleware interfaces. Open Database Connectivity (ODBC) is a common piece of software for this and has been around since the early 1990s. Other common interfaces include the following:

- ADO.NET (used by Microsoft .NET-based applications)
- OLE DB
- Java Database Connectivity (JDBC)

ODBC, being one of the original interfaces for this, is well supported by existing applications, and many of the other interfaces provide bridges for ODBC.

Hive provides several forms of connectivity to Hadoop data through Thrift. Thrift is a software framework that supports network service communication, including support for JDBC and ODBC connectivity. Because ODBC is broadly supported by query access tools, it makes it much easier for business users to access the data in Hadoop using their favorite analysis tools. Excel is one of the common tools used by end users for working with data, and it supports ODBC. (Using Excel with Hadoop is discussed further in Chapter 11, "Visualizing Big Data with Microsoft BI.")

In addition to providing ODBC data access, Hive also acts as a translator for the SQL. As mentioned previously, many users and developers are familiar with writing SQL statements to query and transform data. Hive can take that SQL and translate it into MapReduce jobs. So, rather than the business users having to learn Java and MapReduce, or learn a new tool for querying data, they can leverage their existing knowledge and skills.

Hive manages this SQL translation by providing Hive Query Language (HQL). HQL provides support for common SQL language operations like `SELECT` for retrieving information and `INSERT INTO` to load data. Although HQL is not

ANSI SQL compliant, it implements enough of the standard to be familiar to users who have experience working with RDBMS systems.

Differentiating Hive from Traditional RDBMS Systems

This chapter has discussed several of the ways that Hive emulates a relational database. It's also covered some of the ways in which it differs, including the data types and the storage of the data. Those topics are worth covering in a bit more depth because they do have significant impact on how Hive functions and what you should expect from it.

In a relational database like SQL Server, the database engine manages the data storage. That means when you insert data into a table in a relational database, the server takes that data, converts it into whatever format it chooses, and stores it in data structures that it manages and controls. At that point, the server becomes the gatekeeper of the data. To access the data again, you must request it from the relational database so that the server can retrieve it from the internal storage and return it to you. Other systems cannot access or change the data directly without going through the server.

Hive, however, uses Hadoop as its data storage system. Therefore, the data sits in HDFS and is accessible to anyone with access to the file system. This does make it easier to manage the data and add new information, but you must be aware that other processes can manipulate the data.

One of the primary differences between Hive and most relational systems is that data in Hive can only be selected, inserted, or deleted; there is no update capability. This is due to Hive using Hadoop file storage for its data. As noted in Chapter 8, "Effective Big Data ETL with SSIS, Pig, and Sqoop," Hadoop is a write-once, read-many file system. If you need to change something in a file, you delete the original and write a new version of the file. Because Hive manages table data using Hadoop, the same constraints apply to Hive. There are also no row-based operations. Instead, everything is done in bulk mode.

Another key difference is that the data structure is defined up-front in traditional relational databases. The columns of a table, their data types, and any constraints on what the column can hold are set when the table is created. The database server enforces that any data written to the table conforms to the rules set up when the table was created. This is referred to as *schema on write*; the relational database server enforces the schema of the data when it is written to the table. If the data does not match the defined schema, it will not be inserted into the table.

Because Hive doesn't control the data and can't enforce that it is written in a specific format, it uses a different approach. It applies the schema when the data is read out of the data storage: *schema on read*. As mentioned, if the number of columns in the file is less than what is defined in Hive, null values are returned for the missing columns. If the data types don't match, null values are returned for those columns as well. The benefit of this is that Hive queries rarely fail due to bad data in the files. However, you do have to ensure that the data coming back is still meaningful and doesn't contain so many null values that it isn't useful.

Working with Hive

Like many Hadoop tools, Hive leverages a command-line interface (CLI) for interaction with the service. Other tools are available, such as the Hive Web Interface (HWI) and Beeswax, a user interface that is part of the Hue UI for working with Hadoop. For the examples in this chapter, though, the command line is used.

NOTE **Beeswax and Hue are not yet supported in HDInsight or the Hortonworks HDP 1.3 distribution, but it is under development. In the meantime, the CLI is the primary means of interacting directly with Hive.**

You can launch the CLI by navigating to the Hive bin folder (`c:\hdp\hadoop\hive-0.11.0.1.3.0.0-0380\bin` in the Hortonworks HDP 1.3 distribution with the default setup). Once there, run the CLI by executing the `hive.cmd` application. After the CLI has been run, you'll notice that the prompt changes to hive (see Figure 6.1).

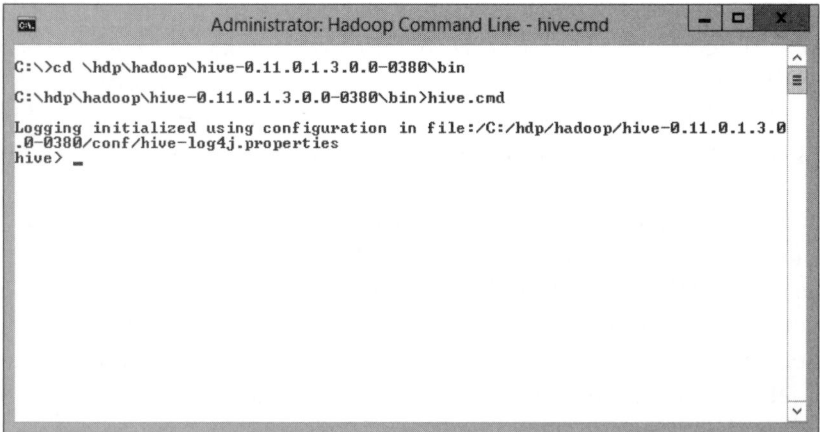

Figure 6.1: Hive CLI Interface

When executing Hive commands through the CLI, you must put a semicolon on each line of code that you want to execute. You can enter multiple lines, and the CLI will buffer them, until a semicolon is entered. At that point, the CLI executes all the proceeding commands.

A useful feature of the Hive CLI is the ability to run `hadoop dfs` commands without exiting. The Hive CLI uses an alias so that you can simply reference `dfs` directly, without the `hadoop` keyword, and it will execute the `dfs` command and return the results. For example, running the following code from the Hive prompt returns a recursive directory listing from the Hadoop file system:

```
dfs -lsr
```

The Hive CLI also supports basic autocomplete; that is, if you start typing a keyword or function and press the Tab key, it tries to complete the word. For example, if you type in `cre` and press Tab, it will complete it to `create`. If you press Tab on a new line, it prompts you if you want a list of all 427 possibilities. The CLI also maintains a history of previous commands entered. You can retrieve these values by pressing the up- and down-arrow keys. If you have a previously entered command selected, you can press the Enter key to run it again.

Creating and Querying Basic Tables

This section covers the basics of creating and organizing tables in Hive, as well as how to query them. If you are comfortable with SQL, you should find the commands familiar.

Creating Databases

Hive databases are essentially a way to organize tables. They are similar to the concept of a schema in SQL Server. In fact, Hive supports `SCHEMA` as a synonym for the `DATABASE` keyword. Databases are most often used to organize tables when there are multiple groups using the Hive server. When a database is created, Hive creates a folder in the Hadoop file system, by default using the same name as specified for the database, with `.db` appended to it. Any objects that are created using that database will be stored in the database's directory. If you don't specify a database when you create a table, it will be created in the `default` database.

To create a database, use the `CREATE DATABASE` command, followed by the name of the database:

```
CREATE DATABASE MsBigData;
```

NOTE **Many commands in Hive support `IF EXISTS` or `IF NOT EXISTS` clauses. Generally, you can use `IF NOT EXISTS` when creating objects, and `IF EXISTS` when removing them. These are used to check whether the target object is in the correct state before executing the command. For example, running a `CREATE DATABASE foo;` command when a `foo` database already exists will result in an error. However, if you use `CREATE DATABASE IF NOT EXISTS foo;`, no error will be produced, and the state of the database won't be modified.**

If you want to see the directories created in Hadoop for the databases, you can run this command: `dfs -lsr /hive/warehouse;`. `/hive/warehouse` is the default location for Hive in Hadoop storage. If you want to place the files in a different location, you can also directly specify the directory for the database using the `LOCATION` clause:

```
CREATE DATABASE MsBigDataAlt LOCATION '/user/MyNewDb';
```

NOTE The default directory for Hive metadata storage can be changed in the `hive-site.xml` file, along with many of the properties that control how Hive behaves. This file is located in the Hive `conf` folder, located at `c:\hdp\hadoop\hive-0.110.1.3.0.0.0-0380\conf` in a standard HDP setup. Be careful when making changes to this file, though; any errors can cause Hive not to start correctly.

After creating a few databases, you may be wondering how to view what's been created and how to remove databases you don't need. The `SHOW DATABASES` command lists the databases, and `DESCRIBE DATABASE` provides the location of the database:

```
SHOW DATABASES;
DESCRIBE DATABASE MsBigData;
```

`DROP DATABASE` removes a database. This also removes the directory associated with the database. By default, Hive does not let you drop a database that contains tables. If you are sure that you want to remove the database and its tables, you can use the `CASCADE` keyword. This tells Hive to remove all contents of the directory. `DROP DATABASE` also supports the `IF EXISTS` clause:

```
DROP DATABASE MsBigDataAlt;
DROP DATABASE MsBigDataAlt CASCADE;
```

Finally, you can use the `USE` command to control what database context will be used if you don't specify one. You'll find this convenient if you work in a particular database most of the time:

```
USE MsBigData;
```

Creating Tables

The basics of creating a table in Hive are similar to typical SQL, but there are a number of extensions, particularly for dealing with different file and record formats. A basic table can be created with the following:

```
CREATE TABLE MsBigData.customer (
  name STRING,
  city STRING,
  state STRING,
```

```
  postalCode STRING,
  purchases MAP<STRING, DECIMAL>
);
```

This table holds some basic customer information, including a list of the customer purchases in a MAP column, where the key is the product name, and value is the amount paid. To copy the schema for an existing table, you can use the LIKE keyword:

```
CREATE TABLE IF NOT EXISTS MsBigData.customer2 LIKE MsBigData.customer;
```

You can use the SHOW command to list the tables in either the current database or other databases. The DESCRIBE command can also be used with tables:

```
SHOW TABLES;
SHOW TABLES IN default;
DESCRIBE MsBigData.customer;
```

NOTE **You might have noticed that no primary or foreign keys are defined on these tables, nor any NOT NULL or other column constraints. Hive doesn't support these options because it doesn't have any way to enforce constraints on the data. In a relational system, these constraints help enforce data quality and consistency and are generally enforced when the data is inserted into a table (schema on write). Hive doesn't control the data, so it can't enforce the constraints.**

Tables can be removed by using the DROP TABLE command, and renamed using the ALTER TABLE statement. Columns can be renamed or have their types changed using CHANGE COLUMN, and they can be added or deleted using ADD COLUMNS and REPLACE COLUMNS, respectively. Replacing columns deletes any column not included in the new column list:

```
DROP TABLE MsBigData.customer2;
ALTER TABLE customer RENAME TO customer_backup;
ALTER TABLE customer_backup
  CHANGE COLUMN name fullname STRING;
ALTER TABLE customer_backup
  ADD COLUMNS (
    country STRING);
ALTER TABLE customer_backup
  REPLACE COLUMNS (
    name STRING,
    city STRING,
    state STRING,
    postalCode STRING,
    purchases MAP<STRING, DECIMAL>);
```

WARNING **Using ALTER TABLE to modify a table changes the metadata for the table. It does not modify the data in the files. This option is useful for correcting mistakes in the schema for a table, but any data issues have to be cleaned up separately.**

As discussed in the "Custom File and Record Formats" section, Hive gives you control over the record format. In the preceding `CREATE TABLE` statement, the Hive defaults are used; it expects text files in delimited format, with `Ctrl-A` (octal `001`) as a field delimiter. To control that format, Hive supports explicitly declaring the format options. The preceding table, with explicit delimiters defined, would look like this:

```
CREATE TABLE MsBigData.customer (
  name STRING,
  city STRING,
  state STRING,
  postalCode STRING,
  purchases MAP<STRING, DECIMAL>
)
ROW FORMAT DELIMITED
  FIELDS TERMINATED BY '\001'
  COLLECTION ITEMS TERMINATED BY '\002'
  MAP KEYS TERMINATED BY '\003'
  LINES TERMINATED BY '\n'
STORED AS TEXTFILE;
```

The file format is controlled by the `STORED AS` portion of the statement. To use the `SEQUENCEFILE` file format, you replace `STORED AS TEXTFILE` with `STORED AS SEQUENCEFILE`. To use custom file formats, you specify the `INPUTFORMAT` and `OUTPUTFORMAT` options directly. For example, here is the specification for the `RCFile` format. The value in the string is the class name for the file format to be used:

```
STORED AS
  INPUTFORMAT 'org.apache.hadoop.hive.ql.io.RCFileInputFormat'
  OUTPUTFORMAT 'org.apache.hadoop.hive.ql.io.RCFileOutputFormat'
```

The row format options are controlled by the `ROW FORMAT` portion. The delimited SerDe is the default. To specify a custom SerDe, use the `SERDE` keyword followed by the class name of the SerDe. For example, the `RegexSerDe` can be specified as follows:

```
ROW FORMAT SERDE 'org.apache.hadoop.hive.contrib.serde2.RegexSerDe'
```

Another important option in table creation is the `EXTERNAL` option. By default, when you create a table without specifying `EXTERNAL`, it is created as a managed table. This means that Hive considers itself the manager of the table, including any data created in it. The data for the table will be stored in a subdirectory under the database folder, and if the table is dropped, Hive will remove all the data associated with the table.

However, if you use `CREATE EXTERNAL TABLE` to create the table, Hive creates the metadata for the table, and allows you to query it, but it doesn't consider itself the owner of the table. If the table is dropped, the metadata for it will be deleted, but the data will be left intact. External tables are particularly useful for data files that are shared among multiple applications. Creating the Hive table definition allows it to be queried using the power of Hive, but it makes it clear that the data is shared with other applications.

When you use the `EXTERNAL` keyword, you must also use the `LOCATION` option:

```
CREATE EXTERNAL TABLE MsBigData.customer (
  name STRING,
  city STRING,
  state STRING,
  postalCode STRING,
  purchases MAP<STRING, DECIMAL>
)
LOCATION 'user/MyCustomerTable';
```

You can the `LOCATION` option with managed tables, as well, but it's not necessary unless you want a table that Hive manages that is also stored in a directory that Hive doesn't manage. For clarity, it's recommended that `LOCATION` be used only with external tables.

WARNING **Be aware that, regardless of whether the table is managed or external, the data is still accessible through the Hadoop file system. Files can be added or deleted by anyone with access to Hadoop. So, even for managed tables, Hive doesn't really take full control of the data files.**

Adding and Deleting Data

Remember from the earlier discussion about differences between Hive and relation systems that Hive uses Hadoop for storage, so it does not support row-level operations. You can't insert, update, or delete individual rows. However, because Hive is designed for big data, you would want to perform bulk operations in any case, so this isn't a significant restriction.

Perhaps the simplest way to add data to a Hive table is to write or copy a properly formatted file to the table's directory directly, using HDFS. (Commands for copying files directly in HDFS are covered in Chapter 5, "Storing and Managing Data in HDFS.")

You can load data from existing files into a table using the `LOAD DATA` command. This is similar to using a `BULK INSERT` statement in SQL Server. All the data in the specified location will be loaded into the table. However, in SQL Server, `BULK INSERT` references a single data file. `LOAD DATA` is usually pointed at a directory, so that all files in the directory can be imported. Another important difference is that, while SQL Server verifies the data in a bulk load, Hive only verifies that the file format matches the table definition. It does not check that the record format matches what has been specified for the table:

```
LOAD DATA LOCAL INPATH 'C:/MsBigData/TestData/customers'
  OVERWRITE INTO TABLE MsBigData.customer;
```

In the preceding statement, `OVERWRITE` indicates that any files in the table's directory should be deleted before loading the new data. If it is left out, the data files will be added to the files in the directory. The `LOCAL` keyword indicates that the data will be copied from the local file system into the Hive directory. The original copy of the files will be left in the local file system. If the `LOCAL` keyword is not included, the path is resolved against the HDFS, and the files are moved to the Hive directory, rather than being copied.

What if you want to insert data into one table based on the contents of another table? The `INSERT` statement handles that:

```
INSERT INTO TABLE customer
  SELECT * FROM customer_import
```

The `INSERT` statement supports any valid `SELECT` statement as a source for the data. (The format for the `SELECT` statement is covered in the next section.) The data from the `SELECT` statement is appended to the table. If you replace the `INTO` keyword with `OVERWRITE`, the contents of the table are replaced.

NOTE Several variations of these statements can be used with partitioned tables, as covered in the section "Loading Partitioned Tables," later in this chapter.

There is also the option to create managed tables in Hive based on selecting data from another table:

```
CREATE TABLE florida_customers AS
  SELECT * FROM MsBigData.Customers
  WHERE state = 'FL';
```

NOTE Hive doesn't support temp tables. You can create tables and populate them easily using the `CREATE TABLE .. AS` syntax, but you must manage the lifetime of the table yourself.

After a table has been loaded, you may want to export data from it. You can use the `INSERT .. DIRECTORY` command for this. `OVERWRITE` indicates that the target directory should be emptied before the new files are written, and `LOCAL` indicates that the target is a directory on the local file system. Omitting them has the same behavior as it had with the `LOAD DATA` command:

```
INSERT OVERWRITE LOCAL DIRECTORY 'c:\MsBigData\export_customer'
  SELECT name, purchases FROM customer WHERE state = 'FL';
```

You can also export to multiple directories simultaneously. Be aware that each record that meets the `WHERE` clause conditions will be exported to the specified location, and each record is evaluated against every `WHERE` clause. It is possible, depending on how the `WHERE` clause is written, for the same record to be exported to multiple directories:

```
FROM customer c
  INSERT OVERWRITE DIRECTORY '/tmp/fl_customers'
    SELECT * WHERE c.state = 'FL'
  INSERT OVERWRITE DIRECTORY '/tmp/ca_customers'
    SELECT * WHERE c.state = 'CA';
```

Querying a Table

Writing queries against Hive is fairly straightforward if you are familiar with writing SQL queries. Instead of focusing on the everyday SQL, this section focuses on the aspects of querying Hive that differ from most relational databases.

The basic `SELECT` statement is intact, along with familiar elements such as `WHERE` clauses, table and column aliases, and `ORDER BY` clauses:

```
SELECT c.name, c.city, c.state, c.postalCode, c.purchases
FROM MsBigData.customer c LIMIT 100
WHERE c.state='FL'
ORDER BY c.postalCode;
```

NOTE One useful difference to note is the `LIMIT` clause. This restricts the query to an upper limit of rows that it can return. If you are used to SQL Server, you might be familiar with the `TOP` clause. `LIMIT` works in the same way, but it doesn't support percentage based row limits. `LIMIT` can prove very handy when you are exploring data and don't want to process millions or billions of rows in your Hive tables.

When you run the `SELECT` statement, you'll notice that the results are as expected, with the exception of the `purchases` column. Because that column represents a collection of values, Hive flattens it into something that it can return as a column value. It does this using Java Script Object Notation (JSON), a standard format for representing objects:

```
John Smith   Jacksonville FL 32226 {"Food":456.98,"Lodging":1245.45}
```

This might be useful to get a quick look at a table's data, but in most instances you will want to extract portions of the value out. Querying individual elements of complex types is fairly straightforward. For `MAP` types, you reference the key value:

```
SELECT c.name, c.city, c.state, c.postalCode, c.purchases['Lodging']
```

If `purchases` were an `ARRAY`, you would use the index of the value you are interested in:

```
SELECT c.name, c.city, c.state, c.postalCode, c.purchases[1]
```

And if `purchases` were a `STRUCT`, you would use the field name:

```
SELECT c.name, c.city, c.state, c.postalCode, c.purchases.Lodging
```

You can use this syntax in any location where you would use a regular column.

Calculations and functions are used in the same way as you would in most SQL dialects. For example, this `SELECT` statement returns the sum of lodging purchases for any customer who purchased over `100` in food:

```
SELECT SUM(c.purchases['Lodging'])
FROM MsBigData.customer c
WHERE c.purchases['Food'] > 100;
```

NOTE One interesting feature of Hive is that you can use regular expressions in the column list of the `SELECT`. For example, this query returns the name column and all columns that start with "address" from the specified table:

```
SELECT name, 'address.*' FROM shipments;
```

You can also use the functions `RLIKE` and `REGEXP`, which function in the same way as `LIKE` but allow the use of regular expressions for matching.

Some functions that are of particular interest are those that deal with complex types, because these don't have equivalent versions in many relational systems. For example, there are functions for determining the size of a collection. There are also functions that generate tables as output. These are the opposite of aggregating functions, such as `SUM`, which take multiple rows and aggregate them into a single result. Table generating functions take a single row of input and produce multiple rows of output. These are useful when dealing with complex types that need to be flattened out. However, they must be used by themselves in `SELECT` column lists. Table 6.3 describes the table-generating functions, along with other functions that work with complex types.

Table 6-3: Functions Related to Complex Types

NAME	DESCRIPTION
`size(MAP | ARRAY)`	Returns the number of elements in the `MAP` or `ARRAY` passed to the function
`map_keys(MAP)`	Returns the key values from a `MAP` as an `ARRAY`
`map_values(MAP)`	Returns the values from a `MAP` as an `ARRAY`
`array_contains(ARRAY, value)`	Returns true if the array contains the value, false if it does not

NAME	DESCRIPTION
`sort_array(ARRAY)`	Sorts and returns the `ARRAY` by the natural order of the elements
`explode(MAP | ARRAY)`	Returns a row for each item in the `MAP` or `ARRAY`
`inline(ARRAY<STRUCT>)`	Explodes an array of `STRUCT`s into a table

NOTE There are also functions for parsing URLs and JSON objects into tables of information that can prove extremely useful if you need to deal with this type of data. For a complete, current list of Hive operators and functions, a good resource is the Hive wiki: `https://cwiki.apache.org/confluence/display/Hive/LanguageManual+UDF`.

Hive supports joining tables, but only using equi-join logic. This restriction is due to the distributed nature of the data, and because Hive has to translate many queries to MapReduce jobs. Performing non-equi-joins across distributed data sets is extremely resource intensive, and performance would often be unreasonably poor. For the same reason, `OR`s cannot be used in `JOIN` clauses.

`INNER`, `LEFT OUTER`, `RIGHT OUTER`, and `FULL OUTER JOIN`s are supported. These function like their SQL equivalents. When processing a `SELECT` with both `JOIN` and `WHERE` clauses, Hive evaluates the `JOIN` first, then the `WHERE` clause is applied on the joined results.

During join operations, Hive makes the assumption that the largest table appears last in the `FROM` clause. Therefore, it attempts to process the other tables first, and then streams the content of the last table. If you keep this in mind when writing your Hive queries, you will get better performance. You can use a query hint to indicate which table should be streamed, too:

```
SELECT /*+ STREAMTABLE(bt) */ bt.name, bt.transactionAmount, c.state
FROM bigTable bt JOIN customer c ON bt.postalCode = c.PostalCode
```

When you are using `ORDER BY`, be aware that this requires ordering of the whole data set. Because this operation cannot be distributed across multiple nodes, it can be quite slow. Hive offers the alternative `SORT BY`. Instead of sorting the entire data set, `SORT BY` lets each node that is processing results sort its results locally. The overall data set won't be ordered, but the results from each node will be sorted:

```
SELECT c.name, c.city, c.state, c.postalCode, c.purchases
FROM MsBigData.customer c
SORT BY c.postalCode;
```

You can use SORT BY in conjunction with DISTRIBUTE BY to send related data to the same nodes for processing so that there is less overlap from sorting on multiple nodes. In the following example, the data is distributed to nodes, based on the state, and then the postal codes are sorted per state for each node:

```
SELECT c.name, c.city, c.state, c.postalCode, c.purchases
FROM MsBigData.customer c
DISTRIBUTE BY c.state;
SORT BY c.state, c.postalCode;
```

Now that you have explored the basic operations in Hive, the next section will address the more advanced features, like partitioning, views, and indexes.

Using Advanced Data Structures with Hive

Hive has a number of advanced features. These are primarily used for performance and ease of use. This section covers the common ones.

Setting Up Partitioned Tables

Just like most relational databases, Hive supports partitioning, though the implementation is different. Partitioned tables are good for performance because they help Hive narrow down the amount of data it needs to process to respond to queries.

The columns used for partitioning should not be included in the other columns for the table. For example, using the customer table example from earlier, a logical partition choice would be the state column. To partition the table by state, the state column would be removed from the column list and added to the PARTITIONED BY clause:

```
CREATE TABLE MsBigData.customer (
  name STRING,
  city STRING,
  postalCode STRING,
  purchases MAP<STRING, DECIMAL>
)
PARTITIONED BY (state STRING);
```

There can be multiple partition columns, and the columns in the PARTITIONED BY list cannot be repeated in the main body of the table, because Hive considers those to be ambiguous columns. This is because Hive stores the partition column values separately from the data in the files. As discussed previously, Hive creates a directory to store the files for managed tables. When a managed table is partitioned, Hive creates a subdirectory structure in the table directory. A subdirectory is created for each partition value, and only data files with that partition value are stored in those folders. The directory structure would look something like this:

```
.../customers/state=AL
.../customers/state=AK
.....
.../customers/state=WI
.../customers/state=WY
```

You can also use the `SHOW PARTITIONS` command to see what the partitions look like for the table. The partitions are created automatically as data is loaded into the table.

When this table is queried with a `WHERE` clause like `state = 'AL'`, Hive only has to process files in the `.../customers/state=AL` folder. Partitioning can drastically impact performance by reducing the number of folders that need to be scanned to respond to queries. However, to benefit from it, the queries have included the partition columns in the `WHERE` clause. One of the available options for Hive is a "strict" mode. In this mode, any query against a partitioned table must include partitioned columns in the `WHERE` clause. This can be enabled or disabled by setting the `hive.mapred.mode` to strict or nonstrict, respectively.

External partitioned tables are managed a bit differently. The partitioned columns are still declared using the `PARTITIONED BY` clause. However, because Hive doesn't manage the directory structure for external tables, you must explicitly set the available partitions and the directory it maps to using the `ALTER TABLE` statement. For example, if the customer example were an external table, adding a partition for the state of Alabama (AL) would look like this:

```
ALTER TABLE MsBigData.customer ADD PARTITION(state = 'AL')
  LOCATION 'hdfs://myserver/data/state/AL';
```

Notice that in this mode you have complete flexibility with the directory structure. This makes it useful when you have large amounts of data coming from other tools. You can get the performance benefits of partitioning while still retaining the original directory structure of the data.

To remove a partition, you can use the `DROP PARTITION` clause:

```
ALTER TABLE MsBigData.customer DROP PARTITION(state = 'AL')
  LOCATION 'hdfs://myserver/data/state/AL';
```

Moving a partition can be done using the `SET LOCATION` option:

```
ALTER TABLE MsBigData.customer PARTITION(state = 'AL')
  SET LOCATION 'hdfs://myserver/data/new_state/AL';
```

Loading Partitioned Tables

When loading data into a partitioned table, you must tell Hive what partition the data belongs to. For example, to load the AL partition of the customer table, you specify the target partition:

```
LOAD DATA LOCAL INPATH 'C:/MsBigData/TestData/customers_al'
  OVERWRITE INTO TABLE MsBigData.customer
  PARTITION (state = 'AL');
```

If you want to insert data into a partition from an existing table, you must still define the partition that is being loaded:

```
INSERT INTO TABLE customer
  PARTITION (state = 'AL')
  SELECT * FROM customer_import ci
  WHERE ci.state_code = 'AL';
```

However, this may not work well if you have a large number of partitions. The `INSERT INTO...SELECT` statement for each partition would have to scan the source table for the data, which would be very inefficient. An alternative approach is to use the `FROM...INSERT` format:

```
FROM customer_import ci
  INSERT INTO TABLE customer
    PARTITION (state = 'AL')
    SELECT * WHERE ci.state_code = 'AL'
    PARTITION (state = 'AK')
    SELECT * WHERE ci.state_code = 'AK'
    PARTITION (state = 'AZ')
    SELECT * WHERE ci.state_code = 'AZ'
    PARTITION (state = 'AR')
    SELECT * WHERE ci.state_code = 'AR';
```

When you use this format, the table is scanned only once. Each record in the source table is evaluated against each `WHERE` clause. If it matches, it is inserted into the associated partition. Because the record is compared against each clause (even if it's already matched to a previous `WHERE` clause), records can be inserted into multiple partitions, or none at all if it doesn't match any clauses.

You can also do dynamic partitioning. This is based on matching the last columns in the `SELECT` statement against the partition. For example, in the following `FROM...INSERT INTO` statement, the country code has a hard-coded value, meaning it is static. However, the state partition does not have a hard-coded value, which makes it dynamic. The `state_code` column is used to dynamically determine what partition the record should be placed in. This isn't based on matching the column name; it's based on ordinal position in the `SELECT`. In this case, there is one partition column, so the last column in the `SELECT` list is used. If there were two partition columns, the last two columns would be used, and so on:

```
FROM customer_import ci
  INSERT INTO TABLE customer
    PARTITION (country='US', state)
    SELECT name, city, postalCode, purchases, state_code;
```

WARNING **Be careful when using dynamic partitioning. It can be easy to inadvertently create a massive number of partitions and impact performance negatively. By default, it operates in strict mode, which means at least some of the partition columns must be static. This can avoid runaway partition creation.**

Using Views

Views are a way of persisting queries so that they can be treated like any other table in Hive. They behave similarly to views in a relational database. You can use `CREATE VIEW` to define a view based on a query:

```
CREATE VIEW customerSales AS
  SELECT c.name, c.city, c.state, c.postalCode, s.salesAmount,
  FROM MsBigData.customer c JOIN sales s ON c.name = s.customerName
  WHERE c.state='FL';
```

Selecting from the view works like selecting from any table, except that the logic of the original query is abstracted away:

```
SELECT * FROM customerSales
WHERE salesAmount > 50000;
```

One of the most powerful uses of views in Hive is to handle complex data types. Often, these need to be flattened out for consumption by users or other processes. If you are using a view, the purchases column in the customer table could be flattened into two columns, and consumers of the view wouldn't need to understand the collection structure:

```
CREATE VIEW customerPurchases AS
SELECT c.name, c.city, c.state, c.postalCode,
  c.purchases['Food'] AS foodPurchase,
  c.purchases['Lodging'] AS lodgingPurchase
FROM MsBigData.customer c
WHERE c.state='FL';
```

You can remove views by using the `DROP VIEW` statement:

```
DROP VIEW customerPurchases;
```

Creating Indexes for Tables

As mentioned in the section on creating tables, Hive doesn't support keys. Because traditional relational databases create indexes by creating stores of indexed values that link to the keys of records with those values, you might wonder how Hive can support them. The short answer is that indexes work differently in Hive. For the slightly longer answer, read on.

When an index is created in Hive, it creates a new table to store the indexed values in. The primary benefit of this is that Hive can load a smaller number of columns (and thus use less memory and disk resources) to respond to queries that use those columns. However, this benefit in query performance comes at the cost of processing the index and the additional storage space required for it. In addition, unlike indexes in most relational systems, Hive does not automatically update the index when new data is added to the indexed table. You are responsible for rebuilding the index as necessary.

To create an index, you use the `CREATE INDEX` statement. You must provide the table and columns to use for creating the index. You also need to provide the type of index handler to use. As with many parts of Hive, indexes are designed to be extensible, so you can develop your own index handlers in Java. In the following example, the `COMPACT` index handler is used:

```
CREATE INDEX customerIndex
ON TABLE customer (state)
AS 'COMPACT'
WITH DEFERRED REBUILD
IN TABLE customerIndexTable;
```

Another option for the index handler is `BITMAP`. This handler creates bitmap indexes, which work well for columns that don't have a large number of distinct values.

The index creation also specifies the table where the index data will be placed. This is optional; however, it does make it easier to see what the index contains. Most of the standard options for `CREATE TABLE` can also be specified for the table that holds the index.

The `WITH DEFERRED REBUILD` clause tells Hive not to populate the index immediately. Rather, you tell it to begin rebuilding with the `ALTER INDEX...REBUILD` command:

```
ALTER INDEX customerIndex
ON TABLE customer
REBUILD;
```

You can show indexes for a table using the `SHOW INDEX` command, and drop one by using `DROP INDEX`:

```
SHOW INDEX ON customer;
DROP INDEX customerIndex ON TABLE customer;
```

Summary

This chapter covered the basics of working with Hive. The commands for creating databases, tables, and views were covered. In addition, the commands for inserting data into those tables and querying it back out were reviewed. Some more advanced functionality around partitions and indexing was also highlighted.

Hive has quite a bit of functionality, and not all the functionality could be covered here due to space constraints. In particular, administration, configuration, and extensibility could require a book unto themselves to cover fully. An excellent reference for this is *Programming Hive* (O'Reilly Media, Inc., 2012), by Edward Capriolo, Dean Wampler, and Jason Rutherglen. However, a good overview of setting up data for querying and implementing some common performance improvements has been provided.

CHAPTER

7

Expanding Your Capability with HBase and HCatalog

WHAT YOU WILL LEARN IN THIS CHAPTER:

- Knowing When to Use HBase
- Creating HBase Tables
- Loading Data into an HBase Table
- Performing a Fast Lookup with HBase
- Defining Data Structures in HCatalog
- Creating Indexes and Partitions on HCatalog Tables
- Integrating HCatalog with Pig and Hive

This chapter looks at two tools that you can use to create structure on top of your big data stored in the Hadoop Distributed File System (HDFS): HBase and HCatalog. HBase is a tool that creates key/value tuples on top of the data and stores the key values in a columnar storage structure. HBase ensures fast lookups and enables consistency when updating the data. It supports huge update rates while providing almost instant access to the updated data. For example, you might use HBase to record and analyze streaming data from sensors providing near real-time agile predictive analytics.

The other tool, HCatalog, provides a relational table abstraction layer over HDFS. Using the HCatalog abstraction layer allows query tools such as Pig and

Hive to treat the data in a familiar relational architecture. It also permits easier exchange of data between the HDFS storage and client tools used to present the data for analysis using familiar data exchange application programming interfaces (APIs) such as Java Database Connectivity (JDBC) and Open Database Connectivity (ODBC). For example using HCatalog you can use the same schema for processing the data in Hive or Pig and then pull the data into a traditional data warehouse contained in SQL Server, where it can easily be combined with your traditional BI systems.

Using HBase

Although HDFS is excellent at storing large amounts of data, and although MapReduce jobs and tools such as Hive and Pig are well suited for reading and aggregating large amounts of data, they are not very efficient when it comes to individual record lookups or updating the data. This is where HBase comes into play.

HBase is classified as a NoSQL database. Unlike traditional relational databases like SQL Server or Oracle, NoSQL databases do not attempt to provide ACID (atomicity, consistency, isolation, durability) transactional reliability. Instead, they are tuned to handle large amounts of unstructured data, providing fast key-based lookups and updates.

As mentioned previously, HBase is a key/value columnar storage system. The key is what provides fast access to the value for retrieval and updating. An HBase table consists of a set of pointers to the cell values. These pointers are made up of a row key, a column key, and a version key. Using this type of key structure, the values that make up tables and rows are stored in regions across regional servers. As the data grows, the regions are automatically split and redistributed. Because HBase uses HDFS as the storage layer, it relies on it to supply services such as automatic replication and failover.

Because HBase relies so heavily on keys for its performance, it is a very important consideration when defining tables. In the next section, you will look at creating HBase tables and defining appropriate keys for the table.

Creating HBase Tables

Because the keys are so important when retrieving or updating data quickly, it is the most important consideration when setting up an HBase table. The creation of the keys depends a great deal on how the data gets accessed. If data is accessed as a single-cell lookup, a randomized key structure works best. If you retrieve data based on buckets (for example, logs from a certain server), you should include this in the key. If you further look up values based on log event type or date ranges, these should also be part of the key. The order of the key attributes is important. If lookups are based primarily on server and then on event type, the key should be made up of Server–Event–Timestamp.

Another factor to consider when creating tables in HBase is normalization versus denormalization. Because HBase does not support table joins, it is important to know how the data will be used by the clients accessing the data. Like most reporting-centric databases, it is a good idea to denormalize your tables somewhat depending on how the data is retrieved. For example, if sales orders are analyzed by customer location, this data should be denormalized into the same table. Sometimes it makes more sense to use table joins. If you need to perform table joins, it can be implemented in a MapReduce job or in the client application after retrieving the data.

To interact with HBase, you can use the HBase shell. The HBase command-line tool is located in the bin directory of your HBase installation directory if you are using HDP for Windows. (Note: The shell is not currently available in HDInsight.) To launch the HBase shell using the Windows command prompt, navigate to the bin directory and issue the following command:

```
hbase shell
```

After the HBase shell is launched, you can view the help by issuing the `help` command. After issuing the `help` command, you will see a list of the various command groups (see Figure 7.1).

```
hbase(main):003:0> help
HBase Shell, version 0.94.6.1.3.0.0-107, r1a62b76bde7776a433ee069ab47ee6270f8992d4, Mon May
20 02:43:24 EDT 2013
Type 'help "COMMAND"', (e.g. 'help "get"' -- the quotes are necessary) for help on a specific
command.
Commands are grouped. Type 'help "COMMAND_GROUP"', (e.g. 'help "general"') for help on a
command group.

COMMAND GROUPS:
Group name: general
Commands: status, version, whoami

Group name: ddl
Commands: alter, alter_async, alter_status, create, describe, disable, disable_all, drop,
drop_all, enable, enable_all, exists, is_disabled, is_enabled, list, show_filters

Group name: dml
Commands: count, delete, deleteall, get, get_counter, incr, put, scan, truncate

Group name: tools
Commands: assign, balance_switch, balancer, close_region, compact, flush, hlog_roll,
major_compact, move, split, unassign, zk_dump
```

Figure 7.1: Listing the various command groups in the HBase shell.

There are command groups for data definition statements (DDL), data manipulation statements (DML), replication, tools, and security. To list help for a command group, issue the `help` command followed by the group name in quotation marks. For example, Figure 7.2 shows the help for the DDL command group (only the Alter command is showing).

```
Command: alter
Alter column family schema; pass table name and a dictionary
specifying new column family schema. Dictionaries are described
on the main help command output. Dictionary must include name
of column family to alter. For example,

To change or add the 'f1' column family in table 't1' from defaults
to instead keep a maximum of 5 cell VERSIONS, do:

hbase> alter 't1', NAME => 'f1', VERSIONS => 5

To delete the 'f1' column family in table 't1', do:

hbase> alter 't1', NAME => 'f1', METHOD => 'delete'

or a shorter version:

hbase> alter 't1', 'delete' => 'f1'

You can also change table-scope attributes like MAX_FILESIZE
MEMSTORE_FLUSHSIZE, READONLY, and DEFERRED_LOG_FLUSH.
```

Figure 7.2: Listing help for the DDL command group.

To create a basic table named Stocks with a column family named Price and one named Trade, enter the following code at the command prompt:

```
create 'Stocks', 'Price','Trade'
```

To verify that the table has been created, you can use the `describe` command:

```
describe 'Stocks'
```

Figure 7.3 shows the output describing the table attributes.

Notice the two column family groups. You can also set attributes for the table/column groups (for example, the number of versions to keep and whether to keep deleted cells).

Now that you've created your table, you're ready to load data into it.

Loading Data into an HBase Table

You can load data into the table in two ways. To load a single value, you use the `put` command, supplying the table, column, and value. The column is prefixed by the column family. The following code loads a row of stock data into the Stocks table:

```
put 'Stocks', 'ABXA_12092009','Price:Open','2.55'
put 'Stocks', 'ABXA_12092009','Price:High','2.77'
put 'Stocks', 'ABXA_12092009','Price:Low','2.5'
put 'Stocks', 'ABXA_12092009','Price:Close','2.67'
put 'Stocks', 'ABXA_12092009','Trade:Volume','158500'
```

```
hbase(main):015:0> describe 'Stocks'
DESCRIPTION ENABLED
{NAME => 'Stocks', FAMILIES => [{NAME => 'Price', D true
ATA_BLOCK_ENCODING => 'NONE', BLOOMFILTER => 'NONE'
, REPLICATION_SCOPE => '0', VERSIONS => '3', COMPRE
SSION => 'NONE', MIN_VERSIONS => '0', TTL => '21474
83647', KEEP_DELETED_CELLS => 'false', BLOCKSIZE =>
'65536', IN_MEMORY => 'false', ENCODE_ON_DISK => '
true', BLOCKCACHE => 'true'}, {NAME => 'Trade', DAT
A_BLOCK_ENCODING => 'NONE', BLOOMFILTER => 'NONE',
REPLICATION_SCOPE => '0', VERSIONS => '3', COMPRESS
ION => 'NONE', MIN_VERSIONS => '0', TTL => '2147483
647', KEEP_DELETED_CELLS => 'false', BLOCKSIZE => '
65536', IN_MEMORY => 'false', ENCODE_ON_DISK => 'tr
ue', BLOCKCACHE => 'true'}]}
```

Figure 7.3: Describing the table attributes.

To verify that the values have been loaded in the table, you can use the `scan` command:

```
scan 'Stocks'
```

You should see the key/values listed as shown in Figure 7.4. Notice a timestamp has been automatically loaded as part of the key to keep track of versioning.

```
hbase(main):026:0> scan 'Stocks'
ROW COLUMN+CELL
ABXA_12092009 column=Price:Close, timestamp=1381194957034, value=2.67
ABXA_12092009 column=Price:High, timestamp=1381194712419, value=2.77
ABXA_12092009 column=Price:Low, timestamp=1381194840880, value=2.5
ABXA_12092009 column=Price:Open, timestamp=1381194255613, value=2.55
ABXA_12092009 column=Trade:Volume, timestamp=1381195075045, value=158500
1 row(s) in 0.0350 seconds
```

Figure 7.4: Listing key/values.

If the key is already in the table, HBase updates the value and creates a new timestamp for the cell. The old record is still maintained in the table.

Using the HBase shell and the `put` command illustrates the process of adding a row to the table, but it is not practical in a production setting. You can load data into an HBase table in several other ways. You can use the HBase tools ImportTsv and CompleteBulkLoad. You can also write a MapReduce job or write a custom application using the HBase API. Another option is to use Hive or Pig to load the data. For example, the following code loads data into an HBase table from a CSV file:

```
StockData = LOAD '/user/hue/StocksTest2.csv' USING PigStorage(',') as
   (RowKey:chararray,stock_price_open:long);
STORE StockData INTO 'hbase://StocksTest'
  USING org.apache.pig.backend.hadoop.hbase.HBaseStorage('Price:Open');
```

Now that you know how to load the data into the table, it is now time to see how you read the data from the table.

Performing a Fast Lookup

One of HBase's strengths is its ability to perform fast lookups. HBase supports two data-retrieval operations: `get` and `scan`. The `get` operation returns the cells for a specified row. For example, the following `get` command is used to retrieve the cell values for a row in the Stocks table. Figure 7.5 shows the resulting output:

```
get 'Stocks', 'ABXA_12092009'
```

```
hbase(main):004:0> get 'Stocks', 'ABXA_12092009'
COLUMN CELL
Price:Close timestamp=1381194957034, value=2.67
Price:High timestamp=1383000037853, value=2.85
Price:Low timestamp=1381194840880, value=2.5
Price:Open timestamp=1381194255613, value=2.55
Trade:Volume timestamp=1381195075045, value=158500
5 row(s) in 0.0420 seconds
```

Figure 7.5: Getting the row cell values.

You can also use the `get` command to retrieve the previous versions of a cell value. The following `get` command gets the last three versions of the high column. Figure 7.6 shows the output:

```
get 'Stocks', 'ABXA_12092009', {COLUMN => 'Price:High', VERSIONS => 3}
```

```
hbase(main):006:0> get 'Stocks', 'ABXA_12092009', {COLUMN => 'Price:High', VERSIONS => 3}
COLUMN CELL
Price:High timestamp=1383001106170, value=2.95
Price:High timestamp=1383000037853, value=2.85
Price:High timestamp=1381194712419, value=2.77
3 row(s) in 0.0520 seconds
```

Figure 7.6: Retrieving previous versions of a cell.

You can query the values in the HBase table using the `scan` command. The following command returns all columns in the Stocks table:

```
scan 'Stocks'
```

You can limit the output by passing filters with the `scan` command. For example, to retrieve just the high price column, you can use the following command:

```
scan 'Stocks', {COLUMNS => ['Price:High']}
```

You can also use value-based filters, prefix filters, and timestamp filters. For example, this filter scans for values greater than 2.8:

```
scan 'Stocks', {FILTER => "ValueFilter(>, 'binary:2.8')"}
```

HBase provides for fast scanning and lets you create some complex querying through the use of filters. Unfortunately, it is based on the JRuby language and can be quite complex to master. You may want to investigate a tool such as HBase Manager (`http://sourceforge.net/projects/hbasemanagergui/`), which provides a simple graphical user interface (GUI) to the HBase database.

Loading and Querying HBase

To complete the exercise in this section, you need to download and install the Hortonworks Data Platform (HDP) for Windows from Hortonworks. (Note: At the time of this writing the HBase shell is not yet exposed in HDP for Windows or HDInsight. It is anticipated it will be available in early 2014.) You can set up HDP for Windows on a development server to provide a local test environment that supports a single-node deployment. (For a detailed discussion of installing the Hadoop development environment on Windows, see `http://hortonworks.com/products/hdp-windows/`.)

In this exercise, you load stock data into an HBase table and query the data using scan filters. The file containing the data is a tab-separated value file named `StocksTest.tsv` that you can download from `http://www.wiley.com/go/microsoftbigdatasolutions.com`. The first step is to load the file into the Hadoop file system. Open the Hadoop command-line interface and issue the following command to copy the file (although your paths may differ):

```
hadoop fs -copyFromLocal
    C:\SampleData\StocksTest.tsv /user/test/StockTest.tsv
```

You can verify the file was loaded by issuing a list command for the directory you placed it in:

```
hadoop fs -ls /user/test/
```

The next step is to create the table structure in HBase. Open the HBase shell and enter the following command to create a table named stock_test with three column families (info, price, and trade):

```
create 'stock_test', 'info','price','trade'
```

You can use Pig Latin to load the data into the HBase table. Open the Pig command shell and load the TSV file using the `PigStorage` function. Replace the path below with the path where you loaded `StockTest.tsv` into HDFS:

```
StockData = LOAD '/user/test/StockTest.tsv' USING PigStorage() as
        (RowKey:chararray,stock_symbol:chararray,date:chararray,
         stock_price_open:double,stock_price_close:double,
         stock_volume:long);
```

Now you can load the HBase stock_test table using the `HBaseStorage` function. This function expects the row key for the table to be pasted first, and then the rest of the fields are passed to the columns designated in the input string:

```
STORE StockData INTO 'hbase://stock_test'
    USING org.apache.pig.backend.hadoop.hbase.HBaseStorage
    ('info:symbol info:date price:open price:close trade:volume');
```

To test the load, you can run some scans with various filters passed in. The following scan filters on the symbol to look for the stock symbol ADCT:

```
SingleColumnValueFilter filter = new SingleColumnValueFilter(
      info,
      symbol,
      CompareOp.EQUAL,
      Bytes.toBytes("ADCT")
      );
scan.setFilter(filter);
```

Managing Data with HCatalog

HCatalog creates a table abstraction layer over data stored on an HDFS cluster. This table abstraction layer presents the data in a familiar relational format and makes it easier to read and write data using familiar query language concepts. Originally used in conjunction with Hive and the Hive Query Language (HQL), it has expanded to support other toolsets such as Pig and MapReduce programs. There are also plans to increase the HCatalog support for HBase.

Working with HCatalog and Hive

HCatalog was developed to be used in combination with Hive. HCatalog data structures are defined using Hive's data definition language (DDL) and the

Hive metastore stores the HCatalog data structures. Using the command-line interface (CLI), users can create, alter, and drop tables. Tables are organized into databases or are placed in the default database if none are defined for the table. Once tables are created, you can explore the metadata of the tables using commands such as `Show Table` and `Describe Table`. HCatalog commands are the same as Hive's DDL commands except that HCatalog cannot issue statements that would trigger a MapReduce job such as `Create Table` or `Select` or `Export Table`.

To invoke the HCatalog CLI, launch the Hadoop CLI and navigate to the bin directory of the HCatalog directory. Enter the command `hcat.py`, which should result in the output shown in Figure 7.7.

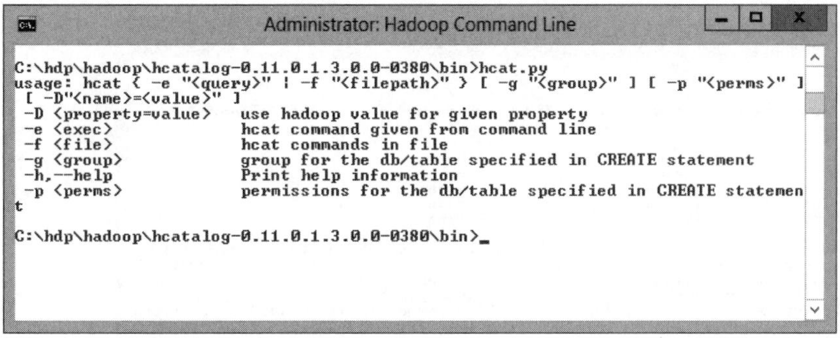

```
Administrator: Hadoop Command Line

C:\hdp\hadoop\hcatalog-0.11.0.1.3.0.0-0380\bin>hcat.py
usage: hcat { -e "<query>" | -f "<filepath>" } [ -g "<group>" ] [ -p "<perms>" ]
 [ -D"<name>=<value>" ]
 -D <property=value>    use hadoop value for given property
 -e <exec>              hcat command given from command line
 -f <file>              hcat commands in file
 -g <group>             group for the db/table specified in CREATE statement
 -h,--help              Print help information
 -p <perms>             permissions for the db/table specified in CREATE statemen
t

C:\hdp\hadoop\hcatalog-0.11.0.1.3.0.0-0380\bin>_
```

Figure 7.7: Invoking the HCatalog CLI.

To execute a query from the command line, use the `-e` switch. For example, the following code lists the databases in the metastore:

```
hcat.py -e "Show Databases"
```

At this point, the only database listed is the default database.

Defining Data Structures

You can create databases in HCatalog by issuing a `Create Database` statement. The following code creates a database named flight to hold airline flight statistics tables:

```
hcat.py -e "Create Database flight"
```

To create tables using HCatalog, you use the `Create Table` command. When creating the table you need to define the column names and data types. HCatalog supports the same data types and is similar to those supported by most database systems such as integer, boolean, float, double, string, binary, and timestamp. Complex types such as the array, map, and struct are also supported. The following code creates an airport table in the flight database to hold airport locations:

```
Create Table flight.airport
(code STRING, name STRING, country STRING,
 latitude double, longitude double)
```

Once a table is created, you can use the `Describe` command to see a list of the columns and data types. If you want to see a complete listing of the table metadata, include the `Extended` keyword, as follows:

```
Describe Extended flight.airport;
```

Figure 7.8 shows this command output.

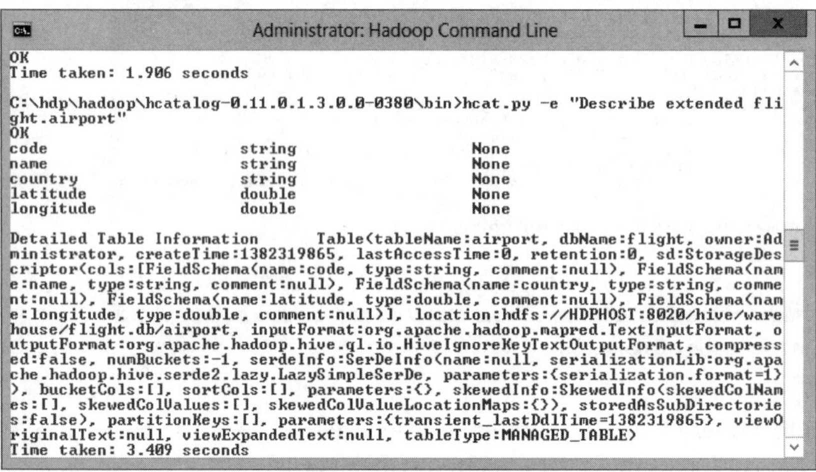

Figure 7.8: Extended description of the airport table.

Once a table is created, you can issue `ALTER TABLE` statements to do things like changing the table name, alter table properties, change column names, and change column data types. For example, the following command changes the table name:

```
ALTER TABLE airport RENAME TO us_airports
```

To add a new column to the table, you use the following code:

```
ALTER TABLE us_Airports ADD COLUMNS (city String)
```

You can also drop and truncate a table.

HCatalog supports the creation of views to filter a table. For example, you can create a Canadian airport view using the following command:

```
Create View canadian_airports as Select * from airport
where country = 'Canada'
```

Views are not materialized and are only logical structures (although there are plans to eventually support materialized views). When the view is referenced in a query, the view's definition is used to generate the rows. Just as with tables, you can alter views and drop views.

Creating Indexes

When joining tables or performing lookups, it is a good idea for performance to create indexes on the keys used. HCatalog supports the creation of indexes on tables using the `CREATE INDEX` statement. The following code creates an index on the code column in the us_airports table. Notice that it is passing in a reference to the index handler. Index handlers are pluggable interfaces, so you can create your own indexing technique depending on the requirements:

```
CREATE INDEX Airport_IDX_1 ON TABLE us_airports (code) AS
'org.apache.hadoop.hive.ql.index.compact.CompactIndexHandler'
with deferred rebuild
```

The `deferred rebuild` command is used to defer rebuilding the index until the table is loaded. After the load, you need to issue an `ALTER` statement to rebuild the index to reflect the changes in the data:

```
ALTER INDEX Airport_IDX_1 ON us_airports REBUILD
```

As with most data structures, you can delete an index by issuing the `DROP` command. The `CompactIndexHandler` creates an index table in the database to hold the index values. When the index is dropped, the underlying index table is also dropped:

```
DROP INDEX Airport_IDX_1 ON us_airports
```

Along with indexing, another way to improve query performance is through partitioning. In the next section, you will see how you can partition tables in HCatalog.

Creating Partitions

When working with large data stores, you can often improve queries by partitioning the data. For example, if queries are retrieved using a date value to restrict the results, a partition on dates will improve performance.

To create a partition on a table, you use the partitioned-by command as part of the `Create Table` statement. The following statement creates a table partitioned by the date column:

```
Create Table flightData_Partitioned (airline_cd int,airport_cd string,
delay int,dep_time int) Partitioned  By(flight_date string);
```

Using the `describe` command, you can view partition information for the table, as shown in Figure 7.9.

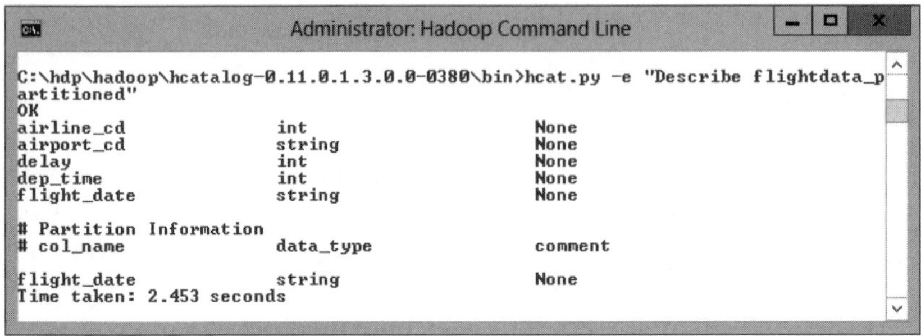
```
C:\hdp\hadoop\hcatalog-0.11.0.1.3.0.0-0380\bin>hcat.py -e "Describe flightdata_p
artitioned"
OK
airline_cd              int                     None
airport_cd              string                  None
delay                   int                     None
dep_time                int                     None
flight_date             string                  None

# Partition Information
# col_name              data_type               comment

flight_date             string                  None
Time taken: 2.453 seconds
```

Figure 7.9: Viewing partition information.

You can create partitions on multiple columns, which results in a separate data directory for each distinct combination of values from the partition columns. For example, it may be beneficial to partition the flight data table by both the flight date and airport code depending on the amount of data and the types of queries. Another option is to further bucket the partitions using `Clustered By` and order the data in the buckets with a `Sorted By` command. The following statement creates a flight data table partitioned by flight date, bucketed by airport code, and sorted by departure time:

```
Create Table flightData_Bucketed (airline_cd int,airport_cd string,
delay int,dep_time int) Partitioned  By(flight_date string)
Clustered By(airport_cd) Sorted By(dep_time) into 25 buckets;
```

When loading data into a partitioned table, it is up to you to ensure that the data is loaded into the right partition. You can use Hive to load the tables directly from a file. For example, the following statement is used to load a file containing daily flight data into a table partitioned by date:

```
LOAD DATA INPATH '/flight/data/flightdata_2013-01-01.txt'
INTO TABLE flightdata PARTITION(date='2013-01-01')
```

You can also use Hive to load data from one table into another table. For example, you may want to load data from a staging table into the partitioned tables, as illustrated by the following statement:

```
FROM flightdata_stg fds
INSERT OVERWRITE TABLE flightdata PARTITION(flight_date='2013-01-01')
SELECT fds.airline_cd, fds.airport_cd, fds.delay, fds.dep_time
WHERE fds.flight_date = '2013-01-01'
```

To load into multiple partitions, you can create a multi-insert statement as follows:

```
FROM flightdata_stg fds
INSERT OVERWRITE TABLE flightdata PARTITION(flight_date='2013-01-01')
SELECT fds.airline_cd, fds.airport_cd, fds.delay, fds.dep_time
WHERE fds.flight_date = '2013-01-01'
INSERT OVERWRITE TABLE flightdata PARTITION(flight_date='2013-01-02')
SELECT fds.airline_cd, fds.airport_cd, fds.delay, fds.dep_time
WHERE fds.flight_date = '2013-01-02'
```

If you have a table partitioned on more than one column, HCatalog supports dynamic partitioning. This allows you to load more efficiently without the need to know all the partition values ahead of time. To use dynamic partitioning, you need the top-level partition to be static, and the rest can be dynamic. For example, you could create a static partition on month and a dynamic partition on date. Then you could load the dates for the month in one statement. The following statement dynamically creates and inserts data into a date partition for a month's worth of data:

```
FROM flightdata_stg fds INSERT OVERWRITE TABLE flightdata
PARTITION(flight_month='01',flight_date)
SELECT fds.airline_cd, fds.airport_cd, fds.delay, fds.dep_time,
fds.flight_date WHERE fds.flight_month = '01'
```

One caveat to note is that the dynamic partition columns are selected by order and are the last columns in the select clause.

Integrating HCatalog with Pig and Hive

Although originally designed to provide the metadata store for Hive, HCatalog's role has greatly expanded in the Hadoop ecosystem. It integrates with other tools and supplies read and write interfaces for Pig and MapReduce. It also integrates with Sqoop, which is a tool designed to transfer data back and forth between Hadoop and relational databases such as SQL Server and Oracle. HCatalog also exposes a REST interface so that you can create custom tools and applications to interact with Hadoop data structures. In addition, HCatalog contains a notification service so that it can notify workflow tools such as Oozie when data has been loaded or updated.

Another key feature of HCatalog is that it allows developers to share data and structures across internal toolsets like Pig and Hive. You do not have to explicitly type the data structures in each program. This allows us to use the right tool for the right job. For example, we can load data into Hadoop using HCatalog, perform some ETL on the data using Pig, and then aggregate the data using Hive. After the processing, you could then send the data to your data warehouse housed in SQL Server using Sqoop. You can even automate the process using Oozie.

To complete the following exercise, you need to download and install the HDP for Windows from Hortonworks. You can set up HDP for Windows on a development server to provide a local test environment that supports a single-node deployment. (For a detailed discussion of installing the Hadoop development environment on Windows, see `http://hortonworks.com/products/hdp-windows/`.)

In this exercise, we analyze sensor data collected from HVAC systems monitoring the temperatures of buildings. You can download the sensor data from `http://www.wiley.com/go/microsoftbigdatasolutions`. There should be two files, one with sensor data (`HVAC.csv`) and a file containing building information (`building.csv`). After extracting the files, load the data into a staging table using HCatalog and Hive:

1. Open the Hive CLI. Because Hive and HCatalog are so tightly coupled, you can write HCatalog commands directly in the Hive CLI. As a matter of fact, you may recall that HCatalog actually uses a subset of Hive DDL statements. Create the sensor staging table with the following code:

```
CREATE TABLE sensor_stg(dt String, time String, target_tmp Int,
actual_tmp Int, system Int, system_age Int,building_id Int)
ROW FORMAT DELIMITED FIELDS TERMINATED BY ',';
```

2. Load the data into the staging table:

```
LOAD DATA Local INPATH 'C:\SampleData\HVAC.csv'
     INTO TABLE sensor_stg;
```

3. Use the following statement to view the data to verify that it loaded. Your data should look similar to Figure 7.10:

```
Select * from sensor_stg Limit 10;
```

```
hive.cmd - Shortcut
hive> Select * from sensor_stg Limit 10;
OK
Date    Time    NULL    NULL    NULL    NULL    NULL
6/1/13  0:00:01 66      58      13      20      4
6/2/13  1:00:01 69      68      3       20      17
6/3/13  2:00:01 70      73      17      20      18
6/4/13  3:00:01 67      63      2       23      15
6/5/13  4:00:01 68      74      16      9       3
6/6/13  5:00:01 67      56      13      28      4
6/7/13  6:00:01 70      58      12      24      2
6/8/13  7:00:01 70      73      20      26      16
6/9/13  8:00:01 66      69      16      9       9
Time taken: 1.891 seconds, Fetched: 10 row(s)
hive> ■
```

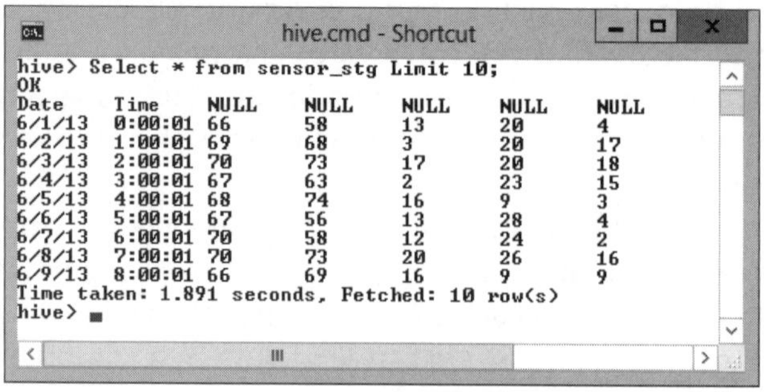

Figure 7.10: Sample sensor data.

4. Using the same process, load the building data into a staging table:

```
CREATE TABLE building_stg(building_id Int, mgr String,
     building_age Int,
hvac_type String, country String)
ROW FORMAT DELIMITED FIELDS TERMINATED BY ',';

LOAD DATA Local INPATH 'C:\SampleData\building.csv'
INTO TABLE building_stg;

Select * from building_stg Limit 10;
```

5. Create tables to hold the processed data. The sensor table is partitioned by the date:

```
CREATE TABLE sensor(time String, target_tmp Int,
actual_tmp Int,delta_tmp Int, building_id Int)
PARTITIONED BY (dt String);

CREATE TABLE building(building_id Int,
building_age Int, hvac_type String);
```

6. Because you are going to join the tables using the building ID, you are going to create indexes for the tables using this column:

```
CREATE INDEX Building_IDX_1 ON TABLE sensor (building_id)
AS 'org.apache.hadoop.hive.ql.index.compact.CompactIndexHandler'
with deferred rebuild;

CREATE INDEX Building_IDX_2 ON TABLE building (building_id)
AS 'org.apache.hadoop.hive.ql.index.compact.CompactIndexHandler'
with deferred rebuild;
```

   Now you can use Pig to extract, transform, and load the data from staging tables into the analysis tables.

7. Open the Hadoop CLI and browse to the bin directory of the Pig installation folder. Issue the following command to launch the Pig CLI, passing in the switch to use HCatalog:

```
pig.cmd -useHCatalog;
```

   This will launch the Grunt, the Pig CLI.

8. Issue the following Pig Latin script to load the data from the staging table:

```
SensorData = load 'sensor_stg'
using org.apache.hcatalog.pig.HCatLoader();
```

   You should see an output message indicating that a connection to the metastore is established.

9. To ensure that the data is loaded, you can issue a `Dump` command to output the data to the screen (which will take a few minutes):

```
Dump SensorData;
```

10. Use the following code to filter out nulls and calculate the temperature deltas:

```
FilteredData = Filter SensorData By building_id is not null;

ProcessedData = Foreach FilteredData Generate dt, time, target_tmp,
actual_tmp,target_tmp - actual_tmp as delta_tmp,building_id;
```

11. The final step is to load the processed data into the sensor table:

```
STORE ProcessedData INTO 'sensor' USING
 org.apache.hcatalog.pig.HCatStorer();
```

Once the table loads, you can close the CLI.

12. Open the Hive CLI and issue the following query to verify that the sensor table has been loaded. Your output should look similar to Figure 7.11. Notice that the data is all coming from the same partition (date):

```
Select * from sensor Limit 10;
```

```
hive.cmd - Shortcut
hive> Select * from sensor Limit 10;
OK
0:00:01 66      58      8       4       6/1/13
6:13:19 68      66      2       3       6/1/13
12:43:51        69      79      -10     7       6/1/13
18:13:20        68      65      3       12      6/1/13
0:00:01 69      60      9       7       6/1/13
6:13:19 69      64      5       7       6/1/13
12:43:51        70      59      11      3       6/1/13
18:13:20        66      73      -7      8       6/1/13
0:00:01 69      55      14      17      6/1/13
6:13:19 69      72      -3      16      6/1/13
Time taken: 0.656 seconds, Fetched: 10 row(s)
```

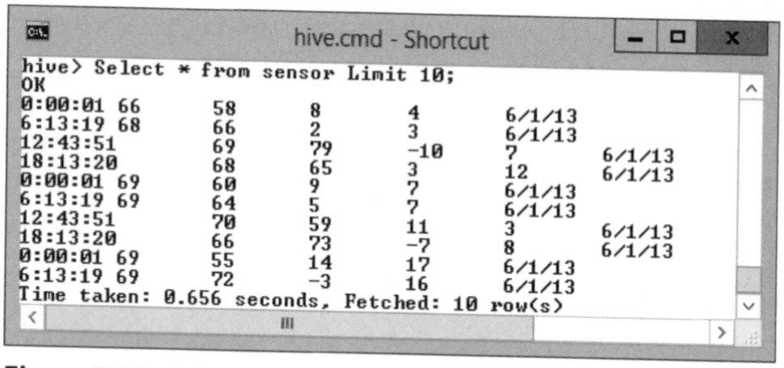

Figure 7.11: Selecting sensor data.

13. Load the building table with the following query:

```
From building_stg bs
Insert Overwrite Table building
select bs.building_id, bs.building_age, bs.hvac_type;
```

14. Now that the tables are loaded, you need to build the indexes:

```
ALTER INDEX Building_IDX_1 ON sensor REBUILD;
ALTER INDEX Building_IDX_2 ON building REBUILD;
```

After the index has been built, the data is now ready to analyze.

You can use Hive to query and aggregate the data. The following query determines the maximum temperature difference between target and actual temperatures for each day and HVAC type:

```
select max(s.delta_tmp), s.dt, b.hvac_type
from sensor s join building b on (s.building_id = b.building_id)
Group By s.dt, b.hvac_type;
```

In Chapter 11, "Visualizing Big Data with Microsoft BI," you will see how you can use the Hive ODBC connector to load and analyze the data in Microsoft's BI toolset.

Using HBase or Hive as a Data Warehouse

Although both HBase and Hive are both considered data warehouse structures, they differ significantly as to how they store and query data. Hive is more like a traditional data warehouse reporting system. It structures the data in a set of tables that you can join, aggregate, and query on using a query language (Hive Query Language [HQL]) that is very similar to the SQL, which most database developers are already used to working with. This relieves you from having to write MapReduce code. The downside to Hive is it can take a long time to process through the data and is not intended to give clients instant results.

Hive is usually used to run processing through scheduled jobs and then load the results into a summary type table that can be queried on by client applications. One of the strengths of Hive and HCatalog is the ability to pass data between traditional relational databases such as SQL Server. A good use case for Hive and HCatalog is to load large amounts of unstructured data, aggregate the data, and push the results back to SQL Server where analysts can use the Microsoft BI toolset to explore the results. Another point to consider is that Hive and HCatalog do not allow data updates. When you load the data, you can either replace or append. This makes loading large amounts of data extremely fast, but limits your ability to track changes.

HBase, however, is a key/value data store that allows you to read, write, and update data. It is designed to allow quick reads of random access data from large amounts of data based on the key values. It is not designed to provide fast loading of large data sets, but rather quick updates and inserts of single sets of data that may be streaming in from a source. It also is not designed to perform aggregations of the data. It has a query language based on JRuby that is very unfamiliar to most SQL developers. Having said that, HBase will be your tool of choice under some circumstances. Suppose, for example, that you have a huge store of e-mail messages and you need to occasionally pull one for auditing. You may also tag the e-mails with identifying fields that may occasionally need updating. This is an excellent use case for HBase.

If you do need to aggregate and process the data before placing it into a summary table that needs to be updated, you can always use HBase and Hive together. You can load and aggregate the data with Hive and push the results to a table in HBase, where the data summary statistics can be updated.

Summary

This chapter examined two tools that you can use to create structure on top of your big data stored in HDFS. HBase is a tool that creates key/value tuples on top of the data and stores the key values in a columnar storage structure. Its strength is that it enables fast lookups and supports consistency when updating the data. The other tool, HCatalog, offers a relational table abstraction layer over HDFS. Using the HCatalog abstraction layer allows query tools such as Pig and Hive to treat the data in a familiar relational architecture. It also permits easier exchange of data between the HDFS storage and relational databases such as SQL Server and Oracle.

Part

IV

Working with Your Big Data

In This Part

CHAPTER

8

Effective Big Data ETL with SSIS, Pig, and Sqoop

WHAT YOU WILL LEARN IN THIS CHAPTER:

- Moving Data Between SQL Server and Hadoop
- Using SSIS to Integrate
- Using Sqoop for Importing and Exporting
- Using Pig to Transform Data
- Choosing the Right Tool

A number of tools are available to help you move data between your Hadoop environment and SQL Server. This chapter covers three common ones: SQL Server Integration Services, Sqoop, and Pig.

SQL Server Integration Services (SSIS) is used in many SQL Server environments to import, export, and transform data. It can integrate with many different data systems, not just SQL Server, and supports a number of built-in transformations. In addition, you can extend it using custom transformations to support any transformations not supported "out of the box." This extensibility enables it to work with Hive as both a source of data and as a destination.

Sqoop is a tool designed to handle moving data between Hadoop and relational databases. Although it doesn't support a full range of transformation capabilities like SSIS, it is easy and quick to set up and use.

Pig enables users to analyze large data sets. It supports a number of built-in transformations for the data, and additional transformations can be added as user-defined functions through custom coding. It was originally developed as a way to reduce the complexity of writing MapReduce jobs, but it has evolved into a fully featured transformation tool for Hadoop data.

Because each of these tools has strengths and weaknesses, the final part of this chapter focuses on helping you decide which tool is the best choice for different scenarios you may encounter when moving your data.

Combining Big Data and SQL Server Tools for Better Solutions

As with many platforms, both Hadoop and SQL Server have strengths and weaknesses. By using the tools together, you can help leverage the strengths of each platform while mitigating the weaknesses.

The Hadoop platform's strengths derive from its capabilities to scale out easily to accommodate growing amounts of data. It also can handle a wide variety of data formats with little up front transformation effort. However, it has few restrictions or validations on the data it stores, and it doesn't have the same end-user capabilities and ecosystem that SQL Server has developed.

SQL Server, however, handles enforcing data quality and consistency much better than Hadoop, and a wide variety of tools and clients enable you to perform different analytic, reporting, and development tasks with SQL Server. Challenges with SQL Server include scaling it to handle massive amounts of data and also support for easily storing loosely formatted data.

Why Move the Data?

When your environment includes both Hadoop and SQL Server, you will sometimes need to move the data between the two systems. One example of this is importing data into Hadoop from an online transactional processing (OLTP) system using SQL Server, such as sales data from an order-processing system.

There are a number of reasons to move data from SQL Server into Hadoop:

- **Archival and data retention:** Hadoop storage can be less expensive than SQL Server, and the costs of scaling up are generally less. In addition, keeping extensive, infrequently accessed historical data in an OLTP database creates overhead that negatively impacts performance. Moving this data to Hadoop can save the physical resources on your SQL Server for processing transactions quickly and efficiently.
- **Analytics:** Hadoop offers tools like Mahout for data mining and machine learning that can be applied to your Hadoop data. These tools leverage

Hadoop capabilities for processing large amounts of data. Moving data from SQL Server to Hadoop enables the use of these tools.

- **Transformation and aggregation:** Data can be transformed in a number of ways on both the SQL Server and Hadoop platforms. However, the Hadoop architecture enables you to distribute data transformations over a cluster, which can dramatically speed up transformation of large amounts of data.

The reverse is also true. You will find the need to extract data from Hadoop and place it in SQL Server. Common scenarios for this include the following:

- **Business analysis and reporting:** SQL Server has more options and more robust end-user tools for doing data exploration, analysis, and reporting. Moving the data into SQL Server enables the use of these tools.
- **Integration:** The results of your Hadoop analytics, transformations, and aggregation may need to be integrated with other databases in your organization.
- **Quality/consistency:** SQL Server, as a relational database, offers more capabilities to enforce data quality and consistency rules on the data it stores. It does this by enforcing the rules when the data is added to the databases, giving you confidence that the data already conforms to your criteria when you query it.

NOTE **SQL Server has more tools available today, but this is changing quickly. More vendors are adding the ability to interact with Hadoop directly into their tools, and the quality of the end-user experience is getting better as the competition in this space increases.**

Transferring Data Between Hadoop and SQL Server

One key consideration for moving data between Hadoop and SQL Server is the time involved. With large data volumes, the data transfers often need to be scheduled for times when other workloads on the relevant servers are light.

Hadoop is optimized for batch data processing. Generally, when writing data to Hadoop, you will see the best performance when you set up the processing to handle large batches of data for import, instead of writing single or small numbers of rows to Hadoop each time. Remember that, by default, Hadoop uses a 64MB block size for files, and it functions best when the file size exceeds the block size. If you need to process smaller numbers of rows, consider storing them in a temporary table in SQL Server or a temporary file and only writing them to Hadoop when the data size is large enough to make it an efficient operation.

When writing data back to SQL Server, you generally want to make sure that the data is aggregated. This will let you write a smaller amount of data to the SQL Server environment. Another concern when writing data to SQL Server is how much parallel write activity you want to allow. Depending on your method of doing the transfer, you could enable writing to the SQL Server from a large number of Hadoop nodes. SQL Server can handle parallel clients inserting data, but having too many parallel streams of insert activity can actually slow down the overall process. Finding the right amount of parallelism can involve some tuning, and requires you to understand the other workloads running on your SQL Server at the same time. Fortunately, you can control the amount of parallelism when moving data to SQL Server in a number of ways, as are covered for each technology.

Working with SSIS and Hive

SSIS doesn't currently support direct connectivity to Hadoop. However, using Hive and Open Database Connectivity (ODBC), you can leverage data in your Hadoop system from SSIS. This involves a few steps:

1. Making sure that Hive is configured properly
2. Verifying that you can access Hive from the computer running SSIS
3. Verifying that the data you want to access in Hadoop has a table defined for it in Hive

After going through this setup, you gain the ability to query your Hadoop data in SSIS (and other tools) as if it resides in a relational database. This offers the lowest-friction approach to using your Hadoop data in SSIS.

Writing data to Hadoop from SSIS is a little more challenging. In Chapter 6, "Adding Structure with Hive," we discussed that Hive only supports bulk insert operations, in keeping with the Hadoop approach of "write-once" large files. Unfortunately, Hive uses some nonstandard SQL to handle these bulk inserts, and the available ODBC drivers don't fully support it. Therefore, writing to Hadoop from Integration Services is best accomplished by writing a file out to the file system and then moving it into the Hadoop file system.

The next sections cover these operations in detail, so that you can configure your SSIS packages to both retrieve data from Hadoop and move data into it. The instructions assume the use of the Hortonworks Hadoop distribution.

Hadoop can be installed on the same computer where you have SSIS installed. However, in a production environment, these will likely be on two different machines. This does present a few additional constraints because SSIS cannot currently interact directly with Hadoop, and without a local installation of Hadoop, it cannot access the Hadoop tools. The approaches to work around these constraints are covered next.

NOTE At the time of this writing, SSIS does not support direct connectivity to the Hadoop file system. However, Microsoft has announced that they are working on a number of additional tasks and components for SSIS to allow for better interaction with Hadoop. These components are planned for release on CodePlex (`http://www.codeplex.com`) as open source.

There are a few options that require a little more setup and some custom coding in SSIS. The Win HDFS Managed Library (`http://blogs.msdn.com/b/carlnol/archive/2013/02/08/hdinsight-net-hdfs-file-access.aspx`) allows you to access the HDFS file system from a script task or component in SSIS. You can also use FTPS (not supported natively in SSIS; it will require a custom task) to upload files to HDFS on the Windows distribution. Finally, you can use WebHDFS, which is a REST API. This can be accessed from a custom script in SSIS.

Connecting to Hive

First, to use the Hive installation, you need to confirm that Hive is configured properly for access over the network. You need to check several things to verify this. First, ensure that the Hive service is started. Next, verify that ports 10000 and 10001 are open for communication on the Hadoop computer. On a Windows machine, you can check this by running the following command from a command prompt:

```
netstat -a > c:\temp\ports.txt
```

It can take some time to complete this command. When it finishes, you can open the file `c:\temp\ports.txt` in `notepad.exe`. This file contains a listing of open ports on the computer. Search the file for 10000 and 10001. If the port is open, you will see lines similar to the following. (The IP address and computer name values may vary, depending on your environment settings):

```
TCP   0.0.0.0:10000  HDP1-3:0   LISTENING
TCP   0.0.0.0:10001  HDP1-3:0   LISTENING
```

If there are no entries for ports 10000 or 10001, you can run the following commands from the command prompt to open them:

```
netsh advfirewall firewall add rule name=AllowHive dir=in
    action=allow protocol=TCP localport=10000-10001
```

You will also need to verify that the computer running SSIS allows outgoing connections on ports 10000 and 10001. You can do that with the following command (note the use of `out` instead of `in` for direction):

```
netsh advfirewall firewall add rule name=AllowHive dir=out
    action=allow protocol=TCP localport=10000-10001
```

WARNING If you are having trouble getting SSIS and Hive to communicate over the network, one troubleshooting step you can take is to disable the firewalls on both computers entirely, using the instructions provided by Microsoft: `http://technet.microsoft.com/en-us/library/cc766337(v=ws.10).aspx`. If this allows the computers to start communicating, it indicates a problem with the firewall configuration. If they still cannot communicate, you have a different issue.

Be aware that disabling the firewall can open up potential security risks and may be prohibited by your network policy. This is recommended only as a troubleshooting step, and you should restore the firewall as soon as you identify the problem.

After opening the ports, verify that the Hive server is running in Thrift mode. You can check this by opening the Hive server's `hive-site.xml` configuration file, which you can find in the Hive installation directory, under the `conf` folder (by default, `C:\hdp\hadoop\hive-0.11.0.1.3.0.0-0380\conf`). Locate the property entry for `hive.server2.servermode`. Make sure that the value of the property is set to `thrift`. This puts the Hive server into a mode that better supports multiple users and enables authentication from external clients. This is required for the Hortonworks ODBC driver to work correctly. The value in the configuration file should look like the following:

```
<property>
  <name>hive.server2.servermode</name>
  <value>thrift</value>
  <description>HiveServer server type: thrift or http</description>
</property>
```

NOTE This file may be locked by the Hive server, in which case you will get an "access denied" error when you try to save changes to it. If this happens, stop the Hive server, save your changes to the configuration file, and restart it.

Installing the Hortonworks ODBC Driver for Hive

Next, you need to install the Hortonworks ODBC driver for Hive, which you can download from `http://hortonworks.com/products/hdp-windows/#add_ons`. You need to install the driver on your SSIS computer. You do not have to install it on the Hadoop machine. After installing the driver, you can configure it from the ODBC Administrator tool included as part of Windows.

NOTE Hortonworks provides both 32-bit and 64-bit versions of their ODBC driver. To use this with SSIS, you'll want to install both versions of the driver. SQL Server Data Tools (SSDT) is a 32-bit application, so it uses the 32-bit version of the driver when you are designing SSIS packages. However, when the package is executed, it is run from a 64-bit process. At that point, it needs the 64-bit version of the driver to be present. This is also the most common mode for use in production.

The ODBC Administrator tool also comes in 32-bit and 64-bit versions. If you want to use a data source name (DSN) to connect to Hive, you can set it up here.

However, you will need to set it up twice, once as 32-bit and once as 64-bit, so that it's available to both types of applications. Using a connection string for connections eliminates the need for this.

Configuring the Hive ODBC Connection

You can configure your Hive ODBC connection in two ways. One option is to configure a DSN. This stores the connection parameter information locally on the computer and results in a simpler connection configuration in SSIS. The other approach is to use a connection string that contains all the parameters for the connection. This option is a little more complex to set up, but it makes your SSIS packages more portable because they don't rely on a DSN being set up on the local computer, and you don't have to worry about setting up both 64-bit and 32-bit versions of the DSN.

The process for setting up either is fairly similar:

1. You start by opening up the ODBC Administrator application, using the 32-bit or 64-bit version.
2. Select the DSN type from the tabs across the top of the administrator interface (see Figure 8.1).
3. Choose the System DSN if you want to store the connection information on the computer, and choose the File DSN if you want a portable connection string. The process differs only in that with a File DSN you have to select a location to store the file. This example will proceed with a file DSN setup because that is a more common scenario.

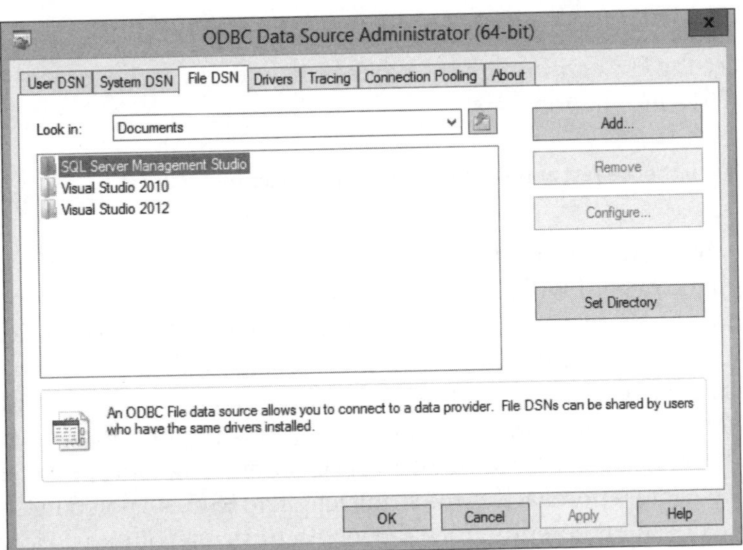

Figure 8.1: ODBC Administrator interface.

4. Add the new connection by using the Add button, and choose the Hortonworks Hive ODBC driver from the resulting wizard.
5. At the next step, choose a location to store the File DSN. You will be opening this file in just a moment, so use an easily accessible location, like the desktop.
6. Finish walking through the wizard, and at the end, you will be presented with the Hive ODBC driver's property screen (see Figure 8.2).

Figure 8.2: Hortonworks ODBC driver properties.

7. Replace the Host entry with the name or IP address of the server hosting your Hive installation.

NOTE If you choose Test at this point, it should connect successfully.

8. The Advanced Options dialog box also contains a few items of interest, though the default will work in most cases. The two properties that you are most likely to need to change under Advanced Options are Rows Fetched per Block and Default String Column Length. Rows Fetched per Block tells Hive how many rows to return in a batch. The default of 10,000 will work in most scenarios; but if you are having performance issues, you can adjust that value. The Default String Column Length property tells the driver what to report back as the string length to SSIS. As noted in Chapter 6, Hive doesn't inherently track the length of string columns. However, SSIS is much more particular about this and requires the driver to report

a value back. This setting controls how long the strings will be. After you have completed the property settings, click OK to save the File DSN.

You can use the resulting file to prepare a connection string.

Now, open the file in Notepad, and you will see a series of names and values in the format `Name=value` that define the parameter values for the connection. You can take these name/value pairs and convert them to a connection string by removing the carriage returns and adding a semicolon between each name/value pair. So, if the original file looked like this:

```
[ODBC]
DRIVER=Hortonworks Hive ODBC Driver
Schema=default
Port=10001
HS2AuthMech=2
Host=Your_Hive_Server
HiveServerType=2
DESCRIPTION=Test
ApplySSPWithQueries=1
```

You should end up with a connection string like this:

```
DRIVER=Hortonworks Hive ODBC Driver;Schema=default;
Port=10001;HS2AuthMech=2;Host=Your_Hive_Server;
HiveServerType=2;DESCRIPTION=Test;ApplySSPWithQueries=1
```

NOTE You may find some names without any specified values in the File DSN. These are properties that are left at their default settings, and they are safe to leave out of the connection string. They were left out of this example for clarity.

WARNING If you attempt to save a File DSN that does not test successfully, you will get a warning message. You can choose to save anyway, but the resulting File DSN will be missing most of the parameters, so it is wise to make sure that your File DSN can be validated while still in the ODBC Administrator interface.

This is the connection string that will be used in the SSIS packages. The next section covers how to set up the package and use this connection string inside it.

Configuring Your Packages

This section assumes that you have some familiarity with SSIS. If you are new to SSIS, you may find the book *Professional Microsoft SQL Server 2012 Integration Services* (Wrox 2012 by Brian Knight and others) a helpful reference. For the most part, working with Hive through ODBC drivers makes it much like working with any other data source in SSIS.

The exception to this, as noted already, is writing data to Hive. Because the ODBC driver doesn't support writing to the Hive database, you must insert data into Hive by accessing the Hadoop Distributed File System (HDFS) and moving files in the appropriate format to the appropriate directory.

NOTE In different SSIS versions, you work with Hive in different ways. SSIS 2008 R2 and earlier support ODBC through an ADO.NET wrapper, whereas SSIS 2012 and later let you access ODBC directly. Generally, direct access results in better performance, so 2012 is recommended for use with Hive, but it's not required.

Another difference between SSIS 2008 R2 and 2012 is that the development environment has changed names. In 2008 R2 and earlier, it is known as Business Intelligence Developer Studio (BIDS). In 2012 and later, it is named SQL Server Data Tools - Business Intelligence (SSDT-BI). It works essentially the same in both versions, so instructions provided for one will apply to the other, unless specifically noted otherwise.

Configuring a Connection Manager for Hive

To extract data from Hive, you can set up an ODBC connection to the Hive database, using the connection string created in the section "Connecting to Hive." The first step in this process is creating a package and setting up a connection manager. If you are using SSIS 2008 R2 or earlier versions, you must use an ADO.NET connection manager to use the ODBC driver:

1. To create a package, choose New Connection from the SSIS menu in Business Intelligence Developer Studio (BIDS).
2. Choose the ADO.NET item from the list.
3. In the resulting screen, make sure that you change the Provider option at the top of the screen to `.NET Providers\ODBC` Data Provider. This uses the ODBC provider through an ADO.NET wrapper.
4. After you have selected the ODBC Data Provider, you can provide either the DSN or input the connection string you created in the section "Connecting to Hive."

NOTE If you are using SSIS 2012 or later, you can take advantage of native support for ODBC by creating an ODBC connection manager. This will present the same interface for selecting the DSN or connection string to use. However, it bypasses the ADO .NET provider selection, and generally performs better at run time, thanks to the skipping of the additional ADO.NET provider layer. To use this, select the ODBC item from the list of connections.

Note that the ODBC connection type will not be displayed when you right-click in the connection manager area of the package designer. You must choose New Connection to display the full list of connections in order to select the ODBC connection type.

After selecting the DSN or adding the connection string to the connection manager, you will have the opportunity to provide the username and password. By default, Hive does not need a password, only the username (hadoop, by default). If you do specify a password, remember that SSIS treats it as a sensitive property, so you will need to encrypt the password or set it when the package is loaded. You can do this through a configuration in 2008 R2 and earlier, or by using a parameter in SSIS 2012 or later.

Extracting Data from Hive

To retrieve data from Hive in SSIS 2008 R2, you can add an ADO.NET Source component to a data flow task (see Figure 8.3). When configuring the source component, select the Hive connection manager, and specify a `SELECT` statement for your Hive table. You can preview the data here as well to confirm that the results are what you expect.

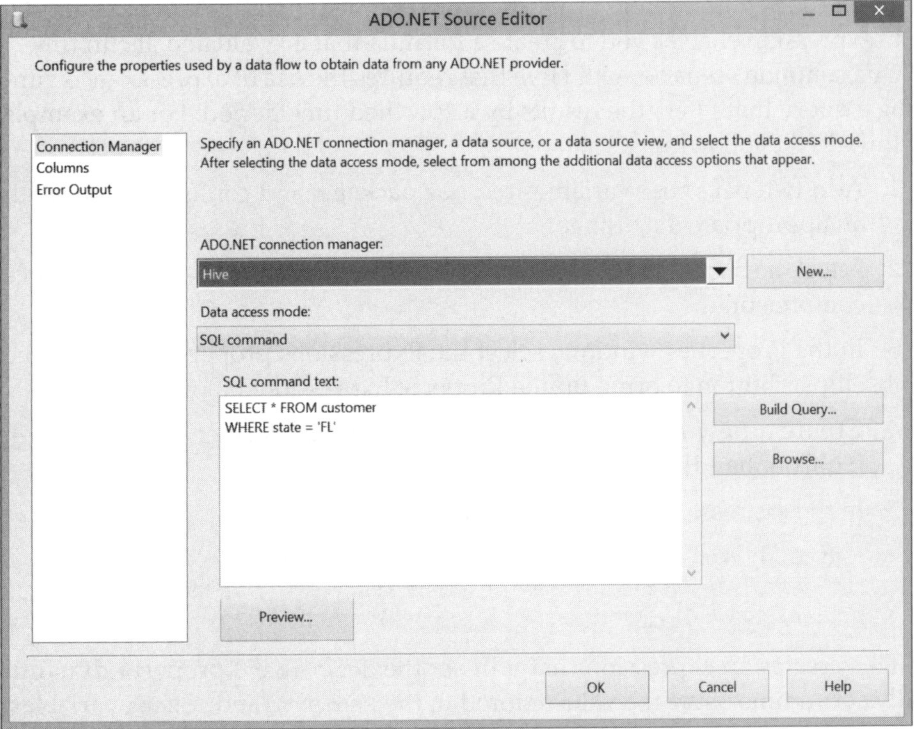

Figure 8.3: ADO.NET Source.

TIP **If you are using SSIS 2012, you can use the ODBC Source instead of the ADO.NET Source to gain a little performance. The interface is almost identical, and setting it up**

is exactly the same as the ADO.NET Source except that you will pick an ODBC connection manager rather than an ADO.NET connection manager.

For the best SSIS experience, make sure that the query being run against Hive returns the smallest number of rows and columns possible. Hive tables can be quite large, so it's important for package performance that you minimize the amount of data retrieved by SSIS. One way to do this is to not use `SELECT * FROM` table in the queries; instead, list the specific columns that you need to use. Also, you will generally want to apply some sort of `WHERE` clause to the query to reduce the number of rows returned.

Making the Query Dynamic

You may have noticed that neither the ADO.NET Source nor the ODBC Source offers the ability to parameterize the queries. In many cases, you will need the `WHERE` clause to be dynamic at run time. To achieve this, you can use expressions on the SQLCommand properties exposed by the source components. An SSIS expression enables you to create a formula that is evaluated at run time.

One common scenario with Hive that requires the use of expressions is running a query that filters the results by a specified time period. For an example of this, do the following:

1. Add two `DateTime` variables to your package, and configure them with an appropriate date range.
2. Select the background of the Data Flow Task containing your Hive source component.
3. In the Properties window, select the Expressions property and click the ellipsis button to bring up the Property Expression dialog.
4. Create a new entry for the property named [NameOfYourSource].[SqlCommand].
5. In the expression, enter the following:

```
"SELECT * FROM Customer WHERE LastSaleDate BETWEEN \"" +
(DT_WSTR, 50) @[User::FromDate] + "\" AND \"" +  (DT_WSTR, 50)
@[User::ToDate] + "\""
```

This creates an expression that will set the `SqlCommand` property dynamically at run time using the values stored in the `FromDate` and `ToDate` variables. If you take this approach, the resulting SSIS package is more flexible and can incorporate dynamic filtering of the Hive source.

WARNING **The use of expressions in SSIS packages can be done in any version of SSIS. However, you want to be aware of an important pre-SSIS 2012 restriction. In earlier versions, expressions could not interact with any string longer than**

4,000 characters, and couldn't return a result longer than 4,000 characters. When creating long SQL statements using expressions, it is possible to exceed this limit. Unfortunately, in this case, the only solution is to reduce the length of your SQL.

Fortunately, SSIS 2012 has removed that restriction, making it much easier to work with if you need to use long SQL queries.

After your Hive data has been retrieved into SSIS, you can use it as you would any other data source, applying any of the SSIS transformations to it, and send it to any destination supported by SSIS. However, data retrieved from Hive often contains null values, so it can be worthwhile to make sure that your SSIS package handles null values appropriately.

NOTE Hive tends to return null values because it applies schema on read rather than on write. That is, if Hive reads a value from one of the underlying files that makes up a table, and that value doesn't match the expected data type of the column, or doesn't have appropriate delimiters, Hive will return a null value for the column. This is good in that it doesn't stop your query from processing, but it can result in some strange behavior in SSIS if you don't have appropriate null handling in your package.

Loading Data into Hadoop

As noted earlier, SSIS cannot write to Hive directly using ODBC. The alternative is to create a file with the appropriate file format and copy it directly to the Hadoop file system. If it is copied to the directory that Hive uses for managing the table, your data will show up in the Hive table.

If your SSIS environment has the Hadoop tools loaded on it, loading data into Hadoop can be as simple as calling the `dfs -put` command from an Execute Process task:

```
hadoop dfs -put \\HDP1-3\LandingZone\MsBigData\Customer1.txt
    /user/MsBigData/Customer1.txt
```

This moves the file from the local file system to the distributed file system. However, it can be a little more complex if you do not have a Hadoop installation on your SSIS server. In this case, you need a way to execute the `dfs -put` command on the remote server.

Fortunately, several tools enable you to execute remote processes. The appropriate tool depends on what operating system is running on your Hadoop cluster. If you are using Linux, you can use the SSH shell application to execute the remote process. To run this from your SSIS package, you can install a tool called puTTy on your SSIS server. This tool enables you to run SSH commands on the remote computer from an Execute Process task.

If your Hadoop environment is hosted on a Windows platform, using the Hortonworks distribution, you can use PsExec, a tool from Microsoft that enables you to execute remote processes on other servers. To use this in SSIS, you call it from an Execute Process task.

NOTE Security issues with PsExec are one of the more common challenges when using it. Make sure that the command line you are sending to PsExec is valid by testing it on the target computer first. Then ensure the user account you are running the PsExec command under has permissions to run the executable on the remote computer. One easy way to do this is to log in to the target computer as the specified user and run the executable. Finally, ensure that the account running the package matches the account you tested with.

Setting up a package to implement this process is relatively straightforward. You set up a data flow task as normal, with a source component retrieving data from your choice of sources. Any transformations that need to be applied to the data can be performed. As the last step of the data flow, the data needs to be written to a file. The format of the file is determined by what the Hive system expects. The easiest format to work with from SSIS is a delimited format, with carriage return / line feeds delimiting rows, and a column delimiter like a comma (,) or vertical bar (|) separating column values. The SSIS Flat File Destination is designed to write these types of files.

NOTE The default Hive column delimiter for flat files is Ctrl-A (0x001). Unfortunately, this isn't supported for use from SSIS. If at all possible, use a column delimiter that SSIS supports. If you must use a non-standard column delimiter, you will need to add a post-processing step to your package to translate the column delimiters after the file is produced.

NOTE If Hive is expecting another format (see Chapter 6 for some of the possibilities), you might need to implement a custom destination using a script component. Although a full description of this is beyond the scope of this chapter, a custom destination lets you fully control the format of the file produced, so you can match anything that Hive is expecting.

Once the file is produced, you can use a file system task to copy it to a network location that is accessible to both your SSIS server and your Hadoop cluster. The next step is to call the process to copy the file into the HDFS. This is done through an Execute Process task. Assuming that you are executing the Hadoop copy on a remote system using PsExec, you configure the task with the following property settings. (You might need to adjust your file locations):

- Executable: `C:\Sysinternals\PsExec.exe`
- Arguments: `\\Your_Hadoop_Server C:\hdp\hadoop\hadoop-1.2.0.1.3.0.0-0380\bin\hadoop.cmd dfs -put \\CommonNetworkLocation\LandingZone\Customer1.txt /user /MsBigData/Customer1.txt`

The Execute Process task can be configured to use expressions to make this process more dynamic. In addition, if you are moving multiple files, it can be used inside a `For Each` loop in SSIS to repeat the process a specified number of times.

Getting the Best Performance from SSIS

As touched on earlier, one way to improve SSIS performance with big data is to minimize the amount of data that SSIS actually has to process. When querying from Hive, always minimize the number of rows and columns you are retrieving to the essential ones.

Another way of improving performance in SSIS is by increasing the parallel activity. This has the most benefit when you are writing to Hadoop. If you set up multiple, parallel data flows, all producing data files, you can invoke multiple `dfs -put` commands simultaneously to move the data files into the Hadoop file system. This takes advantage of the Hadoop capability to scale out across multiple nodes.

Increasing parallelism for packages reading from Hive can have mixed results. You get a certain amount of parallelism when you query from Hive in the first place because it spreads the processing out across the cluster. You can attempt to run multiple queries using different ODBC source components in SSIS simultaneously, but generally it works better to issue a single query and let Hive determine how much parallelism to use.

SSIS is a good way to interact with Hadoop, particularly for querying information. It's also a familiar tool to those in the SQL Server space. Thanks to the number of sources and destinations it supports, it can prove very useful when integrating your big data with the rest of your organization.

Transferring Data with Sqoop

Sqoop is a tool designed to import and export data from Hadoop systems to other data stores, particularly relational databases. This can prove very useful for easily moving data from a SQL Server database into Hadoop or for retrieving data from Hadoop and storing it in SQL Server. Sqoop uses MapReduce to do the actual data processing, so it takes full advantage of the parallel processing capabilities of Hadoop.

One of the reasons that Sqoop is easy to use is that it infers the schema from the relational data store that it is interacting with. Because of this, you don't have to specify a lot of information to use it. Instead, it determines column names, types, and formats from the relational definition of the table.

Behind the scenes, Sqoop is creating logic to read and write the relational data through generated code classes. This means that most operations are performed on a row-by-row basis, so it may not deliver the most optimal performance. Certain databases, like MySQL, do have options to use bulk interfaces with Sqoop, but currently, SQL Server does not.

Sqoop uses Java Database Connectivity components to make connections to relational databases. These components need to be installed on the computer where Sqoop is run. Microsoft provides a JDBC driver archive for SQL Server at `http://msdn.microsoft.com/en-us/sqlserver/aa937724.aspx`. After downloading the archive, you need to extract the appropriate `.jar` file in your Sqoop `lib` directory (on a Hortonworks default installation, `C:\hdp\hadoop\sqoop-1.4.3.1.3.0.0-0380\lib`) so that Sqoop can locate the driver.

Copying Data from SQL Server

To move data from SQL Server to Hadoop, you use the `sqoop -import` command. A full example is shown here:

```
sqoop import --connect
    "jdbc:sqlserver://Your_SqlServer;database=MsBigData;
    Username=demo;Password=your_password;"
  --table Customers
  --m 1
  --target-dir /MsBigData/Customers
```

The first argument of the command, `--connect`, determines what type of driver you will use for connecting to the relational database. In this case, the command is specifying that Sqoop will use the SQL Server JDBC driver to connect to the database.

NOTE **When specifying the connection to the database, you should use the server name or IP address. Do not use localhost, because this connection string will be sent to all the cluster nodes involved in the job, and they will attempt to make their own connections. Because localhost refers to the local computer, each node will attempt to connect to the database as if it exists on that node, which will likely fail.**

You may notice that the `--connect` argument contains the full connection string for the database. Ideally, you will use Windows Authentication in the connection string so that the password doesn't have to be specified. You can also use the `--password-file` argument to tell Sqoop to use a file that stores the password, instead of entering it as part of the command.

The `--table` argument tells Sqoop which table you intend to import from the specified database. This is the table that Sqoop will derive its metadata from.

By default, all columns within the table are imported. You can limit the column list by using the `--columns` argument:

```
--columns "FirstName,LastName,City,State,PostalCode"
```

You can also filter the rows returned by Sqoop by using the `--where` argument, which enables you to specify a where clause for the query:

```
--where "State='FL'"
```

If you need to execute a more complex query, you can replace the `--table`, `--columns`, and `--where` arguments with a `--query` argument. This lets you specify an arbitrary `SELECT` statement, but some constraints apply. The `SELECT` statement must be relatively straightforward; nested tables and common table expressions can cause problems. Because Sqoop needs to split up the data to process it in parallel, you must also provide some additional information:

```
--query 'SELECT customer.*, sales.*
  FROM customer
  JOIN sales on (customer.id == sales.customerId)
  WHERE $CONDITIONS'
--split-by customer.id
```

The `WHERE $CONDITIONS` portion of the query provides a placeholder for the criteria Sqoop uses to split up processing. The `--split-by` argument tells Sqoop which column to use when determining how to split up the data from the input query. By default, if the import is referencing a table instead of a query, the table's primary key is used as the split column.

The `--m` argument controls how many parallel activities are created by Sqoop. The default value for this is 4. Setting it to 1, as in this example, means that the Sqoop process will be single threaded.

WARNING **Although increasing the parallel activities can improve performance, you must be careful not to increase it too much. Increasing the `--m` argument past the number of nodes in your cluster will adversely impact performance. Also, the more parallel activities, the higher the load on the database server.**

Finally, the `--target-dir` argument determines what folder the data will be written into on the Hadoop system. You can control whether the new data is added to an existing directory by using the `--append` argument. And you can import using Hive rather than a directory by specifying the `--hive-import` and `--hive-table` arguments:

```
sqoop import --connect
    "jdbc:sqlserver://Your_SqlServer;database=MsBigData;
    Username=demo;Password=your_password;"
  --table Customers
  --m 1
  --target-dir /MsBigData/Customers --append
```

```
sqoop import --connect
    "jdbc:sqlserver://Your_SqlServer;database=MsBigData;
    Username=demo;Password=your_password;"
  --table Customers
  --m 1
  --hive-import --hive-table CustomerImport
```

NOTE **There is also a Sqoop `import-all-tables` command. This imports all tables and all their columns from the specified database. It functions well only if all the tables have single column primary keys. Although you can specify a list of tables to exclude with this command, it has less flexibility and control than importing individual tables. Because of this, it is recommended that you import tables one at a time in most cases.**

Copying Data to SQL Server

The Sqoop `export` command enables you to export data from Hadoop to relational databases. As with the `import` command, it uses the table definition in the relational database to derive metadata for the operation, so it requires that the database table already exists before you can export data to the database:

```
sqoop export --connect
    "jdbc:sqlserver://Your_SqlServer;database=MsBigData;
    Username=demo;Password=your)password;"
  --table Customers --export-dir /MsBigData/Customers
```

The arguments for the `export` command are similar to the `import` command. However, you have fewer options with the export. `--export-dir` indicates the folder in the Hadoop file system that will be used as the source for records to load into the database. The `--table` argument indicates the relational table that will be populated from Hadoop. Alternatively, you can use the `--call` argument to indicate that a stored procedure should be called for each row of information found in the Hadoop system.

If you do not specify the `--call` argument, by default Sqoop generates an `INSERT` statement for each record found in the Hadoop directory. By specifying the `--update-key` argument and indicating a key column or columns, you can modify this behavior to generate `UPDATE` statements rather than `INSERT`s. You can use the `--update-mode` argument to indicate rows that don't already exist in the target table should be inserted, and rows that do exist should be updated:

```
sqoop export --connect
    "jdbc:sqlserver://Your_SqlServer;database=MsBigData;
    Username=demoPassword=your)password;" --table Customers
  --export-dir /MsBigData/Customers
  --update-key ID --update-mode allowinsert
```

Exports done using Sqoop commit to the target database every 10,000 rows. This prevents excessive resources from being tied up on the database server managing large transactions. However, it does mean that the exports are not atomic and that a failure during execution may leave a partial set of rows in the target database.

The `--m` argument controls the amount of parallel activity, just as it does with the import. The same warnings and caveats apply to its use with export. Particularly in the case of exports, because Sqoop does its operations on a row-by-row basis, running a large number of parallel nodes can have a very negative impact on the target database.

Sqoop is a useful tool for quickly moving data in and out of Hadoop, particularly if it is a one-time operation or the performance is not particularly important.

Using Pig for Data Movement

Pig was originally developed for much the same reasons as Hive. Users needed a way to work with MapReduce without becoming Java developers. Pig solves that problem by providing a language, Pig Latin, that is easy to understand and allows the developer to express the intent of the data transformation, instead of having to code each step explicitly.

Another major benefit of Pig is its ability to scale, so that large data transformation processes can be run across many nodes. This makes processing large data sets much more feasible. Because Pig uses MapReduce under the covers, it benefits from MapReduce's ability to scale across the nodes in your Hadoop cluster.

Pig does come with some downsides. It cannot natively write to other data stores, so it is primarily useful for transforming data inside the Hadoop ecosystem. Also, because there is some overhead in preparing and executing the MapReduce jobs, it's not an ideal choice for data transformations that are transactional in nature. Instead, it does best when processing large amounts of data in batch operations.

Transforming Data with Pig

Pig can be run in a batch or interactive mode. To run it in batch, simply save your Pig commands to a file and pass that file as an argument to the Pig executable. To run commands interactively, you can run the Pig executable from the command prompt.

Pig uses a language, Pig Latin, to define the data transformations that will be done. Pig Latin statements are operators that take a relation and produces another relation. A *relation*, in Pig Latin terms, is a collection of tuples, and a *tuple* is a collection of fields. One way to envision this is that a relation is like a table in a database. The table has a collection of rows, which is analogous to the tuples. The columns in the row are analogous to the fields. The primary difference between a relation and a database table is that relations do not require that all the tuples have the same number or type of fields in them.

An example Pig Latin statement follows. This statement loads information from Hadoop into a relation. Statements must be terminated with semicolons, and extra whitespace is ignored:

```
source = LOAD '/MsBigData/Customer/' USING PigStorage()
  AS (name, city, state,
      postalcode, totalpurchaseamount);
```

In this case, the result of the `LOAD` function is a relation that is being assigned to the alias of `source`. The alias allows the relation to be referred in later statements. Also, while this example declares the fields that will be retrieved, it is not required to define them. In fact, you may have noticed that there is no type definition. Pig can reference fields by ordinal position or name, if provided, and data values will be implicitly converted as needed.

The `LOAD` function is using the `PigStorage()` function. This is the default storage function, which allows access to Hadoop files and supports delimited text and the standard binary formats for Hadoop. Additional storage functions can be developed to allow Pig to communicate with other data stores.

To reduce the number of tuples (rows) in the relation, you can apply a filter to it using the `FILTER` function. In this case, the `FILTER` is being applied to the `source` alias created in the previous statement:

```
filtered = FILTER source BY state = 'FL';
```

The relation produced by this statement is assigned to an alias of `filtered`. You can also group the data using a `GROUP` function. The following statement results in a new relation that contains a tuple for each distinct city, with one field containing the city value and another field containing a collection of tuples for the rows that are part of the group:

```
grouped = GROUP filtered BY city;
```

You can look at this as producing a new table, with any rows belonging to the same grouped value being associated with that row:

```
grouped        | filtered
Jacksonville   | (John Smith, FL, 32079, 10000),
                 (Sandra James, FL, 32079, 8000)
Tampa          | (Robert Betts, FL, 32045, 6000)
               | (Tim Kerr, FL, 32045, 1000)
Miami          | (Gina Jones, FL, 32013, 7000)
```

When you need to operate on columns, you can use the FOREACH function. It is used when working with data like that shown here, because it runs the associated function for each value in the specified column. If you want to produce an average totalpurchaseamount for each city, you can use the following statement:

```
averaged = FOREACH grouped GENERATE group,
        AVG(filtered.totalpurchaseamount);
```

To order the results, you can use the ORDER function. In this case, the $2 indicates that the statement is using the ordinal column position, rather than addressing it by name:

```
ordered = ORDER averaged BY $2 DESC;
```

To store the results, you can call the STORE function. This lets you write the values back to Hadoop using the PigStorage() functionality:

```
STORE ordered INTO 'c:\SampleData\PigOutput.txt' USING PigStorage();
```

If you take this entire set of statements together, you can see that Pig Latin is relatively easy to read and understand. These statements could be saved to a file as a Pig script and then executed as a batch file:

```
source = LOAD '/MsBigData/Customer/' USING PigStorage()
  AS (name, city, state,
      postalcode, totalpurchaseamount);
filtered = FILTER source BY state = 'FL';
grouped = GROUP filtered BY city;
averaged = FOREACH grouped GENERATE group,
        AVG(filtered.totalpurchaseamount);
ordered = ORDER averaged BY $2 DESC;
STORE ordered INTO 'c:\SampleData\PigOutput.txt' USING PigStorage();
```

NOTE **Pig scripts are generally saved with a .PIG extension. This is a convention, but it is not required. However, it does make it easier for people to find and use your scripts.**

Another key aspect of Pig Latin is that the statements are declarative rather than imperative. That is, they tell Pig what you intend to do, but the Pig engine can determine the best way accomplish the operation. It may rearrange or combine certain operations to produce a more efficient plan for accomplishing the work. This is similar to the way SQL Server's query optimizer may rewrite your SQL queries to get the results in the fastest way possible.

Several functions facilitate debugging Pig Latin. One useful one is DUMP. This will output the contents of the specified relation to the screen. If the relation contains a large amount of data, though, this can be time-prohibitive to execute:

```
DUMP source;
```

`DESCRIBE` outputs the schema of a relation to a console. This can help you understand what the relation looks like after various transformations have been applied:

```
DESCRIBE grouped;
```

`EXPLAIN` shows the planned execution model for producing the specified relation. This outputs the logical, physical, and MapReduce plans to the console:

```
EXPLAIN filtered;
```

`ILLUSTRATE` shows the data steps that produce a given relation. This is different from the plan, in that it actually displays the data in each relation at each step:

```
ILLUSTRATE grouped;
```

A large number of other functions are available for Pig. Unfortunately, space constraints do not allow a full listing here. You can find complete documentation on Pig at `http://pig.apache.org`.

Using Pig and SSIS Together

Pig's primary advantage over SSIS is its ability to scale the workload across multiple nodes in a cluster. When you are doing data transformations over large amounts of data, being able to scale out is a significant advantage. Data operations that might otherwise take days to run on a single node may take just hours when spread across multiple nodes. A primary concern for many business users is timeliness. If producing the data they are requesting takes multiple days, that data might no longer be useful.

A proven useful pattern is to offload parts of the data transformation that involve large amounts of data to Pig and then consume the results in SSIS for any final transformation and land the data in the appropriate data store. You can execute the Pig scripts from an Execute Process task, in the same manner used to move files into Hadoop storage from SSIS.

The Pig scripts should produce a delimited text file because this is easy for SSIS to consume. After the output file has been created, you can read the text from the Hadoop file system, or you can access it via a Hive connection in SSIS. From that point, SSIS can use the data as if it came from any other source. This lets you take advantage of parallel processing in Hadoop while still using SSIS capabilities to land the data in any SSIS supported data store.

NOTE If the data is supposed to remain in Hadoop, in most cases it won't make sense to send it through SSIS, because doing so introduces some overhead. Unless you have need of some special transformation in SSIS, using Pig is probably a better option if the source and target are both Hadoop. Even if there is a unique transformation in SSIS, remember that Pig can be extended with custom functions as well. Using

the streaming model for the Pig transformation will even allow you to build these transformations using .NET.

Choosing the Right Tool

You have a variety of options for integrating your SQL Server and Hadoop environments. As with any set of tools, each option has pros and cons too, and the best one to use will vary depending on the use case and specific requirements that you have. In addition, existing skillsets can impact tool choice. It is worthwhile being familiar with the different strengths of each tool, because some scenarios may be much easier to accomplish in one tool or another.

The following sections lay out some of the advantages and disadvantages of each tool, as well as scenarios where you might want to use them.

Use Cases for SSIS

SSIS works well in cases where you have the following:

- Staff trained on SSIS
- The need to do additional transformations on the data after reading it from Hive or prior to writing it to Hadoop
- Performance tuning is important

SSIS is the best fit for shops that are already invested in SSIS and that need to incorporate Hadoop data into existing data-integration processes. However, SSIS does not have an inherent ability to scale out. In cases where there is significant data processing to be done, the best results can come from a hybrid solution leveraging both SSIS and Pig. SSIS delivers the integration with other data sources and destinations, and Pig delivers the ability to scale transformation of data across a Hadoop cluster.

Use Cases for Pig

Pig is best used in the following cases:

- The amount of data to be processed is too much to be handled in SSIS.
- You need to take advantage of the scalability of Hadoop.
- Your IT staff is comfortable learning a new language and tool.
- Your Hadoop data is stored in standard Hadoop binary file formats.

Pig proves quite useful when you need the data transformation to happen on your Hadoop cluster so that the process scales and conserves resources on your SSIS systems. Using it along with SSIS can deliver the best of both worlds: a solution that scales with Hadoop and that has the extensive integration capabilities of SSIS. In addition, if the data doesn't need to leave Hadoop storage, Pig is a natural fit.

Use Cases for Sqoop

Sqoop proves most useful in the following cases:

- There is little need to transform the data being moved between SQL Server and Hadoop.
- The IT staff isn't comfortable with SSIS or Pig.
- Ease of use is a higher priority than performance.
- Your Hadoop data is stored in standard Hadoop binary file formats.

Sqoop primarily comes into play for either simple table replication scenarios or for one-time data import and export from Hadoop. Because of the reduced control over transformations and lack of fine-grained tuning capability, it generally doesn't work as well in production-level data integration unless the integration is limited to replicating tables.

Summary

This chapter reviewed multiple methods of integrating your existing SQL Server environment with your big data environment, along with the pros and cons of each. SSIS was discussed, along with how to set it up for communication with Hive via ODBC and how to get the best performance from it. Sqoop was also covered, as a useful tool for handling bulk data import and export from Hadoop. A third option, Pig, was discussed, with a description of how you can leverage it to take advantage of Hadoop scalability and how it can be part of an SSIS solution to create a better solution overall. The chapter concluded by looking at when each tool is most applicable.

CHAPTER

9

Data Research and Advanced Data Cleansing with Pig and Hive

WHAT YOU WILL LEARN IN THIS CHAPTER

- Understanding the Difference Between Pig and Hive and When to Use Each
- Using Pig Latin Built-in Functions for Advanced Extraction, and Transforming and Loading Data
- Understanding the Various Types of Hive Functions Available
- Extending Hive with Map-reduce Scripts
- Creating Your Own Functions to Plug into Hive

All data processing on Hadoop essentially boils down to a map-reduce process. The *mapping* consists of retrieving the data and performing operations such as filtering and sorting. The *reducing* part of the process consists of performing a summary operation such as grouping and counting. Hadoop map-reduce jobs are written in programming languages such as Java and C#. Although this works well for developers with a programming background, it requires a steep learning curve for nonprogrammers. This is where Pig comes in to play. Another tool available to create and run map-reduce jobs in Hadoop is Hive. Like Pig, Hive relies on a batch-based, parallel-processing paradigm and is useful for querying, aggregating, and filtering large data sets.

This chapter covers both Pig and Hive and will help you to understand the strengths of each. You will also see how to extend Pig and Hive using functions and custom map-reduce scripts. In addition, the chapter includes hands-on activities to help you solidify the concepts presented.

Getting to Know Pig

Pig was originally developed as a research project within Yahoo! in 2006. It became popular with the user community as a way to increase productivity when writing map-reduce jobs. By 2007, Yahoo! decided to work with the open source community to develop Pig into a production-quality product. The open source community embraced the project, and additional features were added such as error handling, a streaming operator, parameter substitution, and binary comparators. Eventually, the entire codebase was rewritten to provide significant performance increases. With the growing popularity of Hadoop and Pig, the open source community continues to improve and augment Pig.

Today, Pig is a high-level scripting program used to create map-reduce functions that are translated to Java and run on a Hadoop cluster. The scripting language for Pig is called Pig Latin and is written to provide an easier way to write data-processing instructions. In the following sections, you'll learn more about Pig, including when to use Pig and how to use both built-in and user-defined functions.

THE DIFFERENCE BETWEEN PIG AND HIVE

The main difference between Pig and Hive is that Pig Latin, Pig's scripting language, is a procedural language, whereas HiveQL is a declarative language. This means that when using Pig Latin you have more control over how the data is processed through the pipeline, and the processing consists of a series of steps, in between which the data can be checked and stored. With HiveQL, you construct and run the statement as a whole, submitting it to a query engine to optimize and run the code. You have very little influence on the steps performed to achieve the result. Instead, you have faith that the query engine will choose the most efficient steps needed. If you have a programming background, you are probably more comfortable with and like the control you get using Pig Latin. However, if you a lot of experience with writing database queries, you will most likely feel more comfortable with HiveQL.

When to Use Pig

It is important that you use the right tool for the job. Although we have all used the side of a wrench to hammer in a nail, a hammer works much better! Pig is designed and tuned to process large data sets involving a number of steps. As such, it is primarily an extraction transform load (ETL) tool. In addition, like all Hadoop processing, it relies on map-reduce jobs that can be run in parallel on separate chunks of data and combined after the analysis to arrive at a result. For example, it would be ideal to look through massive amounts of data measurements like temperatures, group them by days, and reduce it to the max temperature by day. Another factor to keep in mind is the latency involved in the batch processing of the data. This means that Pig processing is suitable for post-processing of the data as opposed to real-time processing that occurs as the data is collected.

You can run Pig either interactively or in batch mode. Typically interactive mode is used during development. When you run Pig interactively, you can easily see the results of the scripts dumped out to the screen. This is a great way to build up and debug a multi-step ETL process. Once the script is built, you can save it to a text file and run it in batch mode using scheduling or part of a workflow. This generally occurs during production where scripts are run unattended during off-peak hours. The results can be dumped into a file that you can use for further analysis or as an input file for tools, such as PowerPivot, Power View, and Power Map. (You will see how these tools are used in Chapter 11, "Visualizing Big Data with Microsoft BI.")

Taking Advantage of Built-in Functions

As you saw in Chapter 8, "Effective Big Data ETL with SSIS, Pig, and SQOOP," Pig scripts are written in a script language called *Pig Latin*. Although it is a lot easier to write the ETL processing using Pig Latin than it is to write the low level map-reduce jobs, at some point the Pig Latin has to be converted into a map-reduce job that does the actual processing. This is where functions come into the picture. In Pig, *functions* process the data and are written in Java. Pig comes with a set of built-in functions to implement common processing tasks such as the following:

- Loading and storing data
- Evaluating and aggregating data
- Executing common math functions
- Implementing string functions

For example, the default load function `PigStorage` is used to load data into structured text files in UTF-8 format. The following code loads a file containing flight delay data into a relation (table) named `FlightData`:

```
FlightData = LOAD 'FlightPerformance.csv' using PigStorage(',');
```

Another built-in load function is `JsonLoader`. This is used to load JSON (JavaScript Object Notation)-formatted files. JSON is a text-based open standard designed for human-readable data interchange and is often used to transmit structured data over network connections. The following code loads a JSON-formatted file:

```
FlightData = LOAD ' FlightPerformance.json' using JsonLoader();
```

NOTE For more information on JSON, see `http://www.json.org/`.

You can also store data using the storage functions. For example, the following code stores data into a tab-delimited text file (the default format):

```
STORE FlightData into 'FlightDataProcessed' using PigStorage();
```

Functions used to evaluate and aggregate data include `IsEmpty`, `Size`, `Count`, `Sum`, `Avg`, and `Concat`, to name a few. The following code filters out tuples that have an empty airport code:

```
FlightDataFiltered = Filter FlightData By IsEmpty(AirportCode);
```

Common math functions include `ABS`, `CEIL`, `SIN`, and `TAN`. The following code uses the `CEIL` function to round the delay times up to the nearest minute (integer):

```
FlightDataCeil = FOREACH FlightData
GENERATE CEIL(FlightDelay) AS FlightDelay2;
```

Some common string functions are `Lower`, `Trim`, `Substring`, and `Replace`. The following code trims leading and trailing spaces from the airport codes:

```
FlightDataTrimmed = FOREACH FlightData
GENERATE TRIM(AirportCode) AS AirportCode2;
```

Executing User-defined Functions

In the preceding section, you looked at some of the useful built-in functions available in Pig. Because these are built-in functions, you do not have to register the functions or use fully qualified naming to invoke them because Pig knows where the functions reside. It is recommended that you use the built-in functions if they meet your processing needs. However, these built-in functions are limited and will not always meet your requirements. In these cases, you can use user-defined functions (UDFs).

Creating your own functions is not trivial, so you should investigate whether a publicly available UDF could meet your needs before going to the trouble of creating your own. Two useful open source libraries containing prebuilt UDFs are PiggyBank and DataFu, discussed next.

PiggyBank

PiggyBank is a repository for UDFs provided by the open source community. Unlike with the built-in UDFs, you need to register the jar to use them. The jar file contains the compiled code for the function. Once registered, you can use them in your Pig scripts by providing the function's fully qualified name or use the `define` statement to provide an alias for the UDF. The following code uses the `reverse` function contained in the `piggybank.jar` file to reverse a string. The `HCatLoader` loads data from a table defined using HCatalog (covered in Chapter 7, "Expanding Your Capability with HBase and HCatalog"):

```
REGISTER piggybank.jar;
define reverse org.apache.pig.piggybank.evaluation.string.Reverse();
FlightData = LOAD 'FlightData'
USING org.apache.hcatalog.pig.HCatLoader();
FlightDataReversed = Foreach FlightData
Generate (origin, reverse(origin));
```

PiggyBank functions are organized into packages according to function type. For example, the `org.apache.pig.piggybank.evaluation` package contains functions for custom evaluation operations like aggregates and column transformations. The functions are further organized into subgroups by function. The `org.apache.pig.piggybank.evaluation.string` functions contain custom functions for string evaluations such as the reverse seen earlier. In addition to the evaluation functions, there are functions for comparison, filtering, grouping, and loading/storing.

DataFu

DataFu was developed by LinkedIn to aid them in analyzing their big data sets. This is a well-tested set of UDFs containing functions for data mining and advanced statistics. You can download the jar file from `www.wiley.com/go/microsoftbigdatasolutions`. To use the UDFs, you complete the same process as you do with the PiggyBank library. Register the jar file so that Pig can locate it and define an alias to use in your script. The following code finds the median of a set of measures:

```
REGISTER 'C:\Hadoop\pig-0.9.3-SNAPSHOT\datafu-0.0.10.jar';
DEFINE Median datafu.pig.stats.Median();
TempData = LOAD '/user/test/temperature.txt'
using PigStorage() AS (dtstamp:chararray, sensorid:int, temp:double);
TempDataGrouped = Group TempData ALL;
MedTemp = ForEach TempDataGrouped
{ TempSorted = ORDER TempData BY temp;
GENERATE Median(TempData.temp);};
```

Using UDFs

You can set up Hortonworks Data Platform (HDP) for Windows on a development server to provide a local test environment that supports a single-node deployment. (For a detailed discussion of installing the Hadoop development environment on Windows, see Chapter 3, "Installing HDInsight.")

NOTE To complete the following activity, you need to download and install the HDP for Windows from Hortonworks or the HDInsight Emulator from Microsoft.

After you have installed the environment, you should see three icons on the desktop for interacting with the Hadoop service. The NameNode maintains the directory files in the Hadoop Distributed File System (HDFS). It also keeps track of where the data files are kept in a Hadoop cluster. Figure 9.1 shows the information displayed when you click the NameNode icon.

NameNode '10.0.2.15:8020'

Started:	Mon Aug 26 16:39:06 PDT 2013
Version:	1.2.0.1.3.0.0-0380, r4c12a850c61d98a885eba4396a4abc145abb65c8
Compiled:	Tue Aug 06 19:39:01 Coordinated Universal Time 2013 by jenkins
Upgrades:	There are no upgrades in progress.

Browse the filesystem
Namenode Logs

Cluster Summary

251 files and directories, 160 blocks = 411 total. Heap Size is 119.28 MB / 3.87 GB (3%)

Configured Capacity	:	49.66 GB
DFS Used	:	8 MB
Non DFS Used	:	15 GB
DFS Remaining	:	34.65 GB
DFS Used%	:	0.02 %
DFS Remaining%	:	69.77 %
Live Nodes	:	1
Dead Nodes	:	0
Decommissioning Nodes	:	0
Number of Under-Replicated Blocks	:	2

Figure 9.1: Displaying the NameNode information

Additional links appear on the NameNode information page for browsing the file system and log files and for additional node information. Figure 9.2 shows the files in the `/user/Dan` directory.

Contents of directory /user/Dan

Goto : /user/Dan [go]

Go to parent directory

Name	Type	Size	Replication	Block Size	Modification Time	Permission	Owner	Group
NYSE_dailyA.csv	file	39.09 MB	1	64 MB	2013-08-02 11:32	rw-r--r--	Dan	supergroup
NYSE_divA.csv	file	218.98 KB	1	64 MB	2013-08-02 12:19	rw-r--r--	Dan	supergroup
sample.log	file	96.94 KB	1	64 MB	2013-08-01 16:07	rw-r--r--	Dan	supergroup

Go back to DFS home

Figure 9.2: Exploring the directory file listing

You can also drill in to see the contents of a data file, as shown in Figure 9.3.

File: /user/Dan/NYSE_dailyA.csv

Goto : \user\Dan [go]

Go back to dir listing
Advanced view/download options

View Next chunk

```
exchange,stock_symbol,date,stock_price_open,stock_price_high,st
ock_price_low,stock_price_close,stock_volume,stock_price_adj_cl
ose
NYSE,AEA,2010-02-08,4.42,4.42,4.21,4.24,205500,4.24
NYSE,AEA,2010-02-05,4.42,4.54,4.22,4.41,194300,4.41
NYSE,AEA,2010-02-04,4.55,4.69,4.39,4.42,233800,4.42
NYSE,AEA,2010-02-03,4.65,4.69,4.50,4.55,182100,4.55
NYSE,AEA,2010-02-02,4.74,5.00,4.62,4.66,222700,4.66
NYSE,AEA,2010-02-01,4.84,4.92,4.68,4.75,194800,4.75
NYSE,AEA,2010-01-29,4.97,5.05,4.76,4.83,222900,4.83
NYSE,AEA,2010-01-28,5.12,5.22,4.81,4.98,283100,4.98
NYSE,AEA,2010-01-27,4.82,5.16,4.79,5.09,243500,5.09
NYSE,AEA,2010-01-26,5.18,5.18,4.81,4.84,554800,4.84
NYSE,AEA,2010-01-25,5.42,5.48,5.20,5.22,257300,5.22
NYSE,AEA,2010-01-22,5.52,5.59,5.31,5.37,260800,5.37
NYSE,AEA,2010-01-21,5.67,5.74,5.37,5.51,264300,5.51
NYSE,AEA,2010-01-20,5.65,5.70,5.53,5.66,244600,5.66
NYSE,AEA,2010-01-19,5.54,5.70,5.54,5.69,368000,5.69
```

Figure 9.3: Drilling into a data file

The Hadoop Map-Reduce Status icon launches the Map/Reduce Administration page. This page provides useful information about the map-reduce jobs currently running, scheduled to run, or having run in the past. Figure 9.4 shows summary information for a job that was run on the cluster.

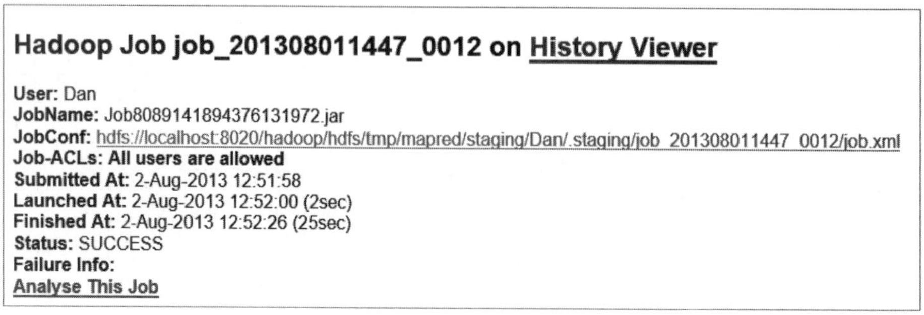

Hadoop Job job_201308011447_0012 on History Viewer

User: Dan
JobName: Job8089141894376131972.jar
JobConf: hdfs://localhost:8020/hadoop/hdfs/tmp/mapred/staging/Dan/.staging/job_201308011447_0012/job.xml
Job-ACLs: All users are allowed
Submitted At: 2-Aug-2013 12:51:58
Launched At: 2-Aug-2013 12:52:00 (2sec)
Finished At: 2-Aug-2013 12:52:26 (25sec)
Status: SUCCESS
Failure Info:
Analyse This Job

Figure 9.4: Viewing job summary stats

The third link is a shortcut to the Hadoop command-line console window displaying the Hadoop command prompt. Using this console, you can build and issue map-reduce jobs and issue Hadoop `File System` (FS) commands. You can also use this console to administer the Hadoop cluster. Figure 9.5 shows the Hadoop console being used to list the files in a directory.

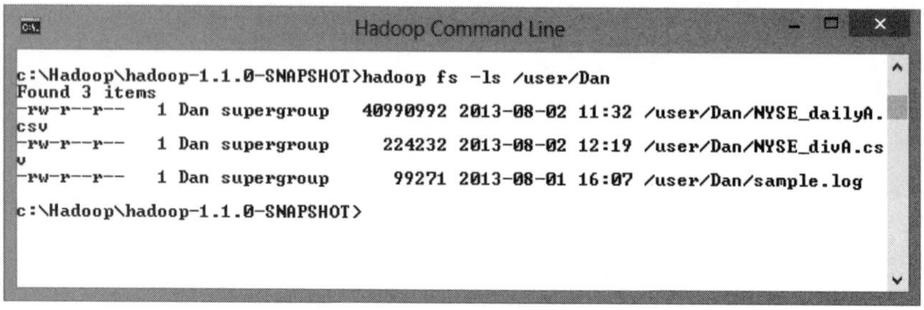

Hadoop Command Line

```
c:\Hadoop\hadoop-1.1.0-SNAPSHOT>hadoop fs -ls /user/Dan
Found 3 items
-rw-r--r--   1 Dan supergroup   40990992 2013-08-02 11:32 /user/Dan/NYSE_dailyA.
csv
-rw-r--r--   1 Dan supergroup     224232 2013-08-02 12:19 /user/Dan/NYSE_divA.cs
v
-rw-r--r--   1 Dan supergroup      99271 2013-08-01 16:07 /user/Dan/sample.log

c:\Hadoop\hadoop-1.1.0-SNAPSHOT>
```

Figure 9.5: Using the Hadoop command-line console

After installing and setting up the environment, you are now ready to implement an ETL process using Pig. In addition you will use UDFs exposed by PiggyBank and DataFu for advanced processing.

The four basic steps contained in this activity are:

1. Loading the data.
2. Running Pig interactively with Grunt.
3. Using PiggyBank to extract time periods.
4. Using DataFu to implement some advanced statistical analysis.

Loading Data

The first thing you need to do is load a data file. You can download a sample highway traffic data file at `www.wiley.com/go/microsoftbigdatasolutions`.

Once the data file is downloaded, you can load it into HDFS using the Hadoop command-line console. Open the console and create a directory for the file using the following code:

```
hadoop fs -mkdir /user/test
```

Next, use the following command to load the `traffic.txt` file into the directory:

```
Hadoop fs -copyFromLocal C:\SampleData\traffic.txt /user/test
```

Once the file is copied into the Hadoop directory, you should be able to browse to the directory and view the data using the Hadoop NameNode link. Figure 9.6 shows the file open in the NameNode browser.

File: /user/test/traffic.txt

Goto : \user\test go

Go back to dir listing
Advanced view/download options

View Next chunk

Timestamp	SensorId	Lane1	Lane2	Lane3	Lane4
1/1/2012 12:00:00 AM	111	61.60	57.20	76.27	88.00
1/1/2012 12:00:00 AM	112	52.80	57.20	54.27	84.48
1/1/2012 12:00:00 AM	113	51.70	71.87	63.07	93.28
1/1/2012 12:00:00 AM	114	57.20	63.07	57.20	91.52
1/1/2012 12:00:00 AM	115	55.00	83.60	83.60	86.24
1/1/2012 12:00:00 AM	116	33.00	86.53	52.80	100.32
1/1/2012 12:00:00 AM	117	33.00	54.27	57.20	86.24
1/1/2012 12:00:00 AM	118	35.20	86.53	55.73	96.80
1/1/2012 12:00:00 AM	119	56.10	82.13	64.53	72.16
1/1/2012 12:00:00 AM	120	55.00	55.73	77.73	88.00
1/1/2012 12:00:00 AM	121	56.10	80.67	73.33	75.68
1/1/2012 12:00:00 AM	122	57.20	73.33	60.13	80.96
1/1/2012 12:00:00 AM	123	64.90	79.20	57.20	72.16
1/1/2012 12:00:00 AM	124	66.00	55.73	64.53	91.52
1/1/2012 12:00:00 AM	125	41.80	55.73	79.20	72.16
1/1/2012 12:00:00 AM	126	41.80	85.07	68.93	82.72
1/1/2012 12:00:00 AM	127	38.50	76.27	55.73	102.08
1/1/2012 12:00:00 AM	128	41.80	52.80	82.13	93.28
1/1/2012 12:00:00 AM	129	45.10	77.73	73.33	80.96
1/1/2012 12:00:00 AM	130	34.10	66.00	73.33	77.44
1/1/2012 12:00:00 AM	131	61.60	86.53	68.93	75.68
1/1/2012 12:00:00 AM	132	50.60	85.07	80.67	82.72
1/1/2012 12:00:00 AM	133	52.80	55.73	86.53	100.32
1/1/2012 12:00:00 AM	134	51.70	85.07	52.80	93.28

Figure 9.6: Viewing the traffic.txt data

Running Pig Interactively with Grunt

From the `bin` folder of the Pig install folder (`hdp\hadoop\pig\bin`), open the Pig command-line console to launch the Grunt shell. The Grunt shell enables you to run Pig Latin interactively and view the results of each step. Enter the following script to load and create a schema for the traffic data:

```
SpeedData = LOAD '/user/test/traffic.txt'
using PigStorage() AS (dtstamp:chararray, sensorid:int, speed:double);
```

Dump the results to the screen:

```
DUMP SpeedData;
```

By doing so, you can run a map-reduce job that outputs the data to the console window. You should see data similar to Figure 9.7, which shows the tuples that make the set of data.

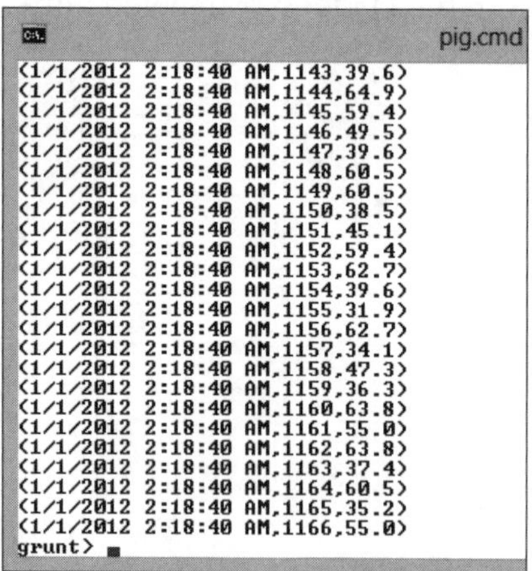

Figure 9.7: Dumping results to the console window

Using PiggyBank to Extract Time Periods

The next step in analyzing the data is to group it into different date/time buckets. To accomplish this, you use functions defined in the `piggybank.jar` file. If that file is not already installed, you can either download and compile the source code or download a compiled jar file from `www.wiley.com/go/microsoftbigdatasolutions`. Along with the `piggybank.jar` file, you need to get a copy of the `joda-time-2.2.jar` file from `www.wiley.com/go/microsoftbigdatasolutions`, which is referenced by the `piggybank.jar` file.

Place the jar files in a directory accessible to the Pig command-line console; for example, you can place it in the same directory as the `pig.jar` file. Now you can register and alias the PiggyBank functions in your Pig Latin scripts. The first function you use here is the `CustomFormatToISO`. This function converts the date/time strings in the file to a standard ISO format:

```
REGISTER 'C:\hdp\hadoop\pig-0.11.0.1.3.0.0-0380\piggybank.jar';
REGISTER 'C:\hdp\hadoop\pig-0.11.0.1.3.0.0-0380\joda-time-2.2.jar';
```

```
DEFINE Convert
org.apache.pig.piggybank.evaluation.datetime.convert.CustomFormatToISO;
```

Use the following code to load and convert the date/time values:

```
SpeedData = LOAD '/user/test/traffic.txt' using PigStorage()
AS (dtstamp:chararray, sensorid:int, speed:double);
SpeedDataFormat = FOREACH SpeedData Generate dtstamp,
Convert(dtstamp,'MM/dd/YYYY hh:mm:ss a') as dtISO;
Dump SpeedDataFormat;
```

After the job completes, you should see data similar to the data shown in Figure 9.8.

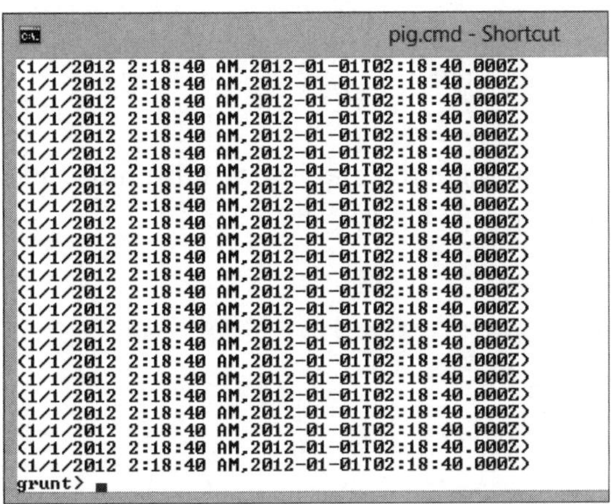

Figure 9.8: Reformatted date/times

Now that you have the dates in ISO format, you can easily strip out the day and hour from the date. Use the following code to create the day and hour fields. The output should match Figure 9.9:

```
REGISTER 'C:\hdp\hadoop\pig-0.11.0.1.3.0.0-0380\piggybank.jar';
REGISTER 'C:\hdp\hadoop\pig-0.11.0.1.3.0.0-0380\joda-time-2.2.jar';
DEFINE Convert
org.apache.pig.piggybank.evaluation.datetime.convert.CustomFormatToISO;
DEFINE SubString org.apache.pig.piggybank.evaluation.string.SUBSTRING;
SpeedData = LOAD '/user/test/trafic.txt' using PigStorage()
AS (dtstamp:chararray, sensorid:int, speed:double);
SpeedDataFormat = FOREACH SpeedData Generate dtstamp,
Convert(dtstamp,'MM/dd/YYYY hh:mm:ss a') as dtISO, speed;
SpeedDataHour = FOREACH SpeedDataFormat
Generate dtstamp, SubString(dtISO,5,7) as day,
SubString(dtISO,11,13) as hr, speed;
Dump SpeedDataHour;
```

```
(1/1/2012 2:18:40 AM,01,02,39.6)
(1/1/2012 2:18:40 AM,01,02,64.9)
(1/1/2012 2:18:40 AM,01,02,59.4)
(1/1/2012 2:18:40 AM,01,02,49.5)
(1/1/2012 2:18:40 AM,01,02,39.6)
(1/1/2012 2:18:40 AM,01,02,60.5)
(1/1/2012 2:18:40 AM,01,02,60.5)
(1/1/2012 2:18:40 AM,01,02,38.5)
(1/1/2012 2:18:40 AM,01,02,45.1)
(1/1/2012 2:18:40 AM,01,02,59.4)
(1/1/2012 2:18:40 AM,01,02,62.7)
(1/1/2012 2:18:40 AM,01,02,39.6)
(1/1/2012 2:18:40 AM,01,02,31.9)
(1/1/2012 2:18:40 AM,01,02,62.7)
(1/1/2012 2:18:40 AM,01,02,34.1)
(1/1/2012 2:18:40 AM,01,02,47.3)
(1/1/2012 2:18:40 AM,01,02,36.3)
(1/1/2012 2:18:40 AM,01,02,63.8)
(1/1/2012 2:18:40 AM,01,02,55.0)
(1/1/2012 2:18:40 AM,01,02,63.8)
(1/1/2012 2:18:40 AM,01,02,37.4)
(1/1/2012 2:18:40 AM,01,02,60.5)
(1/1/2012 2:18:40 AM,01,02,35.2)
(1/1/2012 2:18:40 AM,01,02,55.0)
grunt>
```

Figure 9.9: Splitting day and hour from an ISO date field

Now you can group the data by hour and get the maximum, minimum, and average speed recorded during each hour (see Figure 9.10):

```
SpeedDataGrouped = Group SpeedDataHour BY hr;
SpeedDataAgr = FOREACH SpeedDataGrouped
GENERATE group, MAX(SpeedDataHour.speed),
MIN(SpeedDataHour.speed), AVG(SpeedDataHour.speed);
Dump SpeedDataAgr;
```

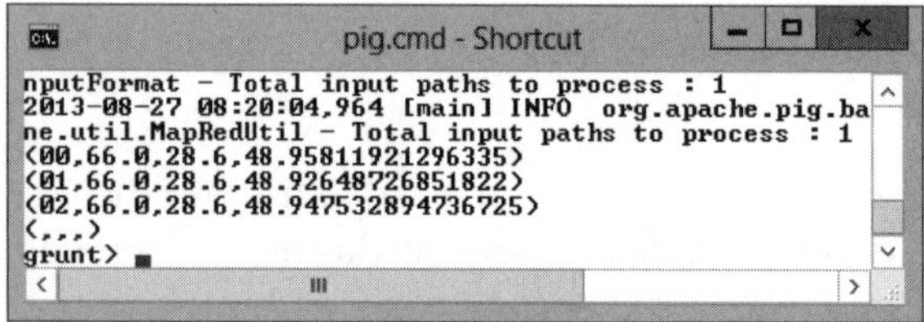

Figure 9.10: Speed data aggregated by hour

Using DataFu for Advanced Statistics

Even though Pig contains some rudimentary statistical UDFs you can use to analyze the data, you often need to implement advanced statistical techniques to accurately process the data. For example, you might want to eliminate outliers in your data. To determine the outliers, you can use the DataFu `Quantile` function and compute the 10th and 90th percentile values.

To use the DataFu UDFs, download the `datafu.jar` file from `www.wiley.com/go/microsoftbigdatasolutions` and place it in the same directory as the `piggybank.jar` file. You can now reference the jar file in your script. Define an alias for the `Quantile` function and provide the quantile values you want to calculate:

```
REGISTER 'C:\hdp\hadoop\pig-0.11.0.1.3.0.0-0380\datafu-0.0.10.jar';
DEFINE Quantile datafu.pig.stats.Quantile('.10','.90');
```

Load and group the data:

```
SpeedData = LOAD '/user/test/traffic.txt' using PigStorage()
AS (dtstamp:chararray, sensorid:int, speed:double);
SpeedDataGrouped = Group SpeedData ALL;
```

Pass sorted data to the `Quantile` function and dump the results out to the command-line console (see Figure 9.11). Using this data, you can then write a script to filter out the outliers:

```
QuantSpeeds = ForEach SpeedDataGrouped
{ SpeedSorted = ORDER SpeedData BY speed;
GENERATE Quantile(SpeedData.speed);};
Dump QuantSpeeds;
```

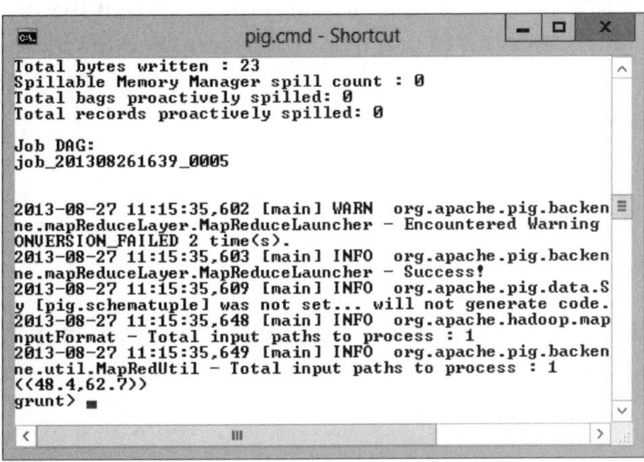

Figure 9.11: Finding the 10th and 90th percentile

Now that you know how to use UDFs to extend the functionality of Pig, it is time to take it a step further and create your own UDF.

Building Your Own UDFs for Pig

Unless you are an experienced Java programmer, writing your own UDF is not trivial, as mentioned earlier. However, if you have experience in another object-oriented programming language such as C#, you should be able to transition to writing UDFs in Java without too much difficulty. One thing you may want to do to make things easier is to download and install a Java interface development environment (IDE) such as Eclipse (`http://www.eclipse.org/`). If you are used to working in Visual Studio, you should be comfortable developing in Eclipse.

You can create several types of UDFs, depending on the functionality. The most common type is the eval function. An eval function accepts a tuple as an input, completes some processing on it, and sends it back out. They are typically used in conjunction with a `FOREACH` statement in HiveQL. For example, the following script calls a custom UDF to convert string values to lowercase:

```
Register C:\hdp\hadoop\pig-0.11.0.1.3.0.0-0380\SampleUDF.jar;
Define lcase com.BigData.hadoop.pig.SampleUDF.Lower;
FlightData = LOAD '/user/test/FlightPerformance.csv'
using PigStorage(',')
as (flight_date:chararray,airline_cd:int,airport_cd:chararray,
delay:int,dep_time:int);
Lower = FOREACH FlightData GENERATE lcase(airport_cd);
```

To create the UDF, you first add a reference to the `pig.jar` file. After doing so, you need to create a class that extends the `EvalFunc` class. The `EvalFunc` is the base class for all eval functions. The `import` statements at the top of the file indicate the various classes you are going to use from the referenced jar files:

```
import java.io.IOException;
import org.apache.pig.EvalFunc;
import org.apache.pig.data.Tuple;

public class Lower extends EvalFunc<String>
{
}
```

The next step is to add an `exec` function that implements the processing. It has an input parameter of a tuple and an output of a string:

```
public String exec(Tuple arg0) throws IOException
{
    if (arg0 == null || arg0.size() == 0)
        return null;
    try
    {
        String str = (String)arg0.get(0);
        return str.toLowerCase();
    }
    catch(Exception e)
    {
        throw new
        IOException("Caught exception processing input row ", e);
    }
}
```

The first part of the code checks the input tuple to make sure that it is valid and then uses a `try-catch` block. The `try` block converts the string to lowercase and returns it back to the caller. If an error occurs in the `try` block, the `catch` block returns an error message to the caller.

Next, you need to build the class and export it to a jar file. Place the jar file in the Pig directory, and you are ready to use it in your scripts.

Another common type of function is the filter function. Filter functions are eval functions that return a Boolean result. For example, the `IsPositive` function is used here to filter out negative and zero-delay values (integers):

```
Register C:\hdp\hadoop\pig-0.11.0.1.3.0.0-0380\SampleUDF.jar;
Define isPos com.BigData.hadoop.pig.SampleUDF.isPositive;
FlightData = LOAD '/user/test/FlightPerformance.csv'
using PigStorage(',')
as (flight_date:chararray,airline_cd:int,airport_cd:chararray,
delay:int,dep_time:int);
PosDelay = Filter FlightData BY isPos(delay);
```

The code for the `isPositive` UDF is shown here:

```
package com.BigData.hadoop.pig.SampleUDF;
import java.io.IOException;
import org.apache.pig.FilterFunc;
import org.apache.pig.data.Tuple;

public class isPositive extends FilterFunc {

       @Override
       public Boolean exec(Tuple arg0) throws IOException {
             if (arg0 == null || arg0.size() != 1)
                    return null;
              try
              {
                    if (arg0.get(0) instanceof Integer)
                    {
                           if ((Integer)arg0.get(0)>0)
                                  return true;
                           else
                           return false;
                    }
                    else
                           return false;
              }
              catch(Exception e)
              {
                    throw new IOException
                    ("Caught exception processing input row ", e);
              }
       }
}
```

It extends the `FilterFunc` class and includes an exec function that checks to confirm whether the tuple passed in is not null and makes sure that it has only one member. It then confirms whether it is an integer and returns true if it is greater than zero; otherwise, it returns false.

Some other UDF types are the aggregation, load, and store functions. The functions shown here are the bare-bones implementations. You also need to consider error handling, progress reporting, and output schema typing. For more information on custom UDF creation, consult the UDF manual on the Apache Pig wiki (`http://wiki.apache.org/pig/UDFManual`).

Using Hive

Another tool available to create and run map-reduce jobs in Hadoop is Hive. One of the major advantages of Hive is that it creates a relational database layer over the data files. Using this paradigm, you can work with the data using traditional querying techniques, which is very beneficial if you have a SQL background. In addition, you do not have to worry about how the query is translated into the map-reduce job. There is a query engine that works out the details of what is the most efficient way of loading and aggregating the data.

In the following sections you will gain an understanding of how to perform advanced data analysis with Hive. First you will look at the different types of built-in Hive functions available. Next, you will see how to extend Hive with custom map-reduce scripts written in Python. Then you will go one step further and create a UDF to extend the functionality of Hive.

Data Analysis with Hive

One strong point of HiveQL is that it contains a lot of built-in functions that assist you in your data analysis. There are a number of mathematical, collection, type conversion, date, and string functions. Most of the functions that are in the SQL language have been included in HiveQL. For example, the following HiveQL counts the flights and finds the maximum delay at each airport from the `flightdata` table. Figure 9.12 shows the output in the Hive console:

```
Select airport_cd, count(*), max(delay)
from flightdata group by airport_cd;
```

Types of Hive Functions

Hive has several flavors of functions you can work with, including the following:

- UDFs
- UDAFs (user-defined aggregate functions)

- UDTFs (user-defined table-generating functions)

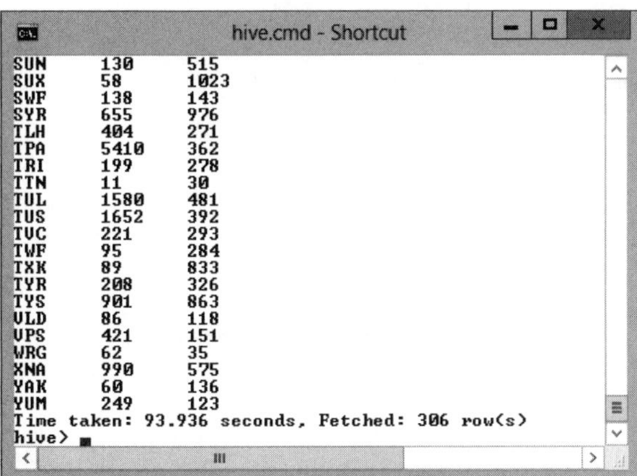

```
SUN     130     515
SUX     58      1023
SWF     138     143
SYR     655     976
TLH     404     271
TPA     5410    362
TRI     199     278
TTN     11      30
TUL     1580    481
TUS     1652    392
TVC     221     293
TWF     95      284
TXK     89      833
TYR     208     326
TYS     901     863
VLD     86      118
VPS     421     151
WRG     62      35
XNA     990     575
YAK     60      136
YUM     249     123
Time taken: 93.936 seconds, Fetched: 306 row(s)
hive>
```

Figure 9.12: Flight counts and maximum delays

UDFs work on single rows at a time and consist of functions such as type conversion, math functions, string manipulation, and date/time functions. For example, the following Hive query uses the date function to get the day from the `flightdate` field:

```
Select day(flightdate), airport_cd, delay
from flightdata where delay > 100;
```

Whereas UDFs work on single rows at a time and processing occurs on the map side of the processing, UDAFs work on buckets of data and are implemented on the reduce side of the processing. For example, you can use the built-in UDAF `count` and `max` to get the delay counts and maximum delays by day:

```
Select day(flightdate), count(*), max(delay)
from flightdata group by day(flightdate);
```

Another type of function used in Hive is a UDFT. This type of function takes a single-row input and produces multiple-row outputs. These functions are useful for taking a column containing an array that needs to be split out into multiple rows. Hive's built-in UDFTs include the following:

- The `explode` function, which takes an array as input and splits it out into multiple rows.
- The `json_tuple` function, which is useful for querying JSON-formatted nodes. It takes the JSON node and splits out the child nodes into separate rows into a virtual table for better processing performance.
- The `parse_url_tuple` function, which takes a URL and extracts parts of a URL string into multiple rows in a table structure.

The file shown in Figure 9.13 contains student data in JSON format.


```
{ "StudentId":"1","StudentData": { "Name":"Dan" , "Major":"Physics" }}
{ "StudentId":"2","StudentData": { "Name":"Jan" , "Major":"Math" }}
{ "StudentId":"3","StudentData": { "Name":"Bill" , "Major":"Art" }}
{ "StudentId":"4","StudentData": { "Name":"Jill" , "Major":"Music" }}
```


Figure 9.13: JSON formatted data

To parse the values from the JSON nodes, you use the `json_tuple` function in combination with the lateral view operator to create a table:

```
Select b.studentid, b.studentdata from studentdata a lateral view
json_tuple(a.jstring,'StudentId','StudentData') b
as studentid, studentdata;
```

Figure 9.14 shows the query output.

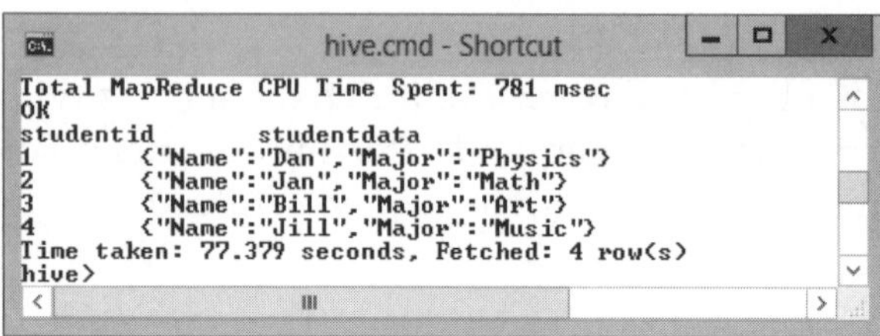

Figure 9.14: Parsing JSON data

Notice that this query did not parse out the nested JSON data from each row. To query the nested data, you need to add an additional lateral view:

```
Select b.studentid, c.name, c.major from studentdata a lateral view
json_tuple(a.jstring,'StudentId','StudentData') b
as studentid, studentdata
lateral view json_tuple(b.studentdata,'Name','Major') c as name, major;
```

Figure 9.15 shows the output with the nested JSON data parsed out into separate columns.

```
hive.cmd - Shortcut
Total MapReduce CPU Time Spent: 936 msec
OK
studentid       name    major
1       Dan     Physics
2       Jan     Math
3       Bill    Art
4       Jill    Music
Time taken: 75.127 seconds, Fetched: 4 row(s)
hive>
```

Figure 9.15: Parsing out nested data

Now that you have expanded out the nested data, you can analyze the data using reduce functions such as counting the number of students in each major.

Extending Hive with Map-reduce Scripts

There are times when you need to create a custom data-processing transformation that is not easy to achieve using HiveQL but fairly easy to do with a scripting language. This is particularly useful when manipulating if the result of the transform produces a different number of columns or rows than the input. For example, you want to split up an input column into several output columns using string-parsing functions. Another example is a column containing a set of key/value pairs that need to be split out into their own rows.

The input values sent to the script will consist of tab-delimited strings, and the output values should also come back as tab-delimited strings. Any null values sent to the script will be converted to the literal string `\N` to differentiate it from an empty string.

Although technically you can create your script in any scripting language, Pearl and Python seem to be the most popular. The code shown in Figure 9.16 is an example Python script that takes in a column formatted as hh:mm:ss and splits it into separate columns for hour, minute, and second.

```
split_time.py - C:\SampleData\s
File Edit Format Run Options Windows Help
#!/usr/bin/env python
import sys
for line in sys.stdin.readlines():
   line = line.strip()
   fields = line.split('\t')
   l = fields[0]
   if len(fields[1].split(':')) == 3:
      h = fields[1].split(':')[0]
      m = fields[1].split(':')[1]
      s = fields[1].split(':')[2]
      t = fields[1]
      print h,"\t",l,"\t",m,"\t",s,"\t",t
```

Figure 9.16: Python script for splitting time

To call this script from HiveQL, you use the `TRANSFORM` clause. You need to provide the `TRANSFORM` clause, the input data, output columns, and map-reduce script file. The following code uses the previous script. It takes an input of a time column and a log level and parses the time. Figure 9.17 shows the output:

```
add file c:\sampledata\split_time.py;
SELECT TRANSFORM(l.t4, l.t2) USING 'python split_time.py'
AS (hr,loglevel,min,sec,fulltime) from logs l;
```

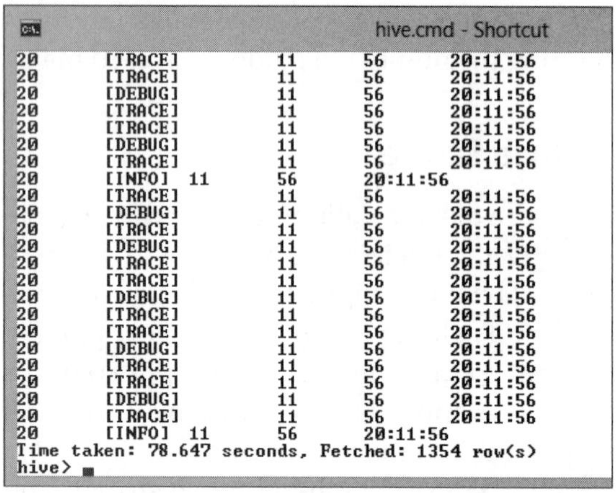

```
hive.cmd - Shortcut
20      [TRACE]         11      56      20:11:56
20      [TRACE]         11      56      20:11:56
20      [DEBUG]         11      56      20:11:56
20      [TRACE]         11      56      20:11:56
20      [TRACE]         11      56      20:11:56
20      [DEBUG]         11      56      20:11:56
20      [TRACE]         11      56      20:11:56
20      [INFO]  11      56      20:11:56
20      [TRACE]         11      56      20:11:56
20      [DEBUG]         11      56      20:11:56
20      [TRACE]         11      56      20:11:56
20      [DEBUG]         11      56      20:11:56
20      [TRACE]         11      56      20:11:56
20      [TRACE]         11      56      20:11:56
20      [DEBUG]         11      56      20:11:56
20      [TRACE]         11      56      20:11:56
20      [TRACE]         11      56      20:11:56
20      [DEBUG]         11      56      20:11:56
20      [TRACE]         11      56      20:11:56
20      [TRACE]         11      56      20:11:56
20      [DEBUG]         11      56      20:11:56
20      [TRACE]         11      56      20:11:56
20      [INFO]  11      56      20:11:56
Time taken: 78.647 seconds, Fetched: 1354 row(s)
hive>
```

Figure 9.17: Splitting the time into hours, minutes, and seconds

The preceding script was a mapping script. You can also create reduce scripts for your custom processing. A *reduce script* takes tab-delimited columns from the input and produces tab-delimited output columns just like a map script. The difference is the reduce script combines rows in the process, and the rows out should be less than the rows put in. To run a reduce script, you need to have a mapping script. The mapping script provides the key/value pairs for the reducer. The Python script in Figure 9.18 is a mapping script that takes the input and checks whether it starts with a `[` character. If it does, it outputs it to a line and gives it a count of one.

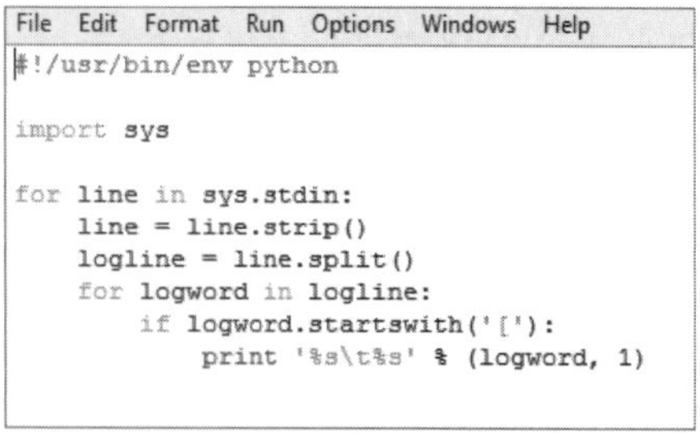

```
File  Edit  Format  Run  Options  Windows  Help
#!/usr/bin/env python

import sys

for line in sys.stdin:
    line = line.strip()
    logline = line.split()
    for logword in logline:
        if logword.startswith('['):
            print '%s\t%s' % (logword, 1)
```

Figure 9.18: Mapping logging levels

Figure 9.19 shows a sample output from the script.

The output from the map script is fed into the reduce script, which counts the occurrence of each log level and returns the total count for each log level on a new line. Figure 9.20 shows the code for the reduce script.

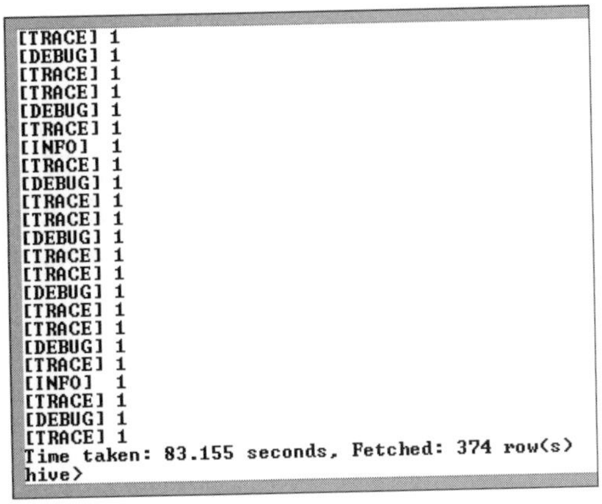

```
[TRACE] 1
[DEBUG] 1
[TRACE] 1
[TRACE] 1
[DEBUG] 1
[TRACE] 1
[INFO]  1
[TRACE] 1
[DEBUG] 1
[TRACE] 1
[TRACE] 1
[DEBUG] 1
[TRACE] 1
[TRACE] 1
[DEBUG] 1
[TRACE] 1
[TRACE] 1
[DEBUG] 1
[TRACE] 1
[INFO]  1
[TRACE] 1
[DEBUG] 1
[TRACE] 1
Time taken: 83.155 seconds, Fetched: 374 row(s)
hive>
```

Figure 9.19: Mapping output

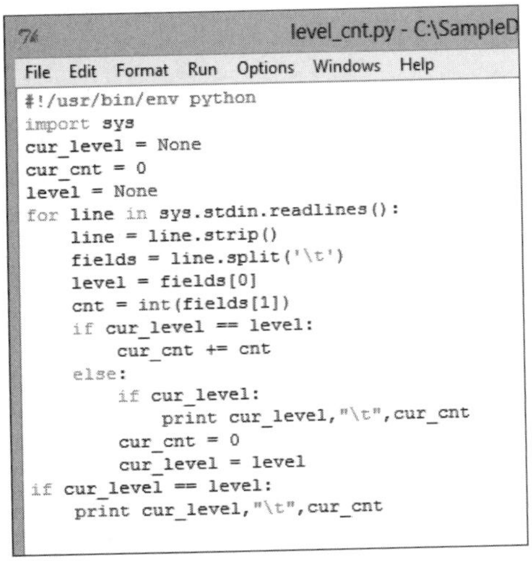

```
level_cnt.py - C:\SampleD
File Edit Format Run Options Windows Help
#!/usr/bin/env python
import sys
cur_level = None
cur_cnt = 0
level = None
for line in sys.stdin.readlines():
    line = line.strip()
    fields = line.split('\t')
    level = fields[0]
    cnt = int(fields[1])
    if cur_level == level:
        cur_cnt += cnt
    else:
        if cur_level:
            print cur_level,"\t",cur_cnt
        cur_cnt = 0
        cur_level = level
if cur_level == level:
    print cur_level,"\t",cur_cnt
```

Figure 9.20: Reduce script to aggregate log level counts

You combine the map and reduce script into your HiveQL where the output from the mapper is the input for the reducer. The `cluster by` statement is used to partition and sort the output of the mapping by the `loglevel` key. The following code processes the log files through the custom map and reduce scripts:

```
add file c:\sampledata\map_loglevel.py;
add file c:\sampledata\level_cnt.py;
from (from log_table SELECT TRANSFORM(log_entry)
USING 'python map_loglevel.py'
```

```
AS (loglevel,cnt) cluster by loglevel) map_out
Select Transform(map_out.loglevel,map_out.cnt)
using 'python level_cnt.py' as level, cnt;
```

Another way to call the scripts is by using the map and reduce statements, which are an alias for the `TRANSFORM` statement. The following code calls the scripts using the map and reduce statements and loads the results into a `script_test` table:

```
add file c:\sampledata\map_loglevel.py;
add file c:\sampledata\level_cnt.py;
from (from log_table Map log_entry USING 'python map_loglevel.py'
AS loglevel, cnt cluster by loglevel) map_out
Insert overwrite table script_test Reduce map_out.loglevel, map_out.cnt
using 'python level_cnt.py' as level, cnt;
```

Figure 9.21 shows the aggregated counts of the different log levels.

```
Job 0: Map: 1  Reduce: 1   Cumulative CPU: 1.874 sec   HDFS
te: 69 SUCCESS
Total MapReduce CPU Time Spent: 1 seconds 874 msec
OK
[DEBUG]         118
[ERROR]         1
[FATAL]         0
[INFO]  26
[TRACE]         221
[WARN]  2
Time taken: 89.272 seconds, Fetched: 6 row(s)
hive>
```

Figure 9.21: Output from the map-reduce scripts

Creating a Custom Map-reduce Script

In this exercise, we create a custom mapping script that takes a set of four measurements and returns the maximum value of the four. Figure 9.22 shows the input file, which you can download from `www.wiley.com/go/microsoftbigdatasolutions`.

Open your favorite text editor and enter the following code. Make sure to pay attention to the indenting:

```
#!/usr/bin/env python
import sys
for line in sys.stdin.readlines():
   line = line.strip()
   fields = line.split('\t')
   time = fields[0]
   sensor= fields[1]
   maxvalue = max(fields[2:5])
   print time,"\t",sensor,"\t",maxvalue
```

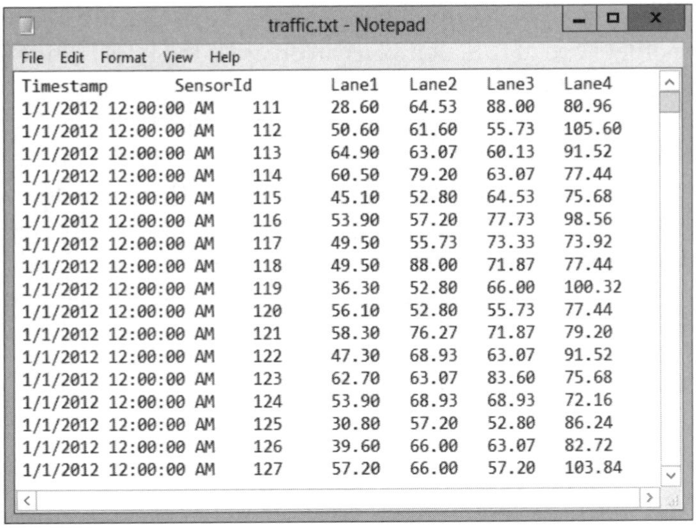

traffic.txt - Notepad

File Edit Format View Help

Timestamp	SensorId	Lane1	Lane2	Lane3	Lane4
1/1/2012 12:00:00 AM	111	28.60	64.53	88.00	80.96
1/1/2012 12:00:00 AM	112	50.60	61.60	55.73	105.60
1/1/2012 12:00:00 AM	113	64.90	63.07	60.13	91.52
1/1/2012 12:00:00 AM	114	60.50	79.20	63.07	77.44
1/1/2012 12:00:00 AM	115	45.10	52.80	64.53	75.68
1/1/2012 12:00:00 AM	116	53.90	57.20	77.73	98.56
1/1/2012 12:00:00 AM	117	49.50	55.73	73.33	73.92
1/1/2012 12:00:00 AM	118	49.50	88.00	71.87	77.44
1/1/2012 12:00:00 AM	119	36.30	52.80	66.00	100.32
1/1/2012 12:00:00 AM	120	56.10	52.80	55.73	77.44
1/1/2012 12:00:00 AM	121	58.30	76.27	71.87	79.20
1/1/2012 12:00:00 AM	122	47.30	68.93	63.07	91.52
1/1/2012 12:00:00 AM	123	62.70	63.07	83.60	75.68
1/1/2012 12:00:00 AM	124	53.90	68.93	68.93	72.16
1/1/2012 12:00:00 AM	125	30.80	57.20	52.80	86.24
1/1/2012 12:00:00 AM	126	39.60	66.00	63.07	82.72
1/1/2012 12:00:00 AM	127	57.20	66.00	57.20	103.84

Figure 9.22: Input traffic data

Save the file as `get_maxValue.py` in a reachable folder (for example, `C:\SampleData`). In the Hive command-line console, create a `speeds` table and load the data from `traffic.txt` into it:

```
CREATE TABLE speeds(recdate string, sensor string, v1 double, v2 double,
v3 double, v4 double) ROW FORMAT DELIMITED FIELDS TERMINATED BY '\t';
LOAD DATA LOCAL INPATH 'c:\sampledata\traffic.txt'
OVERWRITE INTO TABLE speeds;
```

Add a reference to the file and the `TRANSFORM` statement to call the script:

```
add file C:\SampleData\get_maxValue.py;
SELECT TRANSFORM(s.recdate,s.sensor,s.v1,s.v2,s.v3,s.v4)
USING 'python get_maxValue.py'
AS (recdate,sensor,maxvalue) FROM speeds s;
```

The data output should look similar to Figure 9.23.

Creating Your Own UDFs for Hive

As mentioned previously, Hive contains a number of function types depending on the processing involved. The simplest type is the UDF, which takes a row in, processes it, and returns the row back. The UDAF is a little more involved because it performs an aggregation on input values and reduces the number of rows coming out. The other type of function you can create is the UDTF, which takes a row in and parses it out into a table.

If you followed along in the earlier section on building custom UDFs for Pig, you will find that building UDFs for Hive is a similar experience. First, you create a project in your favorite Java development environment. Then, you add a reference to the `hive-exec.jar` and the `hive-serde.jar` files. These are located in the `hive` folder in the `lib` subfolder. After you add these references, you add an `import` statement to the `org.apache.hadoop.hive.ql.exec.UDF` class and extend it with a custom class:

```
package Com.BigData.hadoop.hive.SampleUDF;
import org.apache.hadoop.hive.ql.exec.UDF;
public class OrderNums extends UDF{

}
```

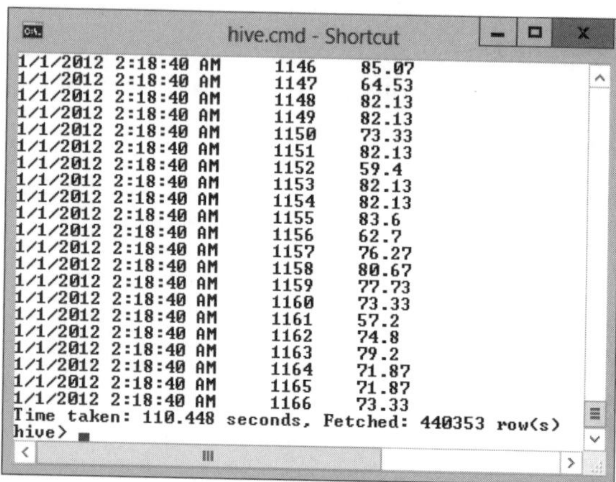

Figure 9.23: Output of the `get_maxValue.py` script

The next step is to add an evaluate function that will do the processing and return the results. The following code processes the two integers passed in and returns the larger value. If they are equal it returns null. Because you are using the `IntWritable` class, you need to add an import for pointing to the `org, apache .hadoop.io.IntWritable` class in the `Hadoop-core.jar` file:

```
package Com.BigData.hadoop.hive.SampleUDF;
import org.apache.hadoop.io.IntWritable;
import org.apache.hadoop.hive.ql.exec.UDF;
public class GetMaxInt extends UDF{

    public IntWritable evaluate(IntWritable x, IntWritable y)
```

```
    {
        if (x.get()>y.get())
            return x;
        else if (x.get()<y.get())
            return y;
        else
            return null;
    }
}
```

After creating and compiling the code into a jar file, deploy it to the `hive` directory. Once deployed you add the file to the hive class path and create an alias for the function using the Hive command line:

```
add jar C:\hdp\hadoop\hive-0.11.0.1.3.0.0-0380\lib\SampleUDF.jar;
create temporary function GetMaxInt as
'Com.BigData.hadoop.hive.SampleUDF.GetMaxInt';
```

You can now call the UDF in your HiveQL. Pass in two integers to get the larger value:

```
select f1, f2, GetMaxInt(f1,f2) from TestData;
```

Figure 9.24 shows the resulting output.

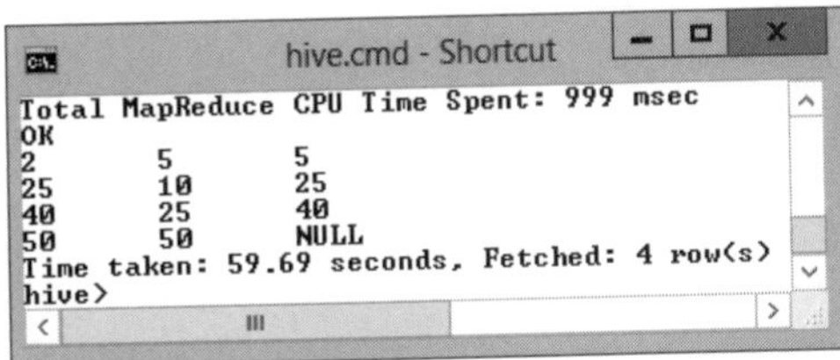

Figure 9.24: Sample UDF output

Once you are comfortable creating custom UDFs for Hive, you can investigate creating UDAFs and UDTFs. You can find more information about creating custom functions on the Apache Hive Wiki (`https://cwiki.apache.org/confluence/display/Hive/Home`).

Summary

In this chapter, you saw how Pig and Hive are used to apply data processing on top of Hadoop. You can use these tools to perform complex extracting, transformation, and loading (ETL) of your big data. Both of these tools process the data using functions created in Java code. Some of these functions are part of the native functionality of the toolset and are ready to use right out of the box. Some of the functions you can find through the open source community. You can download and install the jar files for these libraries and use them to extend the native functionality of your scripts. If you are comfortable programming in Java, you can even create your own functions to extend the functionality to meet your own unique processing requirements.

One takeaway from this chapter should be an appreciation of how extendable Pig Latin and HiveQL are at using pluggable interfaces. This chapter might even jump-start you to investigate further the process of creating and maybe even sharing your own custom function libraries.

Part

V

Big Data and SQL Server Together

In This Part

CHAPTER

10

Data Warehouses and Hadoop Integration

WHAT YOU WILL LEARN IN THIS CHAPTER:

- Understanding the Current "State of the Union"
- Learning About the Challenges Faced with the Traditional Data Warehouse
- Discovering Hadoop's Impact on Data Warehouses and Design
- Introducing Parallel Data Warehouse
- Finding Out About PDW's Architecture
- Grasping the Concepts Behind Project Polybase
- Gaining Insight on How to Use Polybase in Solutions
- Looking into the Future for Polybase

There has never been a more exciting time to be working in the analytics and data warehousing space; and it most certainly is a *space*. Data warehouses should be considered to be a place for free thinking—logical entities that holistically span the business, not physical beings constrained by limits of today's technology and yesterday's decisions. The aspiration for the new world of data is liberty: seamless, friction free-integration across the enterprise and beyond.

Therefore, we start by taking a deeper look at the emerging relationship between data warehouses and Hadoop. The current methods using Sqoop offer limited value, but both data warehouse vendors and Hadoop need more. More importantly, business has demanded more. More so than ever, data warehouse vendors have really had to up their game to demonstrate their value and thought leadership to the enterprise in the face of the disruptive technology that is Hadoop.

This chapter focuses on the changes Microsoft has been making to their data warehouse offerings to address the challenges faced by data warehouses and also how they are embracing Hadoop, offering industry-level innovation to Hadoop integration with Project Polybase. Let's get started.

State of the Union

When I think about data warehouses, I am often reminded of this famous Donald Rumsfeld quote:

> *"There are known knowns; there are things we know that we know. There are known unknowns; that is to say, there are things that we now know we don't know. But there are also unknown unknowns—there are things we do not know we don't know."*

In my mind, I compartmentalize this quote into Table 10.1.

Table 10.1: Compartmentalizing Data Warehousing

	KNOWN KNOWNS	KNOWN UNKNOWNS	UNKNOWN UNKNOWNS
Reporting	☒		
Business Intelligence		☒	
Analytics			☒

Traditional data warehouses have been focused on historical analysis and performance. In other words, we are looking back. At best, we get as far as the *known unknowns*. The fact that we can model, shape, and organize the data is evidence of the fact that we know what we are looking for. Although this is helpful to operationally optimize a business process, it actually isn't "intelligence" and it isn't transformative. It's not going to help us get close to answering the *unknown unknowns*. In actuality, the very fact that we've modeled the data may make it impossible, because in so doing we may have lost subtle nuances in the data that only exist in its raw, most granular form.

However, the beauty of the new world of data warehousing and analytics is that it is all about answering questions. In recent times, advances in technology have enabled us to ask bigger, more exciting, interesting, and open-ended questions—in short *big questions*. The question is what puts the *big* in big data. What's more, we can now answer those big questions.

Challenges Faced by Traditional Data Warehouse Architectures

What is a traditional architecture when it is at home? Every warehouse I come across certainly has some distinguishing features that make it different or special. However, many of these warehouses usually share one very common element in their architecture: they are designed to a symmetric multiprocessor (SMP) architecture; that is, they are designed to scale *up*. When you exceed the capabilities of the existing server, you go out and buy a bigger box. This is a very effective pattern for smaller systems, but it does have its drawbacks. These drawbacks become particularly evident when we start to consider some of the challenges businesses face today. Later in this section we will cover scale-out approaches, but first we will focus on the inherent issues with scale-up.

Technical Constraints

This section identifies, qualifies, and discusses some of the technical challenges facing data warehouses in today's environments. You will recognize many of these challenges from your own environments. This list is not intended to be exhaustive, but it does cover a number of the issues:

- Scaling compute
- Shared resources
- Data volumes and I/O throughput
- Application architecture changes
- Return on investment

Scaling Compute

Scaling compute is hard, especially if you have designed an SMP architecture. You are limited on two fronts: server and software.

Server

The first question to ask yourself is this: How many CPU sockets do you have at your disposal? 1, 2, 4, or 8? Next, what CPUs are you using to fill them? 4, 6, 8, 10 core? At best you could get up to 80 physical cores. With hyper-threading, you could double this figure to get to 160 virtual CPUs. However, in this configuration, not all CPUs are created equally. What do you do after that? Wait for HP to build a server with more CPU sockets on the motherboard? Wait for Intel to release a new CPU architecture? Those often aren't realistic answers and aren't going to be tolerated by a business thirsty for information.

Software

Let's assume that you have the maximum number of cores available to you. In today's market, that means you have a very nice eight–CPU socket server from Hewlett Packard in your data center. Now what? Well, first of all, you need to configure the software to make sure that you are addressing those cores efficiently using a non-uniform memory address (NUMA) configuration. Configuring a server for NUMA is beyond the scope of this book. However, you will have to trust me that this is an advanced topic and generally involves bringing in expert consulting resources to ensure that it is done properly. However, this brings me to my first point: the bigger the server, the greater the need to have an "expert"-level operational team to support it.

It could be argued that this is a one-time cost, so, assuming you know you have to pay it, let's leave it there. Besides, it brings me to the next challenge: generating parallel queries. Even though you might have built a beautiful server and have it expertly configured, you still need to make sure that the database makes that asset sweat—that means running parallel queries.

SQL Server's optimizer *can* generate query plans that use many cores (that is, a parallel plan). This is governed by two factors: the user's query and the cost threshold for parallelism setting.

Depending on the type of query issued by the user, SQL Server may or may not generate a parallel plan. This could be due to a number of reasons. For example, not all operations are parallelizable by SQL Server in a single query.

The key takeaway here is that SQL Server does not offer a mode that *forces* parallelism (a minimum degree of parallelism or MINDOP, if you will). SQL Server only offers a way to cap parallelism using the maximum degree of parallelism (MAXDOP) and the cost threshold mentioned previously.

Remember, SQL Server's query optimizer was not built from the ground up with data warehousing in mind. Over the years, it has had a number of features added to it that make it more suitable to this kind of workload. Nevertheless, it is a general-purpose optimizer and engine with data warehouse extensions.

Sharing Resources

What do we mean by sharing resources? In computing terms we talk about the key resources of CPU, I/O, and memory. Sharing resources is a mixed blessing. SMP data warehouses, for example, often benefit from these shared resources. Think of a join, for instance. We don't think twice about this, but the fact that we have a single memory address space means that we can join data in our SMP data warehouse freely because all the data is in the same place. However, when we think about scaling data warehouses, sharing can often lead to one thing: bottlenecks. Imagine having an Xbox One with only one controller. Only one person gets to have a go while everyone else has to wait.

When a resource is shared, it means that it potentially has many customers. When all those customers want to do is read from the resource, this is a great option. However, if those customers want to write, we hit problems. Resource access suddenly has to be synchronized to maintain the integrity of the write.

In database technology such as SQL Server, such synchronizations are managed. Locks and latches exemplify this concept. Locks deal with the logical updating of data on a data page. Latches are responsible for guaranteeing integrity of writes to memory addresses. The important thing to understand here is that these writes do not happen in isolation. Not only do they have to be synchronized, but they also have to be serialized. Everyone has to take his or her turn. This serialization is required because the resource is shared. So, for example, having a single buffer pool, latch, and lock manager constrains one's ability to scale.

The hardware also suffers the same challenges. Most SQL Server platforms deployed in production today suffer with shared storage, for example. When multiple systems are all accessing the same storage pools via a SAN, then this introduces multiple bottlenecks. Data warehouses are particularly sensitive to this type of resource constraint as they need to issue large sequential scans of data and, therefore, need a very capable I/O subsystem that can guarantee a consistently good level of performance. A server also has limits on the number of PCI cards that can be installed, thus limiting the number of I/O channels and therefore bandwidth it can receive.

To address these challenges both in hardware and software, we need to scale beyond shared resources. We need to "share nothing," and we need to scale out beyond a single set of resources. In our house, we've addressed the Xbox One scalability problem by having multiple controllers. However, that still means we all have to play the same game. The next step would naturally be to have multiple Xbox Ones to resolve that particular problem.

Data Volumes and I/O Throughput

Data warehouses grow. That should go without saying. However, this has not traditionally always been by as much as you might have thought. Of course, as warehouses mature and as businesses grow, more transactions flood in, expanding the need for capacity. However, this type of growth is usually manageable and tends to be measured by a percentage figure.

In recent times, warehouses have grown from gigabyte (GB) scale to terabyte (TB) scale. In an SMP world, that is manageable. Granted, greater care has to be taken to ensure that this data is delivered through the I/O channels at sufficient speed to keep the CPUs busy, but at this scale this has all been managed through reference architectures such as the SQL Server Fast Track Data Warehouse.

Fast Track provides users with tightly scoped hardware configurations that provide a balance of the three key compute resources—CPU, I/O, and memory. This has been coupled with software deployment and development guidance that maximize the benefits of these configurations. With Fast Track I/O, throughput has reached figures of 10GB/sec to 12GB/sec, leading to index and aggregate light designs. Where the response rates have been insufficient, these gaps have been plugged through the use of summary aggregates.

However, limits apply. Even the largest Fast Track deployments tap out at 120TB. That seems like a lot, but even at this scale, queries are starting to suffer from the lack of available throughput. Loading times can also suffer. To maintain the I/O throughput, Fast Track data warehouses must conform to a loading pattern that is optimized for sequential I/O. This loading pattern mandates a final insert using MAXDOP 1, which limits the overall load speed. Furthermore, Fast Track architectures are predicated on the assumption that SQL Server can handle a maximum of roughly 300MB/sec per (physical) core of data. Therefore, the maximum core count places a cap on the storage capacity a system can meaningfully address without adversely affecting query performance.

Moving forward, a 120TB cap might prove to be too small. However, the truth is that 120TB cap is already too small. The rise of Hadoop is testament to that. Data volumes are growing exponentially and are therefore driving storage requirements that need to be measured by a multiplier, not a percentage. That makes an order of magnitude of difference to the size of the warehouse and, as architects, is something we need to design for.

So, where is this data coming from? Well, clearly, we can look to things such as social media, machine data, sensor data, and web analytics as examples of new data sources driving this change. However, there are other reasons too.

Historically, companies (especially in Europe, the Middle East, and Africa [EMEA]) have been good at archiving data and taking it offline (storing it on tape or some other media). Perhaps they've only been keeping a couple of years of data online. This is changing. Companies are being asked to keep more data online, either to feed analytical engines for training new models or for regulatory reasons. Businesses want to query over all their data and are much less tolerant of delays in response while data is retrieved from warm or cold storage.

In addition, companies are starting to exchange and sell data as products to other companies. Retailers have been buying data for years to aid analytics. Consider weather data as a classic example. How will the weather affect sales of ice cream? That seems easy enough. Depending on the granularity of the data requested, that may make a modest bump in the size of a warehouse.

Now consider another source: Think about the location data that your phone offers up to every app provider. Where have you been? What routes do you usually travel? Which shops do you actually visit? All manner of information is suddenly available, providing a much richer data set for analysts to review. However, not only is this data a rich source of information, it is also potentially truly massive. Imagine tacking every telco's warehouse onto yours.

Will Smith was certainly onto something when he portentously starred in *Enemy of the State*.

From a technical perspective, this means that we need more effective ways to hold significantly more data online in readily accessible formats.

Application Architecture Changes

It is often thought that scaling up involves a simple case of buying a bigger box and performing a "lift and shift" of a data warehouse. Nothing could be further from the truth. The data warehouse software will often have to be changed to take into consideration any advantage of the new resources. These changes may be evolutionary, but they certainly are not trivial. What's more, a lot of these costs are hidden costs that are usually not exposed to the business when making the decision to persevere with a scale-up solution. At best, these changes will help to make the most of the new infrastructure. However, let's be clear, such changes do not address the root cause: scaling up has limits that cannot be addressed through these kinds of application changes.

Let's take a couple of examples of typical application changes that are required as you scale up a data warehouse: database layout and fragmentation.

Database Layout

When the time comes to get the "next size up" from your preferred hardware vendor, you want to ensure that you have a balanced configuration of CPU, memory, and storage. This usually means buying a chunkier server and some additional storage trays. Once configured, the database now needs to be created. First, you design the physical architecture of the database; it will differ from the one you had previously, to make sure that you take advantage of the new hardware. At the least, you need to create database files across all the storage trays. However, to balance the data across all the storage, you will probably end up exporting out all the data and reloading it manually.

The export and import time can be lengthy, and it certainly will take the warehouse offline during this time. Depending on the volumes involved, this may require some custom development to intelligently partition and parallelize the process to minimize this outage. The import will also need some careful thought to ensure that the data is both loaded quickly (that is, in parallel) but also contiguously so that the result is a migrated database that supports a good, sequentially scanning workload.

Failure to consider these points will result in a warehouse that either doesn't fully leverage the new hardware or is heavily fragmented and therefore incapable of issuing large block I/O down to the new storage subsystem. This would seriously impact performance, slowing down responsiveness and ultimately impacting the availability of the data warehouse.

Fragmentation

When loading data into a data warehouse, you need to be mindful of fragmentation. Unlike transactional systems (online transactional processing [OLTP]), data warehouses observe a scan-centric I/O pattern that demands largely fragmentation-free tables.

As the size of the tables increase, this issue becomes more apparent and significantly more important. At a small scale, many warehouses benefit purely from moving from legacy, often virtualized, environments to dedicated platforms. The performance bump observed masks the underlying issues of fragmentation in database tables.

However, as the system grows, that performance bump is insufficient. Fragmentation needs to be addressed. This can often lead to a significant rewrite of data warehouse extract, transform, and load (ETL) software. This is no small undertaking. It is often said that the ETL of a data warehouse accounts for 75% of the effort in a data warehouse project. Consequently, these rewrites can attract a significant and often hidden cost. All the business sees is that changes take longer to deliver as service levels suffer.

Return on Investment

When dealing with a traditional SMP warehouse architecture, we have to consider how the costs stack up. Many of the costs when scaling up are clearly understood. If I buy a bigger box with more cores, it will cost me more money. The problem is that, say, doubling the cores doesn't simply double the cost. Often, it is more than double. It's a question of economies of scale, supply and demand, and of course, the fact that building bigger integrated boxes is a more complex and more valuable offering. This translates to nonlinear pricing, which moves further and further away from the line as the offering becomes less of a commodity.

And that's just the technical questions. What about the human resource capital employed to manage this system? As previously mentioned, a bigger, more sophisticated system requires greater levels of technical support and expertise engaged to maximize the investment that even with the best resources is unlikely to continue to achieve linear performance benefits. Can the existing team even maintain it? Can they be trained, or will experts or consultants be required to support and tune the system? These are all open questions that can be answered only by you and your team.

However, what we can say is that we have a system architecture that costs disproportionately more to buy and even more to maintain as it grows. Hardly a scalable model. Clearly, then, we need to look at alternatives (and preferably before issues such as cost force us to).

Business Challenges

In case you hadn't noticed, it's a tough world out there. Competition is rife. The consequences of competition often have brutal outcomes. Failure to change has seen established businesses go to the wall while other new, more dynamic, businesses continue to rise at unparalleled rates. We must adapt to the new economic climate, embracing opportunities and adapting rapidly as business models become stale.

As a result of this ruthless competition, my kids will never know the "joy" of a trip to Blockbusters to rent the latest movie. How many trips did you make only to find they've sold out or gone out of business? My children use online services like Netflix or Lovefilm instead. The thought of going to a shop to rent a movie seems absurd to them. Therefore, to stay ahead, businesses are looking at their data to provide them with genuinely new insights.

The buzz at the moment surrounds predictive analytics. Users want the ability to project and forecast more accurately and look for competitive advantages through new data "products." It's this desire to get into the business of the unknown unknowns that has transformed application architectures and, in turn, data warehouses.

This next section looks at the challenges that businesses face when trying to make informed decisions.

Data Sprawl

Once upon a time, this used to be known as SQL sprawl. However, the reality is that this data is not constrained to disparate databases and also is not limited to the enterprise systems either. Historically, we used to just worry about stovepipe applications.

The challenge here is that the data can come from anywhere. Users are able to collate data from literally any source for their own reporting. The opportunities presented by self-service models has led to a decentralized view of data. This can make certain types of data analysis challenging. Ideally, we want to leverage compute resources as close to the data as possible and integrate these sources in a seamless way.

However, to achieve this we may need to take an increasingly logical view of our data warehouse. We wouldn't, for example, want to move masses of cloud-born web analytics and machine telemetry data down to an on-premise warehouse to perform an in-depth path analysis. The time it would take to continually stream this data may lead to unacceptable latency in our reporting.

This latency may erode the value of the insights presented. Therefore, we might need to take a more practical approach.

24/7 Operations

Business is global—at least that is what all the Hong Kong Shanghai Bank of China (HSBC) adverts keep telling me. This means that there is always someone, somewhere, who is awake and wanting to interact with our services. At least we hope that is the case. What this has led to is considerable pressure being placed on "operational" outages. Backup windows, load windows, and patch management have all felt the force of a 24/7 business.

These days, huge emphasis is placed on loading data really quickly while also having to balance the needs of the business for reporting. We need to build processes that offer balance. It's no good taking the system offline to load data. We need to target the mixed workload.

Near Real-time Analysis

Roll back the time transaction five years and data warehouses were deemed up-to-date when they had yesterday's data loaded inside them. At first there was resistance. Who really needed reporting for the last hour or even quarter of an hour? Roll forward five years and now data warehouses are being used for fraud detection, risk analytics, cross-selling, and recommendation engines to name but a few use cases that *need* near real time.

To get really close to what is happening in real time, we need to take the analytics closer to the source. We may no longer be able to afford the multiple repository hops we traditionally see with traditional architectures. Can we really wait for the data to be loaded into the warehouse only for it to be sucked out by Analysis Services during cube processing? I am certainly seeing fewer people wanting to pay that latency price. Once the data has been integrated, they want their analytical tools to query the data in situ. Therefore, people are looking at relational online analytical processing (ROLAP) engines with renewed interest. The Tabular model, offered by SQL Server Analysis Services, also offers DirectQuery as an alternative.

New Data

It should be no surprise to learn that social media has revolutionized the kind of insights that users want from their warehouse. Brands can be made or destroyed by their perceived online presence. A good, responsive customer support initiative can have a massive multiplier effect to a company's image. Therefore, sentiment analysis applications are big business.

What is possibly not so widely recognized is that all these social media data sources are not "owned" by the enterprise. Companies have been forced to come out of their shells and relinquish some element of control to a third-party site. Want to be on Facebook? Then accept that your page is `www.facebook.com/BigBangDataCo`. That's okay for me; my company is ahem... boutique. However, did you really think you'd ever see Coca-Cola or Nike doing the same thing? What's more, for the first time a company's Facebook page or Twitter handle could actually be more a valuable property and a richer source of analysis than a company's own website.

To complicate matters, the majority of these new properties (Facebook, Twitter, LinkedIn, and so on) typically exist online. We need to integrate with them and possibly third-party engines that provide specific value-added services (such as sentiment analysis) to extract maximum value and insight from the data.

Social media data is just one example. Let's think about machine data for a moment. This dataset is huge. There's a myriad of sensors streaming vast quantities of information, providing a wealth of opportunity for machine learning and enhanced operations. It doesn't all have to be austere factory or plant information either. Think about smart metering in your home, healthcare heart monitoring, and car insurance risk assessment devices (especially for young drivers), all the way to fitness devices such as Fitbit or Nike Fuelband that are so popular these days. All are brilliant new data sources that can be analyzed and would benefit from machine learning. We've moved a long way from just thinking about the web, social media, and clickstream analytics.

For IT we could take data center management as just one example theme. Every server is a rich source of data about the enterprise. Being able to refine data center operations presents organizations with fantastic opportunities for cost savings and streamlined operations. A whole industry has sprung up around what we call *infrastructure intelligence*. One such company is Splunk. They have built a fantastic product for delivering insight on our data centers and are able to crawl and index vast quantities of machine data to provide insight on how our data center is being managed.

However, as with all warehouses, this data provides the most value when we integrate it with other disparate data sources to glean insights and add value to the business. Otherwise, we simply have another (albeit very cool) stovepipe application.

Hadoop's Impact on the Data Warehouse Market

This section delves into the Hadoop developer mindset to understand how the philosophy differs significantly from that of the data warehouse developer. By understanding the approach taken by Hadoop developers, we can set ourselves up for a more informed discussion and identify the most appropriate points of integration between the different environments. Furthermore, we should also identify opportunities to leverage the respective technologies for maximum value. It is important to recognize that both Hadoop and relational databases have distinct advantages and disadvantages. We have to evaluate the scenario. As architects we are obligated to leave our zealotry at the door and search for the optimal solution.

Let's move forward and discuss the following topics:

- Keep everything
- Code first (schema later)
- Model the value
- Throw compute at the problem

Keep Everything

The first rule for the Hadoop developer is to "keep everything." This means keeping the data in its raw form. Cleansing operations, transformations, and aggregations of data remove subtle nuances in the data that *may* hold value. Therefore, a Hadoop developer is motivated to keep everything and work from this base data set.

The advantages here are clear. If I always have access to the raw data online, my analysis is not restricted, and I have complete creative freedom to explore the data.

Coming from a relational database background I was actually quite envious of Hadoop's ability to offer this option. Often, it just isn't feasible to hold this volume of data in a database. The scale at which Hadoop can hold data online is quite unlike anything seen by relational database technology. Even the largest data warehouses will be in the low petabyte (PB) range. Facebook's Hadoop cluster by contrast had 100 PB+ of data under management and was growing at 0.5PB a day. Those figures were released a couple of years ago.

An esteemed colleague and friend of mine in the database community, Thomas Kejser, once proposed an architecture that leveraged Hadoop as a giant repository for all data received by the warehouse thus removing the need for an operational data store (ODS), data vault, or third normal form model. He argues that that the data warehouse could always easily rehydrate a data feed if needed down the road. We'll discuss this in more detail later in this chapter. However, take a look at Figure 10.1 to get your creative juices flowing.

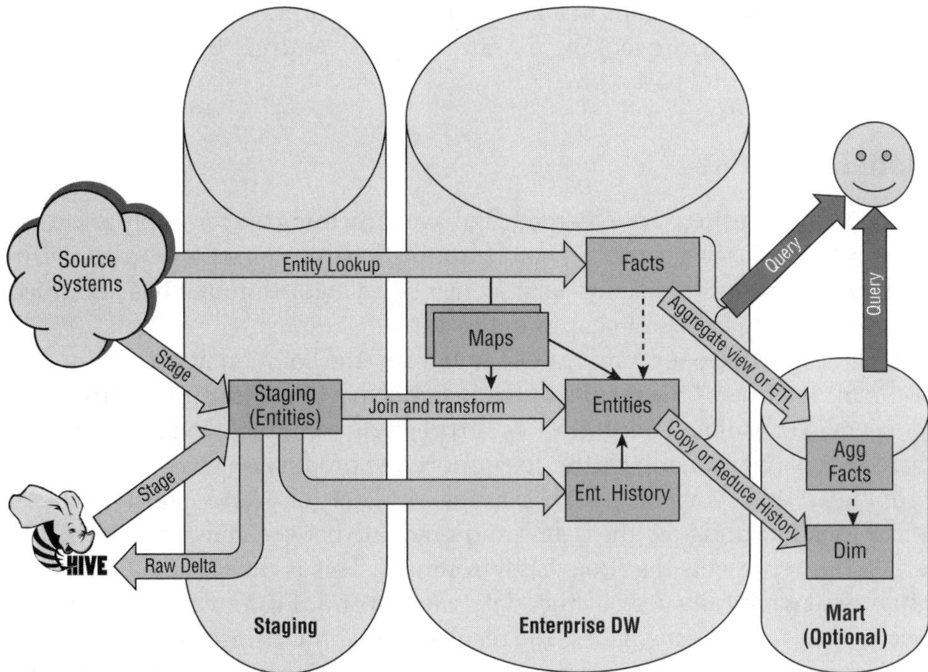

Figure 10.1: Visualizing Thomas Kejser's Big Picture Data Warehouse Architecture

NOTE **You can read more about Thomas' architecture on his blog** `http://blog.kejser.org/2011/08/30/the-big-picture-edwdw-architecture/`.

Code First (Schema Later)

This code-first approach does have other advantages. Cleansing operations, for example, "get in the way" of mining the data for valuable nuggets of information. There is also reduced risk in using code first when you are keeping all the data in its raw form. You can always augment your program, redeploy, and restart the analysis because you still have all the data at your disposal in its raw form.

You can't always go back if you have observed a schema-first approach. If you have modeled the data to follow one structure you may have transformed or aggregated the source information making it impossible to go back to the beginning and reload from scratch. Worse still, the source data may have been thrown away, which could have been collected years ago, it might be difficult or in some cases impossible to get that data back.

Consequently, Hadoop developers tend to shy away from a schema-first/code-later design. They worry less about the structure of the data and instead focus on looking for the value in the data. Remember, Hadoop developers aren't so motivated by plugging gaps in a key performance indicator (KPI) report. Data scientists, especially, are looking for new insights, which is, by its very nature, a more experimental paradigm.

Model the Value

Once a valuable pattern has emerged, we have something we can apply a schema to. However, don't just constrain your thinking when you see the word *model*. In the world of analytics, that model may just be an algorithm that has identified some interesting trends or shapes in the data.

A Hadoop developer may choose to harden the solution at this point and also may "graduate" the results of the insights to a new Hadoop environment for users to consume. This pattern is surprisingly common. Don't assume that there is only one Hadoop cluster to support one production environment.

In Figure 10.2, you can see an example of what the Hadoop environment might look like and how the data could graduate between environments. The far-left bar represents the Bronze environment. This is the raw data and is an environment typically used by the "data scientist" mining for value. As patterns emerge and value is established, the results might find themselves moving into the Silver environment for "power users" or "information workers" to work with. There are usually more power users than there are data scientists. Finally, the data may go through one last graduation phase from Silver to Gold. This might be the environment exposed to the broadest spectrum of the business (that is, the "consumers" of the data). If there are dashboards to be built and so forth, it is likely that Gold is the target environment to perform these tasks.

As the data graduates, we should start seeing other patterns emerge. These patterns aren't constrained to the value *in* the data but also to attributes *of* the data. Typically, we'll see the data take on greater structure to facilitate more mainstream analysis and integration with other tools. Furthermore, we would expect to see improvements in data quality and integrity in these other environments. When we think about integrating this data with the broader enterprise, this becomes increasingly important (because we need to pick our moment when it comes to data integration).

Throw Compute at the Problem

All this flexibility comes at a cost, and that cost is a need to throw greater amounts of compute power at the problem. This philosophy is baked into Hadoop's architecture and is why batch engines like MapReduce exist. MapReduce's ability to scale compute resources is a central tenet of Hadoop. Therefore, Hadoop developers have really taken this to heart.

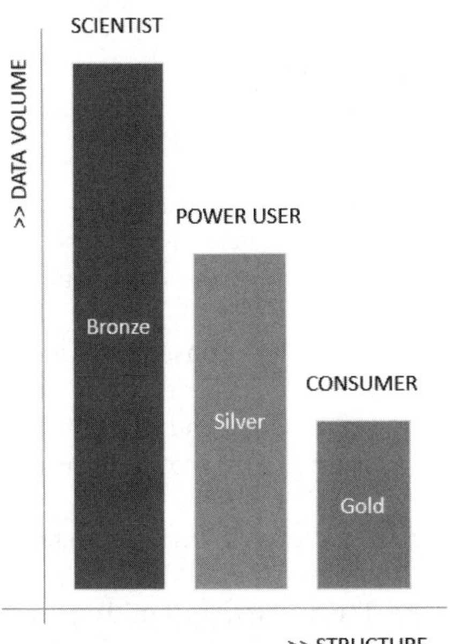

Figure 10.2: Understanding Gold, Silver, and Bronze Hadoop environments

In some cases, there is an overreliance on this compute, which can lead to a level of laziness. Rather than optimize the data processing and possibly leverage other technologies, Hadoop developers can "waste" CPU by re-executing the same MapReduce program over and over. Once the trend has been established, the unknown unknown has been identified. It is now a known unknown.

Remember that the MapReduce program knows nothing about the data in the files contained within the Hadoop Distributed File System (HDFS). This is in stark contrast to the approach taken by relational database systems. The schema and model imposed by a database designer empowers the database engine to hold statistical information on the data held inside the tables. This leads to optimized computing and a significant reduction in compute resources required.

As Hadoop 2.0 takes hold, it will be interesting to see how the Hadoop community adopts other engines. We'll have to see how quickly they move to interactive query with Tez as the underpinning engine, for example. Furthermore, we'll have to wait and see which engine is adopted by the community for other types of problems. The battleground seems drawn for complex event processing, for example. Are you ready for the Flume versus Storm showdown? One thing is certain: how each project leverages the compute at its disposal will be a significant factor. It will, however, only be one factor. Expect ease of programmatic use to be just as important, if not more important. After all, the "winner" will be the project that offers the fastest "time to insight." In the world of Hadoop, insight is king.

Introducing Parallel Data Warehouse (PDW)

Much like the SETI@Home program, Parallel Data Warehouse (PDW) is a scale-out solution, designed to bring massive computing resources to bear on a problem. Both PDW and SETI, therefore, are massively parallel processing (MPP) systems. However, unlike SETI, PDW is designed to support many forms of analysis, not just for searching for alien life.

PDW is a distributed database technology that supports set-based theory and the relational model. This is what sets it apart from Hadoop, even when used with Hive. PDW supports transactions, concurrency, security, and more. All the things you expect from a database, but backed by significantly more resources, courtesy of the scale-out architecture.

Currently, PDW can sometimes be seen by the market as being a niche technology. For starters, Microsoft is not ubiquitously known for building scale-out database technology products. It has one: PDW. It is known for building SQL Server, which is a scale-up solution. It is, therefore, not always at the forefront of architects' minds when building distributed systems. Furthermore, it's often perceived that MPP systems are expensive and, therefore, suitable only for truly massive datasets that are petabytes in size. This is not the way to think about MPP or PDW. MPP solutions aren't as expensive as people think. Likewise, scaling storage capacity is only one goal when using an appliance like PDW. However, it is the most easily understood aspect, and so this is why people talk about it most. I really think it is the least compelling reason.

Consequently, this general lack of brand awareness, coupled with some preconceived technology notions, often results in MPP technology and PDW being eliminated from a solution build before being investigated as an option. This is a real shame. I've seen many customers who would have really benefitted from PDW, but have chosen to implement on SMP technology and have suffered as a consequence. Even when they have heard of PDW, some people have ultimately reached for their security blanket and architected for SMP. I know some of those customers, and they are regretting that decision.

Therefore, in this section we are going to focus on the what, why, and how of PDW so you, the reader, get a much better understanding of why PDW is an important technology that delivers great value to business users. My intention is that you can also use this information to make an informed decision in your next project.

What Is PDW?

PDW is unlike any other technology in the Microsoft Data Platform. For starters, it is not just software, and it's more than hardware plus software. It's an appliance. That means it comes with both hardware and software all preconfigured to offer best practices, high availability, and balanced performance, thus reducing the burden on the developers and the operations team.

The analogy I like to use is that of a kettle. Kettle's do a job for you. They boil water. You could use a pan on the stove, but you don't. If you want to boil water quickly and easily, you buy a kettle. You might look online, read some reviews, and check pricing; but basically, you find one that performs to your needs (and preferably matches the décor of your kitchen). One quick trip to the store and you have a kettle. You unbox it, plug it in, and away you go. You are boiling water, quickly, simply, and efficiently. Remember, though, that it's an appliance. It has a specific purpose; you can't use a kettle to heat soup. (Well, you can, but the result is less than ideal.)

PDW is the same. You can do some research online, pick your preferred hardware vendor (HP, Dell, or Quanta), and decide how much compute resources you want to have at your disposal. You order the kit, and 4 to 6 weeks later a preinstalled, preconfigured rack arrives at your data center. It's unboxed (consider this a white glove service), plugged in, and plumbed into your network. Data warehousing in a box. Note that this is not transactional processing in a box. Remember, we support boiling water, not heating soup with PDW.

NOTE **Quanta have only recently entered the market. At the time of writing the PDW appliance using Quanta is only available in the USA and China. Both HP and Dell are available worldwide.**

Okay, so the question that tends to follow is this: What happens if you want to boil water more quickly or boil greater quantities of water? You simply buy a bigger/better kettle. The same applies with PDW. If you want queries to run faster or you want to handle more data, you can simply extend your appliance to provide you with additional computing resources. The nice part of extending PDW is that the costs are known, predictable, *and* linear. This is one of the key aspects of scale-out solutions. When you extend them you are using more of the same commodity kit.

Contrast this with a normal SQL Server data warehouse build, even one with guidance like a Fast Track solution. These are more like buying a box of Lego. Sure, they come with instructions and guidance on assembly, but it's up to you to assemble it correctly. If you don't follow the instructions you are unlikely to have built the Lego Hogwarts castle you purchased. You are much more likely to have created something completely different. It might look like a castle and feel like a castle but it won't be Hogwarts. The same principle applies to Fast Track.

Furthermore, how do you extend it? Well, extending a server isn't really very simple, is it? It's not like you can graft another couple of CPU sockets onto the motherboard, now is it?

Why Is PDW Important?

PDW is actually branded *SQL Server Parallel Data Warehouse*. This leads to misconceptions about what PDW is or isn't. Actually, it'd be more accurate to say it is Parallel Data Warehouse, powered by SQL Server. There is an important but subtle difference. SQL Server is a mature utilitarian database engine with some enhanced functionality aimed at improving performance for the data warehouse workload. It has a myriad of features and options to support other workloads and products as well. PDW is different. PDW is designed purely for data warehousing. It is built as a black box solution that is designed to streamline development, improve performance, and reduce the burden on operational teams.

However, here is a different way of looking at PDW:

"PDW is the de facto storage engine for data warehousing on the Microsoft Data Platform." — James Rowland-Jones, circa 2013

I realize that I am quoting myself. It's not my intention to be egotistical. However, I do believe it to be true, and I don't know of anyone else who has come out and publicly said anything to the same degree. Besides which, I want to share with you my reasoning. I don't know when I started using it exactly, but it is something that has resonated well with attendees of the PDW training I've given, and I hope that it will resonate with you too.

To help back up my somewhat grandiose hypothesis, I want to draw your attention to the following key points, which I explain more fully in the following sections:

- PDW is the only scale-out relational database technology in the Microsoft Data Platform.
- Data warehouse features come first to PDW.
- PDW is the only Microsoft relational database technology that seamlessly integrates with Hadoop.
- PDW has two functional releases a year.

PDW Is the Only Scale-out Relational Database in the Microsoft Platform

Some attempts have been made at scale-out with the likes of federated databases and distributed partitioned views, but it is also fair to say that SQL Server was designed to scale up. It was also not designed from the ground up with data warehousing in mind. PDW, however, is designed in this way. It is a workload-specific appliance focused on the data warehouse.

The fact that PDW is a scale-out technology is incredibly important. It places Microsoft into the same bracket as other vendors of MPP distributed databases, such as Teradata, Netezza, Oracle, SAP HANA, and Pivotal, with technology that has the ability to scale to the demands of big data projects. The only relational database technology that has any presence in the world of big data involves scale-out MPP databases. Each and every one of them purports to have integration with Hadoop in some form or other. PDW is no exception.

MPP databases offer some compelling benefits for the data warehouse and for big data. The primary benefit is the ability to scale *across* servers enabling a divide and conquer philosophy to data processing. By leveraging a number of servers, PDW can address many more CPU cores than would ever be possible in an SMP configuration.

In its biggest configuration, PDW supports 56 data processing servers (known as compute nodes) comprising the following resources:

- 896 physical CPU cores
- 14TB of memory
- 6PB+ of storage capacity

What is even more impressive is that PDW forces you to use all these resources. In other words, it forces parallelism into your queries. This is fantastic for data warehousing.

Imagine having an option in SQL Server that gave you an option to run with a *minimum* degree of parallelism or MINDOP(448). You can't? No, of course you can't, because there is no such option in SQL Server. With PDW, you have that by default.

UNDERSTANDING MINDOP

448 represents one thread for every distribution on a 56-compute node appliance. There are 8 distributions on each node. In this configuration PDW would issue 448 separate queries in parallel against a distributed table. Hence, MINDOP(448). Fear not, we will discuss distributions and distributed tables shortly. The key takeaway here is that PDW delivers an additional level of parallelism that simply isn't available in SQL Server.

Data Warehouse Features Come First to PDW

Just think about this list of features; all were first in PDW:

- Updateable column store
- Enhanced batch mode for query processing
- Native integration with Hadoop via Polybase
- New Cardinality Estimator

- Cost-based Distributed SQL Query Engine
- New windowing functions including lag and lead

It's a pretty impressive list. I am sure that there are other examples, as well. In the case of Polybase, it is an exclusive feature, as well, which helps to define PDW's unique selling point (USP).

PDW and Hadoop

We just touched on this, and it is worth restating. PDW offers native integration with Hadoop via Polybase—something that we are going to really dive into later in this chapter. The key takeaway here is that Polybase is integrated into a component of PDW, not a component of SQL Server. That component is called the Data Movement Service (DMS).

NOTE **The fact that the DMS was chosen as the integration point means that this feature isn't coming to the box product known as SQL Server anytime soon. The DMS is PDW specific, so if you want to get on the Polybase bus, you will need to buy a PDW ticket.**

PDW Release Cadence

As mentioned previously a few times now, PDW is an appliance, an integrated blend of both hardware and software. This fact has other implications that are less obvious. For example, PDW doesn't *do* service packs. PDW has appliance updates (AUs), with the team committed to delivering an AU every 6 months.

AUs differ from service packs in one notable way. The releases are functional and do not just contain fixes to defects. In actual fact, they are packed full of features targeting the data warehouse work stream. Therefore, the team can rev the product in a much more agile fashion and respond to customer demand as appropriate.

How PDW Works

We are going to start by keeping things simple and build from there. This section is a conceptual introduction to PDW.

PDW uses a single master node known as the *control node* as the front door to the appliance and is the gateway to the data. The data is held on a number of *compute nodes*. The vast majority of data processing occurs in the compute nodes. The ability to continually add compute nodes gives PDW its scale-out ability. The challenge when scaling out is that different subsets of data are held on different nodes and may need to seamlessly move the data to resolve a users' query. PDW achieves this with an external process called the Data Movement Service (DMS).

NOTE The DMS is not part of SQL Server; it is an entirely separate process. When data needs to move across the appliance, DMS moves it. The DMS exists on both the control and the compute nodes and is managed by its own DMS Manager that resides on the control node.

The compute and control nodes are connected together by two networks: Ethernet and Infiniband. The Ethernet network manages basic communication between the nodes: heartbeat, status, acknowledgments, that sort of thing. The Infiniband network is used for moving data. Infiniband is an ultra-low-latency network, which is ideally suited for moving large volumes of data at speed. PDW uses FDR Infiniband, which is capable of sustaining 56Gbps.

When you connect your application, including SQL Server Data Tools (SSDT), you will connect to the control node. The control node accepts the request, generates the DSQL plan and orchestrates a series of highly parallelized operations across the compute nodes, thus achieving scale out. However, the real secret to how PDW works is down to how it creates databases and tables.

Distributed Databases

Think about a piece of toast. That piece of toast is your PDW appliance. Now what do you want to put on that toast? Butter and Marmite, of course!

I LOVE MARMITE

For the international audience who might not understand the reference Marmite is a vegetarian savoury spread made from yeast extract that is itself a by-product of brewing beer. Please head over to `https://www.facebook.com/Marmite` for more details. Better still go and try it! Unless you are in Denmark, of course, where it is banned—only the Danes really understand why. Too bad; I know many of them love it there, too.

Now when spreading butter on your toast, you want to make sure that you get a nice even spread across the slice. Marmite has quite a strong, distinctive flavor, so it's even more important that you get this right. You want to make sure that every bite you take gets a bit of everything; not too much to be overbearing, and not too little so you can't taste it. You want it even. The same applies to PDW. The need to keep things even starts with the database creation:

```
CREATE DATABASE AdventureworksPDW2012
WITH
(
     REPLICATED_SIZE = nn
,    DISTRIBUTED_SIZE = nn
,    LOG_SIZE = nn
,    AUTOGROW = ON | OFF
)
```

That is it! PDW handles the rest. PDW takes this information and converts this into data definition language (DDL) that it can use to drive parallelism in the appliance. Let's look at what `CREATE DATABASE` does and then each of these properties in turn.

Create Database

Although only one `CREATE DATABASE` statement is fired, as shown in the preceding code, many are created. One database is created on each compute node, and one database is created on the control node. What is important to understand is that their purposes differ significantly.

The database created on the control node is there to hold the metadata about the database. This database is also referred to as the *shell database*. Apart from holding all the security configuration, table, and procedure definitions, it also holds all the consolidated statistics from all the other databases held on the compute nodes. The shell database is actually very small; it holds no user data. Its primary function is during query optimization. There's more to come on that topic later in this chapter.

WARNING **Directly Accessing PDW's SQL Servers and the Shell Database**

PDW does not let you directly access the SQL Servers either on the control node or the compute nodes. This is to ensure that no inadvertent changes are made that could damage PDW and potentially void the warranty. Consequently, whilst it is an important component to understand, the shell database is not directly accessible by end users. It's created purely for PDW to use.

Each compute node also has a database created. These databases are where all the user data is stored. These databases have a rather interesting configuration. They consist of 10 separate filegroups that are key to PDW's parallelism. Each database on each compute node has all 10 filegroups. I've detailed them in the all in the matrix shown in Figure 10.3.

I have listed out all the filegroups on the *x*-axis of the matrix and shown compute nodes on the *y*-axis. This symbolizes something important. Every compute node has its own database each with their own set of filegroups. The matrix represents the total number of *buckets* available to PDW for depositing data. This really is the key to how PDW works. The more compute nodes you have, the more buckets.

The filegroups on the x-axis start with some unusually named ones DIST_A - DIST_H. These are called *distributions* and are designed for a certain type of table called a *distributed table*. The next filegroup is called *replicated*. You will notice that there is only one of these. That is significant. This filegroup holds *replicated tables*.

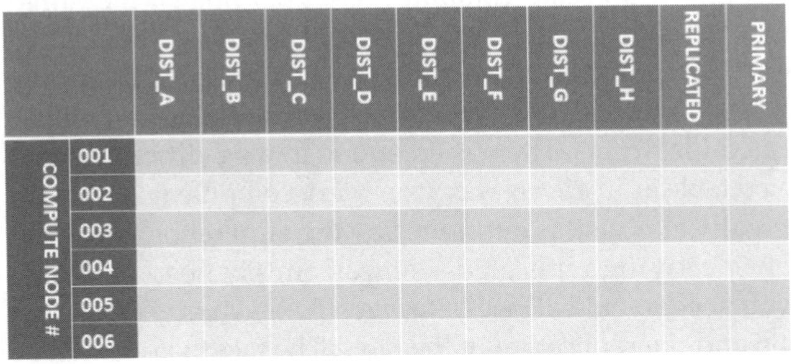

COMPUTE NODE #	DIST_A	DIST_B	DIST_C	DIST_D	DIST_E	DIST_F	DIST_G	DIST_H	REPLICATED	PRIMARY
001										
002										
003										
004										
005										
006										

Figure 10.3: The bucket matrix created by PDW for holding user data

Don't worry if all this talk of different table types is a bit confusing; we are going to talk about distributed and replicated tables later in this chapter. Suffice it to say that PDW supports two types of tables: distributed and replicated. When creating a table, we decide whether we want to distribute the data across the appliance (in which case we use a distributed table) or if we want to replicate the table. Typically, large facts are distributed, and dimensions are replicated. This is not always true, but it is a reasonable starting point.

For completeness, we need to recognize the primary filegroup. The primary filegroup only holds data system table metadata for your database objects just like a regular SQL Server database. The only difference is that we do not let user data go into the primary filegroup. Most of the time, we ignore that it is even there.

You should now see that the `CREATE DATABASE` statement is logical; that is, it is used to create multiple physical databases to support the one database you have specified. To help facilitate this shift from logical to physical, PDW implements a layer of abstraction. An example of that can be seen with the database name. Only the database built on the control node would be given the name you have specified. The databases on the compute nodes have a different name. It follows the convention of DB_ followed by 32 alphanumeric characters. This abstracted name is used on every compute node. PDW exposes this mapping via a PDW-specific catalog mapping view called sys.pdw_database_mappings. Here is some sample code and the results (See Figure 10.4):

```
SELECT d.name
,      dm.physical_name
FROM   sys.databases d
JOIN   sys.pdw_database_mappings dm ON d.database_id = dm.database_id
WHERE  d.name = 'AdventureWorksPDW2012'
```

	database_name	physical_name
1	AdventureWorksPDW2012	DB_c8af3b5b75ae445c8d14ffd7535f646e

Figure 10.4: Logical and physical database names in PDW

Replicated_Size

In Figure 10.4, you can see that we have six compute nodes and one replicated file group per compute node. The replicated size option allows you to size how big each replicated filegroup will be on each compute node. This value is measured in gigabytes (GB) and can be expressed as a decimal. Therefore, a replicated size of 10 will allocate 10GB on each compute node to the replicated filegroup.

Whatever value we specify for the replicated size, this is the value that will be used for all six replicated filegroups. There is no option to have different sizes. Data held in a replicated table is, in effect, a copy on every compute node, which is why the amount actually allocated is multiplied by the number of nodes you have. In reality, when specifying replicated size, you simply need to decide how much capacity you need to hold all the data *once*. PDW actually takes care of the actual allocation and the replication of the table. The fact that we will be holding it six times is really an internal optimization.

The replicated filegroup is only used by PDW when we decide to create a table and specify that we wish to replicate it. Because these tables tend to be our dimensions, we typically expect to see a relatively small size allocated here. If someone had allocated terabytes rather than gigabytes, that would warrant serious investigation.

Distributed_Size

The distributed size value is used differently from the replicated size. The distributed size value provided in the `CREATE DATABASE` statement is actually evenly split across all the distributions to ensure we have the same space available in each bucket for distributed data. Data is then spread across the distributions with each distribution holding a distinct subset of the distributed table data. Again, the value supplied in the DDL statement is also measured in gigabytes and can be expressed as a decimal.

If you remember back to the toast analogy, we also want to spread it as evenly as possible over the appliance. Therefore, if we have 6 compute nodes in our PDW appliance, we also have a total of 48 distributions (8 distributions per node A-H). If I allocate 10TB as my distributed size, I am therefore allocating 1/48 of this to each distribution. In this example, each distribution would be allocated approximately 213.33GB of the available capacity. However, I would have allocated 10TB in total, which I would use for my distributed tables.

Remember, the distributed size is used only by tables that have been specified as distributed. These are likely to be fact tables; so don't be surprised to see a very large number here, a very significant percentage of the total allocated. Furthermore, there is no replication of data in a distributed table. This sets distributed tables apart from replicated tables. In reality, both types of tables rely on disk RAID configurations for data protection.

Log_Size

The log size value behaves similarly to the distributed size, in as much as it is spread evenly across the appliance. Therefore, if I have 6 compute nodes and a 10GB log file, I will split my log file allocation into 6 approximately 1.6GB allocations. Remember that SQL Server doesn't create a filegroup for the log files.

In actual fact, the log file is split further again. PDW doesn't create just one log file for the database. It creates one log file per disk volume instead. With the HP AppSystem for PDW, for example, there are a total of 16 volumes per compute node. Therefore, a 10GB log_size specification for our 6 compute nodes would actually result in 96 log files, with each one being approximately 106.6MB in size. By doing this kind of allocation, PDW ensures that the log file grows evenly across all its available storage and isn't constrained to a single volume. Furthermore, each volume soaks up some of the load from the database log. Typically, the log will be double the size of the largest (uncompressed) file loaded.

Autogrow

PDW will run an autogrow on the database files rather than fail a query that asks for additional capacity when the files are full. In PDW, the autogrow option affects only the databases created on the compute nodes. This is important because PDW's metadata via sys.database_files is a bit misleading. This catalog view shows the information for the shell database held on the control node, not the actual values set against the compute node.

Table 10.2 and Table 10.3 show the actual values set against the compute node.

Table 10.2: Autogrow Settings for Compute Node Database Files (Excluding the Primary Filegroup Data Files)

AUTOGROW	FILE TYPE	ATTRIBUTE	VALUE	COMMENT
ON	ROWS	Max_size	-1	Each data file is not limited by size.
ON	ROWS	Growth	512	Each data file grows by a fixed amount, 512 8KB-pages or 4MB.
ON	ROWS	Is_percent_growth	0	Table grows in fixed amounts, not by percentage.
ON	LOG	Max_size	268435456	Each log file will grow to a maximum of 2TB.

Continues

Table 10.2 *(continued)*

AUTOGROW	FILE TYPE	ATTRIBUTE	VALUE	COMMENT
ON	LOG	Growth	10	Each log file grows by a 10% increment.
ON	LOG	Is_percent_growth	1	Log file grows by percentage increments, not fixed size.
OFF	ROWS	Max_size	-1	Each data file is not limited by size.
OFF	ROWS	Growth	0	Data files are fixed in size and will not grow.
OFF	ROWS	Is_percent_growth	0	Data files not set to grow, so not relevant.
OFF	LOG	Max_size	268435456	Each log file will grow to a maximum of 2TB.
OFF	LOG	Growth	0	Log will not grow.
OFF	LOG	Is_percent_growth	0	Log not set to grow, so not relevant.

Table 10.3: Primary Filegroup Autogrow Settings for Compute Node Database Files

AUTOGROW	FILE TYPE	ATTRIBUTE	VALUE	COMMENT
ON or OFF	ROWS	Size	640	The data file in the primary filegroup is always created at 640 pages or 5MB.
ON or OFF	ROWS	Max_size	-1	The data file in the primary filegroup only is not limited by size.
ON or OFF	ROWS	Growth	10	The data file in the primary filegroup is always allowed to grow by 10%.
ON or OFF	ROWS	Is_percent_growth	1	The data file in the primary filegroup always grows in percentages.

With this information, we can see that PDW handles the data file in the primary filegroup differently from all other files and filegroups. In short, the primary always grows irrespective of the `CREATE DATABASE` setting for `AUTOGROW`. This makes sense; it's not something we've actually specified in the DDL, and the space consumed is tiny. We certainly wouldn't want a DDL request such as `CREATE TABLE` to fail for lack of storage. I have included this here just for completeness of information.

More important is that the other database files and log files are handled differently. Furthermore, these allocations are fixed by the release and do not change (at the time of this writing) based on size of the database; that is, it does not matter whether your database is 1TB or 1PB, the AUTOGROW value is the same. It also doesn't matter whether the filegroup is for distributed or replicated tables, the autogrow works in exactly the same way.

Finally, it should also be clear that PDW is not simply offering up SQL Server functionality. AUTOGROW in PDW is very different than AUTOGROW in SQL Server. Each filegroup type has been evaluated for the AUTOGROW function, and a predesigned, tested configuration is applied on your behalf. This is classic appliance behavior.

Therefore, in conclusion, the AUTOGROW function is really there to prevent failures and 3:00-a.m. alarm support calls! We should definitely be monitoring for consumption of our pre-sized database and log files and be proactive with our management of storage capacity. You can consider it a good practice to preallocate your distributed, replicated, and log sizes for your anticipated growth. A typical projection would be roughly six months to a year. That gives you enough space to fine-tune future allocations without over-allocating in the first instance.

Distributed Tables

Distributed tables are the heart of PDW and are key to understanding its parallelism. In PDW, a table is defined as being distributed when it is created. We pick a column (yes, only one, just like partitioning) and hash the distinct values of this column, allocating each distinct value into one of our buckets. To be a bit more precise, the hash is performed by the DMS as the data is written to the table. Let's look at an example:

```
CREATE TABLE [dbo].[FactInternetSales]
(
[ProductKey] int NOT NULL,
[OrderDateKey] int NOT NULL,
[DueDateKey] int NOT NULL,
[ShipDateKey] int NOT NULL,
[CustomerKey] int NOT NULL,
[PromotionKey] int NOT NULL,
[CurrencyKey] int NOT NULL,
[SalesTerritoryKey] int NOT NULL,
[SalesOrderNumber] nvarchar(20) NOT NULL,
[SalesOrderLineNumber] tinyint NOT NULL,
[RevisionNumber] tinyint NOT NULL,
[OrderQuantity] smallint NOT NULL,
[UnitPrice] money NOT NULL,
[ExtendedAmount] money NOT NULL,
[UnitPriceDiscountPct] float NOT NULL,
[DiscountAmount] float NOT NULL,
[ProductStandardCost] money NOT NULL,
[TotalProductCost] money NOT NULL,
```

```
[SalesAmount] money NOT NULL,
[TaxAmt] money NOT NULL,
[Freight] money NOT NULL,
[CarrierTrackingNumber] nvarchar(25) NULL,
[CustomerPONumber] nvarchar(25) NULL
)
WITH
(       CLUSTERED COLUMNSTORE INDEX
,       DISTRIBUTION = HASH([SalesOrderNumber])
,       PARTITION
               (
               [OrderDateKey]
               RANGE RIGHT FOR VALUES
                      (
                          20000101
                      ,   20010101
                      ,   20020101
                      )
               )
);
```

In the preceding code listing you can see that a lot is familiar to you. However, you can see I have highlighted the key difference: `DISTRIBUTION = HASH([SalesOrderNumber])`. This means that every `SalesOrderNumber` will be hashed and allocated to one of our buckets. It is therefore essential that we pick a value with a good number of distinct values (my rule of thumb is `1000`) to make sure the data is spread evenly across the appliance and avoids something we call *data skew*.

There is actually one consideration that would take precedence over the data skew rule. When large fact tables are joined together (i.e., with a fact-to-fact join), we can often see significant volumes of data being moved across the appliance. This occurs when the two facts are not distributed on the same column. In these situations it is vital that we try to prevent the DMS from moving data to resolve the join. We can achieve this by distributing both fact tables on the same column, ensuring that this column is also used in the join—even if the column is not absolutely required to satisfy the join criteria. The presence of a shared distribution key in the join will prevent a DMS movement of data, which will have a positively dramatic impact on performance. When faced with the prospect of large fact-to-fact joins, data skew is a secondary consideration.

You might be wondering why this table doesn't specify which filegroup it is on. It's a great question. Well, the answer is simply that this table definition doesn't really exist on the compute nodes. PDW does create this table on the control node inside the shell database, though, as you might have suspected. However, after that, PDW has to manage creating one copy of this table for every distribution. Because we have eight distributions per compute node, we need eight different names for this table. The naming convention is similar to the one used for databases `TABLE_32AlphanumerChars_[A-H]`. You can see these table mappings via the `sys.pdw_table_mappings` view:

```
select t.name
,      ptm.physical_name
from   sys.tables t
join   sys.pdw_table_mappings ptm on t.object_id = ptm.object_id
where  t.name = 'FactInternetSales'
```

Figure 10.5 shows the result.

	name	physical_name
1	FactInternetSales	Table_3bb0786f3fe44b718bd8dca6c9acb073_A
2	FactInternetSales	Table_3bb0786f3fe44b718bd8dca6c9acb073_B
3	FactInternetSales	Table_3bb0786f3fe44b718bd8dca6c9acb073_C
4	FactInternetSales	Table_3bb0786f3fe44b718bd8dca6c9acb073_D
5	FactInternetSales	Table_3bb0786f3fe44b718bd8dca6c9acb073_E
6	FactInternetSales	Table_3bb0786f3fe44b718bd8dca6c9acb073_F
7	FactInternetSales	Table_3bb0786f3fe44b718bd8dca6c9acb073_G
8	FactInternetSales	Table_3bb0786f3fe44b718bd8dca6c9acb073_H

Figure 10.5: Comparing logical and physical table names in PDW

As for understanding which column was the one we distributed on, we need a different query. This information is not held on `sys.columns`, and so we need to look into some PDW proprietary extensions for this information:

```
SELECT      t.name                         AS TableName
,           tp.distribution_policy_desc    AS TableDistributionPolicyDesc
,           c.name                         AS ColumnName
,           y.name                         AS DataType
,           c.max_length                   AS DataMaxLength
,           c.precision                    AS DataPrecision
,           c.Scale                        AS DataScale
,           c.collation_name               AS ColumnCollation
,           c.Is_Nullable                  AS ColumnIsNullable
,           cm.distribution_ordinal        AS IsDistributionColumn
FROM sys.columns c
JOIN sys.pdw_column_distribution_properties cm
                                           ON  c.object_id = cm.object_id
                                           AND c.column_id = cm.column_id
JOIN sys.types y                           ON  c.user_type_id = y.user_type_id
JOIN sys.Tables t                          ON  c.object_id = t.object_id
JOIN sys.pdw_table_distribution_properties tp
                                           ON  t.object_id = tp.object_id
```

The abridged results for this query are shown in Figure 10.6. Notice that the `TableDistributionPolicyDesc` column states `HASH` as it is a distributed table and that the `SalesOrderNumber` row has a `1` for the `IsDistributionColumn`.

	TableName	TableDistributionPolicyDesc	ColumnName	DataType	DataMaxLength	DataPrecision	DataScale	ColumnCollation	ColumnIsNullable	IsDistributionColumn
1	FactInternetSales	HASH	ProductKey	int	4	10	0	NULL	0	0
2	FactInternetSales	HASH	OrderDateKey	int	4	10	0	NULL	0	0
3	FactInternetSales	HASH	DueDateKey	int	4	10	0	NULL	0	0
4	FactInternetSales	HASH	ShipDateKey	int	4	10	0	NULL	0	0
5	FactInternetSales	HASH	CustomerKey	int	4	10	0	NULL	0	0
6	FactInternetSales	HASH	PromotionKey	int	4	10	0	NULL	0	0
7	FactInternetSales	HASH	CurrencyKey	int	4	10	0	NULL	0	0
8	FactInternetSales	HASH	SalesTerritoryKey	int	4	10	0	NULL	0	0
9	FactInternetSales	HASH	SalesOrderNumber	nvarchar	40	0	0	Latin1_General_100_CI_AS_KS_WS	0	1
10	FactInternetSales	HASH	SalesOrderLineNumber	tinyint	1	3	0	NULL	0	0

Figure 10.6: Extended table and column properties for distributed tables

This query works just as well for showing off additional data about replicated tables too. Let's look at them now.

Replicated Tables

Replicated tables tend to be smaller tables, typically dimensions, which represent whole copies of data. A replicated table has its entire data set copied to all the compute nodes. Why do this? Well, it really helps when reading the data. At the end of the day, each compute node is a highly tuned SQL Server SMP instance with one buffer pool of memory. To facilitate a join, PDW needs to ensure that all the data is available. By replicating a table, we guarantee that this table at least has all its data available for a local, co-located join.

However, if the join was between two distributed tables, we may have an issue. It's still possible, of course, that both tables may be distributed in the same way; this is often a primary design goal. However, it's not always possible. Under some circumstances, one of the tables may have to be redistributed to make the join compatible. The worst case is realized when either table is distributed on a joining key. In this case both tables need to be redistributed. This is called a double shuffle.

It is important to note that data movement can even happen with a replicated table. When the join is an outer join, this triggers movement because we have to handle the nulls generated by the join.

This is quite an advanced topic, and so we aren't going to be able to cover it here. However, suffice to say that by replicating small dimension tables and inner-joining them to our distribution table, we avert the need to redistribute data because of the join. However, hopefully you can see that we need to pay careful attention to our table design, as it can have a dramatic impact on performance.

Naturally, there is a price to pay for this read enhancement. That price is in the form of delayed writes. Consider for a moment our six-compute-node deployment of PDW. If we have a replicated table, we will need to write the same row six times to ensure consistency. Writes to replicated tables are therefore much slower than to distributed tables. You can imagine that if a user were able to read the data partway through this write that the user would end up with inconsistent results. Therefore, the write is also a blocking transaction.

Under normal operation, these are good trade-offs. The write penalty is a one-time-only operation, and hopefully we can batch these up to maximize efficiency.

Finally, PDW also performs the same abstraction for table names of replicated tables as it does for distributed ones. A slight difference exists, though, inasmuch as we need to create only one mapping name, and so the naming convention differs slightly. For replicated tables, it is `TABLE_32AlphanumericCharacters`. To see the value created, we can use the `sys.pdw_table_mappings` catalog view as before.

Hopefully, you now have an appreciation for the what, why, and how of PDW and are intrigued enough to consider it in your environment. In this next section, we are going to talk about the one feature that's completely unique to PDW—its jewel in the crown, Project Polybase.

Project Polybase

Project Polybase was devised by the Gray Systems Lab (`http://gsl.azurewebsites.net/`) at the University of Wisconsin–Madison, which is managed by Technical Fellow Dr. David DeWitt. In fact, Dr. DeWitt was also instrumental in the development of Polybase, and is himself an expert in distributed database technology.

The goal for Polybase was simple: provide T-SQL over Hadoop, a single pane of glass for analysts and developers to interact with data residing in HDFS and to use that "nonrelational" data in conjunction with the relational data in conventional tables.

The goal was simple, but the solution was not. It was so big that Polybase had to be broken down into phases.

We've talked about Polybase and Hadoop integration a few times in this chapter. This section dives right into it:

- Polybase architecture
- Business use cases for Polybase today
- The future for Polybase

Polybase Architecture

Polybase is unique to PDW. It is integrated within the PDW's DMS. The DMS isn't shipped with any other SQL Server family product. Therefore, I think it's fair to claim Polybase for PDW.

Polybase extends the DMS by including an HDFS Bridge component into its architecture. The HDFS Bridge abstracts the complexity of Hadoop away from PDW and allows the DMS to reuse its existing functionality; namely, data type conversion (to ODBC types), generating the hash for data distribution and loading data into the SMP SQL Servers on residing compute nodes.

This section details the following:

- HDFS Bridge
- Imposing structure with external tables
- Querying across relational and nonrelational data
- Importing data
- Exporting data

HDFS Bridge

The HDFS Bridge is an extension of the DMS. Consequently, it is a unique feature to PDW. Its job is to abstract away the complexity of Hadoop and isolate it from the rest of PDW while providing the gateway to data residing in HDFS. Remember that the world of Hadoop is a Java-based world, and somewhat unsurprisingly PDW is C# based.

The HDFS Bridge then uses Java to provide the native integration with Hadoop. This layer is responsible for communication with the NameNode and for identifying the range of bytes to read from or write into HDFS residing on the data nodes. The next layer up in the HDFS Bridge stack is a Java Native Interface (JNI), which provides managed C# to the rest of the DMS and to the PDW Engine Service.

In Figure 10.7, you can see that the HDFS uses the Java RecordReader or RecordWriter interface to access the data in Hadoop. The RecordReader/Writer is a pluggable element, which is what allows PDW to support different HDFS file types.

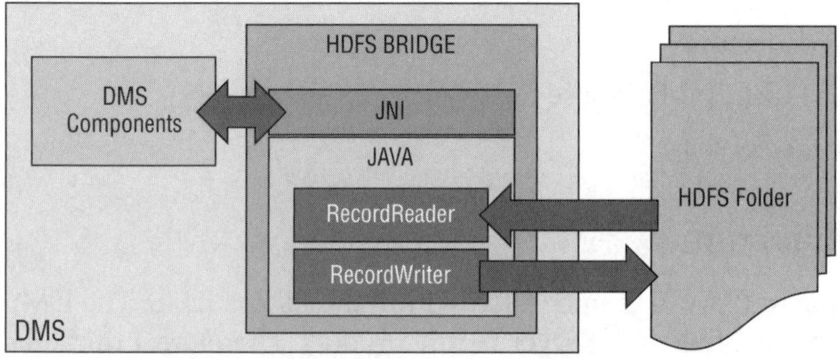

Figure 10.7: HDFS bridge architecture and data flow

Polybase gets much of its power through its ability to parallelize data transfer between the compute nodes of PDW and the data nodes of HDFS. What is interesting about this is that Polybase achieves this transfer with runtime-only execution information.

The PDW Engine uses the HDFS Bridge to speak with the NameNode when handed a Polybase query. The information it receives is used to divide the work up among the compute nodes as evenly as possible. The work is apportioned, with 256KB buffers allocated to stream rows back to the DMS on each compute node. The DMS continues to ingest these buffers from the RecordReader interface until the file has been read.

Imposing Structure with External Tables

PDW uses a DDL concept called an external table to impose the structure we require on the data held in the files of HDFS. The external table is really more akin to a BCP format file or a view than it is a table. (We will look at the internal implementation of external tables shortly.)

It is important to note that the coupling between PDW and Hadoop is very, very loose. The external table merely defines the interface for data transmission; it does not contain any data itself nor does it bind itself to the data in Hadoop. Changes to the structure of the data residing in Hadoop is possible, and even the complete removal of the data is conceivable; PDW would be none the wiser. In tech speak, unlike database views there is no schema-binding option available here. We cannot prevent a table from disappearing in Hadoop by creating an external table. Likewise, when we delete an external table, we do not delete the data from HDFS.

Furthermore, there are no additional concurrency controls or isolation levels in operation either when accessing data through an external table. While there is schema validation against the existing external table object definitions, it is quite possible you may see a runtime error when using Polybase. However, this is part of the design and helps Polybase retain its agnostic approach to Hadoop integration.

External tables are exposed via the sys.external_tables catalog view and in the SSDT tree control. The view inherits from sys.objects, and it exposes to us all the configuration and connection metadata for the external table.

Following is an example of an external table. Imagine if you will that the data for the AdventureWorks table FactInternetSales existed in HDFS. We are still bound by the restriction of having unique names for objects in the same database, so for clarity I have named data residing in Hadoop with an HDFS prefix:

```
CREATE EXTERNAL TABLE [dbo].[HDFS_FactInternetSales]
(
    [ProductKey] int NOT NULL,
    [OrderDateKey] int NOT NULL,
    [DueDateKey] int NOT NULL,
    [ShipDateKey] int NOT NULL,
    [CustomerKey] int NOT NULL,
    [PromotionKey] int NOT NULL,
```

```
        [CurrencyKey] int NOT NULL,
        [SalesTerritoryKey] int NOT NULL,
        [SalesOrderNumber] nvarchar(20) NOT NULL,
        [SalesOrderLineNumber] tinyint NOT NULL,
        [RevisionNumber] tinyint NOT NULL,
        [OrderQuantity] smallint NOT NULL,
        [UnitPrice] money NOT NULL,
        [ExtendedAmount] money NOT NULL,
        [UnitPriceDiscountPct] float NOT NULL,
        [DiscountAmount] float NOT NULL,
        [ProductStandardCost] money NOT NULL,
        [TotalProductCost] money NOT NULL,
        [SalesAmount] money NOT NULL,
        [TaxAmt] money NOT NULL,
        [Freight] money NOT NULL,
        [CarrierTrackingNumber] nvarchar(25)  NULL,
        [CustomerPONumber] nvarchar(25)  NULL

    )
    WITH
    (   LOCATION='hdfs://102.16.250.100:5000/files/HDFS_FactInternetSales'
    ,   FORMAT_OPTIONS
        (
           FIELD_TERMINATOR = '|'
        ,  STRING_DELIMITER = ''
        ,  DATE_FORMAT = ''
        ,  REJECT_TYPE = VALUE
        ,  REJECT_VALUE = 0
        ,  USE_TYPE_DEFAULT = False
        )
    );
```

Looking at the preceding code, you can see that it is indeed more like a BCP format file than anything else. In addition to the column names, types, and null-ability, we can also identify the location of both the cluster and the folder in HDFS holding the data, any field and row terminators, formatting for dates, both the method and the threshold for rejected records, and we can see how PDW should handle missing values when importing data using the `USE_TYPE_DEFAULT` option.

It is important to note, however, that although it doesn't really behave like one, an external table is actually a physical table. However, it is not created in Hadoop, nor is it present on the compute nodes like a normal table would be. It is instead created in the shell database up on the control node. You can see this by looking at the `dsql query plan` commands executed by PDW when we create an external table. In Figure 10.8, you can see the table is indeed created and that the location specifies it as the control node.

As you can see, it is simply a normal table. However, this table is used only to hold statistics and metadata about the table. PDW does not allow any user data to be persisted in the control node. This includes external tables. The metadata includes all the properties we set at creation time of the external table itself. PDW attaches these metadata attributes using the `sp_addextendedproperty` system stored procedure, as shown in Figure 10.9.

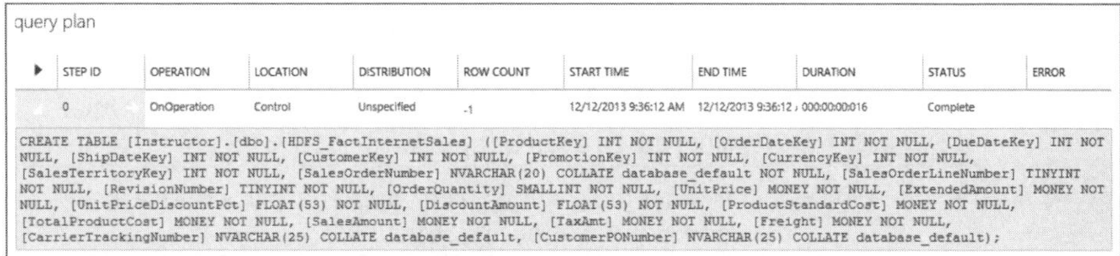

query plan

STEP ID	OPERATION	LOCATION	DISTRIBUTION	ROW COUNT	START TIME	END TIME	DURATION	STATUS	ERROR
0	OnOperation	Control	Unspecified	-1	12/12/2013 9:36:12 AM	12/12/2013 9:36:12 ,	000:00:00:016	Complete	

```
CREATE TABLE [Instructor].[dbo].[HDFS_FactInternetSales] ([ProductKey] INT NOT NULL, [OrderDateKey] INT NOT NULL, [DueDateKey] INT NOT NULL, [ShipDateKey] INT NOT NULL, [CustomerKey] INT NOT NULL, [PromotionKey] INT NOT NULL, [CurrencyKey] INT NOT NULL, [SalesTerritoryKey] INT NOT NULL, [SalesOrderNumber] NVARCHAR(20) COLLATE database_default NOT NULL, [SalesOrderLineNumber] TINYINT NOT NULL, [RevisionNumber] TINYINT NOT NULL, [OrderQuantity] SMALLINT NOT NULL, [UnitPrice] MONEY NOT NULL, [ExtendedAmount] MONEY NOT NULL, [UnitPriceDiscountPct] FLOAT(53) NOT NULL, [DiscountAmount] FLOAT(53) NOT NULL, [ProductStandardCost] MONEY NOT NULL, [TotalProductCost] MONEY NOT NULL, [SalesAmount] MONEY NOT NULL, [TaxAmt] MONEY NOT NULL, [Freight] MONEY NOT NULL, [CarrierTrackingNumber] NVARCHAR(25) COLLATE database_default, [CustomerPONumber] NVARCHAR(25) COLLATE database_default);
```

Figure 10.8: Creating the external table on the control node

The figure clearly shows all the metadata attributes you saw earlier in the DDL, as explained more fully in Table 10.4. A more useful location to see all this data is in the sys.external_tables catalog view.

<table>
<tr><th>STEP ID</th><th>OPERATION</th><th>LOCATION</th><th>DISTRIBUTION</th><th>ROW COUNT</th><th>START TIME</th><th>END TIME</th><th>DURATION</th><th>STATUS</th><th>ERROR</th></tr>
<tr><td>0</td><td>OnOperation</td><td>Control</td><td>Unspecified</td><td>-1</td><td>12/12/2013 9:36:12 AM</td><td>12/12/2013 9:36:12 ,</td><td>000:00:00:016</td><td>Complete</td><td></td></tr>
<tr><td>1</td><td>OnOperation</td><td>Control</td><td>Unspecified</td><td>-1</td><td>12/12/2013 9:36:12 AM</td><td>12/12/2013 9:36:12 ,</td><td>000:00:00:000</td><td>Complete</td><td></td></tr>
<tr><td colspan="10">EXEC [Instructor].[sys].[sp_addextendedproperty] @name=N'pdw_physical_name', @value=N'_979a5b0b0dba451ca4d7c00455e64cd9', @level0type=N'SCHEMA', @level0name=N'dbo', @level1type=N'TABLE', @level1name=N'HDFS_FactInternetSales'</td></tr>
<tr><td>2</td><td>OnOperation</td><td>Control</td><td>Unspecified</td><td>-1</td><td>12/12/2013 9:36:12 AM</td><td>12/12/2013 9:36:12 ,</td><td>000:00:00:000</td><td>Complete</td><td></td></tr>
<tr><td colspan="10">EXEC [Instructor].[sys].[sp_addextendedproperty] @name=N'pdw_distribution_type', @value=N'External', @level0type=N'SCHEMA', @level0name=N'dbo', @level1type=N'TABLE', @level1name=N'HDFS_FactInternetSales'</td></tr>
<tr><td>3</td><td>OnOperation</td><td>Control</td><td>Unspecified</td><td>-1</td><td>12/12/2013 9:36:12 AM</td><td>12/12/2013 9:36:12 ,</td><td>000:00:00:000</td><td>Complete</td><td></td></tr>
<tr><td colspan="10">EXEC [Instructor].[sys].[sp_addextendedproperty] @name=N'pdw_column_delimiter', @value=N'|', @level0type=N'SCHEMA', @level0name=N'dbo', @level1type=N'TABLE', @level1name=N'HDFS_FactInternetSales'</td></tr>
<tr><td>4</td><td>OnOperation</td><td>Control</td><td>Unspecified</td><td>-1</td><td>12/12/2013 9:36:12 AM</td><td>12/12/2013 9:36:12 ,</td><td>000:00:00:000</td><td>Complete</td><td></td></tr>
<tr><td colspan="10">EXEC [Instructor].[sys].[sp_addextendedproperty] @name=N'pdw_string_delimiter', @value=N'', @level0type=N'SCHEMA', @level0name=N'dbo', @level1type=N'TABLE', @level1name=N'HDFS_FactInternetSales'</td></tr>
<tr><td>5</td><td>OnOperation</td><td>Control</td><td>Unspecified</td><td>-1</td><td>12/12/2013 9:36:12 AM</td><td>12/12/2013 9:36:12 ,</td><td>000:00:00:000</td><td>Complete</td><td></td></tr>
<tr><td colspan="10">EXEC [Instructor].[sys].[sp_addextendedproperty] @name=N'pdw_reject_type', @value=N'VALUE', @level0type=N'SCHEMA', @level0name=N'dbo', @level1type=N'TABLE', @level1name=N'HDFS_FactInternetSales'</td></tr>
<tr><td>6</td><td>OnOperation</td><td>Control</td><td>Unspecified</td><td>-1</td><td>12/12/2013 9:36:12 AM</td><td>12/12/2013 9:36:12 ,</td><td>000:00:00:000</td><td>Complete</td><td></td></tr>
<tr><td colspan="10">EXEC [Instructor].[sys].[sp_addextendedproperty] @name=N'pdw_reject_value', @value=N'0', @level0type=N'SCHEMA', @level0name=N'dbo', @level1type=N'TABLE', @level1name=N'HDFS_FactInternetSales'</td></tr>
<tr><td>7</td><td>OnOperation</td><td>Control</td><td>Unspecified</td><td>-1</td><td>12/12/2013 9:36:12 AM</td><td>12/12/2013 9:36:12 ,</td><td>000:00:00:000</td><td>Complete</td><td></td></tr>
<tr><td colspan="10">EXEC [Instructor].[sys].[sp_addextendedproperty] @name=N'pdw_reject_sample_value', @level0type=N'SCHEMA', @level0name=N'dbo', @level1type=N'TABLE', @level1name=N'HDFS FactInternetSales'</td></tr>
<tr><td>8</td><td>OnOperation</td><td>Control</td><td>Unspecified</td><td>-1</td><td>12/12/2013 9:36:12 AM</td><td>12/12/2013 9:36:12 ,</td><td>000:00:00:000</td><td>Complete</td><td></td></tr>
<tr><td colspan="10">EXEC [Instructor].[sys].[sp_addextendedproperty] @name=N'pdw_date_format', @value=N'', @level0type=N'SCHEMA', @level0name=N'dbo', @level1type=N'TABLE', @level1name=N'HDFS_FactInternetSales'</td></tr>
<tr><td>9</td><td>OnOperation</td><td>Control</td><td>Unspecified</td><td>-1</td><td>12/12/2013 9:36:12 AM</td><td>12/12/2013 9:36:12 ,</td><td>000:00:00:000</td><td>Complete</td><td></td></tr>
<tr><td colspan="10">EXEC [Instructor].[sys].[sp_addextendedproperty] @name=N'pdw_use_type_default', @value=N'False', @level0type=N'SCHEMA', @level0name=N'dbo', @level1type=N'TABLE', @level1name=N'HDFS_FactInternetSales'</td></tr>
<tr><td>10</td><td>OnOperation</td><td>Control</td><td>Unspecified</td><td>-1</td><td>12/12/2013 9:36:12 AM</td><td>12/12/2013 9:36:12 ,</td><td>000:00:00:000</td><td>Complete</td><td></td></tr>
<tr><td colspan="10">EXEC [Instructor].[sys].[sp_addextendedproperty] @name=N'pdw_external_uri', @value=N'hdfs://172.16.252.101:8020/files/HDFS_FactInternetSales', @level0type=N'SCHEMA', @level0name=N'dbo', @level1type=N'TABLE', @level1name=N'HDFS_FactInternetSales'</td></tr>
<tr><td>11</td><td>ExternalStatisticsOpe</td><td>Control</td><td>Unspecified</td><td>-1</td><td>12/12/2013 9:36:12 AM</td><td>12/12/2013 9:36:12 ,</td><td>000:00:00:000</td><td>Complete</td><td></td></tr>
<tr><td colspan="10"><Empty></td></tr>
<tr><td>12</td><td>OnOperation</td><td>Control</td><td>Unspecified</td><td>-1</td><td>12/12/2013 9:36:12 AM</td><td>12/12/2013 9:36:12 ,</td><td>000:00:00:000</td><td>Complete</td><td></td></tr>
<tr><td colspan="10">UPDATE STATISTICS [Instructor].[dbo].[HDFS_FactInternetSales] WITH ROWCOUNT = [ROWCOUNT_TEMP_ID_246293], PAGECOUNT = [PAGECOUNT_TEMP_ID_246293]</td></tr>
</table>

Figure 10.9: PDWs external table extended properties

Table 10.4: External Table Extended Properties

PDW EXTENDED PROPERTY NAME	DEFINITION
pdw_physical_name	Internal mapping name of the external table exposed via sys.pdw_table_mappings.
pdw_distribution_type	Determines the table geometry, and in this case identifies the table as an external table. Value = N'External'. Other values are Distributed and Replicated.
pdw_column_delimiter	Identifies the column delimiter used to parse the file in Hadoop when imposing structure.
pdw_string_delimiter	Identifies the string delimiter used to parse the file in Hadoop when imposing structure.
pdw_reject_type	States whether the query error threshold will be measured by VALUE or by PERCENTAGE.
pdw_reject_value	Depending on the reject type, this will either equal the VALUE or PERCENTAGE threshold value before a query will fail.
pdw_reject_sample_value	Defines the number of rows to attempt to load before calculating the percentage of rejected rows.
pdw_date_format	Contains the date format to be used when parsing dates.
pdw_use_type_default	States how to process missing values when importing data from HDFS. 0 = USE NULL. 1 = use the column default.
pdw_external_uri	Holds the URI for the Hadoop location of the data file in HDFS.

Figure 10.9 contains two other steps that are interesting:

- Step 11 - `ExternalStatisticsOperation`
- Step 12 - `OnOperation`

Although step 11 is "empty" (effectively hiding an internal operation), we can infer what action the external statistics operation is performing by looking at step 12. I've copied the code here:

```
UPDATE STATISTICS [Instructor].[dbo].[HDFS_FactInternetSales]
WITH ROWCOUNT  = [ROWCOUNT_TEMP_ID_246293]
,    PAGECOUNT = [PAGECOUNT_TEMP_ID_246293]
```

Clearly, then, PDW is retrieving what statistical data it can from Hadoop to determine the row length, number of rows in a process known as file binding. The file blocks are then allocated across the compute nodes as evenly as possible, for which we need to know the size of the table. This is called the split generation. This step is clearly the first in a long series of optimizations for the future phases of Polybase. Knowing the table size and knowing the row count are important first steps to cost-based optimization on Hadoop data.

Querying Across Relational and Nonrelational Data

"A single pane of glass," that's what Polybase offers the business user—the ability to write a single query that analyzes data across both the relational data warehouse and the nonrelational data held in Hadoop. In that sense, Polybase is a uniter of worlds. Another way of looking at it is that Polybase is like a cow; it has many stomachs to digest data.

By leveraging the existence and structure of the external tables PDW is able to simply write queries against data residing in HDFS.

Consider this simple example (see Figure 10.10):

```
SELECT *
FROM dbo.HDFS_FactInternetSales FIS
OPTION
( LABEL = 'Polybase Read : Q001 : HDFS_FactInternetSales'
)
;
```

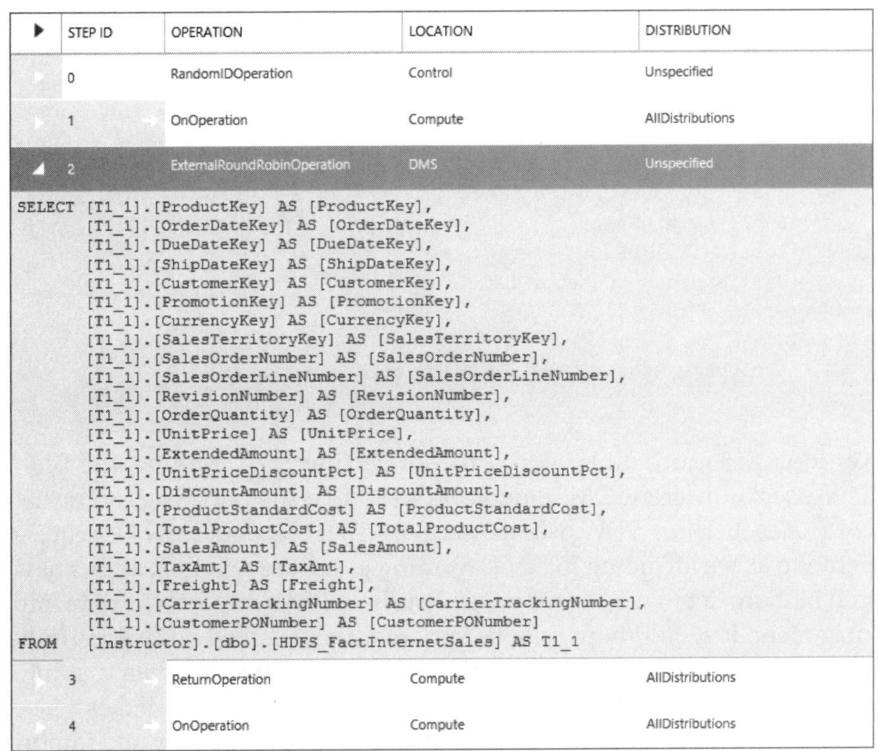

STEP ID
OPERATION
LOCATION
DISTRIBUTION
0 RandomIDOperation Control Unspecified
1 OnOperation Compute AllDistributions
2 ExternalRoundRobinOperation DMS Unspecified
SELECT [T1_1].[ProductKey] AS [ProductKey],
[T1_1].[OrderDateKey] AS [OrderDateKey],
[T1_1].[DueDateKey] AS [DueDateKey],
[T1_1].[ShipDateKey] AS [ShipDateKey],
[T1_1].[CustomerKey] AS [CustomerKey],
[T1_1].[PromotionKey] AS [PromotionKey],
[T1_1].[CurrencyKey] AS [CurrencyKey],
[T1_1].[SalesTerritoryKey] AS [SalesTerritoryKey],
[T1_1].[SalesOrderNumber] AS [SalesOrderNumber],
[T1_1].[SalesOrderLineNumber] AS [SalesOrderLineNumber],
[T1_1].[RevisionNumber] AS [RevisionNumber],
[T1_1].[OrderQuantity] AS [OrderQuantity],
[T1_1].[UnitPrice] AS [UnitPrice],
[T1_1].[ExtendedAmount] AS [ExtendedAmount],
[T1_1].[UnitPriceDiscountPct] AS [UnitPriceDiscountPct],
[T1_1].[DiscountAmount] AS [DiscountAmount],
[T1_1].[ProductStandardCost] AS [ProductStandardCost],
[T1_1].[TotalProductCost] AS [TotalProductCost],
[T1_1].[SalesAmount] AS [SalesAmount],
[T1_1].[TaxAmt] AS [TaxAmt],
[T1_1].[Freight] AS [Freight],
[T1_1].[CarrierTrackingNumber] AS [CarrierTrackingNumber],
[T1_1].[CustomerPONumber] AS [CustomerPONumber]
FROM [Instructor].[dbo].[HDFS_FactInternetSales] AS T1_1
3 ReturnOperation Compute AllDistributions
4 OnOperation Compute AllDistributions

Figure 10.10: Simple Polybase query against data held in Hadoop

PDW is able to use the external table `HDFS_FactInternetSales` to read through to Hadoop and import the data residing in HDFS using a DMS operation called an `ExternalRoundRobinOperation`. This operation imports the buffers as is and simply allocates them on a round-robin basis to the compute nodes. As we do not need to join this table to any others, there is no need for anything more complex. Once allocated, the buffer is simply bulk inserted into a temporary table where it can be easily read by the `ReturnOperation` as shown in step 3 of the plan. The results are then streamed back to the client that issued the original query.

PDW can also initiate joins and aggregations between data held in one of its tables and data held in HDFS. In the following example, PDW is able to read data in HDFS through the same external table `HDFS_FactInternetSales` and subsequently join it to a number of tables in PDW (see Figure 10.11):

```
SELECT [EnglishProductCategoryName]
,      [EnglishMonthName]
,      SUM([TotalProductCost])      AS TotalCost
,      SUM([SalesAmount])           AS TotalSales
FROM dbo.HDFS_FactInternetSales FIS
JOIN dbo.DimCustomer DC
ON FIS.CustomerKey             = DC.CustomerKey
JOIN dbo.DimDate DD
ON FIS.[OrderDateKey]          = DD.[DateKey]
JOIN dbo.DimProduct DP
ON FIS.[ProductKey]            = DP.[ProductKey]
JOIN dbo.DimProductSubcategory DPS
ON DP.[ProductSubcategoryKey] = DPS.[ProductSubcategoryKey]
JOIN [dbo].[DimProductCategory] DPC
ON DPS.[ProductCategoryKey]    = DPC.[ProductCategoryKey]
GROUP BY [EnglishProductCategoryName]
,        [EnglishMonthName]
ORDER BY [TotalSales] DESC
,        [EnglishProductCategoryName]
OPTION
( HASH JOIN
, LABEL = 'Polybase Read : Q002 : HDFS_FactInternetSales'
)
;
```

If you look at Figure 10.11, you will notice that this changes the plan and PDW uses a different DMS operation to source the data. Instead of the `ExternalRoundRobinMove` PDW uses the `ExternalShuffleOperation`. We require this operation as we are going to be performing joins. We will look at this new operation in more detail next as we investigate how PDW imports the data into its environment. It should hopefully be apparent that even when PDW is only reading data from the query perspective, it is, in fact, importing data first into PDW and then selecting from that imported data set. It therefore makes sense to look at the `ExternalShuffleOperation` more from both the query and import perspectives to understand the difference in the respective plans.

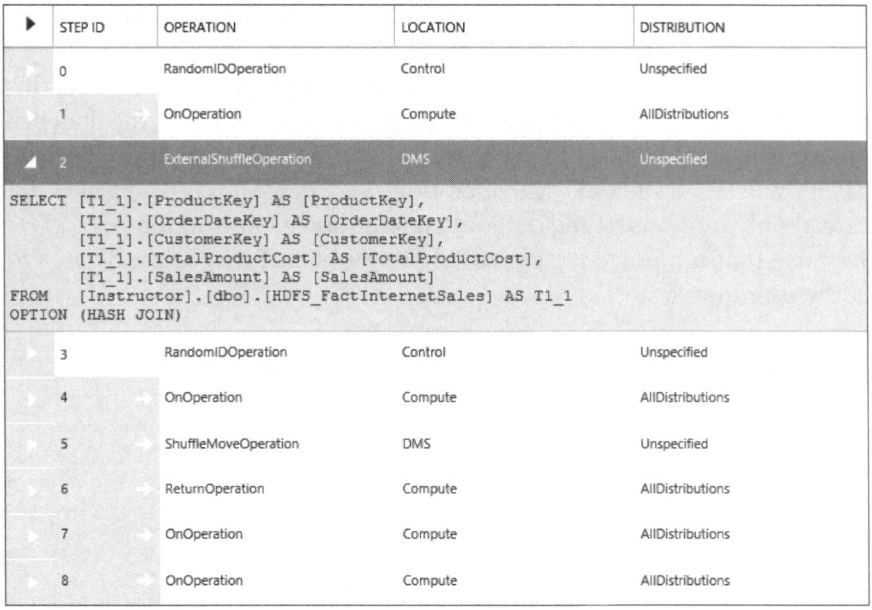

STEP ID	OPERATION	LOCATION	DISTRIBUTION
0	RandomIDOperation	Control	Unspecified
1	OnOperation	Compute	AllDistributions
2	ExternalShuffleOperation	DMS	Unspecified
3	RandomIDOperation	Control	Unspecified
4	OnOperation	Compute	AllDistributions
5	ShuffleMoveOperation	DMS	Unspecified
6	ReturnOperation	Compute	AllDistributions
7	OnOperation	Compute	AllDistributions
8	OnOperation	Compute	AllDistributions

```
SELECT [T1_1].[ProductKey] AS [ProductKey],
       [T1_1].[OrderDateKey] AS [OrderDateKey],
       [T1_1].[CustomerKey] AS [CustomerKey],
       [T1_1].[TotalProductCost] AS [TotalProductCost],
       [T1_1].[SalesAmount] AS [SalesAmount]
FROM   [Instructor].[dbo].[HDFS_FactInternetSales] AS T1_1
OPTION (HASH JOIN)
```

Figure 10.11: More complex Polybase query against PDW and Hadoop data

Importing Data with CTAS

PDW enables the parallel import of data through its `CREATE TABLE AS SELECT` (CTAS) statement. This is akin to a `SELECT INTO` in an SMP environment, but you have some added flexibility in terms of table geometry (distributed or replicated) and indexing.

To import data from HDFS, all you need to do is reference an external table in the `SELECT` part of the CTAS statement. This external table could have been created when the data was originally exported or simply could have been created over existing HDFS data. Either way, you simply reference the external table just like you would any other table. Following is a simple example:

```
CREATE TABLE dbo.FactInternetSales_Import
WITH (DISTRIBUTION = HASH([SalesOrderNumber]))
AS SELECT *
FROM HDFS_FactInternetSales fis
JOIN DimCustomer cus ON fis.CustomerKey = cus.CustomerKey
;
```

To facilitate the move from HDFS, the DMS has introduced a new movement type: the `ExternalShuffleOperation`. This movement selects the data "through" the external table (which provides PDW with the metadata required to access the data from HDFS) and shuffles the data using the DMS hashing function, distributing the data according to the hash (see Figure 10.12); first loading the data into a temp table, known as a Q table and then Inserting that data into the target user table.

The only difference between a query that performs a join and an import at this stage is that the import takes an additional step. An import persists the data in a user-defined table residing in a user database. In contrast, when running a Polybase query, PDW will still issue the DMS operation `ExternalShuffleOperation` but will instead only bulk-insert the data into a temporary table, in tempdb. PDW will then use that temporary table to satisfy joins and where-predicates to answer the user query.

STEP ID	OPERATION	LOCATION	DISTRIBUTION	ROW COUNT
0	OnOperation	Control	Unspecified	-1
1	OnOperation	Compute	AllDistributions	-1
2	RandomIDOperation	Control	Unspecified	-1
3	OnOperation	Compute	AllDistributions	-1
4	ExternalShuffleOperation	DMS	Unspecified	-1
5	OnOperation	Compute	AllDistributions	60398
6	OnOperation	Compute	AllDistributions	-1
7	OnOperation	Control	Unspecified	-1
8	OnOperation	Control	Unspecified	-1
9	OnOperation	Control	Unspecified	-1
10	OnOperation	Control	Unspecified	-1
11	DbccShowStatisticsOperation	Compute	AllDistributions	-1
12	OnOperation	Control	Unspecified	-1

Figure 10.12: Importing data using the DMS and its ExternalShuffleOperation

We can see this clearly when we compare plans. If we look at the plan in Figure 10.9, we can see that there are a total of 13 steps. Step 5 is responsible for the insert of the rows into the table `FactInternetSales_Import`. The row count of 60,398 against step 5 is a telltale sign that this `OnOperation` is performing the insert. If we were to drill in, we'd have seen that the query was a `select` against the temp table with a MAXDOP 1 option applied to ensure a nice, clean, contiguous write into our target. Contrast this with Figure 10.11 and Figure 10.12. Neither query has an `OnOperation` immediately after their DMS operation. Both have moved on to perform other steps to fully resolve their queries. For the simple read, all that is left to do is to perform the `ReturnOperation`, which streams the results back to the client. Our more complex query needs to perform an aggregation that is not distribution compatible (we do not see the distribution key in the group by); therefore, it has to shuffle the data again before moving to its `ReturnOperation`.

However, if we look at the read query plan steps immediately preceding their respective Hadoop DMS operations, we can see that both read queries perform the same steps as the import. The only difference is that import must also create the table `FactInternetSales_Import` and check that the user has the permissions to create a table, which is what it is doing in steps 0 and 1 of its plan in Figure 10.9. Otherwise, these plans are the same.

Owing to the very loose coupling offered by Polybase, it may make sense to move the data into PDW via a CTAS import before executing any further queries. This affords you greater consistency because you will now be querying "your" copy of the data. Now you can guarantee that you are the only person able to edit the data if you so wish. Although this is a disconnected data set from the source, this does have a second added benefit. By moving the data into PDW first, you ensure that future queries on this data will execute more quickly because: a) you will have already imported the data and so won't be paying that write penalty on every execution and b) you can optimize subsequent queries by creating statistics on important columns used by subsequent queries.

Exporting Data with CETAS

PDW uses the same basic mechanism for exporting data as it does for importing. The transfer of data is native and parallel in nature, so we can push the data out very simply, efficiently, and effectively. Ideally, the Hadoop cluster would be attached to the PDW's Infiniband network for maximum performance (although, this would not be a cheap option). A more realistic option is to use 10-Gigabit Ethernet (10GbE).

To export the data, we use a variation on the `CREATE TABLE AS SELECT` method seen when importing data. This time we export data by first creating an external table and then pushing the data through it. This provides us with all the metadata we need to identify the location of the cluster and the format of the delimited file in HDFS. Consequently, the DDL for this action is `CREATE EXTERNAL TABLE AS SELECT` (CETAS). See the following code for a simple example:

```
CREATE EXTERNAL TABLE dbo.HDFS_FactInternetSales
WITH
(
    LOCATION = 'hdfs://102.16.250.100:5000/files/HDFS_FactInternetSales'
,   FORMAT_OPTIONS ( FIELD_TERMINATOR = '|')
)
AS      SELECT T1.*
FROM    dbo.FactInternetSales T1
JOIN    dbo.DimCustomer T2          ON T1.CustomerKey = T2.CustomerKey
OPTION (HASH JOIN);
```

Note that once the CETAS has executed, three things will have happened:

1. An external table will have been created.
2. The data will have been exported.
3. Statistics will have been collected on the exported data.

To export the data, PDW uses a new DMS movement type called the `ExternalExportDistributedOperation`. This operation selects the data out from the compute nodes and pushes it out in parallel to Hadoop. You can see the select used by the `ExternalExportDistributedOperation` in Figure 10.13.

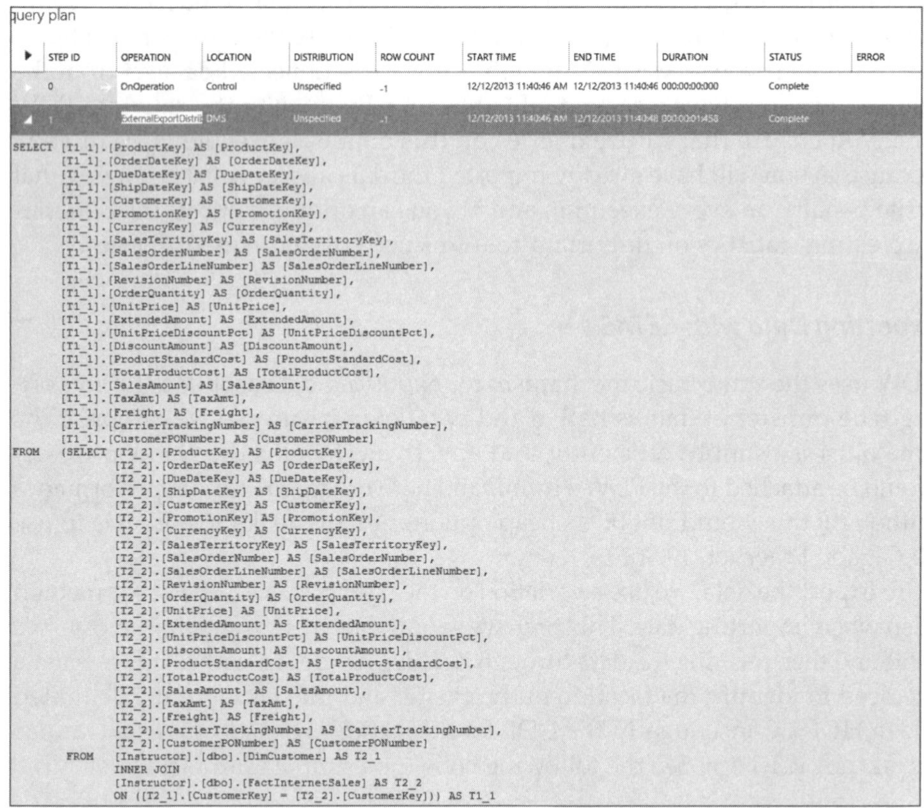
query plan
STEP ID
OPERATION
LOCATION
DISTRIBUTION
ROW COUNT
START TIME
END TIME
DURATION
STATUS
ERROR
0 OnOperation Control Unspecified -1 12/12/2013 11:40:46 AM 12/12/2013 11:40:46 000:00:00:000 Complete
SELECT [T1_1].[ProductKey] AS [ProductKey],
[T1_1].[OrderDateKey] AS [OrderDateKey],
[T1_1].[DueDateKey] AS [DueDateKey],
[T1_1].[ShipDateKey] AS [ShipDateKey],
[T1_1].[CustomerKey] AS [CustomerKey],
[T1_1].[PromotionKey] AS [PromotionKey],
[T1_1].[CurrencyKey] AS [CurrencyKey],
[T1_1].[SalesTerritoryKey] AS [SalesTerritoryKey],
[T1_1].[SalesOrderNumber] AS [SalesOrderNumber],
[T1_1].[SalesOrderLineNumber] AS [SalesOrderLineNumber],
[T1_1].[RevisionNumber] AS [RevisionNumber],
[T1_1].[OrderQuantity] AS [OrderQuantity],
[T1_1].[UnitPrice] AS [UnitPrice],
[T1_1].[ExtendedAmount] AS [ExtendedAmount],
[T1_1].[UnitPriceDiscountPct] AS [UnitPriceDiscountPct],
[T1_1].[DiscountAmount] AS [DiscountAmount],
[T1_1].[ProductStandardCost] AS [ProductStandardCost],
[T1_1].[TotalProductCost] AS [TotalProductCost],
[T1_1].[SalesAmount] AS [SalesAmount],
[T1_1].[TaxAmt] AS [TaxAmt],
[T1_1].[Freight] AS [Freight],
[T1_1].[CarrierTrackingNumber] AS [CarrierTrackingNumber],
[T1_1].[CustomerPONumber] AS [CustomerPONumber]
FROM (SELECT [T2_2].[ProductKey] AS [ProductKey],
[T2_2].[OrderDateKey] AS [OrderDateKey],
[T2_2].[DueDateKey] AS [DueDateKey],
[T2_2].[ShipDateKey] AS [ShipDateKey],
[T2_2].[CustomerKey] AS [CustomerKey],
[T2_2].[PromotionKey] AS [PromotionKey],
[T2_2].[CurrencyKey] AS [CurrencyKey],
[T2_2].[SalesTerritoryKey] AS [SalesTerritoryKey],
[T2_2].[SalesOrderNumber] AS [SalesOrderNumber],
[T2_2].[SalesOrderLineNumber] AS [SalesOrderLineNumber],
[T2_2].[RevisionNumber] AS [RevisionNumber],
[T2_2].[OrderQuantity] AS [OrderQuantity],
[T2_2].[UnitPrice] AS [UnitPrice],
[T2_2].[ExtendedAmount] AS [ExtendedAmount],
[T2_2].[UnitPriceDiscountPct] AS [UnitPriceDiscountPct],
[T2_2].[DiscountAmount] AS [DiscountAmount],
[T2_2].[ProductStandardCost] AS [ProductStandardCost],
[T2_2].[TotalProductCost] AS [TotalProductCost],
[T2_2].[SalesAmount] AS [SalesAmount],
[T2_2].[TaxAmt] AS [TaxAmt],
[T2_2].[Freight] AS [Freight],
[T2_2].[CarrierTrackingNumber] AS [CarrierTrackingNumber],
[T2_2].[CustomerPONumber] AS [CustomerPONumber]
FROM [Instructor].[dbo].[DimCustomer] AS T2_1
INNER JOIN
[Instructor].[dbo].[FactInternetSales] AS T2_2
ON ([T2_1].[CustomerKey] = [T2_2].[CustomerKey])) AS T1_1

Figure 10.13: Exporting data using the DMS and its ExternalExportDistributedOperation

You can also see how the parallel export is achieved by looking at the files created in HDFS by PDW. You can see these files by querying the HDFS file system using the following command in the Hadoop console:

```
Hadoop fs -ls /files/HDFS_FactInternetSales
```

If you look at the Figure 10.14, you can clearly see that a naming convention has been applied to each file. This naming convention helps to explain the parallelism.

The naming convention of the file is as follows (see Table 10.5):

```
QUERYID_DATE_TIME_DISTRIBUTION
```

```
Administrator: Hadoop Command Line
5_20131213_123521_9.txt

:\Hadoop\hadoop-1.1.0-SNAPSHOT>hadoop fs -ls /files/HDFS_FactInternetSales
ound 32 items
-rw-r--r--   3 pdw_user supergroup     524139 2013-12-13 20:56 /files/HDFS_FactInternetSales/QID522665_20131213_123521_0.txt
-rw-r--r--   3 pdw_user supergroup     311973 2013-12-13 20:56 /files/HDFS_FactInternetSales/QID522665_20131213_123521_1.txt
-rw-r--r--   3 pdw_user supergroup     323391 2013-12-13 20:56 /files/HDFS_FactInternetSales/QID522665_20131213_123521_10.txt
-rw-r--r--   3 pdw_user supergroup     313212 2013-12-13 20:56 /files/HDFS_FactInternetSales/QID522665_20131213_123521_11.txt
-rw-r--r--   3 pdw_user supergroup     524181 2013-12-13 20:56 /files/HDFS_FactInternetSales/QID522665_20131213_123521_12.txt
-rw-r--r--   3 pdw_user supergroup     320114 2013-12-13 20:56 /files/HDFS_FactInternetSales/QID522665_20131213_123521_13.txt
-rw-r--r--   3 pdw_user supergroup     120039 2013-12-13 20:56 /files/HDFS_FactInternetSales/QID522665_20131213_123521_14.txt
-rw-r--r--   3 pdw_user supergroup     112038 2013-12-13 20:56 /files/HDFS_FactInternetSales/QID522665_20131213_123521_15.txt
-rw-r--r--   3 pdw_user supergroup     290068 2013-12-13 20:56 /files/HDFS_FactInternetSales/QID522665_20131213_123521_16.txt
-rw-r--r--   3 pdw_user supergroup     524096 2013-12-13 20:56 /files/HDFS_FactInternetSales/QID522665_20131213_123521_17.txt
-rw-r--r--   3 pdw_user supergroup     304118 2013-12-13 20:56 /files/HDFS_FactInternetSales/QID522665_20131213_123521_18.txt
-rw-r--r--   3 pdw_user supergroup      88488 2013-12-13 20:56 /files/HDFS_FactInternetSales/QID522665_20131213_123521_19.txt
-rw-r--r--   3 pdw_user supergroup     296409 2013-12-13 20:56 /files/HDFS_FactInternetSales/QID522665_20131213_123521_2.txt
-rw-r--r--   3 pdw_user supergroup     524078 2013-12-13 20:56 /files/HDFS_FactInternetSales/QID522665_20131213_123521_20.txt
-rw-r--r--   3 pdw_user supergroup     524217 2013-12-13 20:56 /files/HDFS_FactInternetSales/QID522665_20131213_123521_21.txt
-rw-r--r--   3 pdw_user supergroup      80816 2013-12-13 20:56 /files/HDFS_FactInternetSales/QID522665_20131213_123521_22.txt
-rw-r--r--   3 pdw_user supergroup      88417 2013-12-13 20:56 /files/HDFS_FactInternetSales/QID522665_20131213_123521_23.txt
-rw-r--r--   3 pdw_user supergroup     319460 2013-12-13 20:56 /files/HDFS_FactInternetSales/QID522665_20131213_123521_24.txt
-rw-r--r--   3 pdw_user supergroup     524056 2013-12-13 20:56 /files/HDFS_FactInternetSales/QID522665_20131213_123521_25.txt
```

Figure 10.14: Viewing exported data from PDW in HDFS through the Hadoop Console

Table 10.5: HDFS File Naming Convention

ATTRIBUTE	FORMAT	DESCRIPTION
QUERYID	QIDn*	PDW reuses its internally generated, appliance unique, formatted numeric `request_id` that we typically see in `sys.dm_pdw_exec_requests` to mark the export. This enables us to tie the files in HDFS to the query in PDW that exported it. Therefore, n* represents the query in this context.
DATE	YYYYMMDD	Date query started to export data to HDFS. (Note that this is the date in PDW, not the date in Hadoop.)
TIME	HHMMSS	Time query started to export data to HDFS. (Note that this is the time in PDW, not the time in Hadoop.)
DISTRIBUTION	n*	Zero-based number for representing each distribution in the appliance. There are 8 distributions in the appliance per compute node. Therefore, if you have 6 compute nodes, you have 48 distributions. However, the range of these distribution numbers would be 0 to 47 in this instance. The n* in this context would therefore be 0–47.

We can conclude that PDW is creating one file per distribution and that this is how PDW is able to write the data out in parallel. Consequently, we can also conclude that if the data is skewed in PDW, the files in HDFS will be similarly skewed. By default, there will be three copies of the data, and the files will be constituted from 64MB blocks (because this is the block size). We can see the actual size and the number of replicas with our `-ls` command. The value `524139` shown in Figure 10.14 is the size in bytes for the first distribution (that is, distribution 0 or compute node 1 distribution A in PDW parlance). We can also see how many copies of this file we have from `-ls` command. Figure 10.14 shows the value `3` appearing on every row. It's located on the left after the file permissions and is followed by the name of the user (always pdw_user for data written by PDW) responsible for its creation. Sadly, the block size used isn't available through `-ls`.

What about replicated tables? Good question. Replicated tables export only to a single file, so in that sense there is no parallel export of a replicated table.

Aside from the `ExternalExportDistributedOperation` operation, it's basically the same suite of steps taken when an external table is created, including the collection of the table size and row count statistical information, courtesy of `ExternalStatisticsOperation`.

Remember that the external table persists after the CETAS operation. On the one hand, this is helpful for querying or importing the data later on. We also know that we have some statistical data associated with the table. On the other hand, it does prevent you from reexecuting this code (that is, you have to first drop the external table first). (I have to say that it would be really nice if you could just execute this code with a `DROP_EXISTING` instead, because remembering to drop the external table is a pain.)

There is one possible reason for not including `DROP_EXISTING` syntax in the CETAS statement. Simply dropping the external table does nothing to affect the data in Hadoop. This might lead to unexpected behavior for some people. If I did decide to drop the external table and simply reexecuted the CETAS query, I would in effect append the same data to the "table" in HDFS. Remember that the table in HDFS is merely a folder containing files of data. A simple export of data, via CETAS, pushes another new set of files to the same folder within HDFS, which effectively replicates the content. To first properly clean up the data and remove it from HDFS, I must execute a command in Hadoop like the one here:

```
Hadoop fs -rmr /files/HDFS_FactInternetSales
```

Now the data and the folder have been moved to the trash, as you can see in Figure 10.15 (IP address and port blacked out).

Perhaps a more complete extension to CETAS would be `WITH (TRUNCATE, DROP_EXISTING)`. This would both remove the existing external table and fire the Hadoop file system `-rmr` operation to clean up the data residing in Hadoop before the next export. However, at this stage neither `TRUNCATE` nor `DROP_EXISTING` exist at this moment.

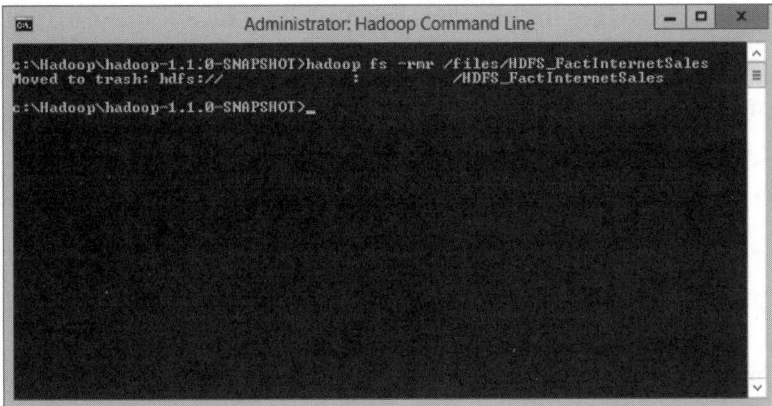

Figure 10.15: Cleaning up directories in Hadoop with -rmr

Business Use Cases for Polybase Today

One of the comments I've heard several times is that Microsoft tends to only talk about what is coming down the line. Although this is both interesting and brings much excitement, it often also leads to frustration as readers, listeners and viewers often end up feeling that there is no immediate use-case for the technology. I am going to try to address that in this section, at least in part. Therefore, in the following subsections, I discuss some of the ideas I've had for how to use Polybase, based purely on the building blocks we have today.

Archiving and Audit

The first scenario I want to suggest is an extension to the archiving solution Thomas Kejser proposed and that I highlighted earlier in this chapter. Thomas suggested that Hadoop and Hive could be a simple place to store source system data, which could both be easily queried and with Polybase now very easily rehydrated if needed. This would enable all sorts of warehouse replay functionality.

My proposed extension for this is to archive snapshot views of data. Suppose, for example, that a user queries a sensitive table. How do you track what the user saw at the time he saw it? One possible solution is to intercept the `SELECT` statement and instead prepend it with a CETAS statement, thus exporting the data into Hadoop creating a formal record of the data viewed.

This data could then be read from that file with a modified `SELECT` against the external table, thus guaranteeing that the same data is read as was recorded against the user accessing the data. These audit snapshots could be implemented in the database itself, but this can sometimes lead to a lot of data being generated and held in a relational store with little requirement to actually do anything with it. This is an attempted low-cost solution to that problem.

In summary, the advantages of this approach are as follows:

- Simple audit process
- Use of low-cost storage
- Reduced complexity for the database
- Removes storage capacity from the database
- Online retrieval if ever required

The primary disadvantage here is the network round-trip.

Data Subsetting and Obfuscation

Time for a variation on a theme: when you need to move data from one environment to another, it is often not a simple case of backup and restore. Consider moving data from production down to development or quality assurance environments. Often you don't want to move all the data, just a meaningful subset for representative testing volumes. More importantly, you want to ensure that no personally identifiable information is exposed in less-secure environments. Therefore, we need a way to both create obfuscated but meaningful subsets of production data.

One option is to leverage the export capabilities of Polybase to perform a high-performance data subsetting and obfuscation routine. Once exported, this data could then be picked up by other PDWs or even other systems from Hadoop. If required, one could also run additional algorithms over the data in Hadoop to provide further obfuscation to the data.

Data Hub/Broker

Like PDW, Hadoop can often be considered as a downstream system. In other words, it receives data from other data sources, which are then brought in for analysis.

Integrating that data into Hadoop does require some additional skills and possible tooling. However, you could mitigate that need by using PDW as a data hub and delivery mechanism for the warehouse and Hadoop environments. This would have some nice benefits:

- No new skills
- No new tools
- Consistency of data
- Streamlined operations through consolidated feeds

Speculating on the Future for Polybase

Sometimes it's worth doing some research and wider reading. You can occasionally come across some hidden gems that make a worthwhile pursuit an invaluable one. Bear this in mind as we dust off our crystal ball and "speculate" on the future for Polybase.

Partitioned Appliance

In the June 2013 sigmod whitepaper authored by Dr. David DeWitt and others titled "Split Query Processing in Polybase," I unearthed the following information morsel: " . . . there are tentative plans to allow customers to partition their appliances into disjoint Hadoop and PDW regions . . ."

This first comment largely speaks for itself. To me, it is clear that the PDW team plans to enable PDW customers to use scale units for Hadoop. I'd expect this to be in addition to the features we have seen in Polybase already. Consequently, as users, I think what we will have is a choice. We can either integrate with Hadoop that's configured inside the appliance and/or integrate with Hadoop outside of the appliance. That'd be a pretty impressive option don't you think? Other vendors tend to favor one deployment model and only work with a single distribution. As we look to the future, the agnostic architecture of Polybase is really starting to show its true worth.

However, before we delve a little deeper into this topic, there is another tidbit of information from the same whitepaper: "There are no plans currently to allow customers to co-locate a SQL Server instance and a Hadoop Datanode."

This makes quite a bit of sense to me. The virtual machines used by PDW for the compute nodes are presized to consume almost all the resources available. Therefore, there isn't much compute processing room for the data nodes. Furthermore, you probably wouldn't want any unpredictable resource contention, which might be another reason to keep the two workloads "disjointed."

One possible advantage of having Hadoop "inside" of PDW is that you might be able to have relational database management system (RDBMS)-like security over the data inside HDFS. As mentioned previously, security isn't exactly Hadoop's forte. However, I would imagine that I can only grant access privileges to people I want to be able to engage on the data, for example.

Another reason might be flexibility. Remember that PDW's configuration is almost completely virtual. The workload definition, for example, is in the compute nodes (a virtual machine). Would it be not be possible therefore to decide that I would like to have four compute PDW nodes with four data nodes one day and six compute and four data the next? Granted, the amount of data committed to any data node(s) would represent an obstacle (data would need to be rebalanced between the remaining compute nodes), but it would in theory at least be possible.

Earlier in the chapter we discussed having separate Hadoop environments for various user personas. A partitioned appliance could be a great location for our power user and consumer community grade data sets, giving them dedicated compute resources that would be very close to the enterprise data held in PDW. This workload isolation would also benefit the data scientists as they wouldn't need to worry about interference from corporate users as much. Naturally, Polybase would be the perfect fit for migrating the data between these Bronze, Silver, and Gold environments. Being able to leverage PDW's ultra-low latency Infiniband network would also come in extremely handy for those challenging ad-hoc queries.

Finally, manageability: from an operational perspective, will a single-managed appliance be more attractive than having two distributed systems and having to manage them separately? There's an opportunity for consolidated management and monitoring here for PDW and Hadoop using a single interface that goes beyond System Center Management Packs. The simplicity of an appliance experience will be a factor for some. That said, I am not sure about this one. Those who have more of a database-centric view of the world might be swayed by such an argument. Having a clean, consistent deployment of Hadoop without any configuration headaches as well having only "one throat to choke" when it comes to support may well prove attractive. However, it would very much depend on the PDW teams' execution focus and priorities. For this to prove really valuable to customers would be a lot of work I expect.

Architecture Versus Implementation

One positive aspect of the Polybase is that, architecturally, it makes no assumptions. Questions concerning data format, data location within HDFS, and number of data nodes, for example, are answered at runtime. This means that the Hadoop ecosystem and PDW can happily coexist without any dependencies.

However, not everything in that architectural vision made the cut when it came to the initial implementation that formed RTM of PDW 2012. One example concerns the format of the data in Hadoop. Although it is true to say that architecturally PDW makes no assumption on the format used to persist the data in HDFS (the HDFS Bridge provides the necessary abstraction), it is not true for the RTM Polybase implementation. At this moment, Polybase supports files in only delimited text format.

That said, I expect to see Polybase supporting other standard file formats and possibly even custom file formats in the future. As long as we can impose that structure on the underlying data file, we should be all good. One example that I could see in the near term is the optimized row columnar (ORC) file format, which has been the subject of much development through the stinger initiative and is very commonly used by Hive users.

Optimized Big Data Queries

In his keynote presentation "Polybase: What, Why, How" at the PASS Summit in 2012 (`http://gsl.azurewebsites.net/Portals/0/Users/dewitt/talks/PolybasePass2012.pptx`), Dr. DeWitt gave some indications to the roadmap of Polybase. At this illuminating session, he broke the roadmap into three phases. Phase 1 is what we have in PDW today, so I won't belabor that. Phase 2 was really focused on using the computational resources of the Hadoop cluster; selectively issuing MapReduce jobs to optimize queries instead of relying on the parallel import functionality that PDW has today. Phase 3 was much heavily caveated. Therefore, it's difficult to read too much into it. However, it was clear that a lot of thought is going into leveraging Hadoop 2.0, Yarn, and Tez. Could we see a more holistic optimizer? Perhaps we'll see PDW dynamically exporting data to Hadoop because it might be more efficient to process the data there for example. Who knows? Suddenly the crystal ball looks a little bit too blurry.

Let's step back to phase 2 then. While highlighting the opportunity for leveraging Hadoop's compute resources, Dr. DeWitt also highlighted several challenges that made me realize that this wasn't simply a case of just getting PDW to issue MapReduce jobs every time a Polybase query is received. In order to decide where and when to use MapReduce, PDW would need additional information fed into it so it could make an informed decision to use it or not. However, put simply, Hadoop did not hold the kind of data required by PDW. It was clearly not going to be a trivial task deriving this information either. We will discuss the kinds of data PDW shortly but first let's understand a bit more about how PDW optimizes a query.

Rather than use a rules engine, PDW uses a cost-based optimizer to determine how to resolve your query in the most efficient manner. Like SQL Server, we create statistics on key columns to help guide the optimizer. In PDW, we create stats on all columns involved in the following areas of a query:

- Joins
- Group by
- Where clause
- Order by

Having these statistical objects created on our tables helps PDW decide on the best MPP plan for your query. In some cases, especially for composite joins, we may even create multicolumn stats to help guide the optimizer further. A multicolumn statistic provides the density of the neighboring column(s) to the optimizer, which can help to influence the type of join chosen. Instead of a nested loop join, which is often undesirable and inefficient in a data warehouse, we might be able to influence the optimizer to choose a hash join, for example. All these techniques are great tuning options for data in your data warehouse.

Hadoop and HDFS do not even hold this basic information. Its approach to data analysis is more sledgehammer based. Remember the Hadoop mindset is to throw compute at the problem.

However, with a system such as Polybase, you really need the statistical information, and a whole lot more. Therefore, in addition to holding statistical information about data held in Hadoop, the Polybase engineers need access to additional information to determine the optimal plan. Consider this list for starters:

- Hadoop cluster size
- Network bandwidth to Hadoop cluster
- Utilization of resources on Hadoop
- Proximity of Hadoop cluster
- Selectivity of predicates for data held in Hadoop
- Semantic differences between Java and SQL

As Polybase evolves and both Hadoop and PDW mature, you could see some really interesting decisions being made. Is 90% of the data in Hadoop, for example? One answer could be to send the remaining data over to Hadoop and process the query there. Is Hadoop busy and data volume reasonable? Move the data to PDW. I am no query processor expert (far from it), but these kinds of possibilities are exciting!

Why Poly *in Polybase?*

If the sole objective of Polybase was to integrate with just HDFS, why call it Polybase? If we look at the definition of *poly*, which is "more than one; many or much" (according to the Collins Dictionary), is this not a clear signal of bigger things to come? Speaking personally for a moment, I'd love to be able to simply reference delimited files exposed on a Windows NTFS file system. I think that would be a really nice extension of this feature and would significantly strengthen PDW's data export functionality. However, I am sure that the cloud will factor into Polybase somewhere. Every product in the Microsoft Data Platform has to have a cloud strategy, and PDW is no exception. If on-premise Hadoop is the cold storage for PDW, could Azure be the deep freezer?

Thinking further ahead, who's is to say that Polybase couldn't be used to integrate with other systems such as SAP Hana or Oracle? After all, a cow has many stomachs. Why can't PDW have many engines? That's certainly something for you to chew on.

Summary

Well, that's about it for PDW and Polybase. I hope you found that interesting, and you learned a bit about PDW and why it is important to the world of data warehousing. However, more importantly, I hope that you are excited about the integration opportunities that Polybase offers us, both now and in the future. It's important to remember that only PDW offers Polybase and Hadoop integration.

Polybase is an enormously strategic piece of technology. Its holistic, agnostic architecture and approach to Hadoop integration opens up the relational world to a whole host of new opportunities. I hope you agree and will give much stronger consideration to PDW and its capabilities for your next project.

This is a rapidly changing and highly dynamic environment. I'm therefore expecting to see lots of great improvements and solutions in the months ahead. Remember PDW also updates with new features twice a year, so the next set of features are never far away!

Summary

CHAPTER

11

Visualizing Big Data with Microsoft BI

WHAT YOU WILL LEARN IN THIS CHAPTER:

- Learning What Microsoft BI Tools Are Available for Big Data Visualizations
- Setting Up the ODBC Driver for Data Access
- Loading Data into a PowerPivot Model
- Adding Measures to a PowerPivot Model
- Creating Pivot Tables to Analyze the Data
- Using Power View to Explore Big Data
- Using Power Map for Spatial Exploration of Data

One of the most important aspects of any business intelligence (BI) solution is making sense of the data to drive intelligent decision-making processes. This usually includes creating visualizations in the form of charts, graphs, and maps that allow the user to easily spot trends and anomalies in the data. The old adage "a picture is worth a thousand words" could not be truer when it comes to data analysis.

Hadoop does not provide native reporting and visualization capabilities, but plenty of tools out there do a good job of providing data visualization. Using standard ODBC drivers, you can easily connect these tools to Hadoop, and use

Hive queries to pull the data into reports and dashboards. Microsoft provides an outstanding set of tools in their self-service BI suite that make it easy to build interactive reports and dashboards. This chapter covers these various tools and how you can use them to gain insight into your Hadoop data repositories.

An Ecosystem of Tools

Microsoft provides a whole ecosystem of tools for reporting on and visualizing data. Which tool you use depends on factors such as data latency requirements, static versus interactive capabilities, and the need to combine data from multiple sources. The following subsections cover the available tools and when you should consider using each.

Excel

Excel is one of the most popular data analysis tools on the market today. Most data analysts are Excel power users and are quite comfortable slicing and dicing data using this tool. This excellent tool proves especially useful for users who want to explore data on their own. They can connect to various data sources, create pivot tables and charts, filter and slice the data, and perform what-if analysis. Excel contains an extensive set of built-in functions to analyze the data, including financial, statistical, and engineering functions. Excel also contains features to help clean the data, such as removing duplicates, consolidating data, and validating data. Figure 11.1 shows some of the menu items on the data tab that help you clean, validate, and shape the data.

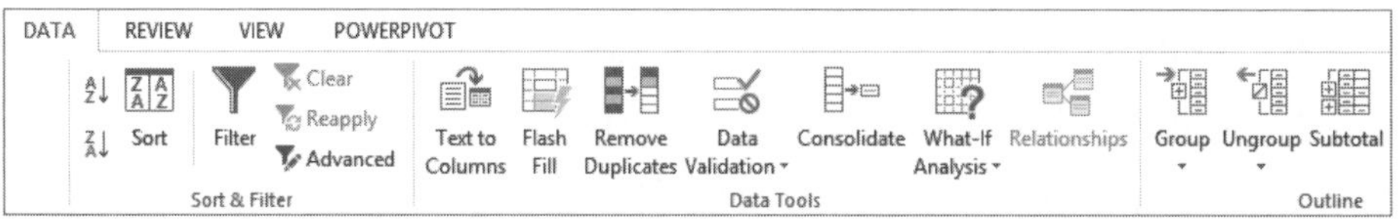

Figure 11.1: Data cleansing features in Excel.

PowerPivot

When the amount of data you need to analyze pushes the limits (about 1 million rows for Excel 2013) of Excel's capabilities, consider moving to PowerPivot. PowerPivot is a free add-in to Excel. It is based on a columnar database structure and data compression that allows it to support millions of rows. It builds on top of Excel's feature set and enables users to create pivot tables and charts and supports slicing and filtering and time-based analysis.

Instead of basing pivot tables and charts on data contained in a data sheet, PowerPivot is based on a data model that contains tables and relationships between the tables. This proves extremely beneficial when the user needs to combine data from various sources into a single mode for the analysis. For example, it is easy to combine data from a relational database with data contained in a Hadoop file structure.

In addition, PowerPivot supports creating custom calculations and measures using Data Analysis Expressions (DAX), a feature that supports efficient querying and sophisticated calculations on very large data sets. Figure 11.2 shows a model being developed in PowerPivot. It is combining census data from Hadoop and rainfall data from a SQL Server database.

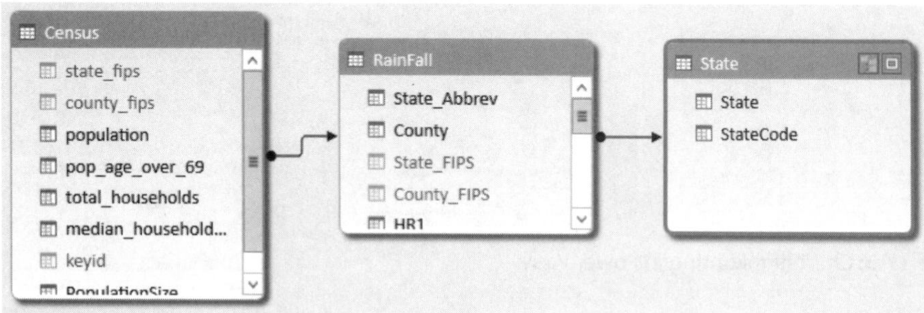

Figure 11.2: Creating a data model in PowerPivot.

Power View

Power View is an add-in to Excel that enables users to create highly interactive data visualizations. You can easily create tables and matrices, along with charts such as bar, pie, line, and bubble charts. Power View reports use PowerPivot models as the data source. Because the model provides both the tables and the relations between the tables, Power View can link the various charts and tables together. Filtering one chart in a view automatically propagates to other visualizations in the same view. Furthermore, if the data model has hierarchies defined, you automatically get the ability to drill up or down through the hierarchy in your charts and matrices. Another useful feature of Power View is support for highlighting, which allows you to examine a subset of the data while still showing the rest of the data. Figure 11.3 shows how highlighting a chart in the view also highlights a chart with related data (State).

If you have data that contains a date/time field, you can create a bubble chart that includes a play axis that shows how the data changes over time. Power View includes a mapping feature that enables visualization of the data on a Bing map layer that includes the ability to zoom in and out. Figure 11.4 shows a map of rainfall for counties in Pennsylvania. The size of the bubble represents the rainfall, and the color of the bubble represents the relative size of the county's population.

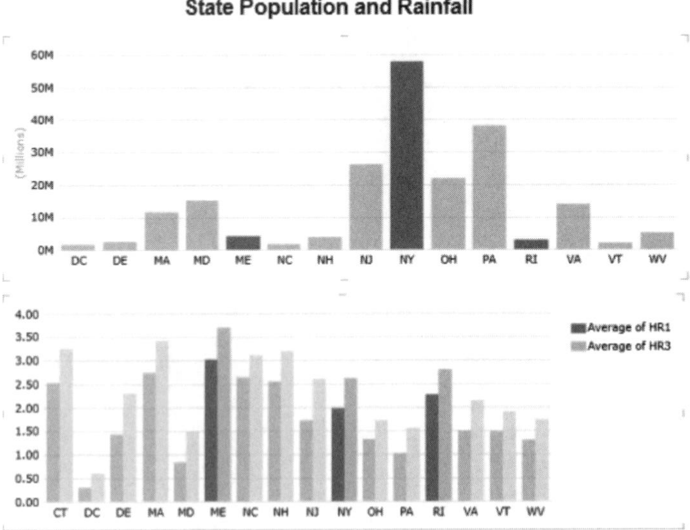

Figure 11.3: Chart highlighting in Power View.

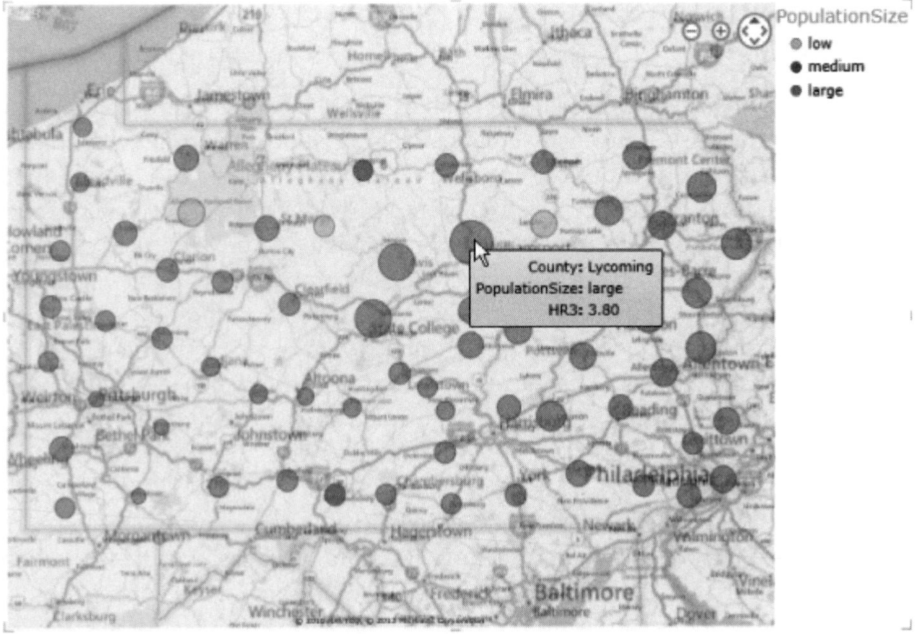

Figure 11.4: Power View map showing rainfall and population data.

Power Map

Although you can create rudimentary maps in Power View, they are limited and do not have much functionality. A much more useful tool for mapping data is Power Map. Power Map is a powerful add-in for Excel that enables you to plot three-dimensional maps for large data sets that contain geospatial data. You can create heat maps, bar charts, and bubble charts. You can also zoom and rotate the maps to gain unique perspectives and insight into the data. If the data is time-stamped, you can even create recordings that show how the data changes over time. One thing to be aware of is that Power Map uses Bing maps to facilitate spatial data exploration and you need to send the data to Bing through a secured connection for geocoding. Figure 11.5 shows rainfall data plotted on a Bing map using Power Map.

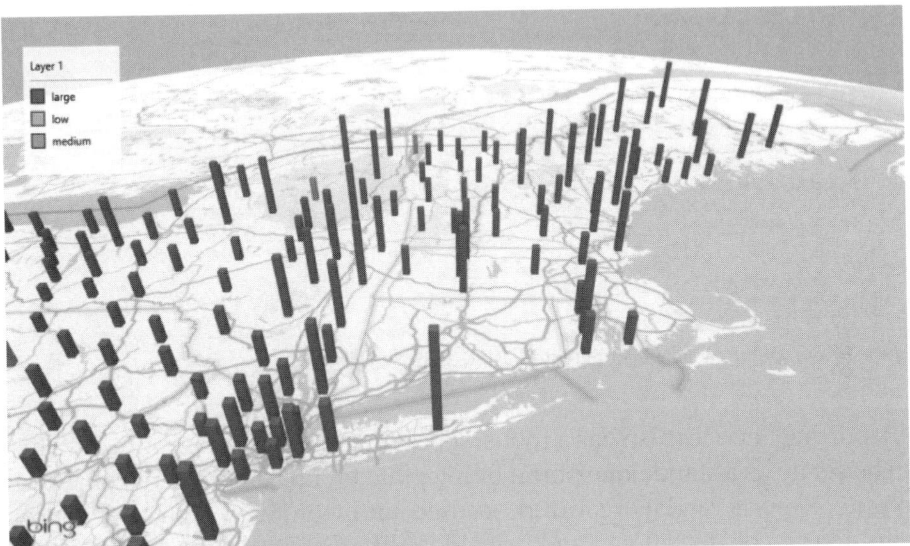

Figure 11.5: Three-dimensional rainfall plot in Power Map.

Reporting Services

Although the preceding tools excel at providing self-service data visualization and exploration, most organizations still need a traditional reporting solution that consists of highly formatted distributed reports. These reports are usually highly structured to meet a specific set of requirements, formatted for printing, and are pushed out to users on a periodic basis.

SQL Server Reporting Services (SSRS) is an excellent tool for creating and managing your structured reporting requirements. It provides a rich development environment, supports conditional formatting, and enables parameter-driven reports and linking of reports for drilling across different views of the data. Reports can include tables, matrices, various graphs, and images. Figure 11.6 shows a typical tabular report created using the report designer.

Sales Order Detail 2008

ADVENTURE WORKS cycles

Sales Order
Order #: SO50750

Bill To: Central Discount Store
259826 Russell Rd. South
Kent, Washington 98031
United States

Ship To: Central Discount Store
259826 Russell Rd. South
Kent, Washington 98031
United States

Contact: Jean Handley Purchasing Manager 582-555-0113
Carina Stanev Purchasing Agent 597-555-0100

Date	Order Date	Sales Person	Purchase Order	Shipment Method
7/31/2009	6/1/2003	David Campbell, Sales Representative 740-555-0182	PO7192170677	CARGO TRANSPORT 5

Line	Qty	Item Number	Description	Tracking #	Unit Price	Subtotal	Discount	Item Total
1	2	CA-1098	AWC Logo Cap	373D-417C-AE	$5.19	$10.37	$0.00	$10.37
2	4	GL-F110-M	Full-Finger Gloves, M	373D-417C-AE	$22.79	$91.18	$0.00	$91.18
3	4	LJ-0192-L	Long-Sleeve Logo Jersey, L	373D-417C-AE	$28.84	$115.36	$0.00	$115.36
4	3	GL-F110-L	Full-Finger Gloves, L	373D-417C-AE	$22.79	$68.38	$0.00	$68.38
5	1	BK-M68B-42	Mountain-200 Black, 42	373D-417C-AE	$1,229.46	$1,229.46	$0.00	$1,229.46
6	1	TG-W091-L	Women's Tights, L	373D-417C-AE	$44.99	$44.99	$0.00	$44.99
7	1	BK-M68S-38	Mountain-200 Silver, 38	373D-417C-AE	$1,242.85	$1,242.85	$0.00	$1,242.85
			Total Discount: $0.00				Total:	$2,802.60

Contact us:

- Phone: 800-ADVENTURE
- Email: help@adventureworks.com
- Fax: 800-555-2424

Figure 11.6: Tabular invoice report created using SSRS.

Reporting Services also has a robust report management environment. This can be set up as a standalone portal or integrated with a SharePoint collaboration site. Reports can be organized, secured, and monitored. The same report definition can be distributed and printed in different rendering formats, such as PDF or Microsoft Word. Reports can be automatically refreshed and delivered through a portal, e-mail, or file share. Another cool feature is the ability to create data-driven report distribution, where the same report can be run using different parameter values depending on who is getting the report. For example, the same report can be rendered using a department ID parameter that is tied to the recipient's department. Figure 11.7 shows a report rendered in a SSRS report portal.

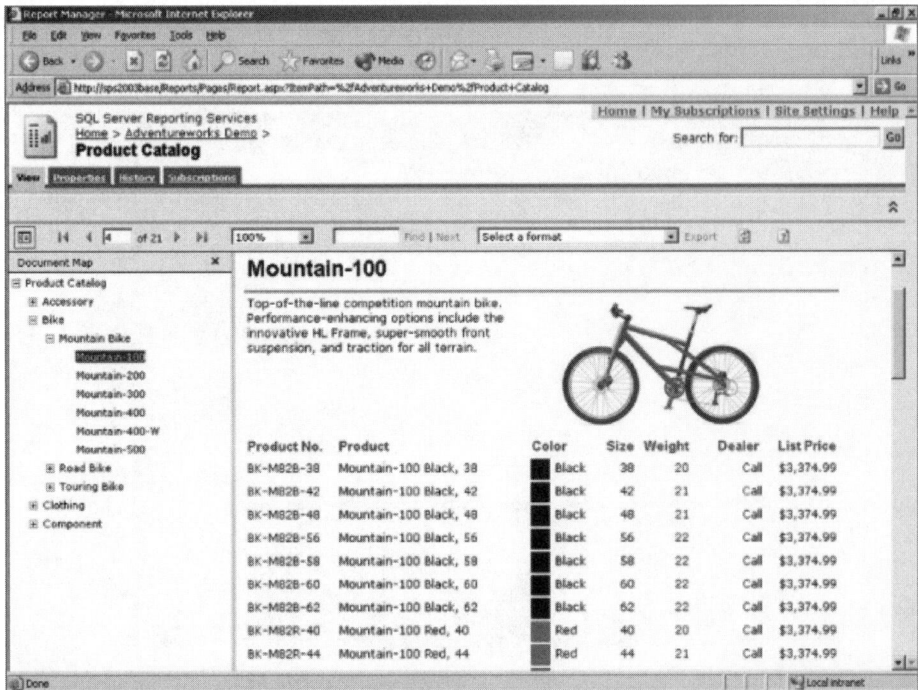

Figure 11.7: SSRS report rendered in a report portal.

Self-service Big Data with PowerPivot

As mentioned previously, you can use PowerPivot to create data mash-ups using data from various sources and combine them into a data model. Because of the underlying database compression and columnar structure, PowerPivot can handle tens of millions of rows. This is the recommended solution when you need to actively slice and dice large amounts of data. In this section, you will set up an ODBC driver to connect to Hadoop and load the data into a PowerPivot model.

Setting Up the ODBC Driver

To load data from Hadoop, you need to install an ODBC driver on the computer on which you are using PowerPivot. Several ODBC drivers for Hadoop are available. Microsoft provides one you can download from their website (`http://www.microsoft.com/en-us/download/details.aspx?id=40886`). The ODBC driver uses Hive and HiveQL to retrieve the data. After you download and install the driver, you need to set up a data source name (DSN) to use in PowerPivot:

1. To begin, launch the ODBC Data Source Administrator and click the System DSN tab (see Figure 11.8).

2. Add a new DSN using the Microsoft Hive ODBC driver, as shown in Figure 11.9.

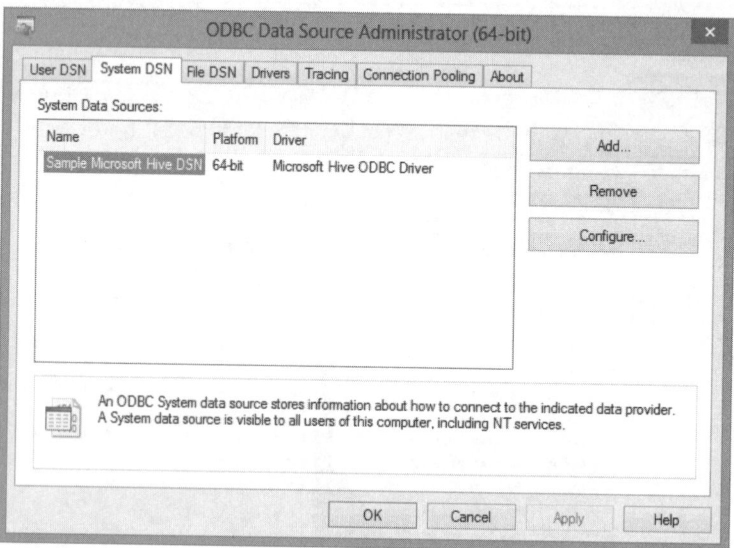

Figure 11.8: Setting up a new system DSN.

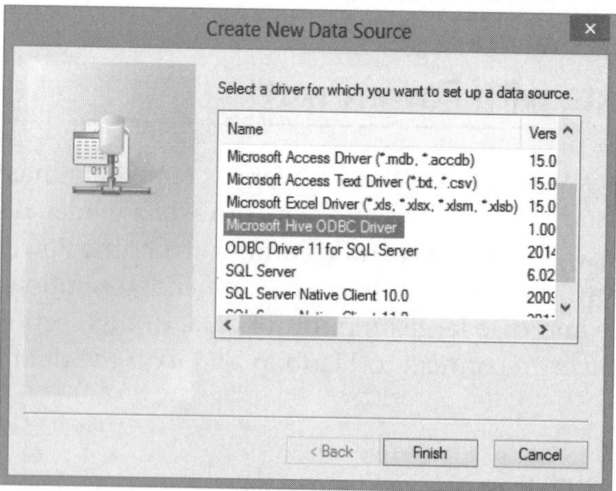

Figure 11.9: Selecting the Hive driver.

3. Fill in the appropriate connection information for your Hadoop cluster in the setup screen shown in Figure 11.10. Remember that your settings will differ. Consult with your Hadoop administrator for the correct settings.

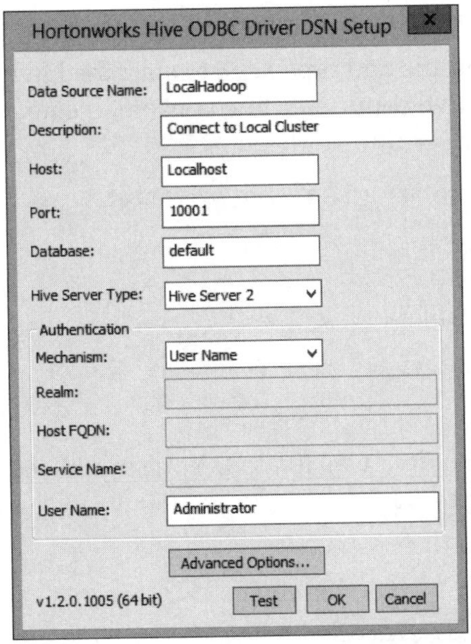

Figure 11.10: Setting up connection information.

Don't forget to verify the connection by clicking the Test button at the bottom of the setup screen.

Loading Data

If you want to follow along loading data into PowerPivot, you can download the sample flight data from (`www.wiley.com/go/microsoftbigdatasolutions`). This contains three CSV files:

- **Flight_Dept_Perf.csv**: Contains flight date, carrier code, airport code, departure times, and departure delays. Although this file only contains flights during October 2012, this is the type of data that would be contained in Hadoop spanning multiple years. A Hadoop map-reduce process would perform an aggregation and load it into a results table that is then consumed by PowerPivot.
- **Carriers.csv**: Contains the carrier codes and names.
- **US_Airports.csv**: Contains the airport code, name, and its latitude and longitude.

You will load the data from these files directly into PowerPivot:

1. Open the Hadoop command line console and type **hive** to start the Hive command-line console. Using the Hive command-line console, create a flight_dept table using the following script:

```
Create Table flight_dept (flight_date string,carrier_cd string,
airport_cd string,dep_time int,delay int)
Row Format Delimited Fields Terminated By ',';
```

2. Use the following script to load the table:

```
LOAD DATA LOCAL INPATH 'c:\sampledata\Flight_Dept_Perf.csv'
OVERWRITE INTO TABLE flight_dept;
```

3. Run the following query to verify the data was loaded. You should see results similar to those shown in Figure 11.11:

```
Select * from flight_dept limit 10;
```

```
hive.cmd - Shortcut
total_size: 13451671, raw_data_size: 0]
OK
Time taken: 1.183 seconds
hive> Select * from flight_dept limit 10;
OK
10/30/2012      DL      LGA     NULL    NULL
10/30/2012      DL      ATL     1110    -5
10/30/2012      DL      BWI     1354    -6
10/30/2012      DL      ATL     1957    -2
10/30/2012      DL      MSP     1548    23
10/30/2012      DL      FLL     1126    -4
10/30/2012      DL      CLT     825     -5
10/30/2012      DL      SAN     642     -3
10/30/2012      DL      MKE     657     -3
10/30/2012      DL      ABQ     841     -4
Time taken: 0.397 seconds, Fetched: 10 row(s)
hive>
```

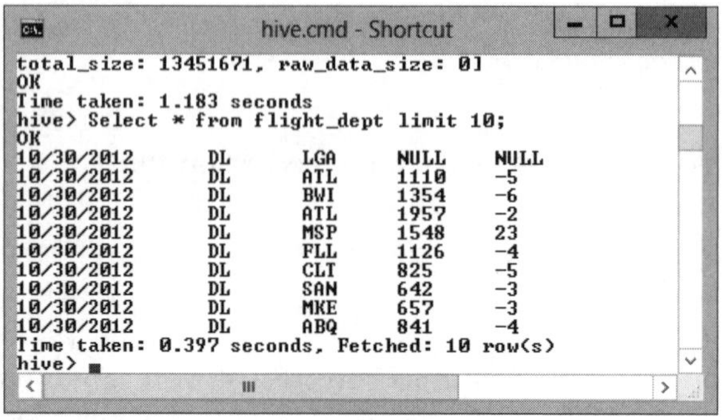

Figure 11.11: Verifying the data load.

4. Now that the data is accessible through a Hive table, you can load it into PowerPivot using the ODBC driver. Open Excel and click the PowerPivot tab. On the PowerPivot tab, click Manage to open the PowerPivot window (see Figure 11.12).

NOTE You may need to enable the PowerPivot add-in if you are using Excel 2013 (see `http://office.microsoft.com/en-us/excel-help/start-power-pivot-in-microsoft-excel-2013-add-in-HA102837097.aspx`).

5. In the PowerPivot model designer, click Get External Data from Other Sources to launch the Table Import Wizard. Select the Others (OLEDB/ODBC) data source, as shown in Figure 11.13, and then click Next.

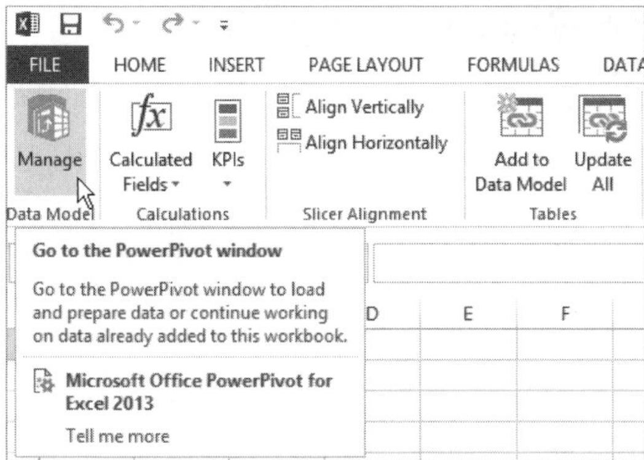

Figure 11.12: Launching the PowerPivot model designer.

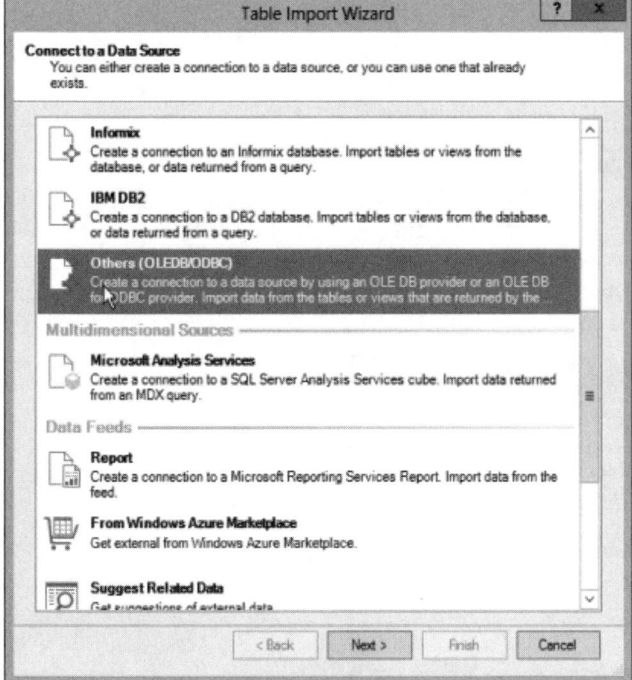

Figure 11.13: Connecting to a data source.

6. In the Specify a Connection String window, click Build to open the Data Link Properties window (see Figure 11.14).
7. From the Provider tab, choose Microsoft OLEDB Provider for ODBC Drivers. From the Connection tab, select the Use Data Source Name option button and choose the DSN you created earlier to connect to your Hadoop cluster and test the connection (see Figure 11.15).

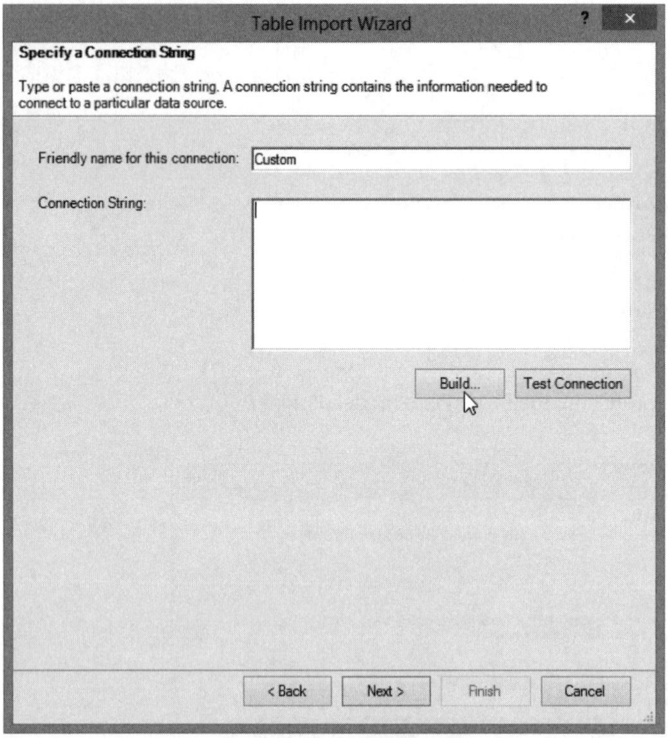

Figure 11.14: Building the connection string.

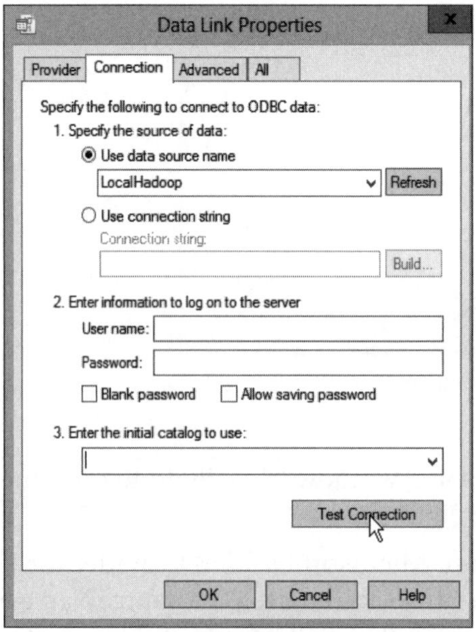

Figure 11.15: Setting data link properties.

8. In the next screen choose to write a query to return the data (see Figure 11.16).

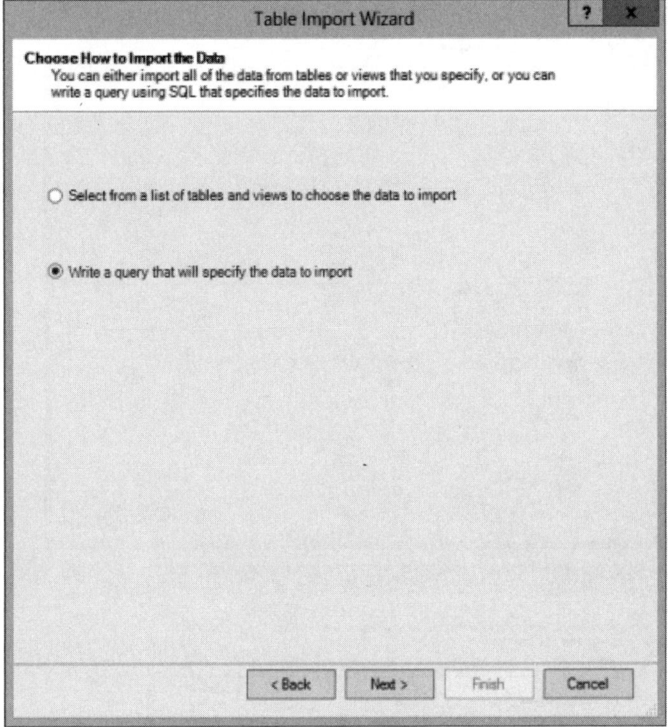

Figure 11.16: Choosing how to import the data.

9. Enter the following query to retrieve the data. If you launch the query designer, you can test the query to see whether you get results back as in Figure 11.17:

```
Select flight_date, carrier_cd, airport_cd, dep_time, delay from
  flight_dept
where delay > 0
```

10. After you have tested the query close the designer, rename the query to **flight_dept** and click Finish. The data will be imported into a table in the model called flight_dept.

    The next step is to import the data contained in the `Carriers.csv` and `US_Airports.csv` files.

11. In the PowerPivot model designer, click Get External Data from Other Sources to launch the Table Import Wizard again. This time select the text file source. Browse to the `Carriers.csv` file and select the Use First Row

as Column Headers check box. Also change the Friendly connection name to **Carriers**. You should see sample data similar to Figure 11.18.

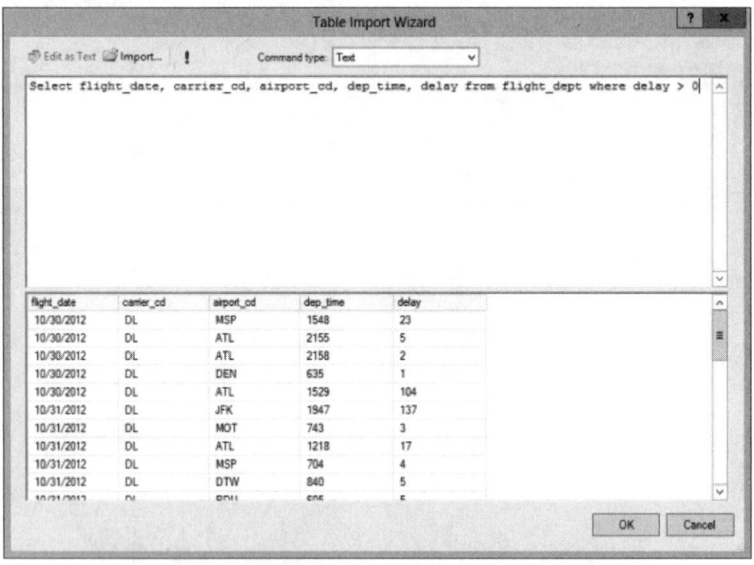

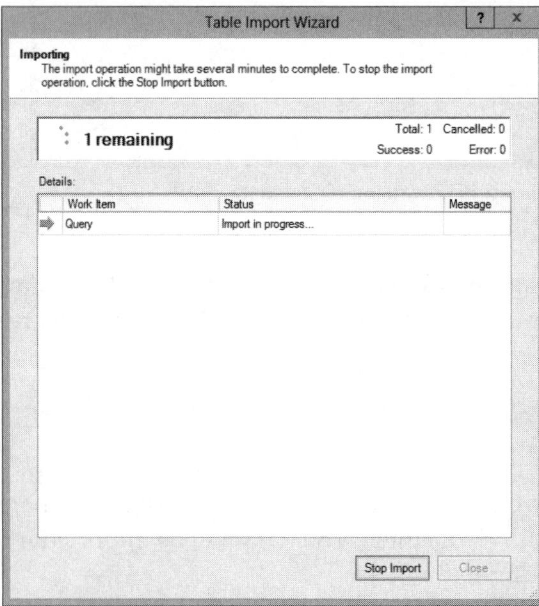

Figure 11.17: Testing the query.

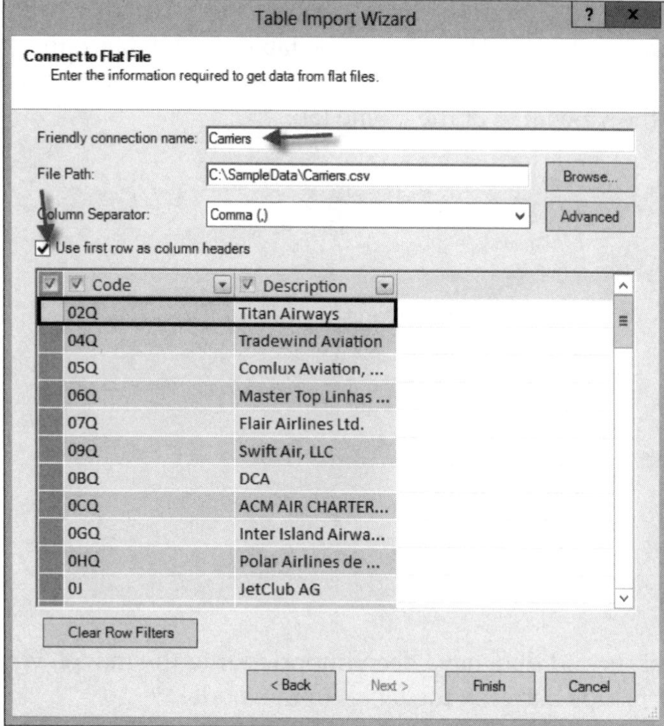

Figure 11.18: Importing CSV data.

12. Repeat the procedure to import data from the `US_Airports.csv` file with a connection name of **US_Airports**. You should end up with three tables in the designer.

You use two views to work with the model: the data view and the diagram view. The data view shows each table in a tab with the data in a grid (see Figure 11.19). The area below the grid is where you define measures such as sum or count to aggregate the data.

flight_date	carrier_cd	airport_cd	dep_time	delay
10/1/2012 12:00:...	WN	MDW	941	1
10/1/2012 12:00:...	WN	MDW	1311	1
10/1/2012 12:00:...	WN	MDW	1701	1
10/1/2012 12:00:...	WN	MDW	601	1
10/1/2012 12:00:...	WN	MDW	2016	1
10/1/2012 12:00:...	WN	MDW	606	1

flight_dept | Carriers | US_Airports

Figure 11.19: The data view of the model.

The diagram view of the model shows the tables and relationships between the tables in the model. Figure 11.20 shows the tables in the diagram view; no relationships are defined between the tables yet. To toggle between the views, click the icons in the View area of the Home tab.

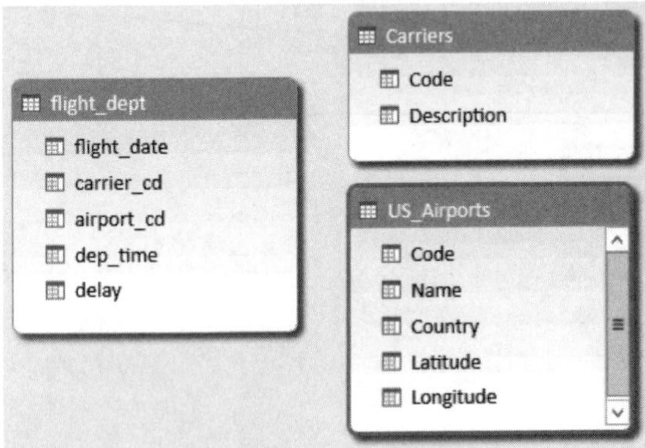

Figure 11.20: The diagram view of the model.

Now that the tables and data have been imported into the model, you need to establish relationships between the tables in the model.

Updating the Model

To establish relationships between the tables in the model complete the following steps:

1. In the diagram view, drag the carrier_cd field from the flight_dept and drop it on the Code field in the Carriers table.
2. Repeat the procedure in step 1 to create a relationship between the airport_cd field in the flight_dept table and the code field in the US_Airports table.
3. Right-click the carrier_cd field in the flight_dept table and select Hide from Client Tools.
4. Repeat the procedure in step 3 for the airport_cd field.

Your model should look like Figure 11.21.

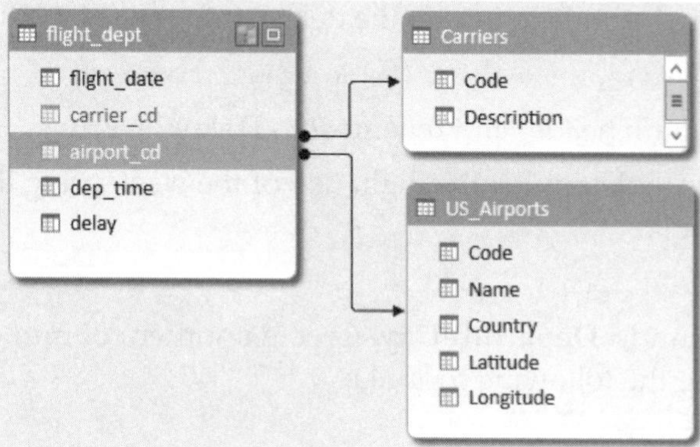

Figure 11.21: The updated model.

The next step you need to do is create some measures in the model that will aid in analyzing the data.

Adding Measures

In this section, you create aggregations to count, average, and find the maximum delays:

1. Switch to the data view of the model and click the flight_dept tab. Select the first cell in the measure area below the grid and add the following DAX code to the formula bar to count the number of delays (see Figure 11.22):

```
TotalDelays:=Count([delay])
```

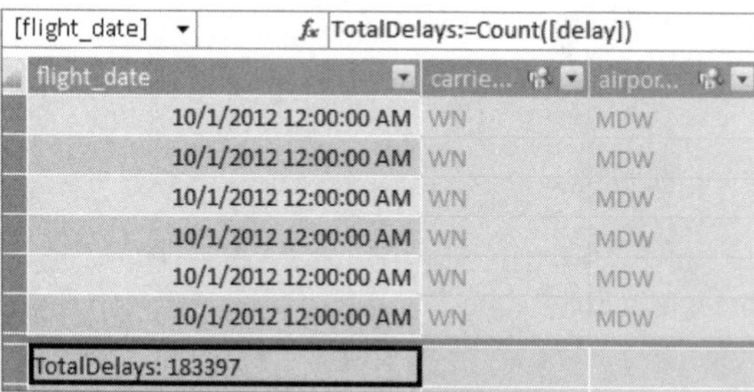

Figure 11.22: Adding a measure to the model.

2. In a similar fashion, add the following measures to the model:

```
MaxDelay:=Max([delay])
AveDelay:=AVERAGE([delay])
```

In addition to measures, you can add calculated columns to the model.

3. Click the cell under the Add Column header in the flight_dept table tab. Enter the following formula to bucket the delays into ranges:

```
=IF([delay]<=15,"small",IF([delay]<=60, "medium","large"))
```

4. Right-click the column header and rename it to **DelaySeverity**.
5. Repeat the process to determine the flight day of the week using the following DAX formula:

```
=Format([flight_date],"DDD")
```

6. Rename the column to **DepartureDay**. Create another column called **DayOfWeek** using the following formula:

```
=WEEKDAY([flight_date])
```

7. Select the DepartureDay column and under the Home tab select Sort by Column. Sort the column by the DayOfWeek column.

Now that the model has been created, you can create pivot tables to analyze the data.

Creating Pivot Tables

To create a pivot table based on the model, complete the following:

1. To create the pivot table, click the PivotTable drop-down on the Home tab of the PowerPivot model designer (see Figure 11.23).

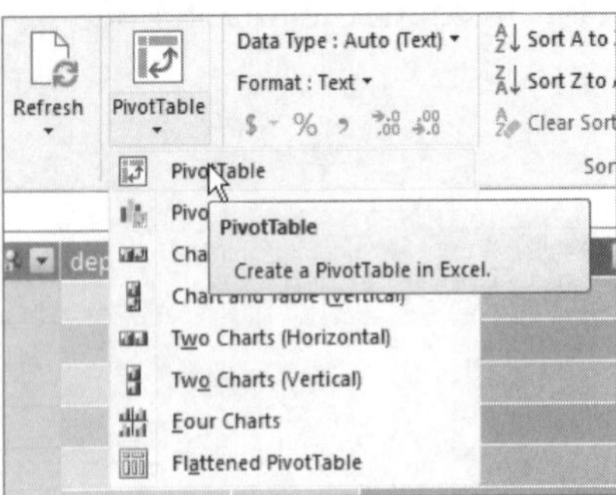

Figure 11.23: Adding a pivot table in Excel.

2. When asked, choose to create the pivot table in a new sheet. You should see an empty pivot table with a pivot table field list that shows the tables and fields in the PowerPivot model. Expand the flight_dept table node and select the TotalDelays and AveDelay fields. Under the Carriers table

node, select the Description field. The pivot table field list should look like Figure 11.24, and the pivot table should be similar to Figure 11.25.

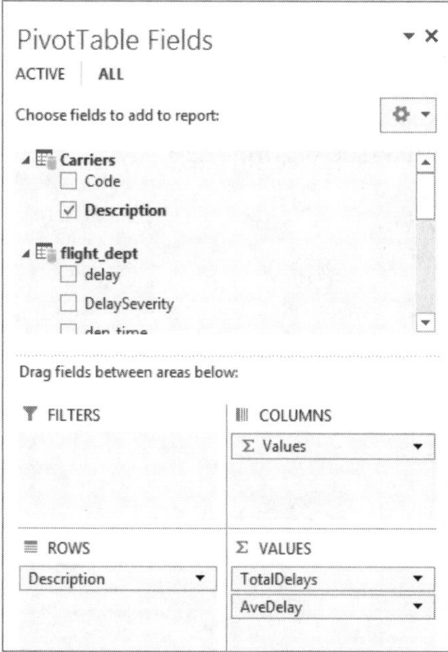

Figure 11.24: The pivot table field list.

Row Labels	TotalDelays	AveDelay
AirTran Airways Corporation	3979	22.53
Alaska Airlines Inc.	2640	38.94
American Airlines Inc.	20376	28.90
American Eagle Airlines Inc.	11041	33.78
Delta Air Lines Inc.	18001	24.28
ExpressJet Airlines Inc.	21398	39.03
Frontier Airlines Inc.	3020	21.05
Hawaiian Airlines Inc.	1144	12.45
JetBlue Airways	6118	29.73
Mesa Airlines Inc.	2312	34.81
SkyWest Airlines Inc.	15528	33.27
Southwest Airlines Co.	48001	19.50
United Air Lines Inc.	20115	26.05
US Airways Inc. (Merged with A	8193	20.66
Virgin America	1531	26.88
Grand Total	**183397**	**27.01**

Figure 11.25: The pivot table showing total delays and average delays.

3. With the pivot table selected, on the Insert tab of Excel, select Slicer. In the Insert Slicers selection window, select DelaySeverity and DepartureDay. Click the OK button to insert the slicers. Clicking the slicers will filter the pivot table.

Along with pivot tables, you can create pivot charts to help easily spot trends in the data, as follows:

1. To create the pivot chart, click the PivotTable drop-down on the Home tab of the PowerPivot model designer.
2. Select the Pivot Chart option and choose to create it on a new sheet.
3. Add the DepartureDay to the Axis, DelaySeverity to the Legend, and the TotalDelays to the Values drop area (see Figure 11.26).

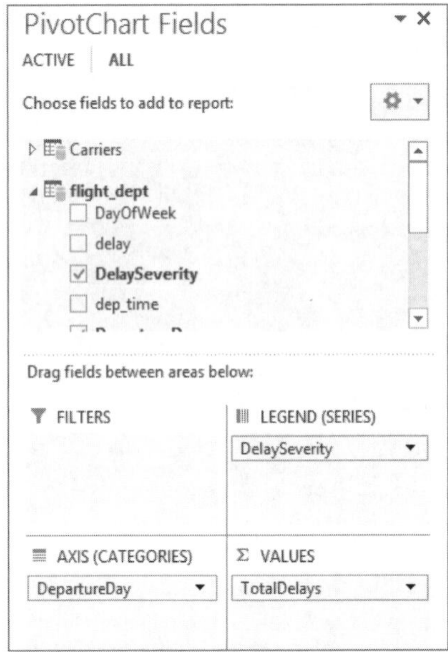

Figure 11.26: Selecting pivot chart fields.

The resulting pivot chart is shown in Figure 11.27.

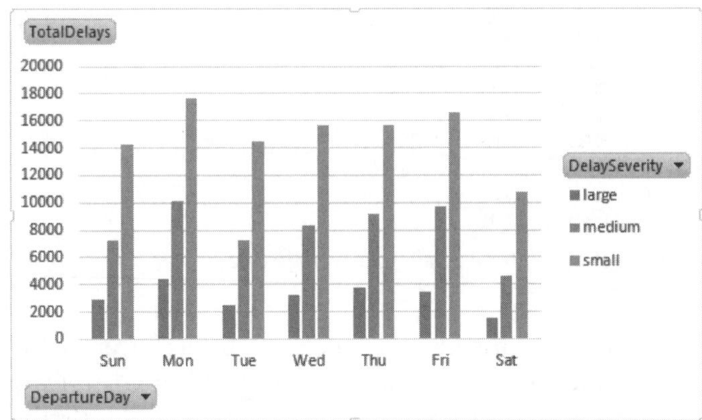

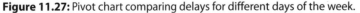

Figure 11.27: Pivot chart comparing delays for different days of the week.

Using PowerPivot models, pivot tables, and pivot charts in combination with Excel formatting, you can create powerful interactive visualizations and dashboards to explore the data. These Excel workbooks can be hosted on SharePoint, where you can automate the refreshing of the data using a schedule. You can also restrict access to the workbooks using SharePoint security.

Rapid Big Data Exploration with Power View

As powerful as the pivot tables and pivot charts are in Excel, unless you are an Excel power user, creating and formatting them can be quite a challenge. With that in mind, Microsoft has created Power View as an add-in for Excel. Power View still uses the PowerPivot model as its data source, but it makes it easier to create highly interactive data visualizations. It is ideal for the Excel casual user who needs to explore the data for trends and insights:

1. Open the Excel workbook you created in the previous section. On the Insert tab, you should see a Power View button. Click the button to launch the Power View designer. It will create a new tab called Power View 1. You should see the Power View Fields window, which contains the tables and fields you created previously in the PowerPivot model (see Figure 11.28). Notice the calculator icon associated with measures you created in the model. In addition, a globe icon is associated with any field that can be interpreted as a geolocation type field, such as latitude, longitude, city, state, or county.

   The design surface includes a view area where you create the visualizations such as charts, tables, and tiles. It also contains a filter area you can use to filter the entire view or individual visualization contained in the view.

   The first step to creating a visualization is to add fields from the field list to the field area below.

2. Drag and drop the DepartureDay and AveDelay to the field drop area. You should see a table created in the view area, as shown in Figure 11.29.

   All visualizations start out as a table that can then be converted to a different type of visualization.

3. Click the table in the view and select the Stacked Column Chart in the Design tab. The table is converted to a stack column chart, as shown in Figure 11.30.

Figure 11.28: The Power View Field window.

DepartureDay	AveDelay
Sun	26.91
Mon	29.74
Tue	24.67
Wed	26.94
Thu	29.10
Fri	26.37
Sat	22.99
Total	**27.01**

Figure 11.29: Creating the initial table.

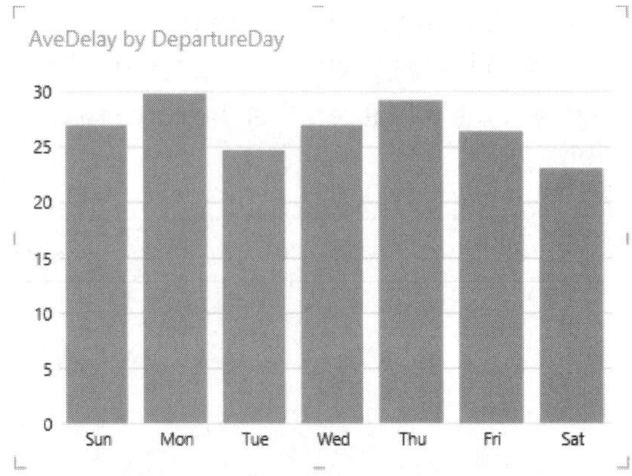

Figure 11.30: Creating a column chart.

4. Drag and drop the Carrier Description field to the filters area beside the view area. Use the filter to select Delta and Southwest airlines. Once the carrier filter is set, drag and drop the Carrier Description field to the Legend drop area, as shown in Figure 11.31. The chart is updated as shown in Figure 11.32.

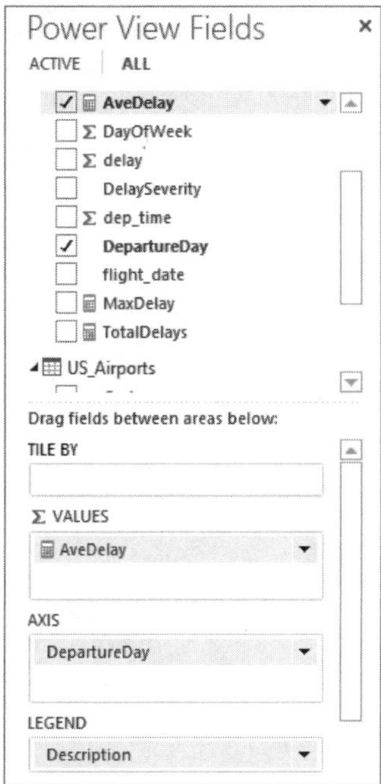

Figure 11.31: Adding carrier description to the legend.

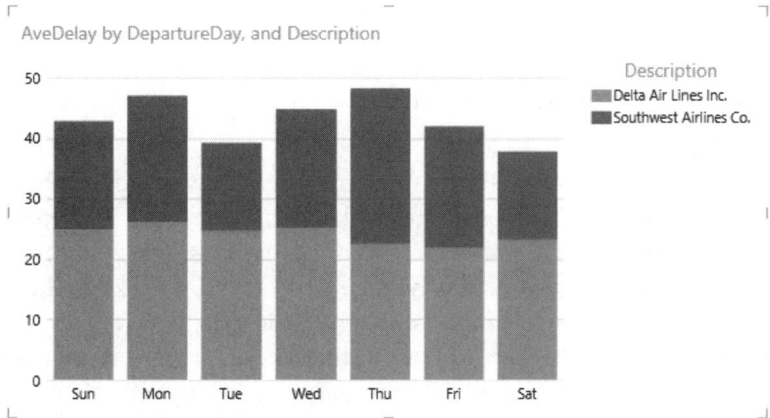

Figure 11.32: The updated stacked column chart.

5. To add another chart to the view, click an empty area of the view. Drag and drop the DepartureDay and TotalDelays to the field drop area in the Power View Field window. Click the resulting table in the view area. Select the Line chart from the Other Chart drop-down on the design ribbon.

   You now have two charts on the same view. Because the charts are based on related fields in the model, highlighting the data in one chart will also affect the other chart. Try clicking the different airlines in the legend of the bar chart and notice how it updates the data in the line chart (see Figure 11.33).

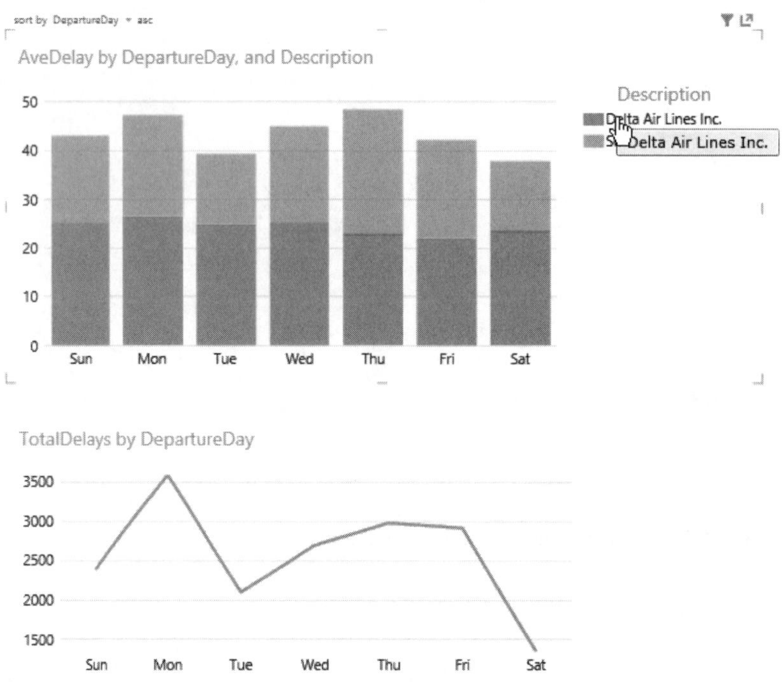

Figure 11.33: Chart interaction in Power View.

Another interesting type of chart you can create in Power View is the bubble chart with an associated play axis. The bubble chart in Figure 11.34 compares the delays for the month of October for four busy airports. The y-axis measures total delays, the x-axis measures the average delays, and the size of the bubble measures the maximum delay. If you click the time axis, you will see how the values change from day to day. It is left to the reader to see whether you can re-create this report.

One of the most interesting ways to analyze data that contains a geographic component, such as latitude and longitude, is to graph the data on a map. In the next section, you will use a new tool from Microsoft, Power Map, to visualize the data.

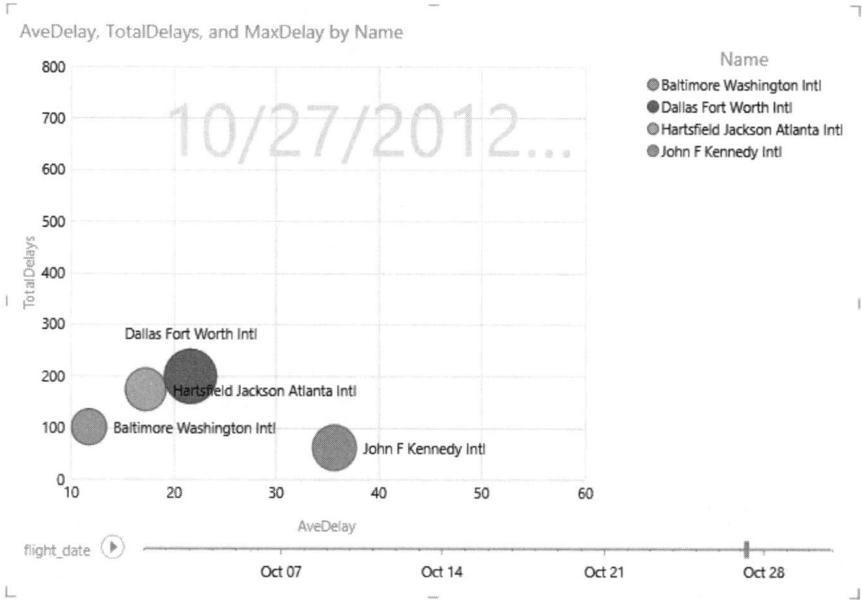

Figure 11.34: A bubble chart comparing airport delays.

Spatial Exploration with Power Map

Although you can create a map-based visualization using Power View and geocoded data such as city and state, it is very limited and provides only two-dimensional maps, where data is represented by the size of a bubble (see Figure 11.4). If you need to conduct more powerful spatial analysis of your geocoded data, Power Map is definitely the tool to use. Power Map is a free add-in to Excel, just like PowerPivot and Power View. It uses Bing mapping technology to create a map layer using geocoded data such as longitude and latitude, city, state, country, and ZIP code. You can display the data on top of the map as a three-dimensional bar chart, heat map, bubble chart, or color shading of regional boundaries. For example, Figure 11.35 shows the rainfall amounts for the various counties as columns and the population of the county represented by the county shading:

1. To map some data using Power Map, open the Excel workbook you used in the previous sections.
2. On the Insert tab, find the Power Map drop-down on the ribbon. Click the drop-down and select Launch Power Map. You should see a global map along with a list of the tables and fields in the PowerPivot model. The first thing you need to do is select the geography data fields to use on the map. Choose the longitude and latitude fields under the US_Airports table (see Figure 11.36).

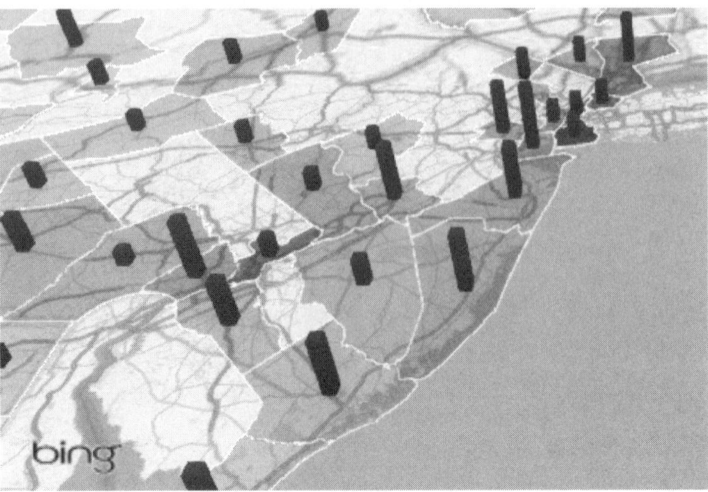

Figure 11.35: Mapping rainfall and county population.

3. Click Next to select the graph type and values to map. Choose the Column type and AveDelay as the height. On the Home tab, click the Map Labels button to show the city names.
4. Rotate and zoom into the map to view the data.
5. You can map several values by dragging additional fields into the height drop box. Drag the MaxDelay field into the Height box. You can either create adjacent columns or stacked columns by selecting the appropriate toggle button above the Height box. Figure 11.37 shows the completed map.

CHOOSE GEOGRAPHY

- flight_dept
  - [ ] DayOfWeek
  - [ ] delay
  - [ ] DelaySeverity
  - [ ] dep_time
  - [ ] DepartureDay
  - [ ] flight_date
  - [ ] AveDelay
  - [ ] MaxDelay
  - [ ] TotalDelays
- US_Airports
  - [ ] Code
  - [ ] Country
  - [x] Latitude
  - [x] Longitude
  - [ ] Name

GEOGRAPHY AND MAP LEVEL

(•) Latitude	Latitude
( ) Longitude	Longitude

Next

Figure 11.36: Selecting the geography fields.

Figure 11.37: Mapping airport flight delays.

6. You can also show how the values vary over time. Drag and drop the flight_date field to the time box under the field list. You should see a play axis appear on the map. Click the Play button and observe how the values change over time.

As you can see, Power Map has some compelling features and allows you to visualize the data in new and interesting ways.

Summary

Humans often rely on visualizations to make sense of data. This usually includes creating visualizations in the form of charts, graphs, and maps that enable the user to easily spot trends and anomalies in the data. Although Hadoop does not inherently provide native reporting and visualization capabilities, plenty of tools are available to consume and visualize the data. In this chapter, you saw how standard ODBC drivers are used to connect Microsoft's BI toolset to Hadoop data. You saw how Hive queries are used to pull the data into Excel and PowerPivot. Using the PowerPivot model, you can build pivot tables and pivot charts in Excel. For even more robust visualizations, you can use Power View to build interactive charts and graphs to present your findings. If you need powerful spatial mapping of the data, you can use Power Map.

This chapter just scratched the surface of the capabilities of these tools. You should definitely dig further into these products. They will undoubtedly become an important part of your BI arsenal.

CHAPTER

12

Big Data Analytics

WHAT YOU WILL LEARN IN THIS CHAPTER:

- Exploring Data Mining and Predictive Analytics
- Using the Mahout Machine Learning Library
- Building a Recommendation Engine on Hadoop

Up to this point, the focus has been on building a foundation that enables you to capture and store large volumes of disparate data. When this data is collected, as you have seen in previous chapters, it can be easily summarized and aggregated using tools built in to the Hadoop ecosystem.

Although this is noteworthy, it alone hardly justifies the time or investment required to implement a big data solution in your organization. The real value for businesses in bringing this data together is that it can be mined for hidden patterns, correlations, and other interesting information that can facilitate better business decision making.

This chapter covers how you can use HDInsight and Hadoop as a big data analytics platform by taking advantage of the Mahout machine learning library to deliver predictive analytics, such as implementing a recommendation engine, and to perform more common data mining in the form of clustering and classification.

Data Science, Data Mining, and Predictive Analytics

Included in just about every big data discussion, the art of data science is one that is built on multiple disciplines. Various skills involving mathematics, statistics, and computer science are combined to allow practitioners in this field, known as data scientists, to broadly explore data and patterns.

Two of the most common techniques used by data scientists to unveil these patterns are data mining and predictive analytics.

Data Mining

Also referred to as machine learning, data mining comes from the computer science field and is a broad term that represents techniques used to discover new information from existing data sets. For many experienced data warehouse and business intelligence professionals, this may be a subject that you are already familiar with.

For those who are not, the distinction is simple. Unlike more traditional business intelligence projects, which merely summarize or aggregate data in various slices, data mining uses specific algorithms to uncover data patterns or trends that would otherwise not be apparent.

To better understand how this applies to big data, review in Table 12.1 some of the more common types of data mining algorithms.

Table 12.1: Common Data Mining Algorithms

ALGORITHM	DESCRIPTION
Clustering	Rather than a specific algorithm, clustering is a category of unsupervised algorithms that groups similar objects into groups or clusters. Typically, a notion of statistical distance is used to calculate distance between objects. Examples of these distance calculations include k-means and Euclidean distance.
Classification	Like clustering, classification is not a single algorithm but a group of algorithms that also group together objects. These algorithms are usually supervised and require both a classifier and a training set of data that helps identify what the groups look like in terms of machine learning. Taken together, classification algorithms can then classify each data point or object into the most appropriate group or bucket.
Regression	An outgrowth of statistics, the regression techniques are used to estimate the relationship between variables. Regression algorithms such as linear regression are commonly used for forecasting important business indicators such as sales volumes.
Association rules	These algorithms are used to explore or discover relationships between objects that exist in large data sets. Common examples of these algorithms include market basket analysis, clickstream analysis, and fraud detection.

Predictive Analytics

A specialization or subset of the broader data mining field, predictive analytics (like other forms of data mining) is interested in identifying patterns. The exception or difference however, is that the patterns identified are used to make a prediction about some behavior or event using the historical data fed to the model.

Examples of predictive analytics are everywhere around you. They are used to determine whether your loan application should be approved, they are the basis of your credit score, they help recommend what movie you should watch or what book you buy, and they often determine whether you are included in a marketing campaign by your favorite retailer.

Taken together, this field is one the primary driving factors for interest in big data and offers huge opportunities for businesses that capitalize on it (by allowing those businesses to transform their data into a competitive differentiator). To paint a clearer picture, let's look at three types of models used in predictive analytics: predictive models, descriptive models, and decision models.

Predictive Models

Predictive models use historic data to make predictions on how likely a defined behavior or action is to occur. These models are often used to improve marketing outcomes by predicting buying behaviors and are also often used to assess credit risks and in fraud-detection systems.

Descriptive Models

Often, a business will want to identify how groups of customers behave. Behavior in this regards is often used to identify customers who are loyal, profitable, or at risk for cancelling your product or service. This is a common scenario used to predict and proactively handle customer churn and is one example where descriptive models excel. Descriptive models, instead of predicting the actions of a single customer, can identify multiple relationships between products and customers and are used to categorize like customers together.

Decision Models

The basis of a decision model is to improve the outcome of some well-defined business decision, taking into account multiple variables. This model uses well-known data (often included historical decision-making data), the business decision and the probability of some result based on the given variables or factors. The results of these models are often used to write business rules found in the line-of-business applications.

With a high-level understanding of the core concepts behind data mining and predictive analytics, we can turn our attention to looking at how Mahout allows you to easily integrate some of these techniques into your big data architecture.

Introduction to Mahout

The preceding section introduced you at a high level to both data mining and predictive analytics and how they apply to big data. If at this point you are worried that you don't possess the skills or background to successfully build and deliver this type of intelligence within your HDInsight platform, fear not!

The remainder of this chapter introduces you to the Mahout machine learning library and explains how you can use it to deliver meaningful big data analytical solutions without a PhD in statistics or mathematics. So, what is this Mahout thing?

Mahout is an open source, top-level Apache project that encapsulates multiple machine learning algorithms into a single library. Like its Hadoop counterpart, the Mahout community is a vibrant and active community that has continually expanded and improved on Mahout.

For a historical perspective, the Mahout project grew out of two separate projects: the Apache Lucene (an open source text indexing project) and Taste (an open source Java library of machine learning algorithms).

Mahout supports two basic implementations. First, is a non-distributed or real-time implementation that involves native non-Hadoop Java calls directly to the Mahout library. The second scenario is the one we are focused on and is accomplished in a distributed or batch processing manner using Hadoop. Both of these scenarios abstracts away the complexity of machine learning algorithms.

The basis of Mahout within the context of big data are four primary use cases:

- Collaborative filtering (recommendation mining based on user behavior)
- Clustering (grouping similar documents)
- Classification (assigning uncategorized documents to predefined categories)
- Frequent item set mining (market basket analysis)

To get started with the Apache Mahout library, you first need to download the project distribution; it is not included by default with HDInsight on Azure platform. To download the required files, visit the Apache project site at `http://mahout.apache.org/`. As of this writing, the currently supported version is 0.7. After you download the `mahout-distribution-0.7.zip` file, extract the contents of using your preferred compression utility.

NOTE **If you are running the Hortonworks Data Platform on premise instead of using HDInsight of Windows Azure, you will find that Mahout is included and is ready to use. No further action is required.**

In the decompressed folder, you'll find the `mahout-core-0.7-job.jar` and the `mahout-examples-0.7-job.jar` (which contains a number of prebuilt samples) files. The `mahout-core-0.7-job.jar` contains prebuilt Hadoop jobs for each of the use cases previously mentioned. These jobs do not require any coding and will generate and run the required MapReduce jobs to implement machine learning algorithms in a distributed environment. To use this jar file, you must upload it either directly to your cluster using the Remote Desktop connection or to the Azure Blob Storage account connected to Azure HDInsight cluster.

NOTE **This section, and the remainder of this chapter, assumes that you have an HDInsight on Windows Azure cluster set up. If you do not have a cluster set up and configured, see Chapter 3, "Configuring Your First Big Data Environment," for further information.**

Building a Recommendation Engine

What caused you to pick up this book? What about the last movie you saw or maybe even the last item of clothing you purchased? Every decision that anyone makes is inevitably based on some preconceived (and often unconscious) opinion. Every day, our opinions develop and become part of the ever-larger library of unconscious factors from which we "borrow" as we face decisions.

Deciding what you like, what you don't, and in some cases what you are indifferent to drives nearly all the purchasing decisions you'll make through your lifetime. Successfully predicting these outcomes is the basis of a recommendation engine.

To set a foundation, let's define what and how a recommendation engine works. First we must start with an assumption that people with similar interests share common preferences. This is a straightforward idea demonstrable by simply looking around at your network of friends and family. Note that this doesn't imply that the assumption always hold true, but it holds well enough to produce meaningful and useful recommendations.

This assumption is the basis of simple recommendation engines and will allow us to generate a recommendation, but what is a *recommendation*? For most, the first thought is some product, good, or service.

However, the recommendation can also be people if it the recommendation engine is implemented on a social media or an Internet dating website, for instance. The truth is that the recommendation can be anything because the recommendation engine doesn't understand the concept of physical things, which is why you will commonly see it referred to as simply an item.

Recommendation engines, for our purpose, use one of two paradigms: collaborative filtering or clustering. Collaborative filtering is highly dependent on both the assumption previously discussed and on historical data.

This historical data records interaction or behavior with the items you are attempting to generate recommendations for. Data that can be used is often split into two distinct groups: explicit and implicit. Explicit data is well-defined data such as purchase or click history. Implicit data, in contrast, is more subjective and includes preferential or product ratings. Table 12.2 provides a more complete list of examples for each category.

Table 12.2: Examples of Explicit and Implicit Data

EXPLICIT	IMPLICIT
Ratings	Purchase history
Feedback	Clicks
Demographics	Browse history
Psychographics (personality/lifestyle/attitude)	
Ephemeral need (need for a moment)	

NOTE One of the most difficult parts of building a recommendation engine is determining how to quantify and weight non-numeric explicit data. Determining the right balance and scale is as much art as science and requires some experimentation.

In the case of implicit data, when used singularly (that is, only purchase history or only click history), it represents a Boolean data type. It is not necessary to represent the negative cases in these models because missing data translates to false. When multiple implicit data points are combined, it is necessary to scale them appropriately.

Clustering, unlike collaborative filtering, focuses instead on an item's taxonomies, attributes, description, or properties. It does not need behavioral or interaction data, and is often a good choice when the data required for collaborative filtering is not available.

To generate recommendations, Mahout supports collaborative filtering and clustering. To understand what each of these are, we can look at the three common recommendation engine implementations:

1. **User-to-user collaborative filtering**: In a user-to-user recommendation implementation, clusters or neighborhoods of similar users are formed based on some user behavior (for instance, purchasing an item or attending a movie). Because similar users are clustered together, these clusters are then used to generate recommendations.
2. **Item-to-item collaborative filtering**: The item-to-item recommendation implementation works in a similar manner to that of the user-to-user implementation, except that it works from the context of an item. Instead of looking at similar users, it uses behavior or interaction with an item

to determine which item to recommend. Let's illustrate this with a more concrete example. If we were evaluating purchase history and everyone who bought the *Star Wars* trilogy also purchased the *Lord of the Rings* boxed set, we would generate a recommendation for *Lord of the Rings* whenever a customer purchases *Star Wars*.

3. **Content-based clustering**: Content-based recommendation engines function in a different manner than the two previously discussed. Instead of looking at behavior or interactions, content-based systems use attributes associated with an item. Item attributes can be anything from physical attributes that describe an item to features or behaviors when describing technology or even people. Examples of this methodology are widely available and can be found on your favorite news aggregator website when similar articles are recommended.

Now that you have a basic understanding, let's look at the specifics for building a recommendation engine using Mahout and HDInsight.

Getting Started

For this demonstration, we are using the GroupLens data set (`http://grouplens.org/datasets/movielens/`). This data set is publicly available and at its largest contains more than 10 million user movie reviews (10,000 movies and 72,000 users). To work with this data set, you must process the data set into a format that Mahout understands.

For the built-in recommenders, the expected data file format is a comma-separated list containing the following data points:

```
<Unique User ID>, <Unique Item ID>, <Numeric Rating>
```

The format of the GroupLens data set is tab-delimited and contains an additional Timestamp column. If you choose, you could process this data set using a C# utility application or MapReduce job to get it into the correct format.

NOTE **A preprocessed file called** `MovieRatings.csv` **is supplied and can be downloaded with the Chapter 12 materials from** `http://www.wiley.com/go/microsoftbigdatasolutions`.

After you have your source data file, you must upload it to your HDInsight cluster. To upload the data file to your cluster and add it to HDFS, follow these steps:

1. Connect to the head node of your HDInsight cluster using Remote Desktop. If Remote Desktop has not been enabled, enable it through the Configuration page and set up an account for Remote Access.

2. Copy and paste the `MovieRatings.csv` file from your local machine to the `c:\temp` folder on the head node of your HDInsight cluster. If the `c:\temp` folder does not exist, you will need to create it first.
3. On the desktop, double-click the Hadoop command prompt to open the Hadoop command line.
4. We will use the Hadoop File System shell to copy the data file from the local file system to the Hadoop Distributed File System (HDFS). Enter the following command at the command prompt:

```
hadoop fs -copyFromLocal c:\temp\MovieRatings.csv
/user/<YOUR USERNAME>/chapter15/input/MovieRatings.csv
```

5. After the command completes, use the following command to verify that the `MovieRatings.csv` file now exists within HDFS:

```
hadoop fs -ls /user/<YOUR USERNAME>/chapter15/input/
```

The data input required to run recommendation jobs using Mahout is now available and ready for processing on HDInsight.

Running a User-to-user Recommendation Job

The first job that we will run will use collaborative filtering to generate user-to-user recommendations for the MovieLens data set. Be sure before continuing that you have deployed the Mahout jar files to your HDInsight cluster before continuing.

Before starting the job, let's delve into what's going to happen once we start the recommendation job. First, we will iterate through each user, finding movies that the user has not previously rated. Next, for each movie that the user has not yet reviewed, we will find other users who have reviewed the movie. We will use a statistical measure to calculate the similarity between the two users and then use the similarity to estimate the preference in the form of a weighted average.

At a high level, we can distill this logic of the recommendation job to the following pseudo-code:

```
for each item i that u has no preference
       for each user v that has a preference for i
             compute similarity s between u and v
             calculate running average of v's preference for i,
weighted by s

return top ranked (weighted average) i
```

Note that this is a drastic simplification of what is really occurring behind the scenes. In fact, we've omitted a key step. If the preceding logic were implemented as is, it would not perform efficiently and would suffer at scale. To remedy this, we could introduce the concept of neighborhoods or clusters of similar users to limit the number of similarity comparisons that need to be made.

A detailed explanation of how this works is beyond the scope of this book, but you can find ample material about how Mahout handles neighborhood formation and similarity calculations on the Mahout website.

With a high-level understanding of how user-to-user recommendations are generated, use the `hadoop jar` command at the Hadoop command line to start the `RecommenderJob`:

```
hadoop jar c:\mahout\mahout-core-0.7-job.jar
    org.apache.mahout.cf.taste.hadoop.item.RecommenderJob
          -s SIMILARITY_PEARSON_CORRELATION
          --input=/user/<YOUR USERNAME>/chapter15/input/MovieRatings.csv
          --output=/user/<YOUR USERNAME>/chapter15/output/
          userrecommendations
```

NOTE **The preceding command assumes that you have placed the Mahout files in a local directory called `c:\Mahout`. If your files are located in another directory, adjust the command so that the path to the Mahout `*.jar` files is correct before using the command.**

The `RecommenderJob` is a prebuilt jar that accepts multiple arguments. At a minimum, you must specify the similarity metric that will be used to determine similarity between users, your input data file, and the path for your recommendation job output.

A number of other job parameters control how the `RecommenderJob` behaves and will allow you to customize it without investing time or effort in coding. Table 12.3 describes these additional job parameters.

Table 12.3: `RecommenderJob` Parameters

PARAMETER	DESCRIPTION
`Input`	Directory containing preference data
`Output`	Output for recommender output
`similarityClassname`	Name of vector similarity class
`usersFile`	User IDs to compute recommendations
`itemsFile`	Item IDs to include in recommendations
`filterFile`	Excludes the item/user recommendations
`numRecommendations`	Number of recommendations per user
`booleanData`	Treat input data as having no preferences values

Continues

Table 12.3 (*continued*)

PARAMETER	DESCRIPTION
maxPrefsPerUser	Maximum preferences considered per user
maxSimilaritiesPerItem	Maximum number of similarities per item
minPrefsPerUser	Ignore users with less preferences than this in the similarity computation
maxPrefsPerUserInItemSimilarity	Maximum number of preferences to consider per user in the item similarity
Threshold	Discard item pairs with a similarity value

Here is a list of the available similarity metrics:

- Euclidean distance
- Spearman correlation
- Cosine
- Tanimoto coefficient
- Log-likelihood
- Pearson correlation

After, the job is started, it will take between 15 and 20 minutes to run if you are using a four-node cluster. During this time, a series of MapReduce jobs are being run to process the data and generate the movie recommendations. When the job has completed, you can view the various outputted files using the following command:

```
hadoop fs -ls /user/<YOUR USERNAME>/chapter15/output/userrecommendations
```

You can find the generated recommendations in the `part-r-00000` file. To export the file from HDFS to your local file system, use the following command:

```
hadoop fs -copyToLocal
/user/<YOUR USERNAME>/chapter15/output/userrecommendations/part-r-00000
c:\<LOCAL OUPUT DIRECTORY>\recommendations.csv
```

You can review the file to find the recommendation generated for each user. The output from the recommendation job takes the following format:

```
UserID      [ItemID:Estimate Rating, ………]
```

An example of the output is shown here:

```
1     [1566:5.0,1036:5.0,1033:5.0,1032:5.0,1031:5.0,3107:5.0]
```

In this example, for the user identified by the ID of 1, we would recommend the movies identified by the IDs 1566 (*The Man from Down Under*), 1036 (*Drop Dead Fred*), 1033 (*Homeward Bound II: Lost in San Francisco*), and so on. The estimated ratings for each of these movies for this specific user is 5.0. You can cross-reference these IDs with the data file provided as part of the GroupLens data set download.

Running an Item-to-item Recommendation Job

In the previous example, we used the GroupLens data set to generate recommendations by calculating similarity between users. In this demonstration, we instead use the notion of item similarity to determine our item recommendations.

For this exercise, you will reuse the GroupLens data set as the format and data requirements for the item-to-item RecommendationJob are the same. In fact, a significant amount of overlap exists between the two jobs, including the job parameters.

In the user-to-user example, the Mahout library uses a similarity metric to form neighborhoods or clusters and then makes recommendations based on reviews by statistically similar users. The item-to-item recommender takes a different approach, instead focusing on items (or in our case, movies).

Much like the former example, the item-to-item recommender must calculate the similarity between movies. To accomplish this, the recommender uses both user reviews and the co-occurrence of movie reviews by users to determine this similarity score. Using this notion of similarity, the job can then generate recommendations based on the provided input.

To generate item-based recommendations, follow these steps:

1. Open the Hadoop command-line console.
2. Mahout uses temporary storage for intermediate files that are output out of intermediate MapReduce jobs. Before you can run a new Mahout job, you need to purge the temporary directory. Use the following command to delete the files in the temporary directory:

   ```
   hadoop fs -rmr -skipTrash /user/<USER>/temp
   ```

3. Enter the Mahout item recommender job to kick off the item-based RecommenderJob:

   ```
   hadoop jar c:\mahout\mahout-core-0.7-job.jar
          org.apache.mahout.cf.taste.hadoop.item.RecommenderJob
          -s SIMILARITY_PEARSON_CORRELATION
          --input=/user/<USER NAME>/chapter15/input/MovieRatings.csv
          --output=/user/<USER NAME>/chapter15/output/
          itemrecommendations
   ```

The item-based RecommenderJob, like the user-based recommender job will take some time to run to completion. After the job successfully completes, you can browse the results in the `/chapter12/output/itemrecommendations` folder in HDFS.

Summary

Big data analytics, and more specifically data mining and predictive analytics, represent the biggest and more potent parts of your big data platform. Taking advantage of this data to gain new insights, identify patterns, and bring out new and interesting information will provide a competitive advantage for those businesses that take the leap.

HDInsight and the Mahout machine learning library make this area approachable by abstracting away the complexity (mathematics and statistics!) generally associated with data mining and predictive analytics.

Mahout provides implementations for clustering, classifying, and (as demonstrated) generating recommendations using the concept of collaborative filtering.

CHAPTER 13

Big Data and the Cloud

WHAT YOU WILL LEARN IN THIS CHAPTER:

- Exploring the Leading Cloud Providers: Amazon and Microsoft
- Using the Amazon Elastic Compute Cloud (EC2) and Microsoft HDInsight Services as Cloud Processing Options
- Hosting and Storing Your Data in the Cloud with Amazon Simple Storage Service (S3) and Microsoft Azure Blob Storage

Although many organizations will inevitably consider an on-premise solution for big data, the broad and ever-expanding appeal of the cloud makes big data approachable to those who would otherwise have neither the resources nor the expertise. The focus of this chapter is threefold. First, we introduce the cloud and look at two of the leading cloud providers: Amazon and Microsoft.

Next, we walk through setting up development or sandbox big data environments to explore the Amazon Elastic Compute Cloud (EC2) service and the Microsoft HDInsight service as cloud processing options.

We then explore two options—Amazon Simple Storage Service (S3) and Microsoft Azure Blob Storage (ASV)—for hosting or storing your data in the cloud. This discussion explains the considerations for cloud storage (pros/cons), reviews best practices for storing your data in the cloud, and identifies proven patterns and tools for loading and managing your data in the cloud.

Defining the Cloud

One of the most overused (and abused) contemporary technology terms is the *cloud*. You've probably seen or heard it used to describe just about everything from distributed computing to the Internet. So, what is it, really? Well, unfortunately, it is a little bit of everything, which is why we will limit our context to that of applications, services, and (of course) data.

By changing the perspective in which we discuss the cloud, we can easily clarify the definition. For our purposes, we will consider the cloud as the hosted virtualization and abstraction of hardware that provides simple and flexible solutions for capacity and scalability. This is sometimes referred to more simply as infrastructure as a service (IaaS). This definition is succinct, but a simple example can provide elaboration.

Consider a scenario such as setting up a Hadoop cluster. In the on-premise world, you have many things to consider. From hardware and software to configuration, numerous areas require a variety of skills and varying degrees of expertise.

Now, consider Hadoop in the cloud. Your cluster will still function the same as if it were running on real, physical hardware in your data center, with the difference being that now everything from the hardware and the operating system to the Hadoop installation and configuration is being provided as a service. This virtualization service abstracts away hardware from the puzzle and means that your cluster, whether 4 nodes or 32, will be seamlessly available and may be distributed over multiple machines (and potentially even across multiple data centers).

This certainly isn't a new concept, but it is an important one, and if it is not immediately evident, consider some of the other benefits of the cloud:

- Getting the hardware/infrastructure right the first time can be almost completely deemphasized. By virtualizing the hardware and abstracting it away as described previously, scaling either up or down after the fact becomes a trivial exercise that can usually be accomplished by little more than the adjustment of a slider bar in an administrative window.
- Clusters can be stood up (created) and shut down in minutes, meaning that they are available when you need them.
- Common infrastructure concerns such as maintenance and redundancy are managed by the cloud provider, freeing you from the concerns such

as hard drive failures, failover for fault-tolerance, and even operating system patches.

Now that you understand the basic value proposition of cloud-based solutions, let's dig deeper into two of the features and offerings of big data cloud providers.

Exploring Big Data Cloud Providers

With the number of cloud service providers offering big data solutions growing at a seemingly endless pace, the environment is dynamic and ever-changing. That notwithstanding, the two market leaders in the space to consider are Amazon and Microsoft.

Amazon

As one of the pioneers with the largest footprint in the big data cloud services space, Amazon offers three relevant services, all of which fall under the Amazon Web Services (`http://aws.amazon.com/`) umbrella.

Amazon Elastic Compute Cloud (EC2)

The Amazon Elastic Compute Cloud (`http://aws.amazon.com/ec2/`) is web-based service that provides resizable compute capacity in the cloud. Amazon offers preconfigured Windows and Linux templates that include a variety of preinstalled application systems. Instances from small or micro to large or high memory/processor capacity can be created. You can easily resize your instances as your computing needs change.

Amazon Elastic MapReduce (EMR)

Built on top of the EC2 service, the Elastic MapReduce service (`http://aws.amazon.com/elasticmapreduce/`) offers businesses a resizable, hosted Hadoop platform for processing large quantities of data. The EMR service supports a number of processing jobs, including MapReduce, MapReduce Streaming (via Java, Ruby, Perl, Python, PHP, R, and C++), Hive, and Pig.

Amazon Simple Storage Service (S3)

The Simple Storage Service (S3) service (`http://aws.amazon.com/s3/`) provides inexpensive, highly scalable, reliable, secure, and fast data storage in the cloud. Data can easily be backed up or even globally distributed and is accessed and managed via a REST API.

NOTE Representational State Transfer (REST) API is a lightweight, stateless web service architectural pattern that is implemented from the HTTP protocol. Commands are generally issued using the HTTP verbs (GET, POST, PUT, and DELETE), making it easier to interact with than traditional SOAP or XML-based web services.

Microsoft

Amazon continues as a leader in this space, but Microsoft (although arriving later) has quickly and dynamically expanded their footprint through innovative and proven solutions in their Windows Azure (`http://www.windowsazure.com/`) offering. Within the context of big data, the services of interest include HDInsight and Azure Blob Storage.

HDInsight

HDInsight (`http://www.windowsazure.com/en-us/services/hdinsight/`) is Microsoft's 100% Apache Hadoop implementation available as a cloud service. You can quickly and easily provision an elastic Hadoop cluster ranging from 4 to 32 nodes that allows for seamless scaling.

Azure (ASV) Blob Storage

Like Amazon's S3 service, the Microsoft Azure (ASV) Blob Storage (`http://www.windowsazure.com/en-us/services/data-management/`) offers a high-performance, reliable, scalable, and secure cloud storage solution that supports backup and global distribution via a content delivery network. In addition to traditional blob storage, the ASV service also supports table-based and queue storage.

Together, both of these service providers offer a first-class storage service and robust, stable processing platform capable of hosting your big data solution. The remainder of this chapter walks you through setting up a sandbox environment for each service provider before demonstrating tools and techniques for getting your data to the cloud and integrating it once it is there.

Setting Up a Big Data Sandbox in the Cloud

Before you dig in and get your hands dirty, both Amazon and Microsoft require that you register or create an account as a condition of service. Amazon will let you create an account using an existing Amazon account, and Microsoft accounts are based on Live IDs.

If you have neither, creating these accounts requires typical information such as name, contact information, an agreement to terms of service, and verification of identity. In addition, both require a credit card for payment and billing purposes.

As mentioned previously, these services are provided on the basis of either compute hours or storage space. Both providers offer a free or preview version that will allow you to try them with little if any out-of-pocket costs, but the payment method you provide will be billed for any overages beyond what's provided as free usage. The tutorials in this chapter assume that you have created accounts for both Amazon and Microsoft.

Getting Started with Amazon EMR

Amazon EMR provides a simple, straightforward method for processing and analyzing large volumes of data by distributing the computation across a virtual cluster of Hadoop servers. The premise is simple and starts with uploading data to a bucket in an Amazon S3 account.

Next, a job is created and uploaded to your S3 account. This job will be responsible for processing your data and can take a number of different forms—such as Hive, Pig, HBase jobs, custom jars, or even a streaming script. (Currently supported languages include Ruby, Perl, Python, PHP, R, Base, and C++.) Your cluster will read the job and data from S3, process your data using a Hadoop cluster running on EC2, and return the output to S3.

NOTE **Hadoop Streaming functions by streaming data to the standard input (stdin) and output (stdout). Executables that read and write using the standard input/output can be used as either a mapper or reducer. For more information on Hadoop Streaming, please visit: `http://hadoop.apache.org/docs/r0.18.3/streaming.html`.**

Before beginning this tutorial, complete the following:

- Create a bucket in your Amazon S3 account, and within your bucket create a folder named `input`. The bucket name must be unique because the namespace is shared globally. (Amazon S3 and its features and requirements are discussed in greater detail later in this chapter.)
- Locate the `wordcount.txt` and `wordsplitter.py` files provided in the Chapter 13 materials (`http://www.wiley.com/go/microsoftbigdatasolutions.com`) and upload the data file to the `input` folder and the `wordsplitter.py` file in the root of your S3 bucket.

Now you are ready to stand up your cluster using the following steps:

1. In a web browser, navigate to the Amazon Web Services portal at `https://console.aws.amazon.com/`. Find and click the Elastic MapReduce link under the Compute & Networking section (see Figure 13.1).

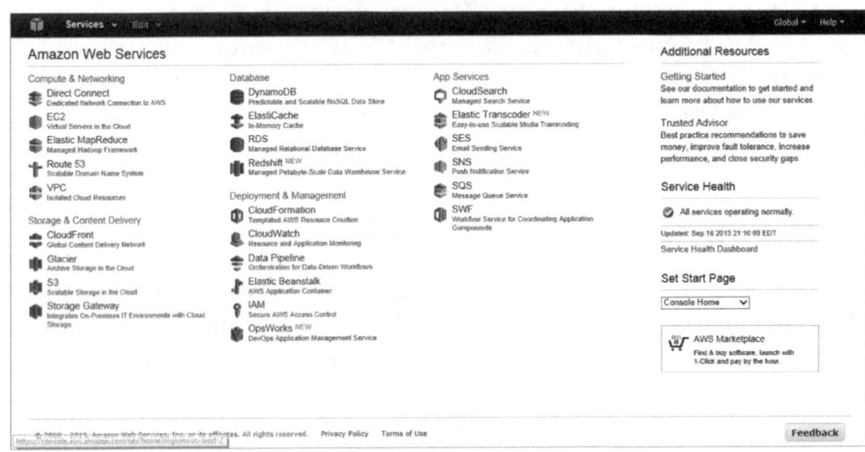

Figure 13.1: The Amazon Web Services portal

2. The Amazon EMR service is built around job flows, which are essential jobs that will process your data. Figure 13.2 shows the Create Job Flow dialog. Begin by clicking the Start Job Flow button.

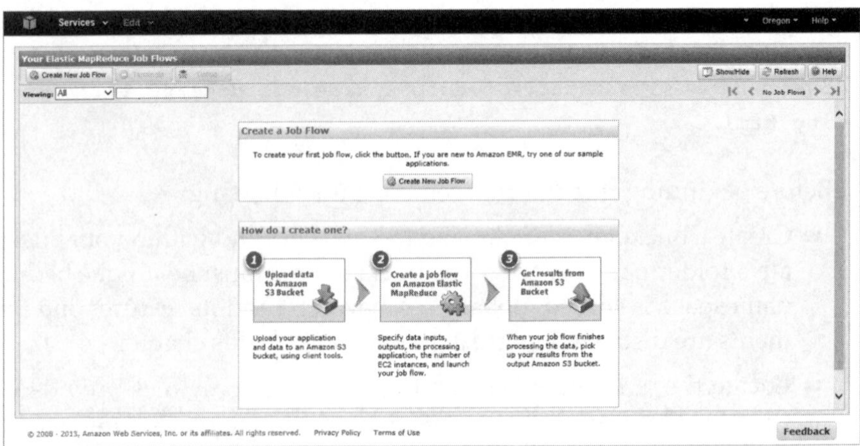

Figure 13.2: Amazon EMR Create Job Flow dialog

3. In the Create a New Job Flow Wizard, define the job settings as described here and illustrated in Figure 13.3, and then click Continue:
   a. Enter **Sandbox Word Count** for your job name.
   b. Keep the default Hadoop distribution, Amazon Distribution.
   c. Use the latest AMI version. As of this writing, 2.4.1 is the current version.
   d. Ensure that the Run Your Own Application option is selected.
   e. Select Streaming as the processing job type.

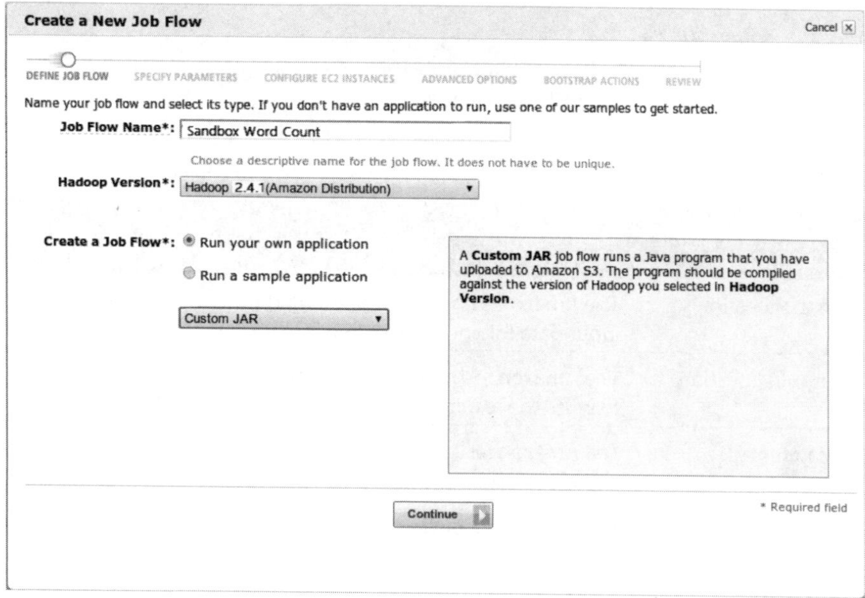

Figure 13.3: Amazon EMR job config

4. Specify the parameters needed to execute your job flow. These include input and output location, mapper and reducer jobs, and any additional arguments required for your job, as shown in Figure 13.4. Table 13.1, elaborates on each option, including the values used for this demo. Note that you must substitute your bucket name throughout this demo. Click Continue when you have finished.

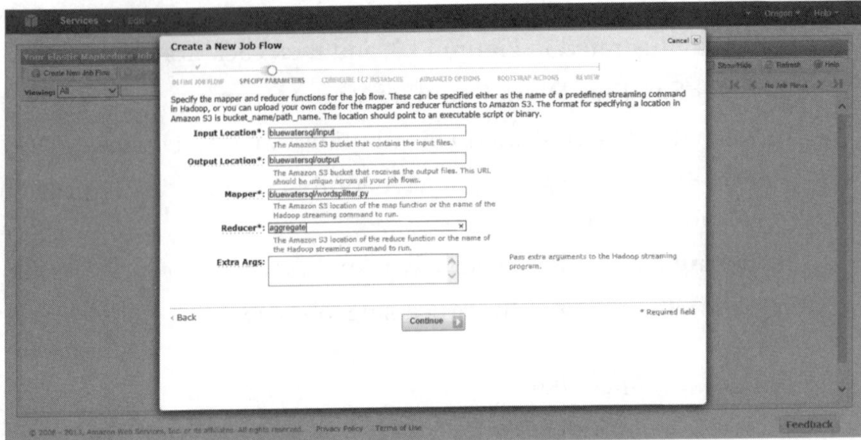

Figure 13.4: Amazon EMR job parameters

Table 13.1: Amazon EMR Job Parameters

PARAMETER/ ARGUMENT	DESCRIPTION	VALUE
Input Location	The Amazon S3 bucket containing the input data for your processing job	`bluewatersql/input`
Output Location	The Amazon S3 bucket that will be used to write the results to	`bluewatersql/output`
Mapper	The Amazon S3 bucket location and name of mapper job	`bluewatersql/wordsplitter.py`
Reducer	The Amazon S3 bucket location and name of the reducer job	`aggregate`
Extra Args	Any additional arguments that are required for the Hadoop Streaming job	

NOTE **For this demo, the built-in `org.apache.hadoop.mapreduce.lib.aggregate` reducer is used in place of a custom scripted reducer.**

5. Now you are ready to specify the number of EC2 instances that form the nodes within your Hadoop cluster. You need to configure three instance types:
   - **Master node:** The head node is responsible for assigning and coordinating work among core and task nodes. Only a single instance of the master node is created.

- **Core node:** These are your task and HDFS data nodes. In addition to specifying the size of each number, you can scale the number of nodes from 2 to 20 nodes.
- **Task node:** These are worker nodes that perform Hadoop tasks but do not store data and can be configured in the same manner as core nodes.

For each of the above node types, you must select the size of the instance and, in the case of core and task nodes, the number of instances you want in your cluster. The size of the instance roughly determines the number of resources (memory, processor, etc.) available for the instance. For this walk-through, small (`m1.small`) instances are plenty. As you work beyond this demo, the number of instances and their size will be dependent on the volume of your data and the data processing being performed. Use the default settings of 2 core nodes and 0 task nodes, as shown in Figure 13.5, and then click Continue.

TIP **The size you specify for your nodes will affect your pricing. To keep size low, use the smallest instance size possible. For more info on the instance sizes available, visit** **`http://docs.aws.amazon.com/ElasticMapReduce/latest/DeveloperGuide/emr-plan-ec2-instances.html`.**

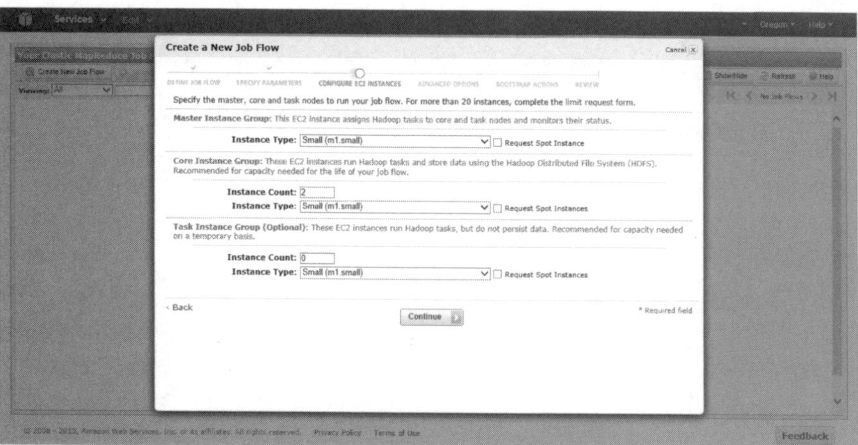

Figure 13.5: Amazon EMR node configuration

6. Accept the defaults for both Advanced Options and Bootstrap Actions by clicking Continue twice.
7. Figure 13.6 displays the final review page before your cluster is created. Verify all parameters are correct, and then click the Create Job Flow button.

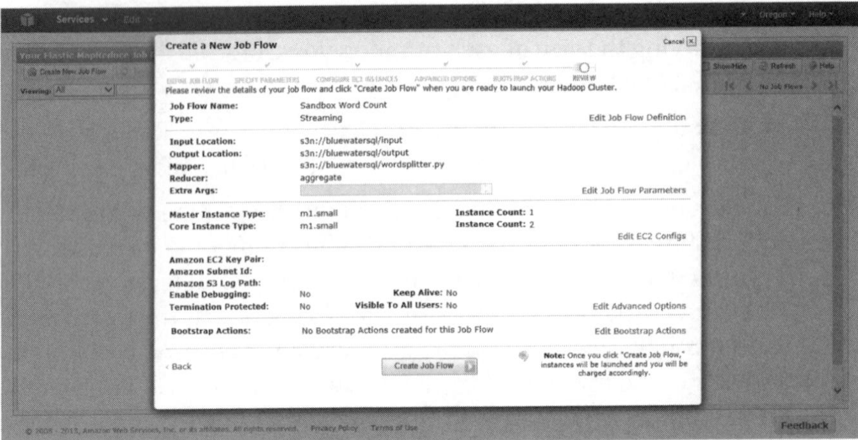

Figure 13.6: Amazon EMR Job review

8. After your job kicks off, you can monitor it from the Elastic MapReduce portal (see Figure 13.7). After the job has been completed, you can download and view the results in the output folder found in your S3 bucket (see Figure 13.8).

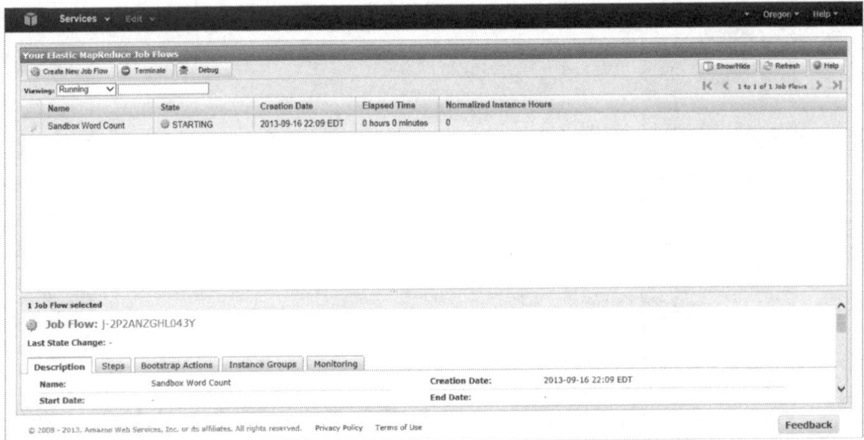

Figure 13.7: Amazon EMR portal dashboard

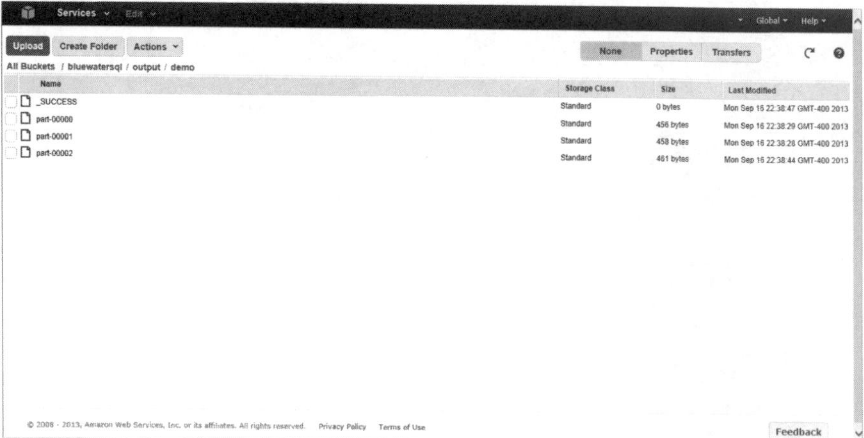

Figure 13.8: Amazon EMR job results

This tutorial demonstrated only the basics required for creating an Elastic MapReduce streaming job and running it on an Amazon EC2 Hadoop cluster. Other cluster types such as Hive, Jar, Pig, and HBase will vary slightly in their setup.

Getting Started with HDInsight

Whereas the Amazon Elastic MapReduce service approach centers on a processing job flow, the Microsoft HDInsight service is more cluster centric. Instead of specifying a job and cluster configuration, HDInsight starts by provisioning the cluster first. Once the cluster is established, one or more jobs can be submitted before tearing the cluster down. To stand up your first HDInsight sandbox, follow these steps:

1. Open your preferred web browser and navigate to `https://manage.windowsazure.com/`. Then log in with your Windows Live account.
2. Before you can begin creating your HDInsight cluster, you must create a storage container. This Azure Blob Storage container will be used to store all the files required for the virtual instances that form your cluster. Click the Storage icon to navigate to the Storage console.
3. From the Storage console, click the New button found in the lower left of the screen to access the New Services dialog shown in Figure 13.9.

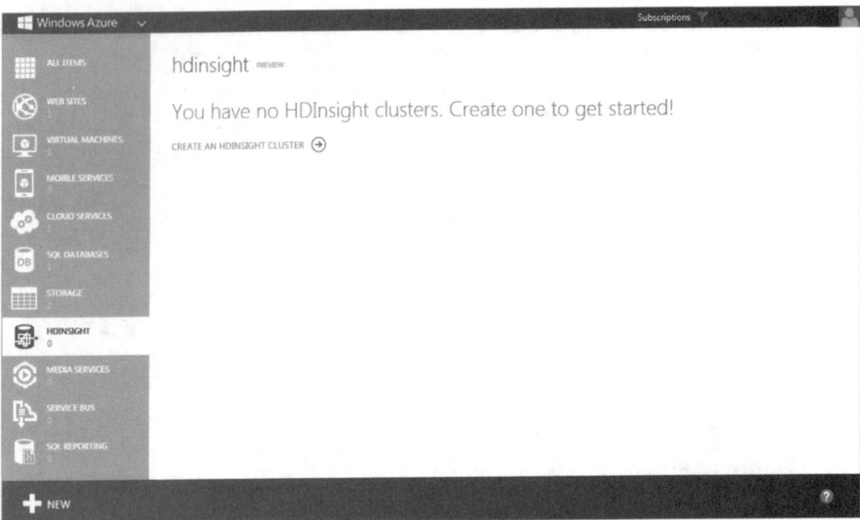

Figure 13.9: HDInsight dashboard

4. Click the Quick Create button, and then select a unique container name. Because the container we are creating will be used for an HDInsight instance, select the West US region. (We will be creating our cluster in the West US region later on.) Note that the Enable Geo-Replication option is selected by default. This option can have a pricing impact on your storage. For evaluation and testing purposes, you can uncheck this box. Figure 13.10 shows the resulting container configuration. Click Create Storage Account when finished.

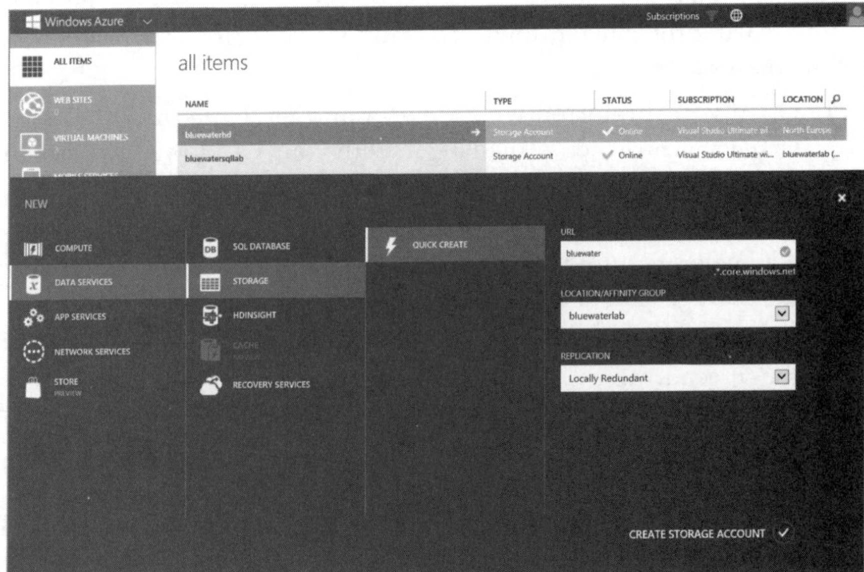

Figure 13.10: Create HDInsight storage container

5. Now you are ready to begin creating your HDInsight cluster. On the menu bar, click the HDInsight icon to navigate to the HDInsight console, and then click the Create an HDInsight Cluster link.
6. We will use the Quick Create option to stand up our HDInsight sandbox. Select a unique name for your cluster. For this demonstration, leave the default of 4 data nodes, and then create your administrator password. Note that the administrator username for your instance is Admin when using the Quick Create option. Finally, ensure that the storage account you created previously is selected. The results should look similar to Figure 13.11. Click the Create HDInsight Cluster button.

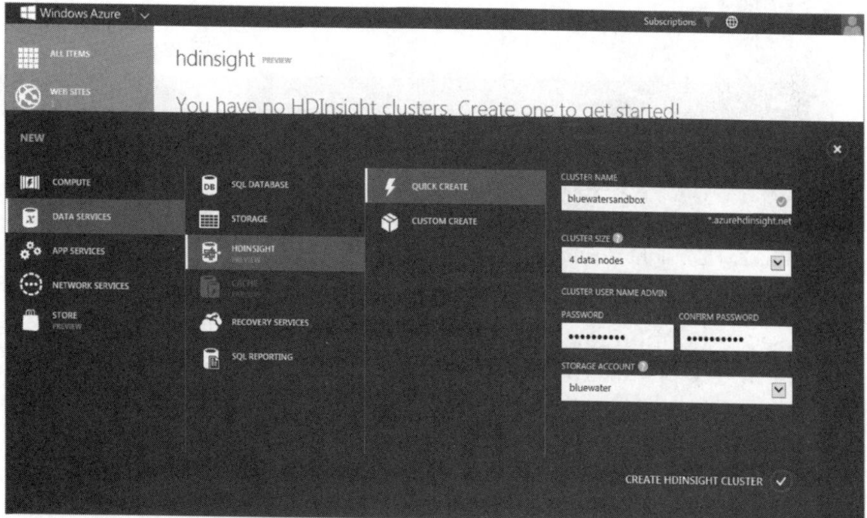

Figure 13.11: Create HDInsight cluster

7. After you have submitted your request for an HDInsight cluster, grab a cup of coffee and relax. It takes between 5 and 10 minutes for your Azure virtual machine configuration and nodes to be built out and made available. You can monitor the progress of your request using the HDInsight console/dashboard. When your cluster is ready, the status will read as Started.

Your HDInsight cluster is now available and is ready for a processing job. To access and manage your new cluster, you can use either Remote Desktop or the HDInsight web console.

To open a Remote Desktop session, select your cluster from the HDInsight console and click the Connect button (see Figure 13.12). An `*.rdp` file is downloaded and contains all the connection information required for the Remote Desktop session. The username mentioned previously is Admin, and the password is the same as you created during setup.

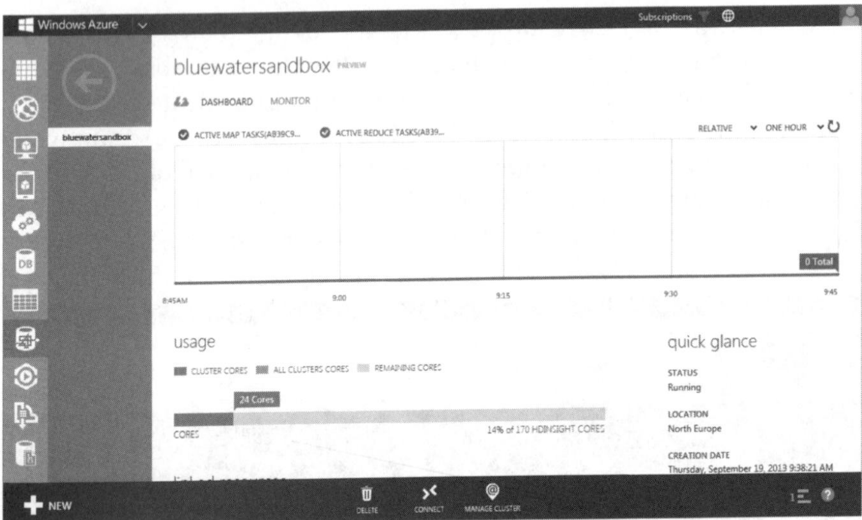

Figure 13.12: HDInsight cluster dashboard

The second option for interacting with your HDInsight sandbox is via the HDInsight web portal. To launch the web portal, click the Manage Cluster link and enter your username and password.

As shown in Figure 13.13, the web portal provides robust access via tiles to key features and functions within your cluster, including the following:

- An interactive console
- Remote Desktop
- A monitor dashboard
- Job history
- Built-in samples
- Downloads and documentation

In addition, you can submit a MapReduce job packaged in a JAR file via the Task tile.

Running a Processing Job on HDInsight

When you set up your sandbox using the Amazon EMR service, your environment centered on a specific processing job. The provision of a cluster was handled in terms of that one specific task. HDInsight takes a different approach from that shown in the preceding demonstration, focusing first on standing up your Hadoop cluster, meaning that to this point, you have not actually processed any data.

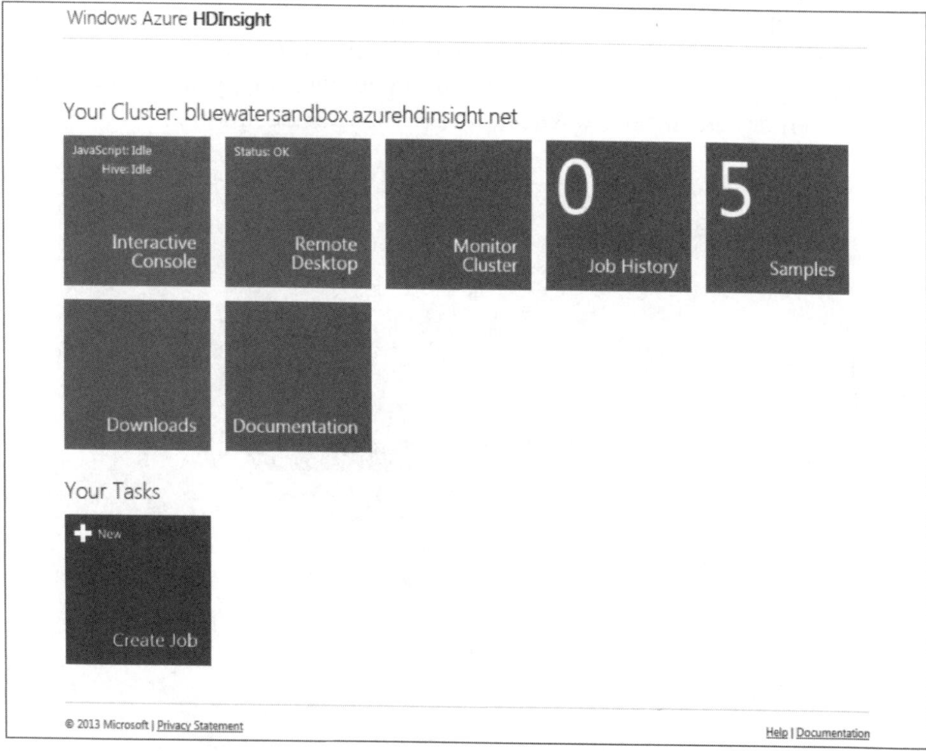

Figure 13.13: HDInsight web portal

To make sure that you understand the differences between the two service providers, create and run a similar word-count job on your HDInsight sandbox by completing the following steps:

1. Download the `wordcount.js` file from the Chapter 13 materials accompanying this book. You also need the `wordcount.txt` file used in the previous demo.
2. From the HDInsight dashboard in the Windows Azure Portal, click your sandbox cluster. Then click the Manage Cluster link at the bottom of the screen.
3. When the management portal has launched, enter your username and password to connect to your HDInsight environment.
4. For this demonstration, use the JavaScript Interactive console. This console is accessed by clicking the Interactive Console tile.

5. To prepare for the job, the data and job scripts must first be available within HDInsight. If you recall from the Amazon EMR demo, you uploaded the files separately. In HDInsight, you can upload both the data and job script files using the interactive console. At the console `js>` prompt, enter or type **`fs.put()`**. This launches a file upload dialog as shown in Figure 13.14. Select `wordcount.txt` from your local file system as the source and enter **`/demo/data/wordcount.txt`** for your destination.

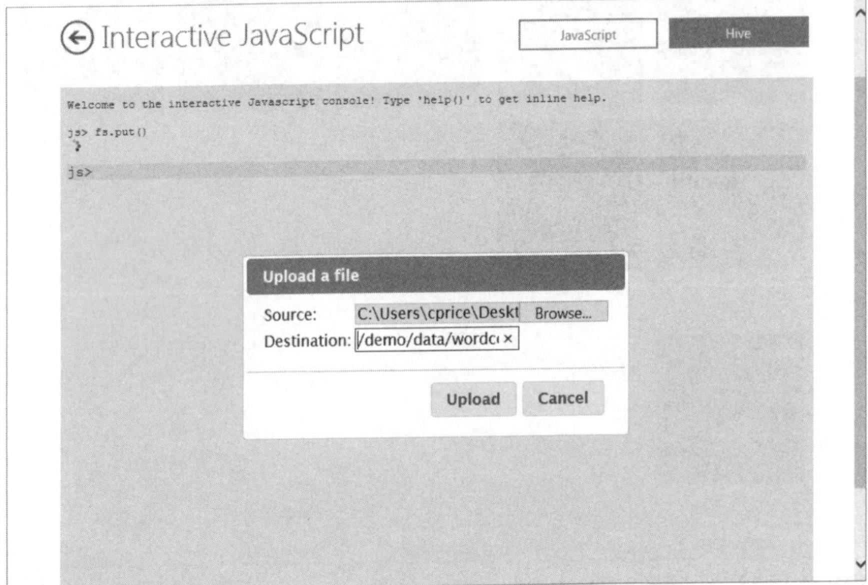

Figure 13.14: HDInsight word count job

6. Repeat Step 5 to upload the `WordCount.js` file using `/demo/WordCount.js` as the destination path. This file contains a streaming JavaScript MapReduce job that will be used to split the words and provide a word count.
7. To confirm that the files exist in your ASV storage account and to demonstrate some of the Hadoop `FileSystem` commands, use the following command, as shown in Figure 13.15, to recursively list the files you uploaded to the demo directory:

```
#lsr /demo/
```

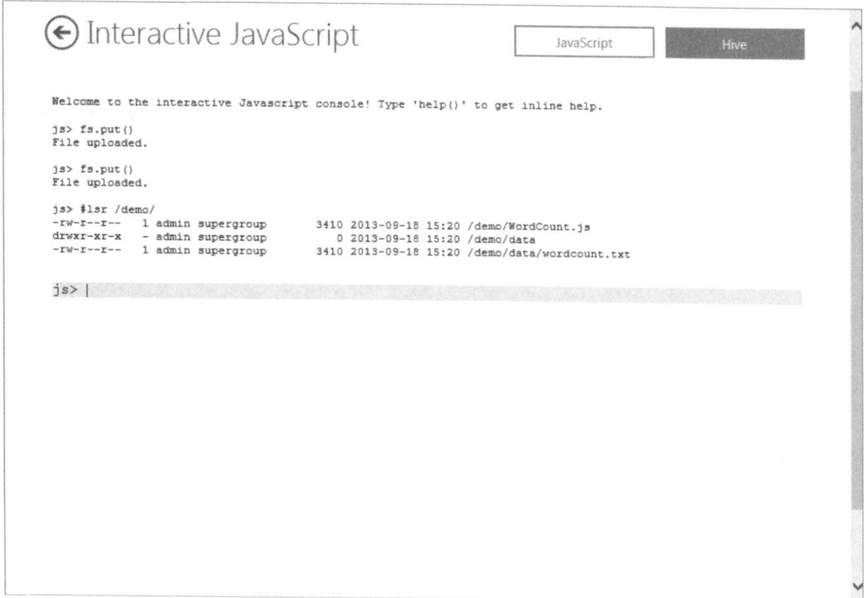

Figure 13.15: HDInsight FS shell

8. You can also browse the contents of the JavaScript file you uploaded to process your data by entering **`#cat /demo/WordCount.js`**. This command reads the file and prints the contents to the Interactive console window.
9. This demo uses both a Pig and MapReduce job to parse the `wordcount.txt` file, count the occurrence of words, and return the top 10 most used words. You can create and execute the processing job by entering the following command:

```
pig.from("/demo/data/wordcount.txt")
.mapReduce("/demo/WordCount.js",
"word, count:long").orderBy("count DESC")
.take(10).to("Top10Words")
```

10. Figure 13.16 displays the result when your command is submitted to your HDInsight cluster. The console will continually update the status as processing proceeds. If you prefer to see the entire job output, click the More link displayed in the job status update. If the More link is not visible, you might need to scroll in the console window to the right.

Figure 13.16: HDInsight JavaScript console

11. When your job completes, you can use the Hadoop `FileSystem` commands to explore the results. The `#lsr Top10Words` command will display the files output by your processing job, and the `#tail Top10Words/part-r-00000` will read and print out the end of your file, as shown in Figure 13.17.

Figure 13.17: HDInsight JavaScript FS command

TIP The Hadoop `FileSystem #cat` command prints out the entire contents of a file to the console window. If you are working with a very large file, this is probably not a desirable function. Instead, you can use the `#tail` function to peek or preview the last kilobyte of the file.

12. Additional functionality beyond the execution of processing jobs is available through your Interactive console. As an example of its flexibility, you could easily chart the top 10 words from the text, as shown in Figure 13.18, using these commands:

```
file = fs.read("Top10Words")
data = parse(file.data, "word, count:long")
graph.bar(data)
```

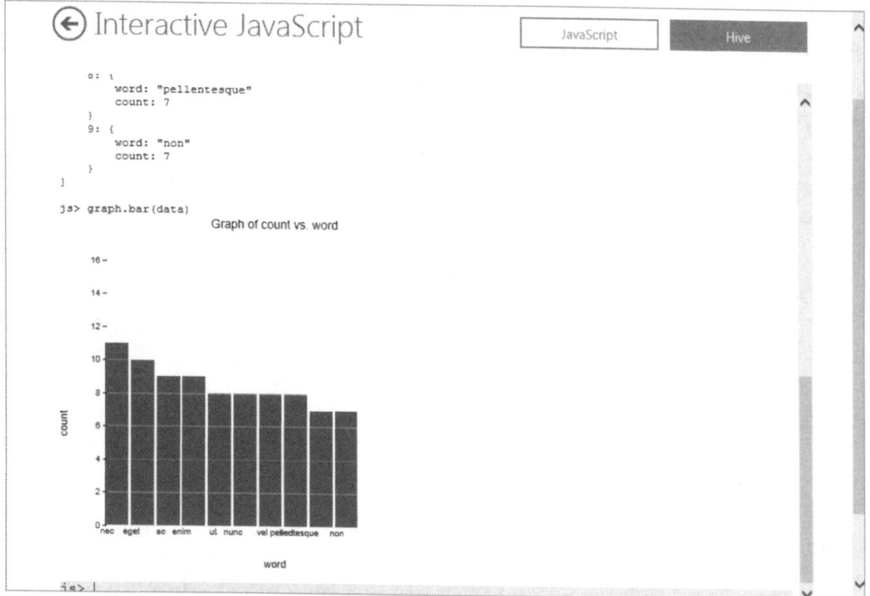

Figure 13.18: HDInsight JavaScript console results

With that, your HDInsight sandbox tour is complete. Unlike the Amazon EMR sandbox, you must manually delete your cluster when you finish. Failure to delete your cluster will result in charges for idle-processing time, which is wasteful and runs counter to the paradigm discussed previously.

Storing Your Data in the Cloud

Previously in this chapter, you worked with cloud storage as you set up and provisioned your Amazon and Microsoft Hadoop clusters. This section looks more closely at cloud storage and some of the common features and rationalizations as they relate to big data.

Storing Data

Storing your big data in the cloud is a more natural fit than it might appear at first glance. Cloud data storage works best when the "write once, read many" or WORM principle is applied. This principle implies that data is written once and read many times from many different sources. This is one of the core principles of big data and Hadoop data systems in general.

Cloud service providers offer cheap, scalable, and redundant data storage that is highly and even globally available when necessary, making it an ideal storage solution for many big data implementations. Regardless of the service provider, the feature set among cloud storage providers is similar, including advanced features such as advanced security options, backup or snapshot capabilities, and content-delivery networks.

Both Amazon S3 and Microsoft Azure Blob Storage are centered on a top-level root directory or container (called a bucket in S3). These containers can contain an unlimited number of files and folders and can scale to any size you require. Likewise, these containers allow you to apply general security and access policies to prevent or allow access as required.

To better illustrate how these containers work, we will use the following example:

- Account: mycorp
- Container/bucket: demo
- Folder: `weblogs`
- File: `server1.csv`

When using Amazon S3, the URL of your bucket is a globally unique name. This results in the URL for your file follows:

```
http://demo.s3.amazonaws.com/weblogs/server1.csv
```

On the Azure Blob Storage service, both your account name and container name are included resulting in a URL that looks like this:

```
http://mycorp.blob.core.windows.net/demo/weblogs/server1.csv
```

Access to both containers is provided via REST web APIs that allow for creating, modifying, and deleting folders and files within the containers. Each API also supports the creation and deletion of containers/buckets on the fly.

Uploading Your Data

Big data presents challenges in terms of how data is processed and managed. If you are going to host your data in the cloud, you are also confronted with the task of efficiently moving your data into the cloud in a timely manner. To assist in the process, you want to consider several best practices, as discussed next.

Location Matters

When you are configuring your containers and buckets, the geographic location that you select during provisioning has a large impact on the file upload latency. If your data center and the servers that are producing the data are located in the southeast United States and the storage container you provision is in the western United States (or worse yet northern Europe), there is additional latency introduced because your data now has to physically travel farther. Make sure that your storage is provisioned correctly by ensuring geographic proximity.

Size Matters

Anytime you move data over any network, especially the Internet, size matters. The bigger the file, the more latency and the greater the likelihood that something will go wrong. This reinforces the obvious, which is why you want to make the files you move to the cloud as small as possible using compression.

You have multiple compression formats and techniques (LZ, zip, deflate, rar) from which to choose. The most popular and widely used in the big data realm is GZip. GZip is a lossless compression technique, which means that statistical redundancies in the data are exploited to shrink the data with no data loss. Libraries to compress and decompress files using the GZip format are available on almost every platform, and most importantly the tools within the Hadoop ecosystem can read directly from a file compressed with the GZip format.

Data Movements

When data is moved, it is usually loaded sequentially (that is, one file after another). This pattern does not scale well when you consider the data volumes typically associated with big data. To provide the scale and throughput required, data movements are usually handled in a multithreaded or parallel fashion. Luckily, the distributed nature of cloud storage lends itself to handling parallel operations.

When planning how your data will move to the cloud, consider the following:

- If your data is being created across many servers, do not create a central collection point. This point will eventually create a bottleneck for your loads. Instead, distribute the responsibility for publishing the data to the cloud to the data producers.
- Consider your tooling. Most modern cloud storage tools support uploading and downloading files in parallel.
- There is a tendency or desire to bundle multiple files into a single compressed file before publishing to the cloud. This process will tax the system responsible for packaging files and slow down your uploads. Multiple small files will always upload faster than a single large or monolithic file.

Exploring Big Data Storage Tools

Amazon S3 and Microsoft Azure Blob Storage provide a robust REST API for integration with their cloud data services. In addition, a number of wrappers function as a layer of abstraction and provide easy access within code; these are available in just about every development language. If you are a developer (or even a closet developer), this may excite you and be exactly what you are looking for. For most of you, however, you will prefer tools that provide the same management and administration capabilities with no coding required.

This section briefly introduces some of the more popular commercial tools available and discusses the AzCopy project. The intent is not to endorse any one tool over another, but instead to make you aware of the current state of the marketplace.

Azure Management Studio

Developed by a company called Cerebata, Azure Management Studio (`http://www.cerebrata.com/products/azure-management-studio/introduction`) is a tool geared toward Microsoft Azure. It is a full-feature product that not only allows for complete administration over your blob storage but also includes other features such as pulling diagnostic and miscellaneous analytical information associated with your account. It also has a number of features built in to enable you to manage your other Azure services. A demo version is available for evaluation, but you have to purchase a license to use this product.

CloudXplorer

Developed by ClumsyLeaf, CloudXplorer (`http://clumsyleaf.com/products/cloudxplorer`) is a lightweight explorer tool for Windows Azure. It is widely used and capable of supporting all needed administrative and management tasks. CloudXplorer offers two versions: one freeware and a Pro version.

CloudBerry Explorer

CloudBerry Explorer (`http://www.cloudberrylab.com/`) by CloudBerry Labs offers versions that work with both Windows Azure and Amazon S3. This tool is also a full-feature product that comes in two versions: freeware and Pro.

AzCopy

Beyond tools offered by third-party providers, within the Windows Azure realm there is an open source, console-based project called AzCopy that enables quick and convenient parallel data transfers (`http://go.microsoft.com/fwlink/?LinkId=287086`). Unlike the tools discussed previously, the sole purpose of this tool is the upload and/or download files to and from your Azure blob storage account. Because it is implemented as a console application, it can easily be scripted for the purpose of automation into your big data movement processing.

Working with AzCopy is easy, and it lends itself nicely to being embedded in jobs or even SQL Server Integration Services packages. The following command format will recursively copy (the `/S` switch) all files from the `c:\logs` directory to the target container:

```
AzCopy C:\logs  https://demo.blob.core.windows.net/logs/ /destkey:key /S
```

The process has built-in parallelism that uses multithreading to simultaneously initiate network connections eight times the number of cores on your server or workstation. This means that for a 4-core machine, 32 simultaneous file transfers to your Azure Blob Storage account would be initiated.

Regardless of the tool you select, the principles for efficiently and effectively transferring data to the cloud remain the same, and all the tools discussed do a good job in helping you effectively and efficiently get your data into the cloud.

Integrating Cloud Data

Once your data is stored in the cloud, integrating it into your Hadoop cluster is a trivial task. Vendors have a done a lot of work to ensure that the links between their cloud storage and cloud computing services are not only seamless but also high performance.

Both S3 and Azure Blob data can be referenced natively within each vendor's respective service using a path that starts with either `s3://` or `asv://` as the path prefix.

Within Microsoft HDInsight, there are three use cases to consider when integrating cloud data stored in Azure Blob Storage, as described next.

Local Container and Containers on the Same Storage Account

Data can be created and read from both the same container and other containers on the same storage account that is used to run your HDInsight cluster. In this scenario, the key required to read from the storage account is already stored in the `core-site.xml`. This allows for full access to the data within these containers.

Public Container

When a container (and the blobs it contains) is marked as public, you can access data directly by specifying a URI path to the blob. The path required varies slightly from the one introduced previously. When accessing a file from a URI, the path format looks like the following:

```
http://<Account>.blob.core.windows.net/<Container>/<Path>
```

The URI required for access to the same file from HDInsight would translate to the following:

```
asv://<Container>@<Account>.blob.core.windows.net/<Path>
```

Private Container on a Separate Account

To connect to a private container on a separate storage account, you must configure Hadoop for access to the container. To make this configuration change, complete the following steps:

1. Use Remote Desktop to connect to your HDInsight cluster by clicking the Configure button on your HDInsight dashboard.
2. In Windows Explorer, navigate to the `C:\apps\dist\hadoop-1.1.0-SNAPSHOT\conf\` directory and open the `core-site.xml` file in Notepad.
3. Add the following snippet of XML, ensuring that you substitute the storage account name and storage account key:

```
<property>
        <name>fs.azure.account.key.<ACCOUNT>.blob.core.microsoft.com
</name>
        <value><KEY></value>
</property>
```

4. Save the changes and close the file.

After you define the account and security key required for access to the container, HDInsight will treat the container as a local container.

NOTE You can easily use the Hadoop `FileSystem` API to manage containers from your HDInsight cluster. A few of the common commands are included here:

- Create a new container

```
hadoop fs -mkdir asvs://<container>@<account>.blob.core
.windows.net/
<path>
```

- List container contents

```
hadoop fs -ls asvs://<container>@<account>.blob.core
.windows.net/<path>
```

- Permanently delete file

```
Hadoop fs -rmr -skipTrash asvs://<container>@<account>.blob.core.
windows.net/<path>
```

Other Cloud Data Sources

Beyond your cloud data, many other cloud data sources may provide value in your big data infrastructure.

Amazon hosts a number of different public data sets, ranging from U.S. census databases to data from the Human Genome project. You can get more information on this data at `http://aws.amazon.com/publicdatasets/`.

Microsoft also hosts a number of different data sources and services through the Windows Azure Data Marketplace. A variety of data is available, ranging from demographic and weather data to business and economic data for banking, finance, and manufacturing. Some data is offered either free of charge or with a free trial; other data is offered via a paid subscription service.

Summary

Getting started with big data does not require a large investment in either time or resources. By leveraging the cloud service providers like Amazon and Microsoft for both storage and computer power, you can easily get started with Hadoop and big data.

Using these services is quick and easy and allows for virtualizing away the hardware and infrastructure while providing a reliable, scalable, cloud-based big data solution.

CHAPTER

14

Big Data in the Real World

WHAT YOU WILL LEARN IN THIS CHAPTER:

- Finding Out How Key Industries Use Big Data Analytics
- Understanding Types of Common Analysis
- Making Analytics Operational in Your Organization

This book has covered numerous solutions so far. This chapter focuses on how the industry leverages these solutions, for example, how the telecommunication industry is planning new development based on customer usage data they are crunching in new ways. This chapter will inspire you and provide ideas (from real-world implementations) for implementing the big data techniques you have learned. Remember, as well, that your clients and employers expect you to "know" these new technologies, so coming to the project table with implementation ideas, in addition to the basic skills, will make you a more valuable team member.

Another concept this chapter covers is how to *fail fast*. After all, a significant benefit of these new technologies is that they provide for quick prototyping and testing cycles, which in turn allow you, faster than ever before, to redirect efforts away from unproductive avenues to more productive solutions. Companies are trying continuously to enhance their analytic capabilities, and through failing and redirecting more rapidly you can help them get to the right solution faster and with less overhead in the process. To start this discussion, let's review some common industry sectors that apply these techniques.

Common Industry Analytics

Industries that use these types of big data analytics include telecommunications, energy, oil and gas, retail, companies that sell data as a service, IT organizations, and large hosting companies such as Rackspace and GoDaddy. In addition, just about every industry's marketing department is interested in things like social sentiment and measuring their brand impact and presence/influence, as discussed later in this chapter.

Telco

In the telecommunications industry, as with any other major commodity, organizations seek consumption details that will enable them to predict bursts of activity and analyze patterns and to then use this information to create valuable offerings for customers. Those offers focus on maximizing new infrastructure development and minimizing wasted effort from construction alliances or new ventures. These analyses attempt to define usage patterns by looking at the types of services that people use. Those services could include Internet, Voice over IP (VoIP), landline telephone, and even mobile.

In consumption analysis, algorithms help us understand where and when, from a consumption perspective, people are spending the most. Is a service/product costing them more to be with this particular provider just because of the way that customers use it? Are they using a service/product more during prime-time hours (which would then influence the pricing model)? These types of models and modeling problems are common, and the solutions explored are usually found in the big data ecosystem.

The Hadoop ecosystem also facilitates the placement of new infrastructure in record time and with increased accuracy (another major analytic area, although not new, in the telecommunications industry). Movement and usage patterns (especially people using their mobile devices for data/voice) significantly influence the placement of this new infrastructure. Tracking users has always been a challenge because of the volume of data such tracking produces. Now, though, all these users can be tracked based on where they move throughout the world and where they're using services. The infrastructure can be improved or enhanced based on these particular usage patterns. That alone can provide a much better experience for the customer, leading to improved customer loyalty and, as customers stay with the same provider, a significant return on investment (ROI).

Energy

In the energy industry, common types of analysis today include survey data information about where people consume different types of energy and analysis of the carbon impact. These analyses seek to predict customer usage and to optimize the availability of multiple fuel types. Although the focus of such analysis is not new (or the result of new and better tools), industry players can complete their analysis with improved levels of accuracy based on significantly larger volumes of data. Those larger volumes of data allow a much more detailed level of analysis for everything from geographic and spatial analysis of three-dimensional survey data to predicting where the most cost-efficient and least environmentally impactful deposits and withdrawal activity could happen.

The energy industry's need to predict customer usage and to optimize the availability of multiple fuel types will continue to grow as the various fuel types become more and more popular (for instance, as geothermal and hydroelectric power begin to move more households away from traditional types of electricity derived from coal or oil). These types of analytics will show whether specific areas of the country could really benefit from the various types of fuel or alternative fuel sources.

Retail

Many of you are already familiar with the types of analysis that retail organizations do. As you shop at Amazon.com, eBay, or any other major retail sites, "you may also like this" sections pop up (known as *market basket analysis*). In large Hadoop implementations, this type of analysis occurs on the fly and behind the scenes based on your shopping cart and your shopping preferences. The companies are running an analytics model designed to tell you about other products/services that you might be interested in. Mahout is the tool in the Hadoop ecosystem that many organizations use to build and leverage these models for testing solution combinations. This market basket analysis value-added service provides recommended tracking for customers, and through tracking customer patterns, it may enable the retailer to sell more and make more money per individual transaction (a key metric in the retail space).

A new type of analytics in the retail space tracks customers as they move through a store. Some organizations do this with a little chip in a shopping cart. Others do it by getting you to install their smartphone application. However these stores physically track customers, the most important piece of information is where customers are spending most of their time. For example, are they spending most of their time shopping for groceries and spending some time in sporting goods? Do they go to automotive every time they come in to buy groceries? These analytics give retailers an incredible amount of insight into how they can stock their stores and how they can organize the floor plans to direct traffic to the areas that will maximize the amount of money they get per visitor.

The last major type of analysis centers on unproductive inventory and stock management. A number of years ago, a Discovery Channel special on Walmart showcased how Walmart was ahead of its time in analytics (in that they could add weather pattern data into their inventory and stock analysis). For example, when a particular type of weather system was coming through the Midwest, they knew that people would buy more of a certain type of Pop-Tarts, and so they could automatically preorder that. Working that into their inventory management system without anybody having to make any decisions is a good example of this type of analysis.

For this type of event analysis, many companies factor in everything from weather data, to traffic data, to the schedule of a big football game or a big political event, to any other event that would drive a lot of tourism. Any retail organization would find it incredibly valuable to integrate any of those types of cyclical population data points. Major retail organizations are already working hard on doing this, and some, like Walmart, have been doing it for a number of years already.

Data Services

In today's economy, an increasing number of organizations provide, as their sole focus, data as a service to other organizations. These organizations take hard-to-get data and amass that data with customer data to provide additional value—everything from integrating weather/population data as a service (as discussed earlier with regard to the retail industry) all the way to mapping data that companies can integrate into their websites for things such as your closest pharmacy or grocery store. They do this by calling a tracking application programming interface (API), and the API takes care of it for them. These data service organizations focus intently on the acquisition and quality of data and being able to scale the response time of the analysis of the particular questions posed. These data companies are very interested in (and in some cases already pioneering) the use of these big data technologies.

IT/Hosting Optimization

Internal IT can also leverage the opportunities presented by Hadoop ecosystem technologies: predicting machine failure, reviewing log data to provide more real-time workload optimization, removing hotspots in a cloud or grid environment, and even reviewing tickets and knowledge bases for common issues using natural language processing. Although this book does not go into detail about natural language processing, many other books do, and many technologies that really excel in natural language processing run in this ecosystem.

Natural language processing comprises a set of tools and software components that developers can leverage to analyze voice recordings or text documents to determine what the user is asking or trying to do. Developers can tell whether the user is happy or sad, positive or negative, forceful or not forceful. We can measure many things through natural language processing, and we can apply simple natural language processing to large call center ticketing systems that large organizations have. Developers can then deal with a significant number of common trouble tickets by either fixing the underlying issue or by providing additional user training. Any of those options may provide significant relief.

In conjunction with real-time machine workload information coming from the logs of large cloud or grid systems, developers can use native ecosystem tools to begin to analyze that data and initiate processes to move the workload to different parts of the cloud. The resultant elasticity and ability to scale more efficiently may thus allow them to be more responsive to their customers.

Marketing Social Sentiment

The ubiquity of social media provides an unprecedented opportunity for marketers. Brands can now understand their influence and presence measurement across a wide variety of populations and geographies. This information has never before been as readily accessible as today, and it is becoming increasingly accessible as new networks and new technologies come online.

Measuring an organization's brand/presence influence with respect to marketing impact is generally referred to as social sentiment analysis. Social sentiment analysis, something that most companies say that they want, usually falls within the purview of the marketing department. Real-world social sentiment analysis considers, among other things, the following:

- Positive and negative statements made about your brand
- Responses (negative and positive) and response time to advertisements played (within specific time periods and via specific modes, such as pop-up ads, referral links, and so on)
- Multiple social network user-population impacts/influences of your brand

Operational Analytics

The concept of operational analytics derives from taking your normal day-to-day operational activities in information technology and combining them as seamlessly as possible with the technologies that are providing your analytics solutions for your customers. A good example of this would be a company that is automatically placing their ads on their web presence based on click-through analysis in real time. Let's explore this more in the following sections.

Failing Fast

Earlier in this chapter, you came across the term *failing fast*. This concept allows you, along with the development team, to redirect your efforts based on any constructive feedback you receive from those who are using your solution. In existing legacy business intelligence (BI) solutions, it can sometimes prove difficult to retrofit a solution based on regular and ongoing feedback. Within the Hadoop ecosystem, the tools provide a more compartmentalized view of the architecture, allowing for more individual retrofitting and adjustment. You will find this point more apparent in the next few sections as you learn how these tools will impact your existing BI and reporting implementations.

A New Ecosystem of Technologies

By this point in the book, you can certainly understand that you can leverage many new technologies and opportunities to do some impressive analytics for your organization. As with any new technology, integrating these technologies can prove challenging (but also beneficial at the same time). The following subsections cover a few of the most common areas where these technologies intersect.

Changing the Face of ETL

Extract, transform, and load (ETL) processes are generally considered the backbone of any BI implementation because they are responsible for moving, cleansing, loading, and reviewing the quality of the data that reports and analytics are based on in today's current systems. The challenge with today's ETL is that it can be difficult to adapt or adjust once a large-scale implementation is in place.

As discussed throughout this book, tools such as Pig and Sqoop provide a less-robust, more-scalable, and more-flexible approach to moving data in and around your environment. In most cases, you will have both your traditional ETL platform, like SQL Server Information Services (SSIS), and an ETL process that works within your project implementation. These work together to move the data back and forth between those environments.

Pig, in particular, provides a robust command-based solution. With this solution, you can do text-based data cleansing and organization aggregation, and you can use the MapReduce framework under the covers to scale the network across many nodes and thus process and move large volumes of data that a normal ETL server may struggle to handle in the same amount of time. Traditional ETL servers use memory-intensive processes to load data into memory, access it very quickly, and perform the appropriate operation (such as cleansing, removing, sorting, aggregating, and so on). Arguably, by combining the capabilities of Pig with additional tools, such as natural language processing and other types of advanced analysis, developers can do things in conjunction with the ETL process that would previously have required a lot more code and a lot more effort to accomplish.

What Does This Do to Business Intelligence?

With all these changes, you are probably asking yourself what this does to BI. The important thing to remember is that nothing changes overnight. Yes, developers do have many new tools and new ways to do some impressive analytics and incredible dedicated visualizations, but these new tools will continue to interact with existing platforms into which you have already invested significant intellectual capital and organizational intellectual property.

BI was originally designed as the analytics platform of the future. Now, though, as the future looms (or as we pass through it), we require additional scalability. BI has successfully demonstrated the value of these types of solutions to so many organizations that they are now struggling to keep up with the volume of data and the types of questions that the users and their customer community want to ask. That represents an incredible value proposition: Users wanting more of your solution (instead of you having to convince users of the utility of BI and solicit customers for it).

The data solutions are giving people and organizations the flexibility to drive types of conversations as never before. That then allows developers to take larger volumes of data that do not fit into traditional BI systems, like a relational database-oriented or online analytical processing (OLAP) cube or a report, and provide a platform where users can analyze all of that data and come up with a subset that they know has real value and real meaning for the organization. After they have identified that subset of information, that subset can be moved into the traditional BI (Business Intelligence) implementation, where the enterprise can begin to consume it and work with it as they would any other data from their sales or customer relationship management (CRM) or reporting system.

This flexibility and agility is something not seen before, but it is similar in some ways to the concept of *self-service BI*. Many of self-service tools (such as Power Query and the Power BI suite from Microsoft) work well with Hadoop and the ecosystem that it runs on. With Hive, developers have the opportunity to quickly publish data to their end users in a relational abstraction format; data that users can query from desktop tools designed to help them be more exploratory in their analysis. You will learn what *exploratory data analysis* means a little bit later in this chapter. For now, just understand that instead of sitting down in the morning and running their normal Monday morning report, we want users to be able to go further. We want users to be able not just to respond to numbers they see on a page, but to be able to make that response a deeper query and a deeper investigation than they can get today—quickly, at their fingertips, without having to request changes or add additional infrastructure from the IT organization.

New Visualization Impact

Resultant from these new types of analysis, methods, and practices for visualizing data are a number of recently published books on best practices for data visualization. Among the valuable material in these books, one good point refers to nonrelational data (such as spatial data or data coming from unspecific file types and government sources): that you can accurately portray the meaning of the data through the way that you visualize it.

Microsoft has advanced visualization tools (for example, Power View and Power Map). Other organizations, such as Tableau, have additional advanced visualizations, and many organizations are looking at a multivendor approach for their reporting and visualization needs as they explore the beginning (and evolving) ecosystem. After all, no one vendor has really cornered the market on visualization. Even open source tools give us a lot of visualization ability right from the command line. As we begin to turn our data into analysis, those graphics can be pulled out directly and put into presentations or shared with our user base.

As all of us are aware, the analysis is only as valuable as the level with which we can communicate it to our end users, executives, and stakeholders. If we cannot visualize and communicate the analysis, its impact, and our recommendations, we will not be successful no matter what technology we are using.

User Audiences

Several user audiences will exist for these types of solutions. So, you want to understand what things each of these user audiences will be most concerned about as you begin to discuss how these new solutions will affect their day-to-day operations. Let's review some of the more important user audiences.

Consumers

Consumers will be some of your easiest customers. They are primarily concerned with where to go to run reports and where to go to direct their data collection activities.

To complete typical jobs, consumers will likely use Hive tables under the covers that you have created and exposed for them. These Hive tables will be the easiest way for them to query underlying data structures, unless they have a tool such as Power Query from Microsoft, which will enable them to go directly to files in the Hadoop Distributed File System (HDFS).

Your consumers will be used to using all of their existing tools, so it is important that you help them understand that many of these tools will continue to be used in exactly the same way, that they do not have to replace their existing enterprise BI environment. We are just adding new data sets to enable them to pull additional information to add value to their existing reports and provide a deeper level of analysis than what they would normally be able to perform. These existing tools (for instance, Excel and Power BI from Microsoft) provide leading-edge capabilities to take advantage of all we are doing with these new tools.

The ecosystem that we cover in this book is providing an additional data platform and a set of capabilities for developers to service additional types of data at volumes that were previously much more difficult (and in some cases prohibitive). With these limitations removed, consumers can now reach a new level of information collection collaboration and management.

Power Users

Power users are going to be some of the most advanced users of these new solutions. They can be doing everything from custom model creation to creating their own Hive tables and writing their own Pig scripts.

These users will demand the most assistance with the actual tools and more assistance with where data is located, how it is being loaded into the system, how they access it, and what kind of metadata is available. Power users will work closely with the developers as the developers build out the functional pieces of the platform, which the power users will then integrate into the system to take something to the next level.

Data Developers

Data developers will be one of your largest and most demanding of all the audiences. In fact, you might be in this category yourself.

Data developers are going to be in charge of everything from sourcing data, to bringing it into the HDFS, loading it into nonrelational data sources such as Mongo DB, and creating Hive tables for users to connect to. And then, most likely, they will be responsible for developing export functionality to dump the subsets of valuable data that users find during analysis out to the format that can then be integrated into the enterprise BI system.

It is this life cycle of identifying data, making it available for exploration, reviewing the results of that exploration, and then taking subsets of value-added data in building integration processes that will keep the new big data developer very busy. This is an extremely exciting time for developers. After all, you get to take all that you have learned about acquiring, cleansing, and managing data and apply it to a set of new tools and thus enable new scalability opportunities and new performance limits that are far beyond what existing systems can offer. If, in addition, you are leveraging the cloud for your biggest solutions, you will have additional opportunities to manage data asynchronously, on-premise solutions, cloud solutions, and enterprise BI solutions wherever they are deployed.

System Administrators

System administrators are usually concerned with ensuring that systems are appropriately deployed and maintained and performing at peak level. In the big data ecosystem, all of these concerns still exist with clusters of the Hadoop nodes within a distributed file system.

Many tools require configuration to control how they scale, how they distribute, and how they manage data across different clusters. Some of these clusters may be on premise, some of them in the cloud, and some of them may be a hybrid scenario where some of the machines are on premise and others are taking advantage of cloud elasticity for seasonal or a particular type of analytic throughput.

System administrators will have their hands full learning all the new configuration options, configuration files, and various other information covered earlier in this book.

NOTE **This book is not an exhaustive reference; you might want to use many other configuration options to manage the environment particular to an organization. It is important to understand all the different options, and there are great references out there to help you do that. You should review the platform documentation for whichever vendor you are using (for instance, Microsoft documentation for HDInsight or the Hortonworks documentation for the Hortonworks Data Platform).**

System administrators will serve as critical partners for data developers of the future because the data developers will rely on a certain amount of scalability and distributed processing power for how they build their applications. It is important that these two groups and roles work together and have a strong relationship to provide the right level of scalability performance and elasticity in these types of environments.

Analysts/Data Scientists

Many analysts and data scientists have been using these tools now for a few years. Their analyses and requirements served as a major driver in the development and enhancement of the tools in this ecosystem. Being able to run statistical models in tools (for instance, predictive analytics in tools such as Mahout) is critical to the success of persons in this role.

Many organizations are still trying to define what it means to be a data scientist in their company, so do not get hung up on the terms *data scientist* or *analyst*. In brief, a data scientist attempts to review internal data along with external data and based on that to then recommend opportunities for the company to measure new things as markers of success or failure for particular projects, divisions, organizations, or markets. For example, many large retail organizations are rapidly growing their data science teams to include people who understand statistics, predictive modeling, regression analysis, market basket analysis, and additional advanced analytics.

Do not worry if you (or your developer) do not yet have all the skills you need. You might want to learn some of them if you find them interesting. However, your main goal is to work with these folks to provide the right platform with the right access to additional data sets and to provide opportunities for them to excel at their job.

Summary

In this chapter you learned how today's common industries are using big data analytics. These industries included telecommunications, energy, retail, data services, and IT/hosting optimization. You also learned how these industries are turning these initiatives from incubation efforts to operational success and how you can do the same thing in your company. You learned about how these solutions will impact different key roles and who the stakeholders will be in your next big data project. Specific things for each of these roles, such as developers and systems administrators, were covered.

You can leverage the new big data technologies covered so far in this book in many different ways. Get creative and share with your organization where you believe they could leverage technology solutions like the ones in this chapter. For more information on specific implementations, ask your platform vendors for customer stories and case studies for a deeper technical description.

Part VI

Moving Your Big Data Forward

In This Part

CHAPTER

15

Building and Executing Your Big Data Plan

WHAT YOU WILL LEARN IN THIS CHAPTER:

- Getting Sponsor and Stakeholder Buy-in
- Identifying Technical Challenges
- Identifying Operational Challenges
- Monitoring Your Solution Post-deployment

Understanding that you need to look at your data infrastructure and reevaluate how you are handling certain sets of data today and in the future is one thing; actually identifying a project and then getting executive sponsor buy-in is another. In most organizations, many opportunities exist for improvement; it's often difficult to find the one opportunity that demonstrates what a new technology or approach can do for an organization while at the same time providing a reasonable return on investment (ROI). In this chapter, we weave throughout the challenges of building and executing your big data plan. Specifically, the chapter begins by looking at how to gain buy-in from sponsors and stakeholders. Then, you learn about technical and operational challenges and how to overcome them. The chapter concludes with a discussion about what you need to do after you've deployed your solution, including how to plan for its growth.

Gaining Sponsor and Stakeholder Buy-in

One of the most difficult things to do when evaluating a new technology is choosing the project. Those of us who come from a technical background tend to look at most projects from that technical angle. We ask ourselves "which one of these applications is a good fit for technology *x*?" The problem with this approach is that it doesn't align itself with business needs. That particular business group might not have the budget for any new projects or hardware. The business group may be perfectly happy with their current application and not want any significant changes. The business group may simply be resistant to change. We have to remember as technologists we love to jump in and learn them. What you may see as a fascinating new product to learn, the business users often see as another new tool they have to learn to get their job done. In this section we will discuss how to match your technologies, like Hadoop, to business needs within your organization.

Problem Definition

In order to match big data solutions to a project, take a step back and look at the different business units in your organization. What are their current challenges and opportunities? Create a quick chart that maps this out. Talk to these groups about their data challenges. You will often hear many of the same statements coming from the groups who may benefit from big data technologies, such as the following:

- The business can't get access to all the relevant data; we need external data.
- We are missing the ETL window. The data we needed didn't arrive on time.
- We can't predict with confidence if we can't explore data and develop our own models.
- We need to parallelize data operations, but it's too costly and complex.
- We can't keep enough history in our enterprise data warehouse.

These are exactly the business units you want to speak with about leveraging big data solutions. The next step is to describe the solution to them without getting too technical. This step is all about the Return on Investment (ROI) to the business unit.

Many people hear about big data and assume that the first project that they take on must be an entirely new project solving a new problem with new data and new infrastructure. Although you can do this, it greatly increases your chance of failure. The reason for this is that there are too many unknowns. You are dealing with new technology (Hadoop, Hive, Pig, Oozie, etc.), new hardware architecture, new solution architecture, and new data. Every one of those unknowns will slow you down and create opportunities for mistakes. Instead, look around at existing solutions and ask yourself and the business group, "What new data elements would make this data and these reports more statistically accurate and relevant?" Whether you have current solutions dealing with fraud detection, churn analysis, equipment monitoring, or pricing analysis, additional data elements can likely be included from either inside or outside your organization that will improve your analytical capabilities.

Finally, it is important to understand that this endeavor is likely to be very visible within your organization. Most every C-level executive has been reading about big data for the last several years and how it will solve many of their data issues. Thus, they will have a great interest in the solution. Also, the initiative isn't trivial, and the budget of the solution alone will garner interest from executives in the company. It is vital that your solution have the sponsorship of one of these C-level executives so that they can represent the solution to the rest of your company. They are your champion. They should be included in regular monthly updates on the status of the projects. Include them on your successes, but also inform them of the roadblocks that are slowing the project down. Your executive sponsor can help rid your organization of those roadblocks to ensure timely completion of the solution.

As part of this process of defining the problem, it is vital to identify your business user population. Your sponsor can usually help direct you to them, but it is up to the solution architect to reach out to this population and interview them. The purpose of the interviews is to identify the key expected outputs of the solution. Of course, simply asking them what they want the solution to do is inappropriate. After all, they are probably not technologists and don't understand the art of the possible with big data. Instead, ask them probing questions, such as the following:

- What does their job entail?
- How do they measure success?
- What are their current challenges with analytics in their group?

The purpose of these queries is to isolate the questions they will want to ask of the data, and for you to determine whether the data you are collecting actually supports the business drivers for the project. As the architect, do not make the mistake of relying on hearsay; instead, go directly to the source to ensure that information has not been lost in translation.

Scope Management

Scope management is vital to the success of any project. From the beginning, you want to define the business needs of the project, data integration with other sources, data latency requirements, and delivery systems. One key aspect of scope management that often goes overlooked is the use of data profiling very early in the process to flush out a couple key issues:

- Can the data support the project expectations?
- How clean is the data, and what steps can be taken to improve it at the source systems?

Additionally, you will need to identify the tools in the presentation layer to ensure you have the appropriate data models to support the tool. Are you going to query the data directly in Hadoop? If so, you need to ensure that all your tools have a solution to allow it to connect to Hadoop. Even if you establish connectivity to Hadoop, you may find that the end user experience isn't as fast as you want it to be. Many architectures move some of the data off of Hadoop and onto a secondary system such as SQL Server or SQL Server Parallel Data Warehouse.

Finally, the presentation layer can be determined. If you are using Power View, do you have the SharePoint infrastructure to host it? If not, are you going to build it? Determine this end-to-end architecture up front as it's vital to establishing the scope of the entire project to know what you are getting into and what kind of buy-in from executives you'll be asking for.

Basing the Project Scope on Requirements

Developing the appropriate business requirements documentation is the first step in assigning the appropriate scope to any project. All features of the project should be mapped back to business requirements. But isn't this big data where we just collect the data in Hadoop and figure out what we want the data for later? No. Every project should have an initial goal; it's also more likely to get funded if the goal is already established. Base the project scope on these goals and objectives.

One key advantage of the big data paradigm is that through the Schema on Read paradigm we may be collecting additional data from sources and storing it for longer periods of time so that we can find additional uses for it. This will usually come out of additional use cases and future projects. For the purposes of the project that is being funded, though, stick with the basics and follow the plan.

Managing Change in the Project Scope

Change is inevitable, but that doesn't mean you should accept all changes. You need a standardized process by which to evaluate changes as to whether they are needed to meet the business requirements. Risks of these changes should be evaluated and weighed along with the benefits before the change is accepted. A simple Excel spreadsheet listing the risk, a description of the risk, and what action is being taken on the risk is needed. An example would be the use of a new technology such as Pig. The risk may be that you plan on using Pig in your solution. The description can include information such as you don't have anyone within the organization who knows PigLatin and thus there is a risk to implementing it incorrectly. The action being taken may be to send someone to training on Pig. Sometimes the risks will outweigh the benefits and prevent changes in scope from occurring. That said, don't let risk be an excuse to prevent change in scope if it is necessary.

Stakeholder Expectations

Most likely any executives that you are working with to implement your new project have read countless stories during the past couple of years about how big data solves everything. This is what you are up against, and setting expectations from the outset is vitally important. Managing FEAR (false expectations about reality) will be a full-time job for someone on your team. As with all projects, this is done through thorough scoping of the project and communication of goals, timeliness of meeting milestones, and addressing and clearing any roadblocks that you encounter along the way.

To manage false expectations, you first have to identify them. Communication with the business sponsor about the goals and desired outputs of the project is key here. For example:

- Does the sponsor expect the project to increase sales 25%?
- If so, what are the underlying assumptions about the data that make him believe this number is possible?
- What are the acceptable variances above and below that number?
- Do all of these assumptions have to come true to make that number?
- If any one of these assumptions is incorrect, what happens to that number?

This is your opportunity to listen to what the sponsor really believes he is paying for. After you have finished listening to the sponsor, restate everything he said as you understand it. Does he agree with your understanding? If so, now you have a starting point for a discussion about reality.

A more formal way to gather these requirements is through a three-step process of elicit, confirm, and verify:

- **Elicit:** What are we going to build?

  Outputs of the elicit phase are objects such as the business requirements document.
- **Confirm:** Is this what you asked for?

  A customer-signed business requirements document.
- **Verify:** Did you get what you wanted?

  A customer-signed business requirements document (if a change occurred).

Defining the Criteria for Success

Defining success criteria for any big data project will vary wildly by projects. Many of the criteria are goal oriented, but some are more budget oriented. Getting the details of these criteria into your business requirements document is imperative for setting yourself up for victory. Table 19.1 shows an example of stating your project success criteria. A simple list such as this allows you to concentrate on the success criteria without worrying about any additional metadata around simply listing them out. Table 19.2 shows an example of listing out the business objectives for the project along with some additional metadata around stakeholders, success, and how to measure. Both of these documents will provide valuable references as your project progresses.

Table 19.1: Examples of Project Success Criteria

Total project cost does not exceed initial budget by more than *Z*%.
Delivery schedule does not exceed project timeline by more than *Z*%
All high priority items identified in the BRD are delivered in the first release.
Daily loads are complete by 6 a.m. daily.

Table 19.2: Examples of Business Objectives and Metadata

BUSINESS OBJECTIVE	STAKEHOLDER	SUCCESS CRITERIA	MEASUREMENT
Identify the Internet display ads that are most successful in driving customers to buy our products online.	Marketing		

Identifying Technical Challenges

No doubt you will encounter technical challenges while building and implementing your big data solution. This section will help you identify some of those challenges before you get started. We'll discuss environmental challenges that you will face and proposed solutions for them. We'll follow that up with additional resources, helping to ensure that your team's skillset is ready for implementing and supporting a big data environment.

Environmental Challenges

There are a few challenges that are specific to your environment that you will have to take into account. Two of the challenges surround your data. Planning for your data volume and the growth through incremental data changes will be vital to your success. Within that data, understanding the privacy laws that surround your data will be critical to both success of the solution and avoiding missteps with governing authorities.

Data Volume and Growth

One of the technical challenges you need to tackle up-front is the initial data volume and growth. You want to consider two important factors here:

- How much total data will comprise the initial project?
- What is the shape of the data files that are going to encompass the initial project?

The initial data volume of the project will give you an idea of the scope of your infrastructure. Second, considering the shape of the files is an important aspect of the initial scoping. Will you be working with a large number of small files or relatively few large files? Hadoop is designed to work with large chunks of data at a time and when the size of files is smaller than 64MB; then it will increase the number of map-reduce jobs necessary to complete any submission. This will slow down each job, potentially significantly. If you are literally talking about thousands or millions of files, each very small (in the low-kilobyte range), you'll probably find it best to aggregate these files before loading them into Hadoop.

Incremental Data

Loading data for any big data or data warehouse solution usually comes in two forms. First you need to load the initial bulk load of history, and then you need to determine an approach to ingest incremental data. Once again, you need to consider the size of the files that you will be loading into the Hadoop Distributed File System (HDFS).

If the files are many but relatively small, consider using Flume to queue them up and write them as a larger data set. Otherwise, write your data to Hadoop from their source using HDFS's `put` command, much like you would into a staging environment for a data warehouse. Write the full data set to Hadoop and then rely on your transform processes in Hadoop to determine duplicates, unwanted data removal, and additional necessary transforms.

Privacy Laws

The issue of privacy and big data is a large and diverse subject that could be a book by itself. These privacy issues cross country and cultural barriers. As you are collecting and storing more data about your customers and augmenting it with additional ambient data from either third parties or from public sources, you must be aware of the privacy laws that affect the customers whose data you are collecting data.

Some data-retention laws require that you keep data for so long once you start collecting it. In the United States, laws such as Health Insurance Portability and Accountability Act (HIPAA) affect the private health information that healthcare providers and insurance companies compile. HIPAA requires that the holder of this health information ensure the confidentiality and availability of the information. Additional regulations such as the Gramm-Leach-Bliley Act are designed such that financial services companies notify their customers, through a privacy notice, how they collect and share their data. The European Union has its own set of much more strict and comprehensive regulations designed to protect consumer information from unauthorized disclosure or collection of personal data.

As a collector of data, it is your responsibility to identify the privacy laws that apply to that data set and the consumers involved. Spend the time to identify the laws that affect the countries of your consumers, your specific industry, and where your data will be located. Understand what data should be de-identified through anonymization, pseudonymization, encryption, or key-coding. Taking the time to understand the laws and comply with them may be the difference between a successful big data project and one that not only gets your organization in hot water but could also be publicly damaging.

Challenges in Skillset

Data analysts usually have a much easier time adapting to the big data environment than database administrators (DBAs). DBAs have a long history of confining data to a particular environment, including managing table space, foreign key relationships, applying indexes, and relying on lots of SQL tuning to solve performance issues. All mature relational database systems have extensive graphical user interfaces (GUIs) that make this job easier. Generally, this has made DBAs relatively lazy over the years. Why spend the time to script out an add column statement when you can do it in 30 seconds in the GUI?

The framework that the Hadoop environment provides is very distributed, with many components that need to be learned so that a team can get them working together for the final solution. A single solution may leverage HDInsight, Hive, Sqoop, Pig, and Oozie. The solution will likely leverage several of these technologies that use a variety of different programming paradigms. (Hive-SQL or Pig Latin anyone?) Don't expect to find any one single person to handle the entire ecosystem himself. This solution will likely require a team of individuals, and they will likely need some help getting ramped up on some or all of the technologies. If you are using existing staff with little to no experience with the Hadoop ecosystem, be prepared to get them some training and to provide ample time for ramp up. You can expect several months of ramp-up time for your staff to get comfortable enough with big data technologies in order for them to create an enterprise ready solution.

Training opportunities abound. Hortonworks provides training for their Hortonworks Data Platform (HDP) on Windows (`http://hortonworks.com/hadoop-training/hadoop-on-windows-for-developers/`). This is a good place to start because they walk through the basics of Hadoop and Hortonworks Data Platform. In addition, they will walk through the ecosystem of C#, Pig, Hive, HCatalog, Sqoop, Oozie, and Microsoft Excel.

Coursera is another great place to provide very applicable training to your employees on big data concepts and technology. Courses on linear algebra provide a good refresher or ramp-up for the concepts and methods of linear algebra and how to use those concepts to think about computational problems that arise in computer science. Several statistics classes provide the principles of the collection, display, and analysis of data to make valid and appropriate conclusions about said data. Other courses that are applicable are Machine Learning, data mining, and statistical pattern recognition classes.

Finally, many universities offer graduate-level courses in big data and business analytics. Universities see the future need for workers able to traverse and understand large sets of data and so are providing the necessary classes to provide that workforce. Carnegie Mellon offers a Masters of Information Technology Strategy with a concentration in big data and analytics (`http://www.cmu.edu/mits/curriculum/concentration/bigdata.html`). The MITS degree provides a multidisciplinary education that allows students to understand and conceptualize the development and management of big data information technology solutions.

Stanford University offers a Graduate Certificate on Mining Massive Data Sets (`http://scpd.stanford.edu/public/category/courseCategoryCertificateProfile.do?method=load&certificateId=10555807`). The four-course certificate teaches "powerful techniques and algorithms for extracting information from large data sets such as the Web, social-network graphs, and large document repositories."

Identifying Operational Challenges

In this section, we'll cover what you need to do to plan for setup and configuration. In addition, we'll discuss what you need to do to plan for ongoing maintenance.

Planning for Setup/Configuration

An early decision that will need to be made is the quantity and quality of hardware on which to run your Hadoop cluster. Generally, Hadoop is designed to be built on commodity server hardware and JBODs (just a bunch of disks).

That doesn't mean that you can run down to your local electronics store and buy a few cheap $800-servers and be good to go. Commodity hardware is still server-class hardware, but the point is that you won't need to go out and spend tens of thousands of dollars per server. You generally purchase two classes of servers for your Hadoop cluster: one for master nodes, and a second one for all the worker nodes.

The master server should have more redundancy built in to it: multiple power supplies, multiple Ethernet ports, RAID 1 for the operating system LUN, and so forth. The master server requires more memory than the worker nodes. Generally, you can start with 32GB of memory for a master server of a small cluster and grow that to as much as 128GB or more for a large cluster that has more than 250 worker nodes.

The worker servers don't need the redundancy of the master server, but need to be built with balance in mind. They need to be able to store the data you have planned for your Hadoop cluster, but they also need to be able to process it appropriately when its time to query the data. You first need to consider how many and what size disks you need. Of course, this depends on the hardware vendor and the configuration of the server that you are purchasing. But after that, you will need to take an educated guestimate of your needs.

The first thing to remember is that you will be replicating your data three times. Assuming that you are using the default replication factor of 3, if you have a need for 100TB of space you will need enough servers so that you can store 300TB of space. But you aren't done yet. You need temporary workspace for queries which can be up to 30% of the drive capacity. Finally, try to always maintain 10% free disk space. History has taught us that when disks have less than 10% free space, performance suffers. Add those requirements up and you are at 420TB of space required. If each server you purchase can store 30TB of data (10 drives × 3TB), you need a minimum of 14 worker nodes for your Hadoop appliance.

THE COMPRESSION FACTOR

You may have noticed that I did not consider compression factor in the previous calculation. You will likely take advantage of compressing data in Hadoop. The Hadoop technologies like Hive and Pig handle various forms of compression very well. So, you may use Zip, RAR, or BZip compression technologies, and getting a compression factor of 5 to 7 times is not unusual. This will reduce the number of worker nodes required to support your solution.

```
Required disk space = (Replication factor)(Total data TB)(1.4)
/ Compression factor
```

Next you need to consider CPU and memory. CPU for each worker node should at a minimum have two quad-core CPUs running at least 2.5GHz. Hex and Octo core solutions should be considered for heavy computing solutions. The newest chips are not necessary because the mid-level chips will generally give you the processing power you need without generating the heat and consuming the electricity of the most powerful chips. Generally speaking, each task that runs inside a worker node will require anywhere from between 2GB and 4GB of memory. A machine with 96GB of memory will be able to run 24 and 48 tasks at any given time. Therefore, a system with 14 worker nodes would be able to run 336 to 672 tasks at any given time. Understanding the potential parallel computing requirements of your solution will help you determine if this is sufficient.

Start the planning and building of your cluster assuming that you will begin with a balanced cluster configuration. If you build your cluster from the beginning with different server classes, different processors and memory, or different storage capacities, you will be spending an inordinate amount of time on resource utilization and balancing. A balanced configuration will allow you to spend less time administering your cluster and more time running awesome solutions that provide value to the line-of-business sponsoring the solution.

Planning for Ongoing Maintenance

There a few tasks that you should be acquainted with in order to perform ongoing maintenance of a Hadoop cluster. In this section we'll cover what you need to know in order to stop jobs, add nodes, and finally rebalance nodes if the data becomes skewed.

Stopping a Map-reduce job

One requirement for a Hadoop administrator is to start and stop map-reduce jobs. You may be asked to kill a job submitted by a user because it's running longer than the user expected. This might result from there being more data than they expected, or perhaps they are simply running an incorrect algorithm or process. When a job is killed, all processes associated with the job are stopped, the memory associated with the job is discarded, and temporary data written to disk is deleted; the originator of the job receives notification that the job has failed.

To stop a map-reduce job, complete the following steps:

1. From a Hadoop command prompt, run `hadoop job -list`.
2. Run `hadoop job -kill jobid` to kill the job.

Adding and Removing Cluster Nodes

Usually data nodes are added because there is a need for additional data capacity. However, it is entirely possible that it may be in response to additional I/O bandwidth needs because of additional computing requirements. Adding the data node is a quick online process of adding the node to the configuration file:

```
hadoop dfsadmin -refreshNodes
```

Rebalancing Cluster Nodes

Hadoop nodes become unbalanced most often when new data nodes are added to a cluster. Those new data nodes receive as much new data as any of the other nodes, but will never catch up to those nodes in the total amount of data stored on it unless you balance the stored data. To balance the stored data, you can run the following command from a Hadoop command prompt,

```
hadoop balancer -threshold N
```

where `N` is the percentage you want the nodes to be within each other. For example, if you want all the nodes to be within 5% of each other for an actual potential of each node being as much as 10% apart in total data stored, run the following:

```
hadoop balancer -threshold 5
```

Once you've created a solution that will benefit your business it's time to hand that solution off to your operations team so that it can operate the daily jobs, respond to user requests, and plan for future growth. In the next section we'll discuss some of the work necessary to make that transition to the operations team effective.

Going Forward

After deploying your solution, you need to continue to monitor its performance and plan for its growth. You learn much more about what to monitor for in Chapter 16, "Operational Big Data Management." For now, we'll limit our coverage to handing the solution off to operations and what needs to happen post deployment.

The Handoff to Operations

The hand off to operations should be thoroughly thought about, discussed, and planned for a long time before the day comes to actually do it. In fact, the handoff to operations should be planned for from day 1 of the project. Questions you should be thinking about include the following:

- Does anyone in operations understand the big data paradigm?
- Does anyone in operations have experience with Hadoop?
- Who or what group is going to operate the solution?
- If the cluster fails at night, how do we notify and respond?
- If a job fails at night, how do we respond?

Other questions should also be discussed from day 1. Why so early? If your organization is spinning up its first big data/Hadoop team for development and there is no one in operations who has any experience in either, it will take them many months to come up to speed on big data and Hadoop (so that they can effectively support it). Why months? Because most likely they have current duties that they have to be responsible for, and other than a few weeks of specialized training, everything else they pick up will be from working part time with the project team. It is vital to the success of the project, though, that you have a skilled and confident operations team ready to support the solution when it is ready to be deployed.

Before deployment of the solution, the development team should work with the operations team to develop a run book that documents the architecture of the solution and provides operations with the responses to specific and expected failures. Typical plans should account for the following:

- If a particular job fails, how to respond. What should one look for to see the state of the job?
- If a node fails, how to respond.
- If connectivity to the source system is down, whom to notify.
- What are the common error messages that your system will surface? What are the steps to resolve these error messages?
- How should the team proactively monitor the environment? For example, performance and space usage trending?

Now that you have developed the run book, you can plan for the handoff to operations and place the solution in production.

After Deployment

During the first week after handing off to operations, the development team and operations need to work closely together to ensure proper knowledge transfer of the solution. Much of this should have been completed through the documentation process of the solution and creation of the run book, but we all have experience where documentation doesn't get read.

Many tasks need to be done to keep the Hadoop cluster healthy and ready to continue to accept more data and to process that data in an acceptable timeframe as defined by your service level agreements (SLAs). These tasks include the previously mentioned job monitoring, managing the various Hadoop-related logs, dealing with hardware failures, expanding the cluster, and upgrading the system software.

Summary

This chapter covered the basics of what you need to know in order to build and plan for you first big data solution. The core ideas delivered are that you need to have sponsorship from executive levels from the beginning and that you need to plan and communicate throughout the process of building your solution. Executive, C-level sponsorship provides you with the influence you need in order to get multiple teams working together to build a new big data solution. Planning for technical and operational challenges requires thinking through what the final architecture will look like and documenting the challenges you will have getting there. Finally, we looked at what it will take to hand off the solution to operations, including developing a run book and monitoring the system for growth.

CHAPTER

16

Operational Big Data Management

WHAT YOU WILL LEARN IN THIS CHAPTER:

- Building Hybrid Big Data Environments
- Integrating Cloud and On-premise Solutions
- Preparing for Disaster Recovery and High Availability in Your Big Data Environment
- Complying with Privacy Laws
- Creating Operational Analytics

Operationalizing your big data solution includes integrating multiple sources, providing a platform for analysis and reporting, and providing analytics for the solution so that you can monitor and improve the environment as needed. All of this requires planning and attention to detail.

This chapter focuses on many of those things that you need to do to make your big data implementation a success. The chapter first focuses on hybrid big data environments, where efficient data movement is key. You will then learn about the possibilities for backups and disaster recovery so that your solution can withstand catastrophes. You'll also take a look at privacy issues to ensure that you are always vigilant with personally identifiable information (PII). The chapter then delves into the analytics you will need to collect to ensure that your solution can grow with the additional demands put on it by growing data sets and user bases.

Hybrid Big Data Environments: Cloud and On-premise Solutions Working Together

The promise of working with an elastic-scale cloud solution such as HDInsight may be intriguing to many organizations. HDInsight in the cloud provides your organization with significant deployment agility. It also provides the infrastructure, high availability, and recoverability that would otherwise take months for most organizations to build themselves.

However, your organization may have hundreds or thousands of users who need access to that data for analysis. The result set of the processing you do on HDInsight may be better lived in your enterprise data warehouse that is sitting in your data center.

Another common scenario in a hybrid environment is when data is born on-premise and you want to take that transactional data and store it in the cloud for additional processing. To do that, you must move a significant amount of data from the data center to the cloud.

Getting these hybrid solutions to work well together is an integral step in the success of your hybrid environment. Throughout this chapter, we examine details of these two scenarios.

When customers ask about hybrid solutions, it is often recommended that customers start with the assumption that data born in the cloud stays in the cloud and data born on-premise stays on-premise. This advice attempts to stem the data movement discussions and complexity of a hybrid environment. It also just makes sense.

With the advent of phones and tablets and their applications, as well as other cloud-based applications, a significant amount of data is being born in the cloud today. The amount of data that requires analytics is exploding. This data can be very large and quickly changing. On-premise traditional solutions and organizations cannot easily handle this complexity and scale.

If possible, your organization should take advantage of cloud-based technologies for the additional required analysis. If you are using HDInsight and have a requirement to drive additional business intelligence (BI) reporting from the resulting data set, look into a Windows Azure SQL Database and Power BI Solution. With these, you can leverage your existing SQL Server development and administration skillset, but with the power, scalability, and cost-effectiveness of the cloud.

However, there may be a requirement that the resulting data set from HDInsight be hosted on-premise. This can be for a variety of reasons. You might have an existing enterprise data warehouse with which you want to integrate. Regulatory reasons might force you to host that data on-premise. Or you may not be able to overcome the internal politics of an organization not quite ready to host all data outside your organization. Whatever the reason, a hybrid solution is in your cards, and you will need to dive into the details of the architecture.

A great deal of data is still being born on-premise within organizations. These organizations may have identified an opportunity to use Hadoop for their data but don't have the capability to host their own Hadoop solution. This scenario may happen for a couple of reasons. First, they might not have the required capital to set up a decent-sized Hadoop cluster. Second, they might not have the staff to do it. This may be especially true if executive management hasn't yet fully come on board with the project.

The game has changed, and you are working through a real paradigm shift. Your architectures will be much more complex in the short term as you struggle to handle an ever-increasing amount of data and analytics you need to apply to that data.

Ongoing Data Integration with Cloud and On-premise Solutions

When developing a hybrid solution, data movement becomes an important consideration. You will be tasked with moving data to and from the cloud. You will need to develop a solution such that you can move that data efficiently to either populate a solution in the cloud with data or to bring data from the cloud to your on-premise environment. You will have three main considerations:

1. What tool to use to move the data to and from the cloud
2. What compression codec to use
3. Whether a hybrid approach is actually the right approach (that is, whether you should look at going all cloud or all on-premise)

You can use a number of tools to move data between your on-premise solution and the cloud. The recommended approach is to use the data movement tools that Microsoft has built right in to the Azure HDInsight PowerShell Scripts. Using PowerShell may be the most straightforward way of moving data from your on-premise environment to Windows Azure blob storage. The first thing you need to do is install Windows Azure PowerShell and then Windows Azure HDInsight PowerShell.

NOTE **Follow the instructions at the following website to get Windows Azure HDInsight PowerShell installed and configured for your environment:** `http://www.windowsazure.com/en-us/manage/services/hdinsight/install-and-configure-powershell-for-hdinsight/`.

For example, the following script will upload the `1987.csv` file from my local drive to the `airlinedata` container with a blob name of `1987`. The first set of parameters provides the details for where to put the data in Windows Azure, the second set of parameters tells us what data to put there. We then open up the connection and, using the `Set-AzureStorageBlobContent` command, we copy the data to Windows Azure:

```
#Configure Azure Blob Storage Parameters
$subscriptionName = "msdn"
$storageAccountName = "sqlpdw"
$containerName = "airlinedata"
$blobName = "1987"

#Configure Local Parameters
$fileName ="C:\Users\brimit\SkyDrive\AirStats\1987.csv.bz2"

# Get the storage account key
Select-AzureSubscription $subscriptionName
$storageaccountkey = get-azurestoragekey $storageAccountName
| %{$_.Primary}

# Create the storage context object
$destContext = New-AzureStorageContext -StorageAccountName
$storageAccountName -StorageAccountKey $storageaccountkey

# Copy the file from local workstation to the Blob container
Set-AzureStorageBlobContent -File $fileName -Container $containerName
-Blob $blobName -context $destContext
```

Integration Thoughts for Big Data

Your big data solution should not exist in isolation. To get the most benefit out of the solution, it should not be built for just a couple of data scientists who will use it to do analysis in which they publish sporadic reports of their findings. If it does exist in isolation, you are not extracting the value out of it that it contains.

Your big data solution needs to be integrated into the rest of your analytics and BI infrastructure. When you integrate your solution with your existing data warehouse and BI infrastructures, more corners of your organization can learn to gain insights from the additional data brought into your organization.

NOTE **Don't worry, you've done data integration before. Your big data solution is now just another data source, albeit with possibly more data, different data types, and new structures that you've never dealt with before. But those are challenges, not barriers.**

You likely already have a data warehouse environment that is a subject-oriented reporting environment tightly constrained around dimensional data that drives reports your organization relies on. The data that lives in this data warehouse is likely driven from your transactional environments.

Your new big data environment now houses additional data that likely wasn't cost-effective to store in your existing data warehouse (perhaps because the data was either too big or too complex for efficient storage). Most solutions will include having a subset of subject matter experts who will be hitting this data directly using the skills learned in this book to extract new insights. But inside of this data is a subset of data that could augment what is already stored in your existing data warehouse and that could potentially make it much more interesting and valuable to your traditional BI analyst. Our goal is to identify this data and provide an integrated solution for your organization.

These hybrid solutions, shown in Figure 16.1, including Hadoop, a data warehouse, and a BI environment are the near future state of a typical analytics environment. Although it makes sense to store log files, social network feeds, user location data, telemetry data, and other big data sources in Hadoop, this isn't the only thing that can benefit from this data. Your traditional data warehouse can take in some of this data to enhance its value.

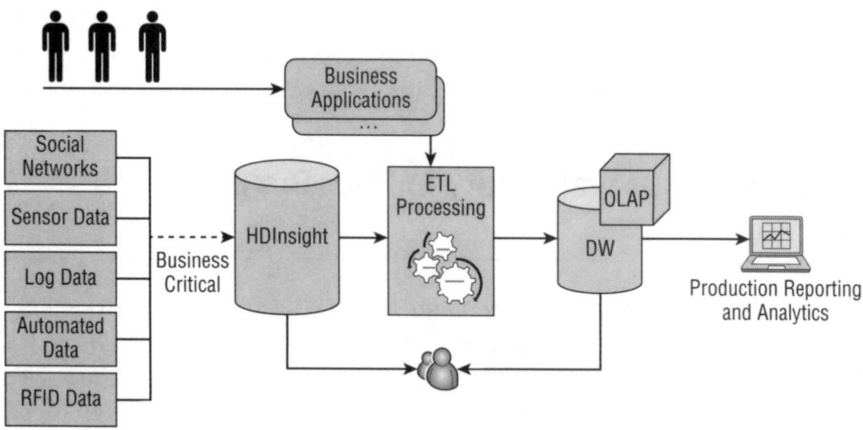

Figure 16.1: The modern data warehouse

You might be thinking, "Okay, this sounds good, but how do I know which data should be integrated into my current data warehouse?" Well, this is where you trust your data scientists who have access to the data in Hadoop and the subject matter experts who explore your current data warehouse solution daily.

The data scientists will explore the data and look for relationships among the new data being collected. They will also most likely be extracting some of your subject-oriented warehouse data into Hadoop to help augment their data sets. As they explore the data and find relationships in the data, they will identify what is useful to the organization. It might sometimes be of use one time and thus the analysis is done, the report is written, and lessons will be learned. Many other times, though, they will find insights in the data that can be reused and watched for on a regular basis. It is this data that they have identified you want to operationalize into your solution.

After the data has been identified, you want to operationalize the solution. This means building the extract, transform, and load (ETL) layer to move data from Hadoop to your data warehouse. Here is where we will likely deviate from your traditional processes of using a tool like SQL Server Integration Services (SSIS) to do the ETL. The reason for this is that we have already loaded the data onto an immensely powerful data processing engine named Hadoop. Therefore, a recommended approach is to do the transform directly on Hadoop and stage the data in Hadoop in the form needed to move to your data warehouse solution.

This is where Pig proves to be incredibly powerful and the right tool for the job. A Pig script that takes your semistructured data and moves the data through a data flow and creates a structured staging table is the efficient way to take advantage of your 8-, 32-, or 128-node Hadoop cluster. This is certainly more efficient than pulling all of that data off of Hadoop into a single SSIS server to transform the data for inserting into the data warehouse. Once the data has been staged in Hadoop, you can use Sqoop to move the data directly from Hadoop into the data warehouse tables where the data is needed.

Backups and High Availability in Your Big Data Environment

How well can your organization withstand the loss of your big data environment? Do you need 100% uptime? What happens if a natural disaster affects your data center, making it no longer viable? These are questions every IT shop should be asking itself when building their big data environment. The answers to these questions will influence your high-availability and disaster recovery solutions.

High Availability

High availability is the approach taken to ensure service level availability will be met during a certain period of time. If users cannot access the system, it is unavailable. Thus, any high-availability approach that you design for your big data solution should be to ensure that your users can access the system up to and beyond the service levels you have determined are appropriate for that system.

The service level availability that you determine will have a significant impact on your high-availability design. Some organizations will determine that they need 99.9% uptime, whereas others will be primarily using their big data solution for reporting and analysis and will come to a number closer to 95% being appropriate for them. Although 4.9% doesn't sound like a big difference, that is a total of almost 18 days per year in downtime.

There are two different types of downtime that you must be concerned with: scheduled and unscheduled downtime. Scheduled downtime is the type of downtime that occurs when you schedule maintenance on your system. For example, you could be scheduling downtime for applying a patch of your software that requires a reboot of the system. In addition, you may schedule downtime for an upgrade of your system software.

In contrast, unscheduled downtime arises from unplanned events such as hardware or software failures. This unscheduled downtime could occur for many reasons from as mundane as a power outage to as significant as security breach such as a virus or other malware. In addition, events that cause downtime include network outages, hardware failures, and software failures.

For scheduled maintenance, you will need to shut down the NameNode service. To ensure the controlled shutdown of the service, follow these steps:

1. Shut down the NameNode monitoring agent:

   ```
   service stop hmonitor-namenode-monitor
   ```

2. Shut down the NameNode process:

   ```
   service stop hadoop-namenode
   ```

When maintenance is complete, follow these steps:

1. Start the NameNode process:

   ```
   service start hadoop-namenode
   ```

2. Start the NameNode monitoring agent:

   ```
   service start hmonitor-namenode-monitor
   ```

3. Verify that the monitoring process has started:

   ```
   service status hmonitor-namenode-monitor
   ```

An important concept to understand is that Hadoop has significant high-availability and robustness features built in to it to withstand unscheduled downtime. Hadoop is built with the understanding that hardware does fail. One of the architectural goals of the Hadoop Distributed File System (HDFS) is the automatic recovery from any failures. With hundreds of servers in your big data solution, there will always be some nonfunctional hardware, and the architecture of HDFS is intended to handle these failures gracefully while repairs are made. The three places of concern are DataNode failures, NameNode failures, and network partitions.

A DataNode may become unresponsive for any number of reasons. It might simply have a hardware failure such as a motherboard failure, it could have a replica become corrupted, and hard drives will fail, along with many other reasons equipment fails. Each DataNode sends a heartbeat to the NameNode on a regular basis. If the NameNode does not receive a heartbeat message, it marks the DataNode as dead and does not send any new data requests to the DataNode. Any data that was on that DataNode is not available to HDFS anymore, and now that data's replication factor will likely be below that specified, which will kick off re-replication of that data to another DataNode.

Another reason Hadoop clusters become nonresponsive is due to NameNode failures. NameNodes are most likely to fail because of misconfiguration and network issues. This is similar to our collective experience with Windows cluster failovers, where it is usually not hardware issues that cause failovers but external issues such as Active Directory problems, networking, or other configuration issues. Pay heed to these external influences as you diagnose failures within your environment.

In this section we examined some basics into planning for high availability. In the next section, we will dive a bit into what happens if something does go wrong—preparing for and dealing with disaster recovery.

Disaster Recovery

By now, you should be aware that Hadoop has many high-availability features built in to it to prevent failures. As you probably know by this point in your career, despite all the features included in products and all the planning we can do, disasters happen. When they do, your service level agreements with your user community will help determine what your recovery strategy will be.

For example, if you incur a complete data center loss because of a natural disaster, how important will it be to recover your Hadoop infrastructure? It may be very low on your priority list, behind many other applications in your organization. Applications such as the transactional systems that run your business and create revenue will likely take priority. In addition, you might have many other customer-facing applications that need to be up before you need to have your big data solution up. You will likely also have applications that your internal customers need to have available to service customers; call centers and financial reporting come to mind. Your organization may have other applications such as your e-mail system that needs to be up and running so that communication may happen. Next, you might have a data warehouse and BI environment that needs to be available to drive internal reporting of month-end processes. Finally, your big data solution may need to be re-created within a few weeks to drive your analytical decisions.

If you need to be backed up within a day, you need to have a different disaster recovery plan. You can back up your Hortonworks Data Platform (HDP) clusters to an external backup Hadoop cluster using DistCp. DistCp stands for distributed copy and is a bulk data movement tool. By invoking DistCp, you can periodically transfer HDFS data sets from the active Hadoop cluster to the backup Hadoop cluster in another location.

To invoke DistCp, run the following command:

```
hadoop distcp hdfs://nn1:8020/foo/bar \  hdfs://nn2:8020/bar/foo
```

The namespace under /foo/bar on nn1 will expand into a temporary file, partition its contents among a set of map tasks, and start a copy on each TaskTracker from nn1 to nn2.

You must use absolute paths with DistCp. Each TaskTracker must be able to communicate with both the source and destination systems. It is recommended that you run the same version protocols on both systems. The system should be acquiesced at the source before invoking DistCp. If there are clients writing to the source system while DistCp is being run, the copy will fail.

Table 16.1 describes some of the import options for DistCp.

Table 16.1: Import Options for DistCp

FLAG	DESCRIPTION
-p[rbugp]	Preserves r: Replication number b: Block size u: User g: Group p: Permission
-i	Ignores failures
-log <logdir>	Outputs logs to <logdir>
-m <num_maps>	Maximum number of maps for copying of data
-update	If source size different from destination size, it will get overwritten. The default is not to overwrite as long as the file exists.

Big Data Solution Governance

As you your big data environment develops, you must mature your ability to govern the solution. Preferably, you will have a team dedicated to governing the environment. What does governance mean in this instance? These team members are the gatekeepers of Hadoop. Specifically, this team will be designed to manage the rules of engagement for your Hadoop clusters. The kind of questions that they will answer include the following:

- What are the use cases that go onto the cluster?
- How do users apply for access to the cluster?

- Who owns each set of data?
- What are the user quotas?
- What are our regulatory requirements around information life cycle management?
- What are our security and privacy guidelines?
- How do external systems interact with the system?
- What should be audited and logged?

If there are new questions about the rules of engagement for the cluster, the big data governance team will answer those questions and set up the rules. Essentially, when it comes to big data, this governance team owns the roadmap for your IT organization to get it from its current state to some preferable future state. The need for the governance team is that there is a lot of change occurring around data in general and big data in particular. Having a team focused on where your organization needs to go allows the operations team to focus on the current state and implementing the rules established by the governance team.

The role of the operations team is to implement the above. The operations team is responsible for auditing and logging the information determined by the governance team as being important. The operations team is responsible for security and privacy of the data as outlined by the governance team. The operations team is responsible for implementing the quotas determined for users and providing access to approved users as determined by the governance team. Ideally, you want different people on the operations team and on the governance team.

Creating Operational Analytics

Hadoop is a complex distributed system, and monitoring it is not a trivial task. A variety of information sources within Hadoop provide for monitoring and debugging the various services. To create an operational analytics solution, you must collect these monitors and store them for correlation and trending analysis.

A solution included with HDP is the HDP monitoring dashboard. This solution uses two monitoring systems, called Ganglia and Nagios, to combine certain metrics provided by Hadoop into graphs and alerts that are more easily understood by administrators and managers alike. Using the HDP monitoring dashboard, you can communicate the state of various cluster services and also diagnose common problems.

When it comes to monitoring Hadoop, in many respects it differs little from monitoring a database management system. I like to refer to several system resources as the canaries in the coal mine. These resources—CPU, disk, network, and memory—are vital to the performance of any system retrieving, analyzing, and moving data. The utilization of these resources both as a point-in-time resource, and viewing them as a trend over time provides valuable insight into the state and health of a system.

For Hadoop, we want to monitor these values for both the NameNode and DataNodes. For the NameNodes, we want store and analyze the individual values. For DataNodes, it is usually good enough to report on the aggregated values of all DataNodes so that we can understand overall cluster utilization and look for one of these particular resources causing a performance bottleneck because of overutilization. In particular, you should monitor the following:

- % CPU utilization and periodic (1-, 5-, 15-minute) CPU load averages
- Average disk data transfer rates (I/O bandwidth) and number of disk I/O operations per second
- Average memory and swap space utilization
- Average data transfer rate and network latency

System Center Operations Manager for HDP

At the time of this writing, HDP for Windows does not include interfaces for open source monitoring services such as Ganglia or Nagios. These services are designed to consolidate information provided by Hadoop into a more centralized and meaningful summary of services-related statistics in graphs and alerts. On the other hand, Microsoft and Hortonworks have collaborated to provide an Ambari System Center Operations Manager (SCOM) solution. With this solution, SCOM can monitor availability, capacity, and the health of the cluster and provide you valuable metrics, graphs, and key performance indicators. In this section we'll look at the overall capabilities of the Ambari MP for SCOM, walk through the installation of the product, and finish by examining specific monitoring scenarios.

The Ambari project is aimed at making it easier to manage a Hadoop cluster. Amabari provides an interface and Rest APIs for provisioning, managing, and monitoring a Hadoop cluster. Its interface is typically a Hadoop management web UI that is powered by those Rest APIs. The Management Pack for SCOM leverages those Rest APIs in order to provide the same monitoring capabilities as the Ambari web UI, but in a familiar enterprise solution like SCOM. Ambari SCOM will first automatically discover all nodes within a Hadoop cluster, then proactively monitor availability, capacity, and health, and finally provide visualizations within for dashboards and trend analysis.

The Ambari SCOM architecture is made up of several discrete installations across your environment. Included in the architecture are the Ambari SCOM Management Pack that extends SCOM to monitor Hadoop clusters.

The Ambari SCOM server component gets installed inside the Hadoop cluster to monitor Hadoop and provide the REST API interface for the SCOM management pack. A SQL Server 2012 instance database will be created for storing the Hadoop metrics that you collect for SCOM. Additional components include a ClusterLayout ResourceProvider so that Ambari can read your `clusterproperties.txt` file to automatically understand your cluster layout for configuration, a Property ResourceProvider that interfaces between the Ambari SCOM Server and SQL Server, and a SQLServerSink that consumes metrics from Hadoop and stores them in SQL Server. At the end of the installation, you will have a solution, such as the one shown in Figure 16.2, that monitors Hadoop will alert you on certain faults and will take performance metrics, aggregate them, and store them in SQL Server and SCOM.

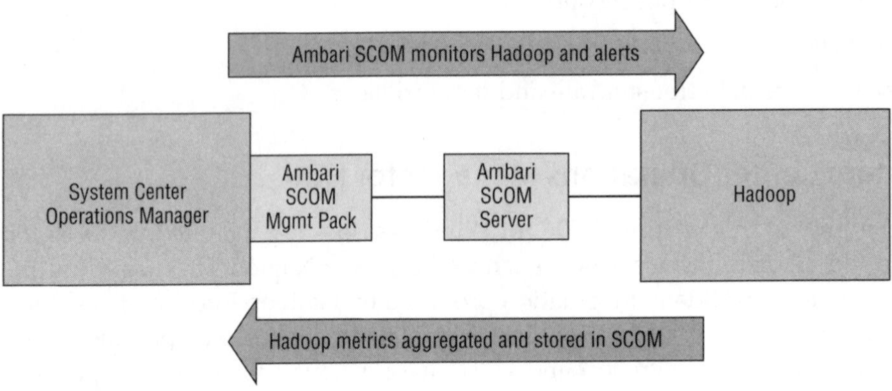

Figure 16.2: Ambari SCOM High Level Architecture

Installing the Ambari SCOM Management Pack

Installing the Ambari SCOM Management Pack is much like installing HDP 1.3 in that there are a number of steps involved in a number of locations and you must follow directions very closely. Take your time and be cautious with this installation. You'll be:

- Configuring SQL Server
- Installing the Hadoop Metrics Sink
- Installing and configuring the Ambari SCOM Server in your cluster
- Installing and configuring the Ambari SCOM Management Pack in SCOM

We are making an assumption that you already have a SCOM Server set up within your environment to take advantage of the Management Pack. If you don't, you can download a preview virtual machine from Microsoft: `http://www.microsoft.com/en-us/download/details.aspx?id=34780`.

To get started, download the Ambari SCOM Management Pack here: `http://hortonworks.com/products/hdp-windows/#add_ons`.

Configuring SQL Server

First, you will need to configure a SQL Server for the Ambari SCOM database. If you don't have a SQL Server, you will first need to do the installation and come back to this series of steps. The steps involved for configuring SQL Server are:

1. Configure SQL Server to use "mixed mode" authentication. Open SQL Server Management Studio and connect to SQL Server. Right-click on the server and choose Properties. Change Server Authentication to SQL Server and Windows Authentication mode. Click OK.
2. Confirm SQL Server is enabled to use TCP/IP and is active. Open SQL Server Configuration Manager and choose SQL Server Network Configuration. Drill down to Protocols for MSSQLServer and find TCP/IP over to the right. If it is disabled, double-click on TCP/IP and enable it. Then follow the additional instructions about restarting your SQL Service.
3. Create a username and password for the Ambari SCOM MP to capture metrics and store them on SQL Server.
4. Extract the contents of the `metrics-sink.zip` package and open the `Hadoop-Metrics-SQLServer-CREATE.ddl` script in SQL Server Management Studio. Alternatively you can open it in Notepad and copy and paste the script into a New Query window in SQL Server Management Studio.
5. Execute the DDL script from Step 4 to create the Ambari SCOM database called HadoopMetrics.

Installing the Hadoop Metrics Sink

In these next steps, we will prepare the Hadoop Metrics Sink files to be used later in the process.

1. Create a `c:\Ambari` folder on each host within the cluster.
2. Retrieve the Microsoft JDBC Driver 4.0 for SQL Server `sqljdbc4.jar` file from here (`http://www.microsoft.com/en-us/download/details.aspx?id=11774`). Download the Linux version of the driver, extract it within the Downloads folder, and then find the `sqljdbc4.jar` file in the extraction. Copy and place this `sqljdbc4.jar` file on each node in the folder created in step 1 (`c:\Ambari`).

3. Retrieve the `metrics-sink-version.jar` file from the `metrics-sink.zip` package extracted during the SQL Server configuration and place it on each node in the folder created in step 1. Your `c:\Ambari` folder should now look like Figure 16.3, with only these two files.

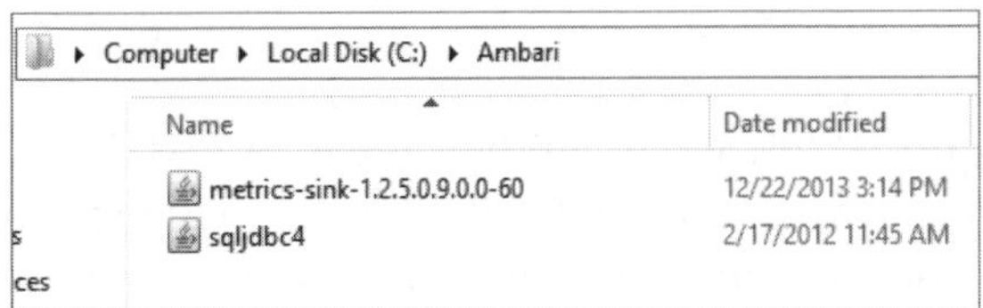

Figure 16.3: Ambari folder on each node in the cluster

Now you must set up the Hadoop Metrics2 Interface on each node in the cluster. This will allow it to use the SQLServerSink and send the metric information from your Hadoop cluster to SQL Server.

1. Edit the `Hadoop-metrics2.properties` file on each node in the cluster located by default at `{C:\hadoop\install\dir}\bin` folder. On your single node cluster from Chapter 3, "Setting Up for Big Data with Microsoft," this location is `c:\hdp\hadoop\hadoop-1.2.0.1.3.0.0-380\bin\hadoop-metrics2.properties`. Replace Server, port, username, and password with the SQL Server name and port that you configured earlier, along with the username and password that you created for access to the HadoopMetrics database. Your `Hadoop-metrics2.properties` file should look similar to Figure 16.4 when you are done:

```
*.sink.sql.class=org.apache.hadoop.metrics2.sink.SqlServerSink

namenode.sink.sql.databaseUrl=jdbc:sqlserver:
//[server]:[port];databaseName=HadoopMetrics;user=[user];password=
[password]
datanode.sink.sql.databaseUrl=jdbc:sqlserver:
//[server]:[port];databaseName=HadoopMetrics;user=[user];password=
[password]
jobtracker.sink.sql.databaseUrl=jdbc:sqlserver:
//[server]:[port];databaseName=HadoopMetrics;user=[user];password=
[password]
tasktracker.sink.sql.databaseUrl=jdbc:sqlserver:
//[server]:[port];databaseName=HadoopMetrics;user=[user];password=
[password]
maptask.sink.sql.databaseUrl=jdbc:sqlserver:
//[server]:[port];databaseName=HadoopMetrics;user=[user];password=
[password]
reducetask.sink.sql.databaseUrl=jdbc:sqlserver:
//[server]:[port];databaseName=HadoopMetrics;user=[user];password=
[password]
```

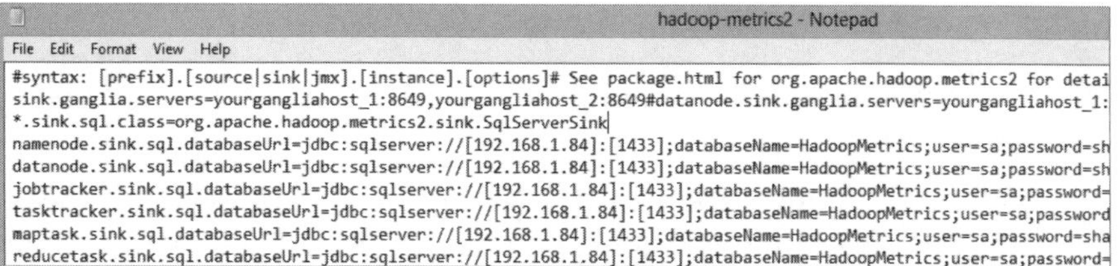

Figure 16.4: Completed hadoop-metrics2.properties file

2. Next, you need to update the Java classpath for each Hadoop service to include the `metrics-sink.jar` and `sqljdbc4.jar` files. You can find these files in the `{c:\hadoop\install\dir}\bin` folder. On your single node cluster, you can find these files at `c:\hdp\hadoop\hadoop-1.2.0.1.3.0.0-380\bin\`. You will need to update the historyserver, tasktracker, jobtracker, datanode, namenode, and secondarynamenode files with the following information:

```
<arguments>... -classpath ...;C:\Ambari\metrics-sink-1.2.5.0.9.0.0-
60.jar;C:\Ambari\sqljdbc4.jar </arguments>
```

   In other words, add both the metrics-sink and sqljdbc4 paths to the classpath so that they are locatable by the service. You may have more success putting them at the front of the class path rather than appending them. One way to find the correct files for the addition of these paths is to search for *.xml files within the `bin` folder. Each one of these files needs to be updated. Also, pay attention to the metrics-sink version number and change it as appropriate. You may have a newer metrics-sink file version than in the Ambari documentation or listed here in this chapter. Finally, if you have a multiple node cluster, don't forget to do this on each node in the cluster.

3. Restart Hadoop. From a command prompt, run `stop_local_hdp_services.cmd` and then run `start_local_hdp_services.cmd`. If your cluster is more than one node, be sure to also run `stop_remote_hdp_services.cmd` and `start_remote_hdp_services.cmd`.

   If everything was successful, all your services will start back up as expected.

4. To verify metrics collection, connect to the SQL Server where you installed HadoopMetrics and run the following query:

```
SELECT * FROM HadoopMetrics.dbo.MetricRecord
```

If you are successfully collecting metrics, you will have a result set from this query.

Installing and Configuring the Ambari SCOM Server

Now it is time to install and configure the Ambari SCOM Server within your Hadoop cluster:

1. Determine which node in the cluster you will be running the Ambari SCOM Server. In our single node cluster from Chapter 3, we'll install it along with the other services. In an enterprise cluster, you will want to install this on another node within the cluster.
2. Create a new folder: `c:\ambari-scom`.
3. Extract the `server.zip` file from the original downloaded zip file into the `c:\ambari-scom\` folder. There are three packages in this file that we will install.
4. Extract the `ambari-scom-server-`*`version`*`-lib.zip` contents locally.
5. Extract the `ambari-scom-server-`*`version`*`-conf.zip` contents locally.
6. Open the `Ambari.properties` file within the configuration folder you just extracted in step 4. Update the server, databasename, user, and password to the information for your SQL Server hosting the HadoopMetrics database.
7. Open a command prompt and run the `org.apache.ambari.scom.AmbariServer` class to start the Ambari SCOM Server.

   You may need to make a few changes to the following code based on where you have installed components. You may want to type it in Notepad first, before cutting and pasting it into the cmd prompt:

   ```
   java -server -XX:NewRatio=3 -XX:+UseConcMarkSweepGC
   -XX:-UseGCOverheadLimit -XX:CMSInitiatingOccupancyFraction=60
   -Xms512m -Xmx2048m -cp
   "C:\Users\Administrator\Downloads\hdp-1.3.0.0-GA\hdp-1.3.0.0-GA;
   c:\ambari-scom\server\conf;c:\ambari\sqljdbc4.jar;
   c:\ambari-scom\server\ambari-scom-server-1.2.5.0.9.0.0-60.jar;
   c:\ambari-scom\server\lib\*" org.apache.ambari.scom.AmbariServer
   ```

8. Verify that the Server API is working by entering this site from the Ambari SCOM server: `http://localhost:8080/api/v1/clusters`. You should receive back a page like Figure 16.5. If you are receiving any error messages, stop here and pay close attention to your paths in step 7.

http://localhost:8080/api/v1/cl Waiting for localhost

{ "href" : "http://localhost:8080/api/v1/clusters", "items" : [{ "href" : "http://localhost:8080/api/v1/clusters/ambari", "Clusters" : { "cluster_name" : "ambari", "version" : "HDP-1.3.0" } }] }

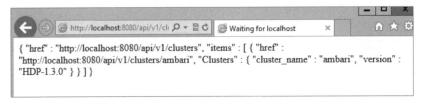

Figure 16.5: Verifying the Server API

9. Within the previously extracted `ambari-scom` folder, find the `ambari-scom.msi`. Run the `ambari-scom.msi` installer. The Ambari SCOM setup appears. Fill it in as appropriate and click Install. An example is shown in Figure 16.6 with the Start Services optionally checked.

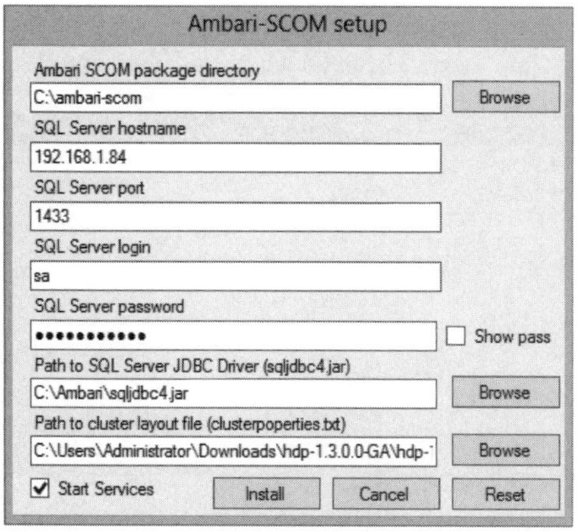

Figure 16.6: Ambari SCOM setup configuration

Once the install is complete, there are new links on the desktop for Start Ambari SCOM Server, Browse Ambari PAI, and Browse Ambari API Metrics. Go ahead and Start Ambari SCOM Server by clicking on the desktop shortcut.

Installing and Configuring the Ambari SCOM Management Pack

You are now ready to install the SCOM Management pack on the SCOM server. In the next steps, you will import the Management Pack, create the Run As Account, and finally configure the Management Pack.

1. On the server running Windows Server 2012, SCOM, and SQL Server, extract the `mp.zip` folder from the `Ambari-scom-version` folder from earlier steps.
2. Open System Center Operations Manager, click on Administration, and from the Tasks portal, under Actions, choose Import Management Packs.
3. Within the Import Management Packs dialog box, choose Add ➢ Add from Disk. If prompted to search the online catalog, choose No. Browse for the management packs where you extracted the `mp` folder. Choose all three files by clicking the first and then Shift-clicking the last. After all are chosen, Click Open. This brings you back to the Import Management Packs page with your three MPs added, as shown in Figure 16.7. Choose Install.

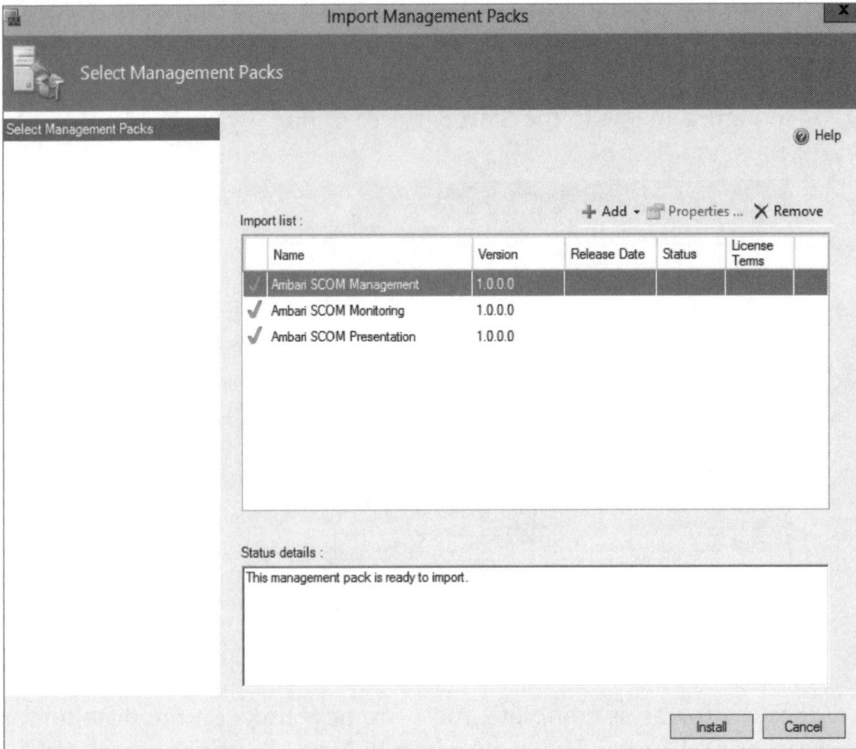

Figure 16.7: Selecting the management packs to import

Now that the management packs are imported, the next step is to create a Run as Account to speak with the Ambari SCOM Server installed within your cluster.

1. Go to Administration…Run as Configuration…Accounts. In the Tasks panel, select "Create Run as Account…".
2. You will now walk through the Create Run As Account Wizard. You start on the introduction page. There is nothing to do here, so click Next.
3. On the General Properties page of the Create Run As Account Wizard, choose a Run As account type of Basic Authentication. Give it a display name such as `AmbariSCOM`.
4. On the Credentials Properties page, choose an Account Name and Password for connecting to the Amabari SCOM server. The defaults are "admin" and "admin". Because you didn't configure these earlier, enter the defaults.

5. On the Distribution Security page, choose the Less Secure option. Click Create.
6. On the Completion page of the Run As Account Wizard, choose Close.

Now that you have configured the Run as Account, the last task that you need to accomplish is configuring the management pack. This will allow SCOM to speak with the Ambari SCOM Server in your Hadoop cluster:

1. Click on Authoring...Management Pack Templates...Ambari SCOM. On the right side is a task panel with the option to Add Monitoring Wizard. Click Add Monitoring Wizard.
2. On the Select Monitoring Type page of the Add Monitoring Wizard, choose Ambari SCOM. Click Next.
3. On the General Properties page, provide a name such as `AmbariSCOM`. Below, on the Select destination management pack, choose New.
4. On the General Properties page of the Create Management Pack wizard, choose a name such as `Ambari SCOM Customizations` and click Next.
5. On the Knowledge page of the Create Management Pack wizard, choose Create.
6. Back on the General Properties page of the Add Monitoring Wizard, ensure the destination management pack is the Ambari SCOM Customizations MP, and click Next.
7. On the Hadoop Details page, provide the Ambari URI. Provide either the Hostname or the IP of your Ambari-SCOM server in your Hadoop cluster. Also, choose the AmbariSCOM credentials for the Credentials Run as Account. The Hadoop Details page should look similar to Figure 16.8. Click Next.
8. On the Watchers Node page of the Add Monitoring Wizard, click Add. This will take you to the Select Proxy Agent dialog. On this page you will choose the Watcher Node that will monitor Hadoop. Click Search and choose an available watcher node. Click OK. This will take you back to the Watcher Nodes page on the Add Monitoring Wizard. Click Next.
9. Complete the Wizard by clicking Create on the Summary page.

Congratulations, you have completed the install of the Ambari SCOM Management Pack. You can now explore your Hadoop cluster statistics by going back to the Monitoring Page in SCOM and choosing Ambari SCOM. You can explore your choices of Ambari SCOM folders in Figure 16.9.

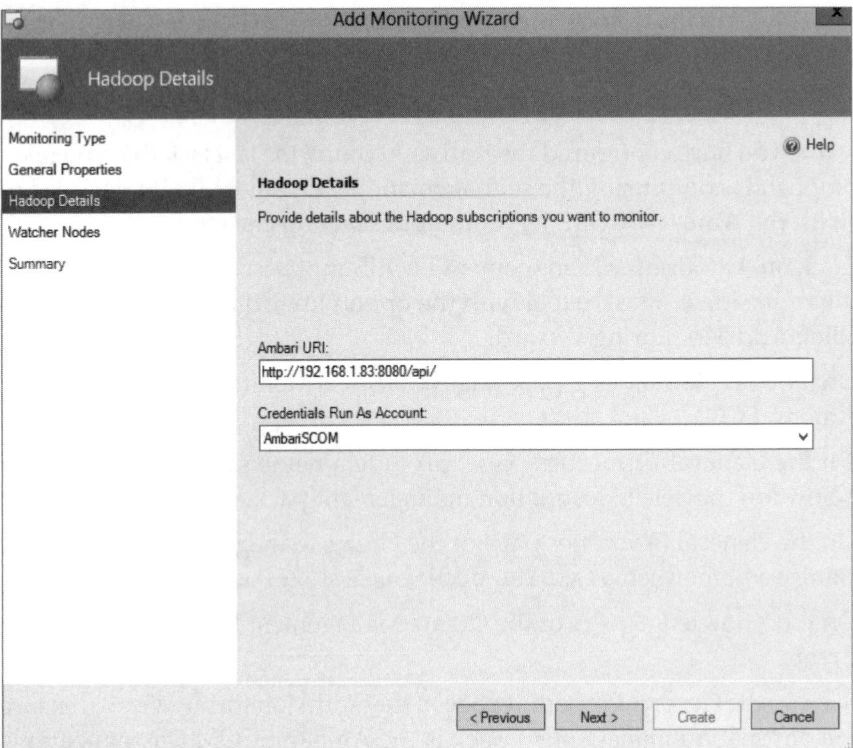

Figure 16.8: Hadoop details for Ambari SCOM MP

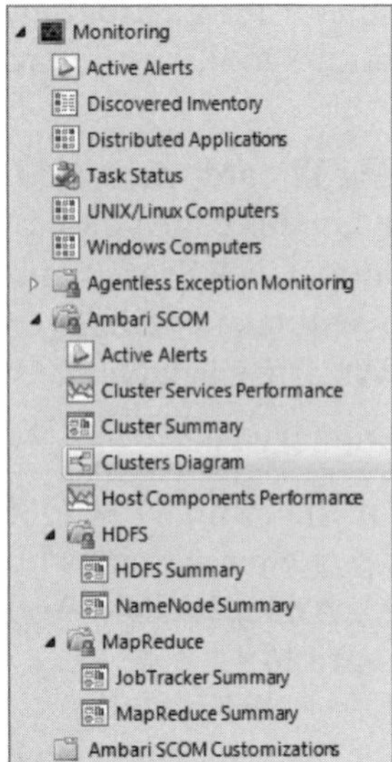

Figure 16.9: Ambari SCOM folders

It will take a few minutes for SCOM to start collecting statistics from your cluster, so the first good place to look is the Clusters Diagram page. Figure 16.10 shows our cluster build from Chapter 3. While it's a single node cluster, you can see all the services running and their status based off of the green check marks.

The whole purpose of going through the pain of this section is so that you can monitor your Hadoop clusters from a central location. Essential to any good monitoring solution is the ability to alert you when something goes wrong and to monitor history of performance so that you can look back in time. In the next section, we'll take a closer look at the capabilities of the Ambari SCOM Management Pack.

Monitoring with the Ambari SCOM Management Pack

The alerts shown in Table 16.2 are configured by Ambari SCOM.

Table 16.2: Alerts Configured by Ambari SCOM

NAME	ALERT MESSAGE	THRESHOLD
Capacity Remaining	Capacity remaining in HDFS is low if percentage of available space is less than the threshold.	30-Warning 10-Critical
Under-Replicated Blocks	Warns if the number of under-replicated blocks in the HDFS is above the threshold.	1-Warning 5-Critical
Corrupted Blocks	Alerts if there are any corrupted blocks.	1
DataNodes Down	Warns if the number of DataNodes that are down is greater than the threshold in the percentage.	10-Warning 20-Critical
Failed Jobs	Alerts if percentage of MapReduce jobs are greater than the threshold.	10-Warning 40-Critical
Invalid TaskTrackers	Alerts if there are any invalid TaskTrackers.	1
Memory Heap Usage	Warns if JobTracker memory heap grows to more than the threshold.	80-Warning 90-Critical
Memory Heap Usage	Warns if NameNode memory heap grows to more than the threshold.	80-Warning 90-Critical
TaskTrackers Down	Warns if the number of TaskTrackers that are down is greater than the threshold in percentage.	10-Warning 20-Critical
TaskTracker Service State	Warns if the TaskTracker service is not available.	

Continues

Table 16.2 *(continued)*

NAME	ALERT MESSAGE	THRESHOLD
NameNode Service State	NameNode service is not available.	
Secondary NameNode Service State	Secondary NameNode service is not available.	
JobTracker Service State	JobTracker service is not available.	
Oozie Server Service State	Oozie Server service is not available.	
Hive Metastore State	Hive Metastore server is not available.	
HiveServer State	HiveServer service is not available.	
WebHCat Server Service State	WebHCat Server service is not available.	

On the left side of the SCOM interface, you can browse the Hadoop cluster by traversing the Ambari SCOM tree. Figure 16.9 showed the various diagrams and reports you can navigate to. Reports of great interest are the Cluster Summary, HDFS Service Summary, HDFS NameNode, MapReduce Summary, and the Jobtracker Summary. We'll examine each report for the benefits it provides.

The HDFS Service Summary provides summary insight into files, blocks, disk I/O, and remaining capacity. For the File Summary, it provides insight into how many files have been appended, deleted, and created. In addition, it lets you know how many total files are stored in HDFS. Blocks Summary provides data on under-replicated blocks, corrupt blocks, missing blocks, and total blocks in the system. Ideally, everything should be zero except Total Blocks. If there are corrupt or missing blocks, it's possible some DataNodes are down or your replication factor for those blocks was 1 and there are no files from which to create new blocks. The disk I/O Summary page provides detail on the total bytes read and written in the system. Finally, the Capacity remaining provides the total amount of space left in the system in a nice trending graph. Figure 16.11 provides a nice view of this set of SCOM graphs.

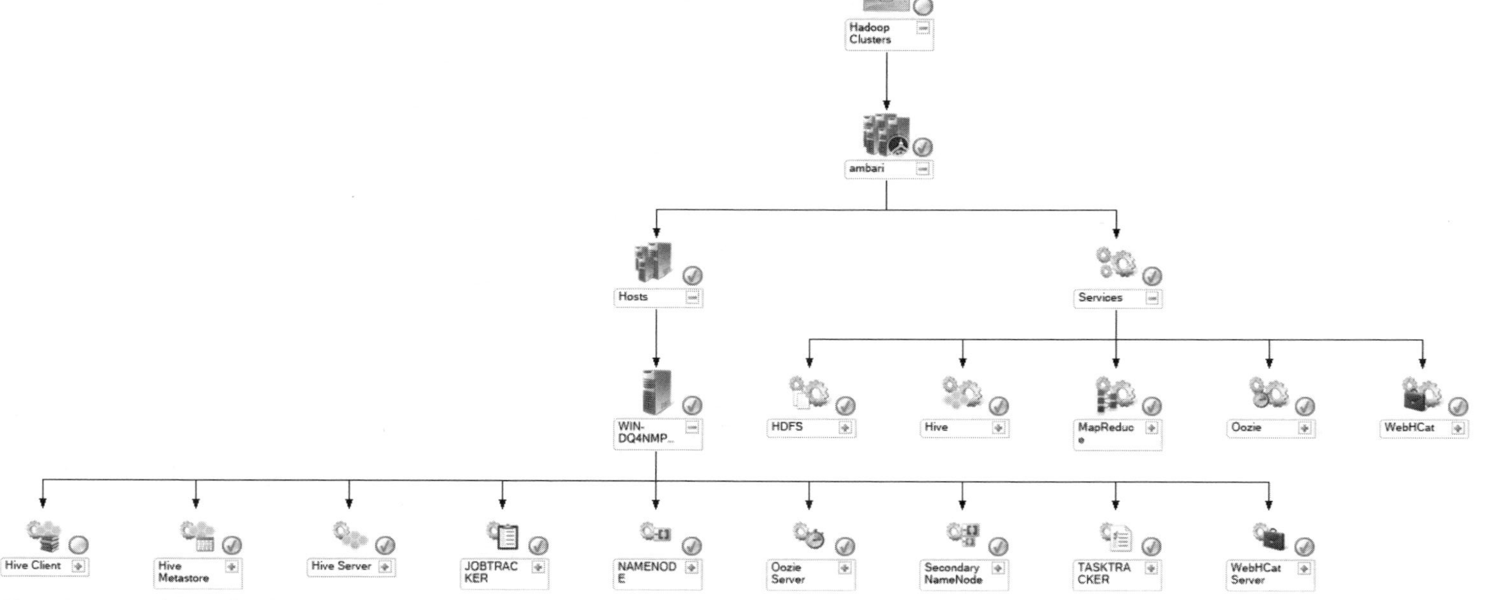

Figure 16.10: Cluster diagram

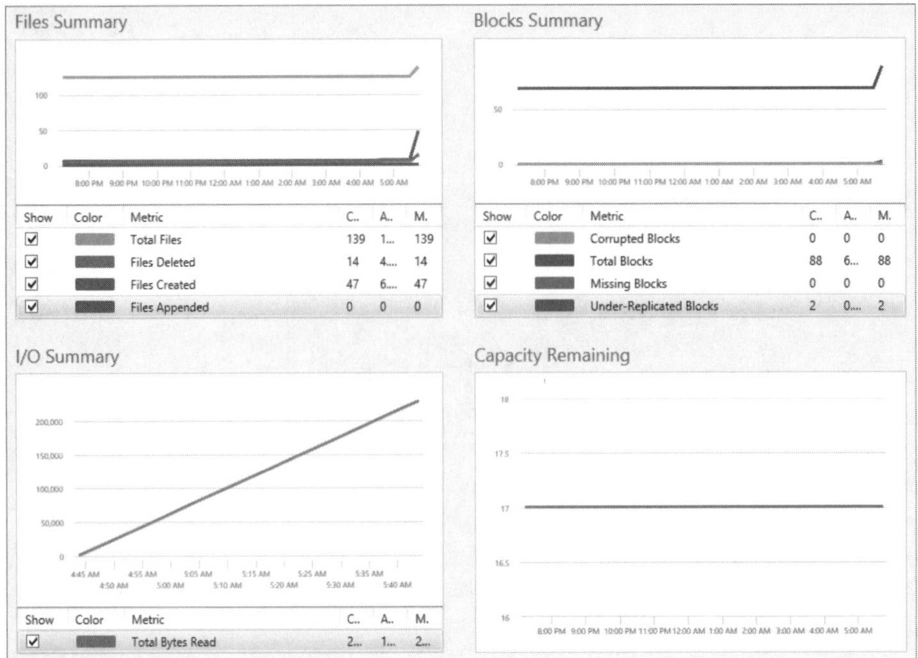

Figure 16.11: HDFS Service summary

The HDFS NameNode Summary graph provides the particulars for performance information for the NameNode. Specifically the summary set of graphs details memory heap utilization, threads status, garbage collection time in milliseconds, and average RPC wait time. The memory heap utilization is important to monitor because as your cluster grows in the number of files it needs to keep track of, then the amount of memory needed to maintain file location will also continue to grow. The graph will show you the difference between memory committed and memory used. The Threads Status report details how many Threads are runnable, blocked, and waiting. There are also the Garbage Collection Time and Average RPC Wait Time reports. If the RPC wait time is high, a job or an application is performing too many NameNode operations. Figure 16.12 shows the NameNode summary graphs.

The MapReduce Service Summary shows summary trends of jobs, TaskTrackers, slots utilization, and total number of maps compared to total number of reducers. The Jobs Summary report details jobs submitted, jobs failed, jobs completed, and jobs killed. The TaskTrackers Summary report provides information on TaskTrackers decommissioned, TaskTrackers blacklisted, TaskTrackers graylisted, and number of TaskTrackers. The Slots Utilization graph shows reserved and occupied reduce slots and reserved and occupied map slots. Finally, the Maps vs. Reducers reports details the number of running map and reduce tasks over time. You will likely visit this summary page often when users are complaining about slow performance, as it will give you quick insight to the aggregate activity on the cluster. Figure 16.13 shows the MapReduce Summary report.

Figure 16.12: NameNode summary

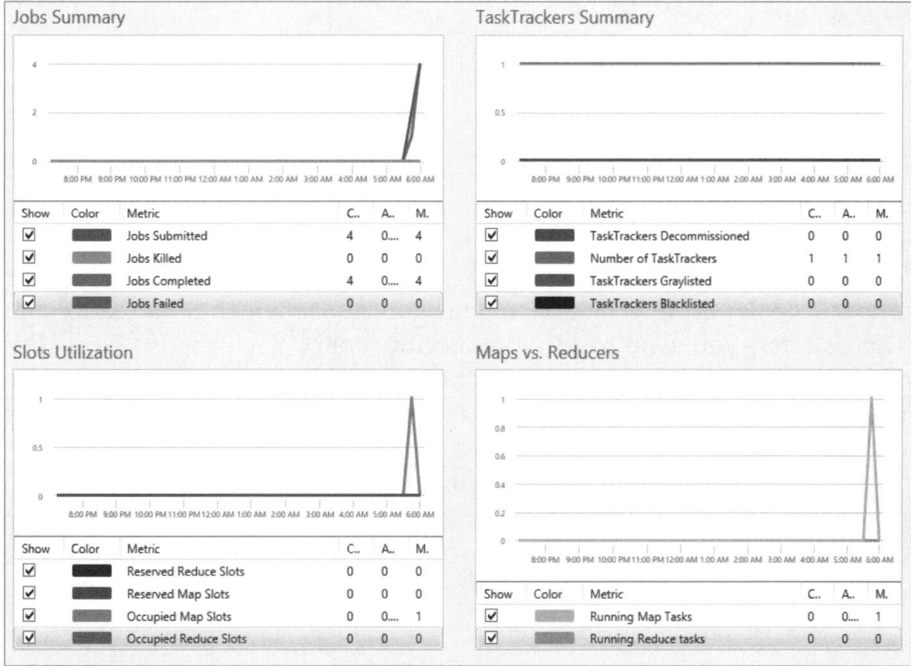

Figure 16.13: MapReduce summary report

Finally, the JobTracker Summary provides details into the memory heap utilization, threads status, garbage collection time, and average RPC wait time (see Figure 16.14). The Memory Heap Utilization graph shows memory heap committed and used for the Jobtracker Service. The Threads Status report shows the threads runnable, waiting, and blocked. The Garbage Collection Time graph shows the time in milliseconds that it takes to run garbage collection. The Average RPC Wait Time Graph shows wait time. If the average RPC wait time grows significantly, look for jobs running a very large number of short running tasks.

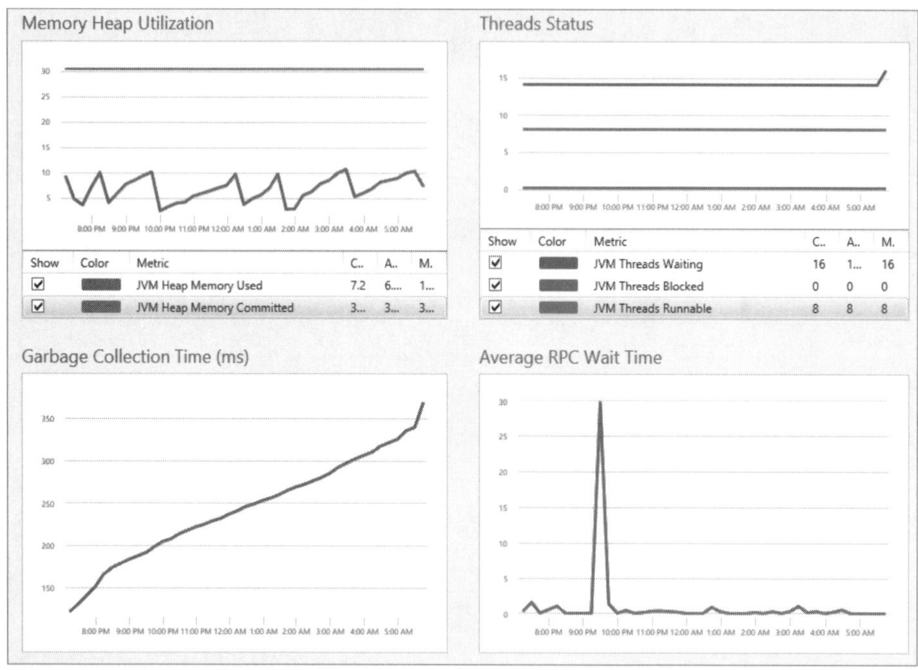

Figure 16.14: Jobtracker summary

Finally, you can create your own reports by using the Cluster Services Performance Report interface. Here you can choose which MapReduce and HDFS counters you want to add to a specific report. You can also right-click within the graph to change the timeframe of your choosing. This graph can also show alerts and maintenance windows as defined by you. Figure 16.15 shows the Cluster Services Performance report.

Now that you have set up and understand the default reports and alerts that come with the Ambari SCOM Management Pack, you will want to continue to explore and customize the solution. The first step you should take is adding the necessary counters to each cluster node to capture the performance information